Mark Lemon

Leyton Hall

And other Tales

Mark Lemon

Leyton Hall
And other Tales

ISBN/EAN: 9783337122218

Printed in Europe, USA, Canada, Australia, Japan

Cover: Foto ©ninafisch / pixelio.de

More available books at **www.hansebooks.com**

LEYTON HALL

AND OTHER TALES.

BY

MARK LEMON,

AUTHOR OF
"WAIT FOR THE END," "FALKNER LYLE," "JEST BOOK," ETC.

NEW EDITION.

LONDON:
WARD, LOCK & CO., WARWICK HOUSE,
SALISBURY SQUARE, E.C.
[*The right of translation is reserved.*]

CONTENTS.

CHAP.	PAGE
LEYTON HALL:—	
I.—THE SCRIVENER OF BREAD STREET	1
II.—TAVERN TALK	12
III.—TOUCHED BY EVIL	23
IV.—REVENGE	36
V.—THE KING'S ROGUES	50
VI.—REUBEN'S REMORSE	58
VII.—THE TRYSTING-PLACE	68
VIII.—GONE	80
IX.—WALTER AND TABITHA IN THE CITY	93
X.—THE DEBAUCH	105
XI.—MAUD'S INNOCENCE PROVED	117
HEARTS ARE TRUMPS: A Dramatic Story:—	
I.—THE TEMPTER	128
II.—"WHEN GREEK MEETS GREEK"	134
III.—THE PROMISE	142
IV.—JOE AND SUSAN	148
V.—A PROPOSAL OF MARRIAGE	154
VI.—THE EXPOSURE	160
VII.—THE DENOUEMENT	167
MIND YOUR OWN BUSINESS: A Dramatic Story:—	
I.—THE OLD BEECH TREE	177
II.—MR. ODDIMAN'S INTERFERENCE	187
III.—CONTENTMENT	196
IV.—MEDDLING AGAIN	199
V.—MR. SMYTHE'S NATURAL ELEMENT	204
VI.—RECLAMATION	211
VII.—THE RETURN HOME	215
VIII.—MR. SMYTHE'S NEWS	218
IX.—"I SHALL 'MIND MY OWN BUSINESS.'"	221

CHAP.	PAGE
THE TALKING SHELL: A TALE FOR THE YOUNG :—	
I.—THE STORY OF THE PEARL	226
II.—CONTINUATION OF THE STORY OF THE PEARL	237
III.—" REMEMBER ! "	242
FLOWERS AND THORNS	249
WHAT CAME OF KILLING A RICH UNCLE ONE CHRISTMAS TIME :—	
I.—" YOU ARE SO PRETTY "	269
II.—THE PONY-RIDING ARRANGEMENT	271
III.—SWEETHEARTS	273
IV.—MISS BEADLE'S MARRIAGE	275
V.—FINANCIAL	279
THE GHOST DETECTIVE	289
A CHRISTMAS IN A JEW'S HOUSE	301
A CHRISTMAS HOLIDAY LESSON :—	
I.—CHRISTMAS EVE	318
II.—CHRISTMAS TIME	330
AUNT SALLY'S CHRISTMAS BOXES :—	
I.—JOHN CRASS	339
II.—AUNT SALLY	343
III.—COURTING	347
IV.—ONE OF AUNT SALLY'S DISCOVERIES	353
V.—THE CHRISTMAS BOXES	356
CHRISTMAS EVE IN A NIGHT TRAIN	362

LEYTON HALL.

CHAPTER I.

THE SCRIVENER OF BREAD STREET.

IT was two o'clock on November the 3rd, ——. The wind from the river swept in cold gusts through New Palace Yard, at Westminster, and the leaden clouds above hung low and rain-laden. Notwithstanding the dreary and uncomfortable state of the weather, groups of men were standing about, some seeking shelter from the wind behind the buttresses of the old Hall; others, with their short cloaks wrapped closely around their shoulders, crouched behind the conduit, whose trickling waters were occasionally scattered like raindrops by the gusty wind. Grooms were leading about pad horses, whose long tails, depressed as they were between their hindquarters, fluttered in the breeze like tattered streamers. Whenever anyone came forth from the Hall, men's faces were turned towards him, and speculation became rife among the gazers.

"The House sits later than I thought for, Master Goring," said a white-haired man in a dark suit of cloth, to another who appeared of the middle class—a trader, perhaps from the City of London.

"I thought they would have risen an hour agone,' replied

the man addressed; "but it's likely that one of the right sort has got the ear of the House, and is telling it our grievances. Heaven knows they are many enow to take time in the telling."

"Past two o'clock," said the first speaker, looking at a ponderous watch which he carried in a side-pocket of his doublet. "I shall tarry no longer, but back to the city. Wilt take a cast in my wherry, Master Goring?"

"I thank thee, no," replied Goring; "I shall bide the end of the sitting, as to-day's doings will be a straw to show which way the wind is to blow for many days to come, I fancy." The two men shook hands and parted.

"Do you know yon gentleman that has just come forth?" asked Goring, of a bystander. "He must be of the court party, by his gay plumage."

"Yea, friend; 'tis Sir Philip Warwick, a good gentleman enough in the main, but a coxcomb withal. He speaks to Master Edward Leyton, who comes out of my county, Darbyshire."

The two gentlemen referred to by the speakers strolled leisurely across the open space, and appeared to be making for the stairs, where several barges and wherries were in waiting, despite the coldness of the day.

"You have had a long sitting, Sir Philip," said Master Leyton; "what has caused it?"

"A bear-baiting, or something akin to it," replied Sir Philip; "for some of our new members are more fitted to hound on a mastiff at the Blind Bear than to address a conclave of gentlemen."

"So much I gathered as I walked in the hall, where I had appointed to meet my scrivener; but I was an hour behind time, and so lost my man. I overheard some sourfaced knaves exulting in what was to happen. Their man seemed to be the member for Cambridge. Who is he?" asked Leyton.

"An ill-conditioned fellow, to judge by his outward man," replied Sir Philip, "though of gentle blood enough. He was speaking when I left the House. You must have heard of the man, Cromwell—Oliver Cromwell?"

"What, that disloyal knave!" cried Leyton. "I never saw the man; but he is always ready, I have heard, to stir up strife, and to claim strange privileges for the people. What manner of man is he?"

"When I entered the House," replied Sir Philip, "I saw a gentleman was speaking, very ordinarily apparelled, for it was a plain cloth suit, which seemed to have been made by an ill country tailor ; his linen was plain, and not very clean, and I was struck by a spot or two of blood upon his little band, which was not much larger than his collar. His hat was without a band, his stature of good size, his sword stuck close to his side, his countenance swollen and reddish, his voice sharp and untuneable, and his eloquence was full of fervour, for the subject-matter would not bear much of reason."*

"I' faith ! thou hast noted him wel', Sir Philip," said Leyton.

"Yes ; and the fellow will be heard of either as a politician, or — a brewer of double ale," replied Sir Philip, laughing. "He presented a petition from that outspoken rogue, John Lilburne, the sturdy London 'prentice, who hath been whipped and imprisoned for circulating the *Histriomastix*, and other scandals of the scurrilous Prynne. There were other petitions from like fellows, but I escaped, and am now for the three o'clock ordinary at Spring Gardens. Wilt with me?"

"I' faith ! I more incline to a good dinner than a cold voyage in a Thames wherry," replied Leyton ; "but the business I have on hand presses, and I have already missed my scrivener once to-day. One word at parting. I am no great politician, Sir Philip, but I bode evil days from this license of speech now permitted. I would, if I had a place in the House, cry out against such boldness as is now common, or some of us will have to 'boot and saddle' before we are many years older."

Sir Philip shrugged his shoulders. "There must be work on Tower Hill before that, perhaps, Master Leyton. In the meantime I shall make the most of the present, and—it is a quarter to three o'clock. God'den."

Leyton returned his salute and then walked to the stairs, his presence provoking the usual clamour among the watermen who contended for his custom.

The tide was fortunately running down, as the awning of the boat which Leyton had selected afforded but slight protection against the wind. The pair of oars, however, made

* See Sir Philip Warwick's "Memoirs," pp. 246, 247.

short work of the distance between Westminster and Paul's Wharf, where Leyton landed, and then made the best of his way to a scrivener's in Bread Street.

The scrivener was the same persons as had spoken to Master Goring in Palace Yard. Leyton apologised for his want of punctuality in keeping his appointment, and was assured that the detention was of small consequence, inasmuch as the scrivener's curiosity to learn the result of the long morning's sitting of the newly assembled Parliament had made him in no hurry to return to the city. The scrivener asked Leyton if he had heard aught of the matter debated.

"There has been a stormy sitting, as I learned from Sir Philip Warwick, and much that sounded like treason, to my thinking," replied Leyton; who then repeated, in part, the conversation he had had with his friend.

"I guessed as much," said the old scrivener, sadly. "We are at the beginning of evil days, Sir; unless more pains are taken to avoid them than has been done of late."

"I am of your opinion," replied Leyton.

"But our governors lack the wisdom to do so, I fear me," said the scrivener, with a deep sigh. "Woe to those who drive matters to extremity, and set brother against brother, as in the days of the Roses!"

"Again I am with you," replied Leyton; "but better hard knocks and cracked crowns, than this continued fret and perilous uncertainty."

"A civil war is a frightful calamity," said the old man; "and to that we are hastening. The people against their king. Woe to those who make the necessity for such a bloody arbitration!"

"And such, I take it, are those who countenance rude praters like Master Cromwell and his fellows," replied Leyton, warmly.

"Then, were a civil contest to arise, you would side against the people?" asked the scrivener, abruptly.

"I would chop off my right hand rather than draw sword for such malcontents," answered Leyton; adding, "And so would every true English gentleman. God bless the king!"

The old scrivener continued silent for a few moments, seemingly trimming a pen, but in reality, struggling to suppress words which he knew it might be unsafe to utter.

"Well Master Leyton," he said, at length, "we will end this

unprofitable talk, and to your business. I trust not to make further transfers of your good acres?"

"Yes," replied Leyton; "but not to satisfy the greed of usurers, albeit to assist in the consummation of what many would think the greatest folly I have yet committed."

"I listen," said the scrivener, after a short pause.

"I am about to marry," continued Leyton, "and some men call that folly. But I—I have the fairest, gentlest, noblest excuse for it that ever man had. The lady has a fair dowry that I desire to be settled upon herself. Here, on this paper, I have set down the amount and all other needful particulars."

The scrivener took the proffered paper, and, having read it carefully, said:—

"I give you my gratulations, Master Leyton, on such a promising union. Mistress Maud Netherby comes of a goodly stock—a very goodly stock."

"By the tone of your speech, my old friend," replied Leyton, "you seem to think the luck is all on one side, and that is mine. Is't so?"

"Not altogether as you say," answered the scrivener; "and you must pardon what I am about to advise. My cousin—younger than me by some half-score years—was thy mother, Master Leyton; and so, in some case, thou art of my blood, and blood, it is said, is thicker than water. I had a strong love for thy mother also, and that—pardon me—has, in part, descended to her son. Your generous nature has made you wasteful of your means, and what you said but now, assures me that you will be equally prodigal of life and safety should the unrelenting folly and oppression of our rulers drive the people to rebellion. Pray hear me out. A resolved people must be conquerors in the end, and victors are not always generous or just. Let me advise, then, that for the sake of thy wife and of the children that may be born to ye, Mistress Leyton's dowry be charged upon your own estate."

"Ha! ha!" Leyton laughed. "Thou mayst spare thy breath, old friend. I came for that purpose also, knowing how I have been tempted, and might be again. Here is set down what I desire to be conveyed to her and the Leytons *in futuro*—nearly all that I have left, except our old Manor House, Leyton Hall, and enough of acres to make it seem unlike a prison."

The old scrivener, having read the paper, took Leyton's hand and pressed it kindly, saying :

"You have acted wisely—generously ; and should you keep in the same mind as to the cause you will elect to serve in this common strife—for come it will, unless God, in His good providence, take away the makers of the people's discontent—thou wilt have preserved to those you are bound to love what otherwise might have been sacrificed."

"I do not share your fears, old friend, even if rebellion stalks the land," replied Leyton. "But let the deeds be drawn. I am impatient to get home again, and would fain take with me your sheepskins. It is rough travelling at this time of year in Derbyshire, and I have no wish to put ice and snow between me and my ladye-love."

"I have an abstract of your property," replied the scrivener, "and by the day after the morrow all shall be ready."

As there were other clients waiting an audience with the scrivener, Master Leyton took his departure, and shortly afterwards entered the Mermaid tavern to satisfy a very excellent hunger which oppressed him.

At the time appointed, Master Leyton was again in the scrivener's house in Bread Street, and found the deeds awaiting his approval and signature.

"They will require a witness to their due execution," said the scrivener, "and I will go seek one."

The old man left the room, and returned shortly, accompanied by a gentleman of about two-and-thirty. His hair was long, and curled upon his shoulders. His fine face, brilliant eyes, and magnificent head, gave assurance of no common man.

"This is my son, Master Leyton," said the scrivener, "who chances to be with me, and he will attest your signature."

Leyton instantly rose up and bowed with unaffected reverence, scarcely having power to say : "I am honoured, indeed, by such a witness."

The old scrivener then read aloud the contents of the two deeds, and when he had ended, Leyton affixed his signature in due form.

The witness then attested, and wrote in bold characters John Milton—a name to become a household word wherever men spoke "his land's language." The old House—we had almost written Temple—in Bread Street has nearly perished, one room only being preserved, and forming part of an adjoining warehouse. It is still remembered as "Milton's Room."

Master Leyton set out for Derbyshire on the following day, and though he and his serving-man Reuben Studley, were well mounted, they did not reach the Manor House at Leyton until after a week's hard riding.

But then Edward Leyton was to be rewarded for that long and perilous journey before the great Hall put on its Christmas garnishing of holly and ivy green. Maud Netherby was to be mistress at the Hall; and of the long line of Mistress Leytons which had preceded her, none could have been fairer or more worthy of a husband's love. And so perfect was Leyton's happiness, that for a while he closed his ears to the rumours which reached even into Derbyshire, of the troublous doings which were disturbing men's minds in almost every part of England. There were stirring "newes" at times which curdled men's blood, or roused the anger of the loyal adherents to kingly prerogative.

Edward Leyton, when he heard those rumours of wars, reproached himself for his disloyalty in not joining the standard of his king; but then he had been married not two short years, and his little Alice just learned to call him father. But he could not rest in Derbyshire. No; he and his wife should go to London for awhile, leaving their child with the careful nurse who had had charge of it from its birth—and the separation was the first great sorrow Maud had ever known.

"A month will soon pass, darling," said Leyton, as he held his wife's tear-covered face between his hands, "and then you shall return; but to London I must go—for—for very weighty reasons. Shall I go alone?"

"No, dearest," replied Maud, throwing her arms around her husband's neck. "You would be so lonely now in that great city. Would you not?"

"Truly yes, love."

"And Alice will be well cared for, and nurse Gibson will send us a post in a fortnight with news of home affairs; so that will make our separation seem of less account. Kiss me."

Master Leyton was a good husband and did as he was

bidden. The next day at sunrise, the horses which were to convey the travellers to London were at the door. Maud was a good horsewoman, and could manage her pretty grey gelding to admiration; but twenty miles a day over rough roads were more than Leyton would permit her to encounter in the side-saddle. Reuben Studley was, therefore, mounted on a strong roadster, that looked like a likely charger, should his master need such at any time ; and behind him was a well-stuffed pillion with a footboard, so that Mistress Leyton might sit as easily almost as in her cushioned chair at Leyton Hall.

Her pretty face was stained by tears, and her bright hazel eyes were filled with tears also, and their pretty lids were red from weeping, and their long lashes were wet and glittering with the water which had welled up from her maternal heart. But Leyton wisely took no apparent notice of her sorrow, but kissed her, as he handed her up to the horse-block that she might mount with ease behind the favoured Reuben. Somewhat like Chaucer's "Wife of Bath," upon her pillion

"Easilie she satte
Ywimpled well and on her hed a hatte ——"

whilst a long cloth robe lined with white rabbits' skins covered her body and feet, so as to bid defiance to the sharp October wind blowing up the avenue of old elms right into the Hall, making sundry pikes and swords and sylvan weapons jingle on the walls. As the cavalcade (the word, though somewhat hackneyed, is expressive) passed down the avenue, the rooks, which had long colonised in the old trees, rose up from them and made a noisy chorus, as though bidding Master Leyton farewell, if not a God speed.

Maud with her cavalier and Leyton led the way, whilst behind followed a horse-boy on a stout galloway, and leading a sumpter-horse laden with the lady's and the master's body-gear. Also with two leather bottles, one filled with Canary wine, and the other with a compound of strong waters, prepared according to a family recipe, and held to be infallible in the cure of catarrhs and the colic. There was also a bag of manchets for the lady's eating, and some slices of brawn, a neat's tongue, and a cold capon, stowed away in two small panniers, to be ready for an emergency. These were needful precautions for a journey of some hundred and thirty odd miles, when Charles the First was king, and long after. The roadside inns were not always provided with other than the coarse fare which satisfied such wayfarers as farmers and hucksters of all sorts, who were generally hungry enough to have eaten their spur-leathers, provided they could have washed the provender down with plenty of thick glutinous ale from a black jack, whose very reek would have intoxicated a modern fine gentleman.

As the party made progress, Leyton was distressed to hear how unpopular the king had become, and not without reason it seemed, if the grievances of which men complained were real and not imaginary. However much Leyton might be disposed to admit the reasonableness of much of the discontent which reached his ears, he was too loyal by education and prejudice to feel other than a stronger desire to throw in his fortunes with the king. And he would do so, when he had learned in London in what manner service could be best rendered to his master's cause.

Master Leyton had had some sore experience of tavern charges in his youthful days, and though it was necessary to put up at the Bell Inn, in Aldersgate, on his arrival in London, he had determined to find lodgings with some reputable person as soon as possible. His friend Mr. Milton was, therefore, consulted, and some pleasant lodgings in Clerkenwell, from which there was a view over the open fields of Islington and Highgate, were secured for the month which was to be passed in London.

Maud had never been in the great city, and her surprise and admiration were continually excited by what she saw around her. The stores of wealth in the traders' booths—the innumerable houses stretching on all sides of her—the great river Thames, covered with its gay barges and wherries—the vast St. Paul's, with its ages of histories—the conduits casting their jets of water from morning till night, and some with quaint devices playing on bells, and so marking the flight of time. Then the playhouses and shows where other causes of wonder and delight, as Maud thought what pleasure she should some day give her darling Alice by recitals of all sh. had seen in marvellous London.

As Leyton and his wife d both connexions living in the city and suburbs, time was never unemployed, and but for the unsettled state of public affairs, this London visit would have been one of those "greenest spots," to be recalled in after years, with all its pleasant memories, when the sky is dark and the storm is raging.

Maud's beauty and Leyton's free, honest, and cheerful bearing, drew around them many of the idlers about the town, and before two weeks had passed, the lady had become a toast, and her husband the prince of good fellows.

But such pleasant days were not to last. The contention between the king and the Commons grew fiercer every day. The Attorney-General appeared at the bar of the House of Lords and accused Lord Kimbolton, and five members of the House of Commons, of high treason. The resistance of the accused led to graver complications, and at last the king, accompanied by three or four hundred armed men, entered Westminster Hall, and demanded the five gentlemen impeached, calling Mr. Pym and Mr. Holles by name, but no answer was made. When the king left the House, the members sat mute for a few seconds, and the cry of " Privilege " burst forth, and the House instantly adjourned.

The alarm in the City was general, and Leyton and those, his friends, who were known to side with the king, stood in some danger, as it was rumoured that the cavaliers were coming to fire the city. The king going to Westminster "in a warlike manner" roused the popular indignation, and committees were appointed to sit, one at Merchant Taylors' Hall, and another at Grocers' Hall. The king, resolute in his determination to maintain his prerogatives, rode into the City without a guard—to show his affection, he said, and to assure them that he should proceed against the men accused of treason in a legal way, for which reason he called upon the citizens to give them no shelter in the city. But, as Clarendon records, " he departed without that applause and cheerfulness which he might have expected from the extraordinary grace he vouchsafed to them." As the king passed along Cheapside, attended only by his master of the horse and a few lacqueys, on his way back to Whitehall, Leyton stood bareheaded opposite Bow Church and made a respectful obeisance, which was acknowledged by a royal smile. As he continued to gaze after the king, his eyes fell on the old scrivener and his son, who remained covered, and indeed scarcely looked in the direction of the royal party. Leyton was annoyed at what he felt to be a marked show of disloyalty, and he resolved to rebuke it. With this intention he followed the scrivener and his son into their house in Bread Street, where he always met with a kindly welcome.

"Art thou from Guildhall?" asked the scrivener; "as I hear, the king met with a cold reception."

"Not only in the Hall, Master Milton," replied Leyton, "but in the goodly street of Cheap, where such men as thou and thy most worthy son gave him scant homage."

"I only pay homage," said the scrivener, "where I acknowledge worthiness. Would that I could lend thee my eyes and my understanding, and so win thee from a bad cause."

"If there is to be a choice of action," said Leyton, "I hold to my allegiance, which some good men in all else seem to put off like their gloves."

"Is there no allegiance due to the people?" asked the scrivener.

"The pople!" repeated Leyton, contemptuously.

"Ay, the people, Sir," said the scrivener's son, who had hitherto remained silent. "The king, as all other kings have done, holds his authority from the people for their good, and not his own. Then may people, as oft as they shall judge it for the best, either choose him or reject him, retain him or depose him, though no tyrant, merely by the right of free born men to be governed as seems to them best."* These opinions he supported with Scriptural quotations, to the confusion of Leyton, who could give no reasons for his devoted adherence to the king, further than that as he came of a loyal race he required no other inducement to peril life and fortune, like a true English gentleman. He could only urge that as the Parliament had invaded the rights of the Crown by the passing of the Militia Bill, he should prefer the rule of one to the tyranny of many.

* Milton's "Tenure of Kings," paragraph 17.

CHAPTER II.

TAVERN TALK.

THE circumstances which followed the assembling of the Parliament of 1640—the Long Parliament, as it came to be called—are so well known, as scarcely to need recapitulation. An alliance had been entered into with the Scotch ; bill after bill had passed the House of Commons, by which the assumed prerogatives of the king had been greatly curtailed ; bishops had been excluded from Parliament and all sway in temporal affairs, and clergymen removed from the commission of the peace. Laud had been sent to the Tower, Strafford executed, to the shame of his ungrateful master, Essex made general for the Parliament, and the king's standard had been set up at Nottingham, as we have already recorded. A few days were to bring on the fatal fight of Edge Hill, when the slain would be counted by thousands.

"Times grow worse and worse, neighbour," said John Ingrain, a mercer in Cheap.

"Nay, neighbour, rather say better," answered Ralph Clicker, the cordwainer; "better as every day clips our tyrant's claws."

"I know no tyrants," replied John, "but these howling Independents."

"Of whom I am one, neighbour Ingrain," said the cordwainer.

"More shame of thee to confess to such disloyal connexions," answered John Ingrain. "You and your fellows would let no man have a free conscience to think and act for himself, but ——"

"Tut! tut!" said the cordwainer, "you shall not anger me. We have lived good neighbours these twenty year, and may so still."

"Not a day longer, Ralph Clicker," cried John Ingrain, whose ledger showed the good reason he had for standing by the Whitehall and Somerset House party. "I will not hold with any that cannot cry 'God save the king, and down with Parliament.'"

Having discharged himself of so much loyalty, John Ingrain turned on his heel, and left his old friend the cordwainer, without even the courtesy of "good day, neighbour."

And thus it was wherever men met together. Old friends debated until they parted enemies. Fathers, brothers, sons, set aside their natural relation to each other until the great strife, which was to succeed, became inevitable. So much of the history of the time was needful to our story; but we shall henceforth have to deal with other domestic commotions, in which the contests were long and fierce, and pregnant with many changes of fortune.

The old Mermaid, in Bread-street, had maintained somewhat of its former repute, when the great wits of Eliza and James made it their Helicon. The larder, opening to the street, was generally supplied with tempting delicacies; and the name of Jacob Magnus, inscribed beneath "a wondrous fishy woman," painted on the signboard, was in high favour with those who loved a tankard of good ale or a flask of good wine.

It wanted an hour to noon, and the large room of the tavern was being prepared for the reception of those guests who needed a morning draught, or a light snack "to close the orifice of the stomach," as Bobadil hath it, until the hour of dinner, which then had grown to be as late as three o'clock.

"Now, Thomas Handy, bestir thyself," said Mistress Magnus, a buxom, bustling dame of five-and-thirty years of age; "wipe the dust from the settles; polish the silver breakers, that any dulness of the liquor may be overlooked for the brightness of the cup."

"Yea!" replied the young man addressed, in the affected drawl already adopted by the frequenters of the conventicles ; and Thomas, though a tapster, had sought to be one of the chosen. "Yea ; the vessels of pewter shall be even as the vessels of silver, and the inside of the platter shall be as clean as the out."

"Ay, ay, Thomas," said Mistress Magnus, "I know thou art a goodly lad ; but as thou art slow at work as well as slow of speech, rub on in silence."

It was well for Thomas that he obeyed his mistress, as his master, Jacob Magnus—who was not over-tolerant of the new doctrines—arrived, bearing a well-filled basket on his arm, which he had carried from Stock's Market, by 'Change.

"Here, you Tom Tapster, help me with my load," bawled Jacob, who could hardly place his burthen upon the table ; "the weight of four goodly capons, a dozen of quails, and as many dried neats' tongues, has tired me sorely. A pint stoup of Rhenish, mistress, for I'm oozing like a Virginny planter." Jacob certainly had earned his draught, as his moist brow and reddened face attested.

When Mistress Magnus brought the wine, Jacob eyed the quantity for a few moments, and said—

"Jane Magnus, thou art a wicked woman ! If thou wouldst not cheat thine own father, thou wouldst thy wedded husband, for this tankard is two pegs, at least, short measure."

"It is too much as a morning draught for a man who drink the hours round, as you do, Jacob," was the tart reply.

"All in the way of my calling, dame," replied Jacob, raising the tankard to his lips, but pausing before he touched the liquor to utter in a low voice, " Here's health to the king, and damn the Parliament."

"Hist !" interposed his wife. "If the Parliament gets upsides, as some say it will, such foolish toasting may find thee a halter."

"Lord ! if they were to hang me !" cried Jacob, laughing aloud. "I hope they'll give me the choice of a gallows—my own sign iron—fair promise methinks of good entertainment within, eh, dame ?" and Jacob's fat sides shook again.

"Ever at thy senseless jests, Jacob," said Mistress Magnus.

"Nay, if thou art to be a hempen widow," replied Jacob, "doth it not show my care of thee ?"

"Of me ?"

"Ay, for when thou hast leaked as many tears as a woman

of thirty ought to do over a husband of forty ——" Jacob paused, as though struck with some sudden fancy which he could not suppress—" Lord ! to see *that* face in three rows of crimped crape like a garnish of chitterlings !"

" Go on, husband ; I am ever a butt for thy humour."
Jacob laughed out his laugh and then continued—

" So when I am hung up like a fatted calf at Christmas-tide, to show how sack possets and choice pickings can feed a man, will not some spare liver be emboldened to seek thy love and thy larder ! make thee his wife, and ——" again Jacob's playful fancy cut short his period—" Ho ! ho ! to see thee a bride again in white dimity gown and sarsenet hood ! Everything white but thy face, and that—a Hecla—a volcano surrounded by snow !"

Jacob's laughter was infectious, not with Mistress Magnus, but it moved Thomas the drawer, who became mirthful exceedingly.

Dame Magnus was not a woman at any time to put up with an indignity quietly, not even from Jacob, except when they were alone, and with no witness to the offence—but from her own tapster ? No ! and Thomas Handy was surprised in the midst of his mirth by the receipt of a stinging clout on the ear, which made his eyes emit as many sparks as the fiery dragon on Lord Mayor's day.

" Laughing at my cost, ungrateful varlet ! " and the cuff was repeated. " Now join thy master's coarse jest an' thou durst, fellow. Take the basket and bestow the capons and quails in the larder before the Common Council return from the Guild."

Jacob restrained his pleasantry at this indication of his wife's temper, as he, too, was not altogether unacquainted with the burning sensation affecting the ears of Thomas, and from a similar cause. Jane had given Jacob her hand on other occasions than when they stood at the altar of Bow Church plighting their troth, and endowing each other with their worldly gear.

It was well that silence reigned, as two gentlemen who had recognised each other at the door of the tavern, now entered for a morning draught of mulled sack, for though it was but the latter end of October, the weather was damp and cold enough to make the warm potation acceptable. Two silver tankards, each containing about half a pint of wine, were soon placed on the table, and a slice or two of salted neat's tongue, which

Jacob knew would often act "as a shoeing horn" to draw on more liquor, though one of the guests, Master Richard Cotterell, seldom needed any other provocative to his wine than the continual thirst which afflicted him morning, noon, and night.

"Welcome back to England, Newberry," said Cotterell, taking his small modicum of wine at a draught.

"Thanks, old *camarado*," replied Newberry, drinking more sparingly. "I am glad to have met you. I thought I could not have forgotten the roll of that goodly carcase as it made up Bread Street."

"I have a style—a manner," said Cotterell, "and one that hath won the favourable glance of many a bright eye in this city of Lud."

"Still the same song, Dick," said Newberry, laughing. "Woman! woman!"

"With the old burthen, wine! wine!" replied Cotterell, and then beating his silver cup on the table summoned Tom Handy.

"Another cup—or stay—I have been upon the river this hour past, and am cold about the midriff, so make the draught a pint, as the wine is somewhat of the weakest. And now tell me—how likest thou Italy?"

"As a drone doth honey, Dick," replied Newberry. "Dark, melting beauties meet you at every turn, and by a sigh—a glance—whisper of moonlight and mischief."

"Tom, the sack!" bawled Cotterell. "Fore heaven! I am half inclined to make a pilgrimage to that land of love, but for two reasons."

"Hey! what! Reason stay Dick Cotterell from his humour?" asked Newberry, with affected surprise. "Reason! Why, they have named a ward in Bedlam after thee—Cotterell's ward. Don't talk of reason!"

"One is this, Ralph," replied Dick, holding up a leathern purse but lightly stocked evidently. "It barely serves a poor foot gentleman who is content to pace Paul's walk for company. You see one of my reasons which tells me that the glowing pleasures of the South are as unattainable as—true measure at a vintner's." Cotterell was helped to his metaphor by the reeking tankard just placed before him, and which proved that Mistress Magnus treated her guests no better than her husband.

Whilst Cotterell was testing the flavour of his new supply,

Master Leyton entered the room unnoticed by the toper, and took his seat at an adjoining table.

"A draught of Canary, lad, and a news letter if thou hast one," said Leyton in answer to Tom Handy's bow.

"The newspaper, the *London Gazette*, is beside thee, Sir. It is filled with good tidings. The train bands have declared for Parliament," drawled Tom.

"Cease your disloyal prate!" said Leyton, "and bring my liquor."

The tapster's remark, however, made Leyton refer with eagerness to the *Gazette*, and read with much interest the news contained in its two octavo pages.

Whilst Leyton was thus engaged, Newberry, at Cotterell's solicitation, had had his cup replenished.

"And now, Ralph, for my other reason," said Dick, assuming a sadly sentimental tone. "I am in love."

"I never knew thee out of it," replied Newberry, laughing.

"True," said Dick, "like a timid swimmer I have long disported in shallow waters; but now I have plunged into an ocean that seems to have no soundings."

"Zounds, man!" said Newberry, "thy case is serious. In such a depth of love nothing can save thee but the lightness of thy wit. Is she so fair?"

"Fair! Let me drain my tankard," replied Dick, suiting the action to the word. "For even I dare hardly attempt to paint her to thee with so cold a fancy as now possesses me. No; Tom Handy, half a measure of sherris!"

The loud tone in which Cotterell now spoke attracted the notice of Leyton towards the speaker.

"Ho! ho! Master Dick Cotterell. I'll keep *perdu* and perchance pick some jest out of his boasting," thought Leyton.

Dick did not wait for the wine, but assuming an attitude somewhat like one he had seen Lacy assume on the stage, he spouted rather than said—

"Poets have nigh exhausted their imageries of beauty! Lilies and roses are as common in their rhapsodies as emptiness in the pockets! The stars—though no two are of size—have been purloined for the eyes of a thousand Chloes! Nightingales have been caged in throats barred with pearl, and Asia has been traversed for perfumed sighs and ivory fingers."

"Then are such similies unworthy of thy lady-love?"

asked Newberry, imitating Cotterell's humour. "How describe her?"

"As a woman!" said Dick, elevating his hand and then kissing his fingers to some invisible creation of his fancy. "A mortal creature, glowing with health. Her carriage free as though she were conscious of her power—her disposition mirthful as though she had never yet been sad; whilst in her eye there lurks a tell-tale glance that says, 'I could love thee, Dick, if thou darest ask me!'"

The wine had certainly warmed Dick's imagination.

"And hast answered her?" asked Newberry with a smile.

"Ay! by gentle pressures of the hand! posies of double meaning!" replied Dick.

"But hast never spoken plainly to her?" asked Newberry.

"Never!" replied Dick. "Plain speaking was not made for lovers: Cupid converses by hieroglyphics. A wink—put that into words, and my lady pouts; let it have no sound, and my lady smiles. A gentle pressure of my lady's fingers runs through every artery to her heart. Put *that* in words, and cinq-deuce to ace you get your *mittimus*—the sooner, if the lady's married!"

Newberry made some reply which did not reach Leyton, as he had risen, feeling that he had no right to listen longer, even for the jest's sake.

"There's no trusting to connubial honour, Master Cotterell," he said, advancing to where the boaster was seated, and tapping him on the shoulder; "the common danger makes all husbands common informers, and I have been eavesdropping."

"Leyton!" exclaimed Cotterell, much more confused than any friend would have imagined Dick Cotterell could have been at the detection of an intrigue.

"So! why, thou lookest as ruffled as a Friesland hen," said Leyton, laughing.

Dick instantly recovered his self-possession, and answered, gaily—

"Why, man, it's not every shoulder can bear such a salutation in these unsettled times; and, as I am about to join the army, I have no desire to be clapped up in the Fleet."

Leyton was polite enough to laugh at Dick's jest, and then said—

"Your friend and I are strangers."

"Sir Ralph Newberry—Master Edward Leyton," replied Dick, introducing the strangers, who mutually expressed the pleasure they received at being made known to each other. The conversation then turned to what Leyton had overheard.

"I fear Master Dick flies his hawk at any man's pigeon," said Newberry.

"Not I—not I!" replied Cotterell, with what might have been affected earnestness. "Zounds, man! wouldst thou make Leyton jealous?"

"Because I have a wife whom the world calls fair?" asked Leyton, with a smile. "Make me jealous? No, Master Cotterell. I can know a woman fair, and believe her honest—mirthful, yet guileness—married, yet constant. Make my creed yours, Dick, and you will really love where now you only covet."

"Hark to him, Ralph!" replied Cotterell. "Dost mark how married men become decoys in the cause of Hymen, like fowlers' birds, to lure others to the net?"

"For what reason?" said Newberry.

"I know not," answered Dick, "unless it be that their bachelor recollections intrude on their matrimonial felicity, and they would lesson their dangers."

"A sorry jest, Master Cotterell," replied Leyton, rather gravely.

"What! hath it made thee sad!" said Dick, the wine speaking. "Thou canst not fear for thine own sweet bird?"

"Not I," answered Leyton, colouring with some feeling of anger; but remembering to whom he was speaking, he added lightly—"It would need a more cunning fowler than Master Cotterell to lure her to his springe. To prove that I neither fear thee, Dick, nor doubt her, thou shalt drink to her health and our old friendship, if thou and Sir Ralph will have your dinner at my lodgings."

The persons addressed readily accepted Leyton's invitation. As it was now full noon, and Leyton having some business, he said, with a scrivener hard by, the friend's separated, Cotterell promising to be Newberry's pilot to the lodgings of the entertainer.

As soon as Leyton had left the tavern, after a brief colloquy with Jacob Magnus, Cotterell drained what remained of his wine, and then, addressing Newberry in a whisper, said—

"Ralph, my friend, I've had a narrow escape from an early grave."

"What mean you?" asked Newberry, surprised at the change in Dick's manner.

"One question more from you had unplugged my mouth, and opened our friend Leyton's eyes," answered Dick.

"Do I guess what you would say?" asked Newberry. "Is your fair enslaver——"

"Mistress Leyton! and thou shalt judge if she be not all I have pictured her to thee. Had I confessed as much in Leyton's hearing, I should have had that country-made whinger of his in my body, for I never could fight in a bad cause, or with a wronged husband."

"Then better throw up the chase, Dick," said Newberry. "Leyton seems an honest gentleman, and ——"

"He has invited me to dinner, and to try conclusions with the lady," replied Cotterell; "so, Tapster Tom, bring our reckoning. What say you for a walk as far as Westminster? There is a main of cocks fought to-day, and we may have an hour's sport."

Sir Ralph agreed to this proposal of disposing of their time until dinner; and, having paid their reckoning, they walked leisurely westward.

Master Leyton was known to mine host of the Mermaid, not only as a customer, but as the master of his niece Tabitha, who had been engaged as waiting-woman to Mistress Leyton, on her arrival in London, at the recommendation of some one acquainted with Magnus. It was, therefore, with no surprise that Tabitha received a visit from her Uncle Jacob, although it was barely one o'clock, an hour when the Mermaid was beset by dinner-seekers among the citizens; but Jacob cared little about his outgoings and incomings, knowing he had a careful helpmate, and there was little liquor to be had by invitation from the thrifty traders, who only dined at the Mermaid from some domestic necessity.

Tabitha, after saluting the rubicund cheek of her uncle, did make inquiry what had brought him from his home at midday?

"Why, thy master, having a keen nose for good venison, hath ordered a pasty that hath done good service in my larder this se'nnight," replied Jacob, with a chuckle. "It wanted a new master."

"La, uncle!" said Tabitha, "hast thou no conscience?"

"As much as is good for a taverner, niece, who desires to pay scot and lot and live," replied Jacob. "The pasty is worthy the high destiny awaiting it. It will go down none but gentle gullets, as Master Cotterell and a Sir Ralph—Sir Ralph—I forget the name—will be anon here to dine with your master. Should they come before Master Leyton returns, they are to be invited in."

"Ne'er fear, uncle," said Tabitha, with a sigh; "Master Cotterell will need but little pressing, my mistress being within!"

Jacob gave a short, knowing whistle.

"Sets the wind in that quarter?"

"Oh, if I had not a good conscience!" said Tabitha, who, having a sneaking kindness for Tom Handy, had acquired something of the cant of the conventicle.

"What's the wench mean?" asked Jacob, with the curiosity peculiar to his class.

"Uncle!" answered Tabitha, solemnly, "what means three new dresses within the month? A tailor has but now brought home a gown that must trail like the court ladies'—half a yard at least. Then mistress has learned to part her hair on her forehead into small ringlets and round it into a knot at the top—Queen's fashion, it is called. She hath a laced handkerchief and a falling band that sets off her pretty country face. Why all this?"

"Because Mistress Leyton is a woman," answered Jacob, "and knows how to please herself and her husband."

"Would it please her husband, think ye, uncle," said Tabitha, rather wickedly, "to see how certain gallants among his acquaintance make eyes at my mistress, or to know that money—silver, ay, even gold—has been forced into my hands to deliver posies and scented gloves to my mistress?"

"And you did not return the money, nor your mistress the gloves, I'll be sworn," said Jacob, laughing.

"Then you would be forsworn, uncle," replied Tabitha. "My mistress would have none of them—yes, the posies now and then; though I must own I never saw her overstep the bounds of modesty."

"And the money, Tabitha?" asked Jacob.

"I was always too frightened when it was given me than to do other——"

"Than put it in thy pocket," said Jacob; "an' thou'dst been a fool not to have done so."

"Yes; perhaps so, uncle," replied Tabitha; "but my conscience sometimes reproves me for it. It seems so like ——"

"The profits of a waiting-woman's place, that is all, niece," said Jacob.

"And how is my aunt!" asked Tabitha, satisfied by her uncle's opinion as to the propriety of her conduct, and desirous to change the conversation to a subject of some interest to her.

"Thy aunt! Marry, she has made up her mind to be a widow; and so is always ailing, Like a pair of bellows, she is ever sighing to blow me into a flame, which I can only quench by drinking. The sexton will charge her double for me, that's one comfort," said Jacob, laughing.

"Don't talk in that profane manner, uncle," replied Tabitha. "Death is a frightful thing!"

"Yes, to old maids and bachelors," replied Jacob; "but la! your married man fears it not, having encountered the worst that can befall him—a wife!"

"And how — and how is Thomas Handy?" asked Tabitha, with affected carelessness.

"Nigh ready for the barber," replied Magnus; "for his head grows thick enough for a block for periwigs."

"Fie, uncle!" said Tabitha, colouring slightly. "But Thomas hath a good conscience, and that will give him strength."

"Heaven send it may!" replied Jacob; "but now he seems to trust to ox-beef and double ale, to my cost. But take away the pasty, and give me my basket, that I may be making my way home again in time for our ordinary."

Tabitha had been so little pleased by Jacob's remarks about Thomas Handy, that she did not seek to detain her uncle, and received his parting salute with something very like a pout upon her lips.

CHAPTER III.

TOUCHED BY EVIL.

LEYTON was not very well pleased with himself for the part he had taken in the morning's conversation at the tavern ; and he felt that he had done Maud wrong in allowing her in anyway to have been made the subject of such loose jesting. He was almost angry with himself, having invited Cotterell to meet Maud at dinner, after the avowal he had made of his libertine character.

The custom of the time allowed great latitude of conduct ; but the introduction of a professed seducer seemed an insult to the virtuous wife. There were other thoughts which obtruded themselves, and made Leyton more uncomfortable than he had been throughout his whole married life. He could not dismiss Cotterell's light boasting as altogether without foundation ; and Leyton thought that possibly some fair, frail woman, had stopped to regard the impudent *roué*, while she was trusted and loved by some doating husband like himself. He strove to repel such thoughts ; and felt that to entertain them for a moment longer than it was possible to dismiss them, was a wrong to Maud—his loving, devoted Maud.

Neither had the business which had taken him to his scrivener, Master Milton, been of the pleasantest character, connected as it was with a prospective scene of sorrow and difficulty. Leyton's loyalty had been so roused since he had been in London, where hourly news of king and Parliament were to be had, that he had resolved no longer to postpone the offer of his services to his Sovereign, although it involved the disturbance of his domestic peace, and his separation from his young and lovely wife and his darling Alice.

Leyton was fully sensible of the sacrifice he was making, and of the chances of danger which attended it; and he had, therefore, made a full disposition of his remaining property to his wife and daughter. The painful announcement of his intention to join the king's forces had yet to be made; and he knew it would prove to be a great sorrow, as whenever he had remotely alluded to the possibility of such a demand being made upon him, and upon all true English gentlemen, Maud had shown by her tears how terrible would be the contingency.

H e paused for a few moments at the door of his lodging, hoping to regain his usual cheerfulness before meeting Maud; and, having succeeded in part, he knocked at the door, which was opened by Reuben.

"Have my friends arrived!" Leyton asked, as he gave Reuben his hat and gloves, and walking-cane.

"We have many callers, Sir," replied Reuben, quietly; "Sir William Royston, Captain Carr, and another gentleman that you met at the Bowling-alley."

At another time, Leyton would have received this information as no unusual summary of their morning visitors, but now a cloud came upon his open brow, and a sigh escaped from his broad bosom. Reuben noted both; and his thick, black brows closed nearly, as though a sudden pain or a sudden pleasure that he would fain conceal had affected him.

"Maud is wrong," thought Leyton, "to hold these morning levees of light-brained idlers when I am absent." But checking the ungenerous inference that might have followed, he said aloud, "Yet why should I deny her the homage she commands and merits? Where is your mistress, Reuben?"

The question was answered instantly by Maud running playfully from an inner room, and throwing her arms around her husband's neck. Having kissed him, she said, "You have returned sooner than I had looked for, Edward."

"Not sooner than to be welcome, eh, sweetheart?" asked Leyton.

"You would not ask me such a question if thou couldst doubt my answer," replied Maud again kissing him. "Where hast thou been?"

"To Master Milton, the scrivener, to make my will?" answered Leyton smiling.

"What put such a thought into thy head as making of thy

will?" asked Maud, opening her large hazel eyes to the full.

"No more than this: that, should I die, thou shouldst not go undowered to thy second husband."

"My second husband!" The large hazel eyes closed instantly.

"Yea; as thou art already provided with a choice of suitors, I thought I had better provide for my departure," said Leyton. The words came unbidden, and were spoken.

"There is now unkindness in your jesting," replied Maud, tears stealing down her cheeks. "I know none but are thy friends—none that breathe a word beyond the limits of innocent gallantry—none that would dare aver that he looked on me but as thy wife, and the guardian of thy honour."

"I do believe so, dearest," said Leyton, pressing Maud to his bosom. "Forgive me my idle words."

"Yes, if thou wilt go presently to Master Milton, and bid him send thy will to make tailors' measures; it may then benefit some of the gallants thou hast given me."

"I will do anything to please thee, sweetheart," replied Leyton, saluting the pretty lips that pouted to be kissed. "To prove to thee that when away I am always mindful of thy pleasure, I have invited your especial favourite, Master Cotterell, to dine with us to-day."

"So I have learned," said Maud, "and some other friend. Tabitha and I have been making preparations to receive them."

A smart knocking at the door announced the arrival of their visitors—at least, Maud said so.

"That is merry Master Cotterell's knock, I'm certain. I know it, because it seems an echo of his laugh."

Leyton smiled at this conceit, and remembered it hereafter.

Reuben having introduced the guests, Cotterell advanced to Mistress Leyton, and presented her with a bouquet of flowers—then to be gathered in many a fair garden of old London city.

"Madam," said Dick, bowing formally, "like a devout gallant, I make my matin offering to my loveliest saint."

As much extravagance of compliment was permitted in society, Maud accepted the flowers, and replied, archly,—

"A proper type of so general a worshipper, as here is the queenly rose and the humble violet—love's myrtle and a sprig of rosemary."

"I see my error," said Dick, softly; "to-morrow I will bring only myrtle."

Maud felt a blush rise to her cheek—she knew not wherefore—as she answered,—

"My husband seems to have forgotten us. Edward, our new guest ——" But Maud started with surprise, and exclaimed—"Sir Ralph Newberry!"

"Maud Netherby!"

"The same, Sir Ralph," said Leyton, also surprised; "though now Mistress Leyton. You are known to each other?"

"Yes, Edward," replied Maud. "When quite a child, Sir Ralph was my lover, and as faithful a knight as ever chased butterflies or gathered hazel-nuts for his lady-love. We have met rarely since then; the last time, if I remember aright, was six years ago."

"Quite six years," replied Sir Ralph. "I was then on the point of obeying my father's commands to travel."

"A wonder, Cotterell!" said Leyton, "a woman keeps a secret! For nearly two years have we been man and wife, and this love-passage of my fair dame hath never been mentioned."

"Would'st thou have me show thee a catalogue of my toys?" asked Maud, with a little laugh.

"Yea, if they were all such dangerous playthings as the gallant Sir Ralph Newberry," answered Leyton, smiling also. "Really, Sir Ralph, I shall grow jealous of you. He was a wise limner that painted Cupid blind."

"You hear, Sir Ralph, what my husband thinks," said Maud, laughing.

"I hear but what he *says*," replied Sir Ralph.

"Still as I think," said Leyton. "Look at a woman by Hymen's flambeau, and you detect her mortality."

"Then Jove keep me a bachelor, as I prefer the society of angels!" exclaimed Cotterell, bowing to Mistress Leyton.

"Thank you, Master Cotterell," replied Maud, with a graceful bend of her pretty head. "Here is Tabitha to bid us to dinner, and to put an end to my husband's ungallant speeches."

The dinner, though hastily arranged and prepared, was an evidence of good house-wifery, and the pasty from the Mermaid remained untasted on the sideboard. There was some sensible conversation between Sir Ralph and Leyton, and plenty of fulsome compliment from Master Dick, who became more figurative and ridiculous as the wine circulated. Maud at last rose to leave the table, but her depaiture was delayed by the entrance of Reuben, who brought a letter tied with black silk and sealed with black wax, for Master Richard Cotterell. The letter had followed him to the Mermaid, and had been sent on by Jacob Magnus.

"Ill tidings, I fear?" said Leyton.

"I trust there is mourning enough on the outside," said Dick, "to give me no cause for more within. If, as I opine ——" he had opened the letter, and, having read a few sentences, hurled it aloft and danced about like a wild Indian. When he had expended so much of his superfluous gratification as could be disposed of by his legs, he threw himself into a chair and gasped out,—

"Leyton, Newberry—dear lady—gratulate me!—envy me! —pardon me! I am a made man!—a man of gold—of lands and houses, rivers and mountains! My old Welsh uncle has died without a will, and I am heir to the scrapings of sixty years! Read, Leyton, what some blessed goosequill has written; and, Ralph, a brimming glass of that old Burgundy, if you love me!"

Leyton read the letter, and found that it contained the good news for Dick which he had described in such a remarkable manner. Although there seemed to be nothing in this accession of fortune to Cotterell which could have more interest for the Leytons than the natural gratification of two generous natures at the success of a friend, yet it was so used in the time to come as to be productive of the most serious consequences to both.

The news of the Battle of Edgeul, or Edge Hill, reached London on the 24th of October, and both the friends and the enemies of the king claimed the victory. The excitement became intense in the city, and almost led to open warfare within the walls, between the cavaliers and roundheads, as the two parties were now coming to be designated.

Leyton hesitated no longer as to the course he should pursue. He therefore made secret preparations for Maud's return to Derbyshire, entrusting her safe conduct to the faithful Reuben.

Leyton mistrusted his own firmness to resist the remonstrances of Maud against his determination to join the king's army. He knew how great would be her sorrow, how passionate her grief, and loving her as he did, he could not trust himself to encounter such a painful struggle. He therefore wrote her a long and earnest letter, wherein he set forth his strong sense of duty to his king, his detestation of the insolence of the overbearing puritans, who threatened to ride roughshod over all the gentle blood in the land, and to institute the worst tyranny that could afflict his country. He thought and spoke as did many a true gentleman of that unhappy period, and in whom the whole chivalry had not been extinguished, and who drew his sword in the king's cause because the quarrel was the king's.

Leyton bade Maud be brave as she was loving, and by her avowed resignation to the sacrifice he was making, induce other true men to strike for the true king. That she would find a solace in the training and companionship of their darling Alice, so that when peace should come—as it would in a few short weeks, perhaps—their lives would be made happier for this transient sorrow. He told her, also, that if Leyton Hall should be too lonely for her comfort, she had his full consent to take residence with her sister Constance, or to make such other disposition of herself as pleased her. And then, with many honied phrases and earnest prayers for their quick reunion, he bade her farewell.

It needed many readings of this cruel epistle before Maud could fully understand the misery which had come to her. Many readings—as her streaming eyes blotted out the words that conveyed the terrible intelligence that *he* had gone to encounter danger of suffering or of death ! Oh, what an appalling thought ! She must be in some oppressive dream —some hideous nightmare that terrified her soul, and from which she could not free herself, strive how she might. Left her !—gone without one parting kiss !—gone without seeing their darling, and to such perils as she had never thought within the scope of their peaceful lives !

For a time poor Maud appeared to be stunned by her grief, and she remained in a kind of stupor, until tears—blessed tears ! rushed freely from her eyes and gave her relief. With more calmness, she re-read all that Leyton had written, and after a while she seemed to comprehend the reasoning of her husband. Tabitha, a kindly girl at heart, though endowed with the cupidity of a waiting-woman, showed her sympathy by her silence, as she knelt by her mistress, and pressed the unresisting hand, cold--almost as cold as death could have made it.

"Dear, noble, gallant husband!" Maud said, at length ; "I thought I could not love thee more from any act of thine! But I do—dear Edward, I feel I do—for this chivalric sacrifice of all most dear to you. No word of mine shall be said to win you from the path of honourable duty. And yet ——" she added after a pause, "and yet, if ill should befall thee— wounds, sickness—and I not by your side to watch and comfort. Oh, merciful Father! give me courage and strength to endure." She fell upon her knees, and so remained praying to the only certain Comforter.

The next day, and the next, brought occasional paroxysms of grief; but they were mitigated as time went on. In one matter she showed disobedience to her husband's commands. She refused to leave London for the present. Knowing that the king's forces, which Leyton had joined, were in the neighbourhood of Brentford, Maud encouraged the hope that Leyton might not find service suitable to his position, or that some happy circumstance might put an end to the threatened strife, and then she should be near—ready to welcome back her soldier, whatever had been his fortune.

She therefore wrote a loving missive to Leyton, resolving to dispatch it by Reuben so soon as she could learn the whereabout of her husband. The Battle of Brentford was fought with doubtful success (so history records), but the boastful Londoners engaged in the fray claimed the victory as against the king. Maud wondered—affrighted at her own conjectures—if Leyton had borne a part in it! And if so, with what result? Now she saw him as the leader of a successful charge—then he laid stricken down, hacked and bloody among the slain. These conflicting fancies became almost unendurable—perhaps would have proved so, had not a messenger brought a ragged piece of paper, on which was rudely scrawled: "Victory! dear Maud! All well. A thousand kisses!—E. L. P Rupert's quarters."

Her first impulse was to journey to Brentford; but Reuben besought her friends to dissuade her from so rash an undertaking, and she yielded to remonstrance only on condition that Reuben should convey her letter to his master.

The faithful servant was delighted at such a charge, and having, through the interest of Master Cotterell (who had returned to London) obtained a safe conduct pass from

Denzil Holles, to whom Dick was known, was soon on his way to Brentford.

Rather more than a week had elapsed since Leyton had left for the army, and during that time Mistress Leyton's friends had not neglected her. Master Cotterell had been regular in his visits, so anxious was he to learn tidings of Leyton, whose rashness he condemned, until Maud requested that her husband's conduct should remain unquestioned.

"To hear is to obey, dear lady," said Cotterell, with affected humility; "but why a man should fly the heaven of such a home for the *inferno* of a camp, for any king or potentate in Christendom, exceeds my poor comprehension."

Maud merely bowed, as though wishing to avoid the subject.

It has been in the experience of many, that when beset by some great apprehension or heavy sorrow, the afflicted seem to accept any grotesque or even childish circumstance with an appearance of satisfaction strangely opposed to all that might have been thought a solace in affliction.

It was thus with Maud, who listened to Cotterell's fulsome compliments and idle gossip with a patience which gratified, whilst it rather surprised that unprincipled gentleman.

Cotterell's unexpected acquisition of wealth came at a time when he had gathered much experience from that stern teacher, necessity; and though he was sufficiently profuse in his expenditure, he indulged in no wasteful extravagance, to the disappointment of many of his old boon companions. Indeed, he appeared to control his propensity for deep potations and midnight orgies to which he had been heretofore addicted, as though he were resolved to live more "cleanly, like a gentleman," now that he had the means to purchase other appliances to enjoyment. He affected not to comprehend the causes of dissension between king and Parliament, and resolutely eschewed all discussion of politics, at a time when the talk of men—and women also —was rarely of anything else. This change of conduct could hardly be called reformation, as Richard Cotterell had devoted himself to the accomplishment of an object which was even more opposed to honour and morality.

It was late in the afternoon of the second day succeeding the battle of Brentford, that Reuben, after many difficulties, reached the quarters of Prince Rupert. Nor was it then easy to find his master, who, having joined very recently held no command, but served only as a volunteer. Leyton, had, however, distinguished himself somewhat during the action, and from that circumstance Reuben was at last enabled to find out where he was quartered. Never was messenger or missive more welcome, and a couple of gold pieces rewarded his perseverance and fidelity.

It is needless to say how Maud's letter was read and re-read by him who loved her so well, or how proud he felt of the true wife who valued her husband's honour more than her own peace.

And then Leyton questioned Reuben, who told him—
"Mistress was sorely afflicted, Sir, when first she learned your departure, and Tabitha had fears that she would have gone distraught at times."

"Poor child!" said Leyton; "but when you left her she was more at ease, Reuben?"

"Oh yes, Sir, and had been for many days past—after she had written that letter. She was prevailed on to see company, and many of her friends came around her, Master Cotterell almost—ay, quite—daily, Sir."

A slight flush rose to Leyton's cheek when he heard this.

"My mistress—as, perhaps, she has told you, Sir—doth refuse to return to the country ——"

"Until she has heard from me," said Leyton.

"Likely, Sir," replied Reuben. "I take it, it is still your wish that she go there?"

"It is so; and I will write her to that effect," said Leyton, "though there are scant means of doing so. I must ask among my comrades for pen and paper."

But Leyton was prevented making the inquiry, as a trumpet sounded a summons to saddle.

"To horse, men!" said a cornet, entering the guard-room where the above colloquy was taking place; "the king departs for Oatlands, and we are his escort."

Leyton was too young a soldier, too fond a husband, to receive this order without a mental murmur; but he knew he must obey, and therefore he spoke a few earnest words of message to his wife, and amongst others an earnest request that she would forthwith return to Leyton Hall while the state of the roads made such a journey possible.

How coldly were Leyton's loving words delivered, and how much his request that Maud should return home sounded like a command, as Reuben repeated it!

Maud reluctantly prepared to obey—the more reluctantly, as she had received news from home assuring her that her darling Alice was thriving as heart could desire, and— he — her husband — was in the midst of dangers, and tidings of him would rarely reach her in the lonely country home.

All was ready for her journey, but there was to be a long delay, as the winter set in early, and a heavy fall of snow made travelling, as it was then, impossible.

The attention which had been called to Leyton's gallantry at Brentford fight had reached the ears of Rupert, and he was appointed to a cornetcy in a troop especially devoted to the charge of the king's person. His majesty had gone into winter-quarters at Oxford, and thither Leyton had accompanied him. For many weary weeks he lay there without the possibility of hearing from his beloved Maud, or of communicating with her, so unsettled was the country—so difficult the means of conveyance. The condition of poor Maud was still more distressing. Separated from her husband, in ignorance of his state, constantly beset with loving fears for his safety, no active duties to occupy her thoughts, what could she do but weep and pray for him? The accident of the weather kept her also from her child, and her wifely solicitude was only exchanged for her maternal anxieties; and at times she accused herself of selfishness in having kept away from Alice to be nearer to her husband. The cruel snow fell and melted ; fell again, and remained long upon the ground, and Reuben pronounced the roads to be impassable. Poor Maud! She who had been so happy until the beginning of that civil strife which was to make fair England a land of lamentation.

It is not to be wondered at that one so placed should be glad to welcome the visits of friends and acquaintance, or that she should listen still patiently to the light conversation of merry Master Cotterell. She had no interest in what he said ; but the sound of his voice, the effort of listening to his words, changed the painful current of her thoughts, and she appeared grateful for the relief.

Cotterell's vanity was flattered by her attention, and his sinfulness was encouraged by it—deceived by it.

After a morning visit, and when he had used bolder words and phrases than he had ever ventured upon, Maud, when left alone, began to recall some of the expressions he had used, and a sudden alarm seized upon her. Surely he, her husband's friend, could have had no hidden meaning in what he had said? He could not have intended to convey to her sentiments which he would not have dared to disclose in the presence of her husband? The more she thought over the interviews of the last few days, the more she became frightened at the construction which could be put upon them ; and so strong became her terror at her own conclusions, that she struck, almost unconsciously, the little silver bell which summoned Tabitha, with the intention of forbidding Cotterell's admission to her presence for the future.

Tabitha did not answer on the instant, and when she came into the room her manner was confused, as though something had occurred to startle the good conscience of which she was in the habit of boasting. She merely said, "A letter for you, Madam," and having delivered it, left the room.

Maud tore away the silk which bound the paper, expecting—as she always did when letters came to her—that the missive contained news of her child or husband. With beating heart and tearful eyes she began the perusal of what was written ; but as she proceeded, a deathly paleness came over her face, until, crushing the paper in her hands, and then casting it from her, she sank back in her chair, and burst into an agony of tears.

What had so moved her?

The letter was from Cotterell, although the cowardly libertine had withheld his signature. Maud knew that no other friend would have dared to have addressed her as that wicked letter spoke to her. It read thus :—

"FAIREST OF CREATED BEINGS !—

"Ovid tells how Icarus, flying too near the sun, fell into the sea and perished. Though fearing to fall like him —for thou art to me the sun of my existence—the intensity of my love makes me brave the danger. Fear bids me destroy this missive ; but the memories of stolen glances and gentle words bid me withhold my hand ——"

Maud had read no more, but cast the letter away.

When the first expression of her indignant grief had subsided, she rose up and walked about the room almost bewildered. What should she do? Fly at all hazard to her husband. She only knew by rumour where it was likely he might be found! No, that course was hopeless. There were pens and paper on her table. She would write to the villain who had so insulted her—yes, write calmly to him if she could, and forbid him her house. She could hardly master her thoughts sufficiently to be coherent in what she wrote.

"I have long esteemed you as a dear friend; but what has passed during the last few days had somewhat prepared me for thy letter ——"

She threw down the pen! To write to such a man in answer to such a letter seemed treachery to her absent husband. *He* would have answered only with his sword. As she thought thus, a feeling of sickness and a faintness came upon her, and she again struck the bell for Tabitha, who arrived just in time to see her mistress's head fall upon her shoulder, and the mockery of death come into her face.

Tabitha instantly called for Reuben, and by his assistance Maud was conveyed to her chamber, after being partially restored by such appliances as were then in use.

When Reuben returned to the room where his mistress had been sitting, his quick grey eye glanced about as though seeking the cause of Maud's sudden illness. The crumpled paper still lay upon the ground. He picked it up and read it slowly, very slowly. There was a smile upon his lips when he had finished. On the table were the few lines that Maud had written. Reuben read those also, and then he folded the sheet of paper and placed it with Cotterell's letter in a pocket inside the breast of his doublet. He then stood with folded hands and upturned eyes and compressed lips, as though he were looking perhaps back into the past, perhaps forward into the future.

After a time he walked stealthily to the door of Maud's chamber and listened for a few moments, but possibly hearing nothing, he clasped his hands above his head, and muttering either a prayer or a malediction, walked silently out of the room.

The next morning Maud gave orders to prepare for the journey home, nothing would stay her longer—not even the prospect of broken roads, streams flooded by the melting snow; the bitter frosty air, or the certainty of cold and cheerless lodgings at the miserable roadside inns! She felt she had been touched by evil, and needed the pure embraces of her child to make her clean again.

CHAPTER IV.

REVENGE.

THE civil war was now at its height. It would be only repeating the history of the times to particularise the events in which Leyton was compelled to take a part, as Prince Rupert had conceived an extraordinary liking for him, and continually employed him in conveying verbal communications between himself and the king, as the roads were so possessed by scouts, that it was not prudent on all occasions to commit to writing the projects of the royalist commanders. From the same cause, Leyton had not been able to write or to receive letters before he was appointed on secret service to the queen, and to the honour of forming part of her escort when she fled to France.

The letter which Leyton had written, informing Maud of this new service, was unluckily intercepted, and as the matter it contained was considered to be of importance to the State, it was detained, and Maud therefore was left in ignorance of her husband's departure from England.

During this time, Leyton Hall—one of the moated manor houses, built early in Elizabeth's time, on the site of a dismantled stronghold — had been frequently occupied by the troops of king and parliament, until Mistress Leyton determined to take up her residence in a small house on the confines of the park. She was accompanied thither by her waiting-maid and nurse, and only two other domestic servants, whilst Reuben and a part of the household remained at the hall. Maud had changed greatly since the

cruel separation from her husband, and at times she fell
into deep despondency, from which it required all Tabitha's
cleverness to rouse her. Little Alice was generally the
medium employed, but it sometimes happened that the very
endearments of the child only served to increase the
mother's depression. The consequence of these attacks
was a nervous excitability, which made Maud painfully
sensitive, and apprehensive of evil to those whom she loved,
and an impulsiveness was induced which not unfrequently
gave her attendants some discomfort and much anxiety.
No tidings of Leyton had reached Maud for some weeks,
and yet news of recurrent conflicts came by an occasional
news-letter, or was narrated by one of the wandering
pedlars who sought for custom at the door.

It was early June, when towards the close of the afternoon, a servant in the livery of Mistress Leyton's only sister,
Constance Gray, rode to the house, and delivered a letter
marked, " Haste—post haste." The horse on which the man
rode was covered with foam, and though he had travelled
only twenty miles, as the crow flies, he had been nearly three
hours upon the road.

The letter just received contained painful news for Maud.
Her sister was thought to be at the point of death, caused by
the sudden intelligence that her husband, Cecil Gray, had
been mortally wounded in a skirmish, and was then being
borne secretly to his house. Maud was implored to come at
once to Constance, but to conceal if possible from everyone
the supposed cause of her sister's illness. To read was to
be obeyed, and horses were forthwith ordered from the Hall;
the messenger's tired beast being left to recover from its
fatigue, whilst the servant—who requested to be permitted
to return as Maud's guide—was mounted upon the horse
usually ridden by Reuben. Having embraced her darling
Alice, Maud with a heavy heart started, late as it was in
the day, to attend her stricken sister. It was well she had
done so, as before the noon of the next day Constance died,
after exacting from her sister a promise to adopt as her own
an infant boy named Walter, should it please providence to
decree the death of her wounded husband, Cecil Gray.

Gray only lived long enough to look upon the pale face of
his dead wife, and to kiss his little son, comforted at his
death by the promise which Maud had given, and which she
felt assured that Leyton would approve.

The necessary preparations for the obsequies of the departed, and the performance of them, occupied about ten days—ten short days fraught with such evil to Maud Leyton, that the whole colour of her life was changed by it.

Captain Leyton—he was captain now—had returned to England with a message from the queen ; and as the king lay at Uxbridge, thither Leyton went, and was most graciously received. Without difficulty he obtained permission to visit his family; and late on the night of the fourth day, he arrived at his ancestral home. He was fortunate, he thought, to find it unoccupied by strangers ; and with beating heart he entered the old hall, and then hurried unannounced to the chamber where he expected to find Maud. Neither light nor fire burned in the once cheerful room ! He called Maud's name—none answered ! A chill fell upon his heart, as though some terrible evil was at hand. He called again ; and Reuben entered the room, bearing a light, and followed by one of the lower servants, with materials for producing a fire.

"What means this, Reuben?" asked Leyton. "Where is your mistress?"

Reuben pointed to his fellow-servant, as though to intimate that silence in her presence was desirable.

"Cease your mumming, Sirrah," cried Leyton ; "and speak out. Leave the room, wench ; and now speak, fellow."

Reuben crouched so low before his master that he might almost be said to be kneeling, as he faltered out—

"Oh, my honoured master, would that any tongue but mine had given you this sorry welcome to your home."

Leyton stamped his foot impatiently on the ground, and said, "Where is your mistress—dead or ill?"

"I hope neither," replied Reuben ; "though heaven knows, there are worse things than death and sickness !"

Leyton caught the fellow by the throat, and hardly forbore dashing his fist into the man's affrighted face, as he exclaimed—

"What damnable story art thou hatching? What dost thou mean, varlet?"

"Since you must hear the truth, dear master, better hear it from me that has served you long and truly than from others."

Leyton sank upon a chair ; and, with staring eyes and parted lips, listened to what Reuben told him.

It was a strange story, and a wicked one. Reuben said that, two days gone, Mistress Leyton, accompanied by her waiting-woman only, had suddenly disappeared late at night, and unknown to everyone at the Hall; that the horse-boy had saddled mistress's horse, and also the one usually ridden by Reuben, placing upon the latter a pillion for the waiting woman. There was a grey gelding left in the stable, which had belonged to the man who accompanied Mistress Leyton in her flight.

What was Leyton to guess from this?

Reuben dare not surmise—it was not for a serving-man to do so; but Reuben told that Mistress Leyton, though sorely grieved when Master Leyton left to join the king's army, soon appeared—as Reuben had said before—to regain her pleasant mood and cheerful bearing; and her lodgings were, as had been the case before his master left, the morning rendezvous of the gayest gallants of the town. Reuben had often wondered how she could find spirits for such entertainment as she gave to those springals, of whom Master Cotterell was ever the most favoured.

Leyton's cheek went pale, and then blood red almost, at Reuben's words. Reuben knew how thoroughly his master trusted his fair wife; and had, therefore, never sought to learn more than a faithful servant was bound to know, and had often chided others who had made free with the name of his mistress—nay, had often reproved Tabitha for receiving gifts from more than one of the gallants visiting their lodgings, and of whom none were so prodigal as Master Cotterell.

A sharp, short imprecation escaped from Leyton's lips—
"What more?"

At last Mistress Leyton returned to Leyton Hall; but she appeared ever restless and desponding, brooding hour by hour together, as though she missed the gaiety of the town, and prized no longer the country pleasures, which, in aforetime, had contented her. After awhile—she had been much apart from all—she decided upon quitting the hall, and taking up her abode at the small Grange, which stood at the borders of the park, contenting herself with the attendance of Tabitha, her maid, the nurse and two other servants. Reuben saw her but seldom, his business being at the Hall. At last, three days before the arrival of Leyton, the mistress had disappeared none knew whither.

"And the child—the child Alice?"

"Was at the Grange."

What was the meaning of all Leyton saw and heard? What did Reuben wish him to understand — to guess at from what he had said?

Reuben remained silent until Leyton, drawing his sword, declared he would kill him where he stood, if he held back any further knowledge which he had, and which could elucidate the mysteries.

Reuben then produced from an inner pocket of his doublet a small packet of papers carefully tied together.

"You have insisted upon this evidence being given, master; and I pray thee, hold me harmless from its consequences," said Reuben. "The day after my mistress fled I went into her room at the Grange, and lying on her open writing-table I found these papers; they may have a better meaning for you than I have been able to assign to them."

With trembling hands and burning eyes, Leyton unfolded and then read the papers—

"Fairest of created beings! Ovid tells how Icarus, flying too near the sun, fell into the sea and perished. Though fearing to fall like him—for thou art to me the sun of my existence — the intensity of my love makes me brave the danger. Fear bids me destroy this missive; but the memories of stolen glances and gentle words bid me withhold my hand." Leyton paused, and ground his teeth together, to suppress any expression of his anger. "If this missive be not my destruction, place to-night a candle in the window of thy chamber—as Sappho showed on the shores of the Hellespont a beacon to her Leander." "Cotterell's hand,'fore heaven!" exclaimed Leyton. "If he's above ground ——" But he had opened the other folded paper, and what he saw made him stagger as though he had received a blow.

It was Maud's writing—his own Maud's—and what had she written?

"I have ever esteemed thee as a dear friend? but what has passed during the past few days had somewhat prepared me for thy letter——" Nothing more!—what more was needed? The light, vain woman, who could, when peril surrounded her husband, court the silly flatteries of such creatures as Reuben had described, could only be destined to one end. And yet, how had Leyton been deceived? He had never detected anything to awaken a suspicion that

Maud was such a mindless wanton! but men had been deceived — the wiser the more readily — since the world began: none so blind as those who loved as fondly as he had done. He who could not remember to have seen a fault in Maud—yet, being mortal, she must have shared the common lot, and had some imperfections.

Reuben did not let him doubt, when the doubt was in Maud's favour. With the perseverance of a sleuth-hound, he hunted the absent woman down; he needed no substratum of truth for what he told his half-maddened master; but with the skill of the Evil One he invented lie upon lie, until Leyton in his frenzy cursed his unhappy wife, and with the dawn of the next day had left Leyton Hall, taking with him his little daughter Alice, and Reuben for her attendant.

Tedious as the journey to London was, of necessity, it seemed doubly irksome now to Leyton, who counted every minute lost which kept him from his revenge upon Cotterell, and who he believed was certain to be found or heard of in the old city. At last London was reached; and having carefully bestowed Alice with an aunt of Reuben, Leyton commenced his search for Cotterell, utterly regardless of the expiry of his leave of absence, and bent only upon one object—the destruction of his destroyer. He went the round of Cotterell's usual haunts, and learned at all of them that he had been absent more than a fortnight. This circumstance was only a confirmation of Cotterell's villany and Leyton's dishonour. It was almost maddening to leave London and his great wrong unrequited; but his duty to his king—now seemingly approaching the consummation of his fate—compelled him to abandon for the present a meeting with Cotterell. Having provided a nurse for Alice, Leyton prepared a document, by which he constituted Reuben his steward and custodian of Leyton Hall.

"You will be master until my return, Reuben," Leyton said —"if ever I go back to that dishonoured house. Should she," he paused, and the quivering of his lips betrayed with what effort he controlled the tears welling from his heart. "Should she," he said, with great effort, "ever return, and need other help than she can command from her friends, spare nothing of mine—house nor land—that can give her comfort."

The strong man could say no more, or his "mother's weakness" would have shamed him.

We will not speak of Maud for the present, but follow Leyton to the strife which was awaiting him.

The king had gone to Hull House, near Harborough, with the van of his army, the rear being encamped at Naseby. Rupert was at Harborough, and thither Leyton made his way, and was heartily welcomed by his brave commander.

"You are a laggard, Captain Leyton," said Rupert, "and I feared that to-morrow's sport would have been had without you. We shall have hot work, I promise you."

"The hotter the more welcome, your highness," replied Leyton. "I am in fighting humour, and I trust to your favour for a post where I may rid me of it."

"Never fear, *camarado !*" replied the prince; "we will not be far asunder."

Leyton rejoiced in this near approach to a bloody contest, as, for a time, he looked upon the prospect of death almost with a desire for its accomplishment, but then two great aspirations found a place in his thoughts, and he cared to live—one was the hope of meeting Cotterell—another his parental desire to be the guardian, the guide, the father to his deserted innocent—his Alice—"sole daughter of his house and heart."

The story of Naseby Field is still told by those who dwell about it. Mill Hill is shown, where Fairfax had taken position on the 14th June, 1645—the right commanded by General Cromwell and the left by Ireton. On the opposite hill was the king's battle, and between them, you are still shown where Rupert made his desperate charge—where Cromwell, shouting his battle cry, "God is our strength," drove back Langdale's horse—where, after three hours of fierce fighting, the army of King Charles was routed, never to re-assemble in defence of its royal master.

"We, after three hours' fight, very doubtful," Cromwell wrote to Mr. Speaker, "at last routed his army; killed and took about 5,000—very many officers, but of what quality we know not. We took also about two hundred carriages, all he had; and all his guns, twelve in number."

Laconic as this despatch is, it contained the materials for the history of England for the next fifteen years.

The king's cause was now utterly lost, although the war continued in various parts of the kingdom. Leyton, however, had obtained his discharge from Prince Rupert before that general's departure from Bristol. He knew that he incurred some danger from the victorious party by appearing openly in London, but he disregarded such peril in his desire to find the man who had wronged him so much. They met at last in the room of the Mermaid where we were first introduced to Cotterell. Although Leyton had been wronged only in intention by his false friend, Cotterell was so oppressed by the sense of the injury he had contemplated, that his bearing towards Leyton was that of a self-convicted man.

The two men were alone in the room. Leyton fixed his eyes upon his foe, the while his brows almost met, and his features, bronzed by exposure in the camp, became almost blackened by the rush of blood to their surface.

Cotterell saw at a glance he had been detected or exposed, and, cowering almost, he stepped backward, as though fearing some violence from Leyton.

Leyton spoke not a word, but quietly unfolding Cotterell's letter to Maud, and which he had never parted from since Reuben gave it to him, he held it out for Cotterell's inspection.

As the man thus silently accused made no sign—spoke no word, Leyton said—

"Do you know that letter? Was it yours?"

Cotterell instinctively placed his hand upon his sword. The action was a sufficient acknowledgment.

"You own it, despicable villain!" cried Leyton; and then, calmly folding the offending paper and replacing it in his bosom, he drew his sword, and called to Cotterell to do the same.

"Draw villain!—draw instantly! Let me not commit murder?"

"Leyton, hear me ——"

"Not if I were your confessor, you treacherous villain!" replied Leyton. "Has your hot blood grown cold? Let that warm it;" and with the flat of the blade of his sword he struck Cotterell sharply on the arm.

Cotterell was no coward, but conscious of the wrong he had intended Leyton, he would have avoided the chance of doing him any bodily injury. He knew himself to be a perfect swordsman, but what Leyton lacked in skill he now made up in impetuosity. With a fury which nothing could withstand, he pressed Cotterell into one corner of the room, and disregarding all the usual forms of attack and defence, appeared likely to overcome his adversary by mere physical force. Cotterell defended himself manfully, skilfully, for some time, but at last Leyton seized his opponent's sword in his left hand, ungloved as it was, and attempted to wrench the weapon away from him.

"Madman!" cried Cotterell; "I will not be butchered! quit my sword;" but as Leyton struggled till he had obtained possession of the weapon, Cotterell drew out a small wheel-lock pistol, and fired full in the face of Leyton.

The wounded man uttered a cry and fell senseless to the ground.

The report of the pistol and the previous noise had brought Magnus and his people to the place of encounter, and more than one was a witness of Cotterell's act.

"You will bear witness, all of you," said Cotterell, "that I shot in self-defence!"

"You did! you did!" replied Magnus; "I will take oath to't," and would have done so on the bare word of such a customer as Master Cotterell. "But be advised by me, Sir. Our city magistrates are cold-blooded fellows, Master Cotterell, and would clap you up for trial an' you were taken before them. Get you gone down to the river. If Master Leyton be dead, he will give us some trouble. If he be only stunned, as I fancy, he will give more; but that will be paid for, so no matter."

Cotterell was fully sensible of the soundness of this advice, and before the confusion had subsided, he made the best of his way down Bread Street, and taking boat at the stairs, was rowed to Southwark, whence, if need be, he could get to the coast, and so be out of harm's way.

An apothecary was soon found, and he, after an examination of the wounded man, pronounced the wound not mortal, although he feared the shot had destroyed the sight of both the patient's eyes, but of that he could not be certain. His conjecture proved, alas, to be true, and when Leyton recovered from his wound, it was to find himself in total blindness.

Leyton had felt his supposed dishonour so acutely that he had carefully avoided the society of all his former friends, and now when this calamity had overtaken him, he resisted all the entreaties of Jacob Magnus (to whom he was known), that any intimation of his condition should be communicated to friend or foe.

Jacob was always a man to mind his own business, especially if he were well paid for it, and Leyton, with a true knowledge of mine host, had taken effectual means to secure the silence of Jacob and his household.

As soon as Leyton had quite recovered his strength, he made arrangements for the care of Alice, and hearing that his friend and general, Prince Rupert, had departed for Sicily, Leyton determined to follow him there, more from the influence of habit than from any seeking for sympathy which the rough soldier might have accorded to his tried companion in arms.

Reuben was secretly summoned to town, but only to receive certain instructions for the future; but much of his responsibility was removed, the Parliament having sequestrated Leyton Hall, as being the property of a recusant, and one of the enemies of the people. Not one word of Maud passed the lips of either master or servant, and she who had been so beloved was now as the dead—ah! far less than the dead —to the husband who had loved her so fondly.

When Reuben parted for the last time, perhaps, from the master whom he had so cruelly abused, he went direct to the woman he had called his aunt, and who had charge of little Alice.

He closed the door of the room where his aunt was seated carefully after him, having first looked out on to the landing as though to be sure he had not been watched or followed.

"Well, aunt," he said, in a low, hoarse whisper, "I have done what I swore to do ten long years ago."

The old woman so addressed waved her head to and fro, as though deprecating what Reuben had done.

"I know! I know!" she said. "I know what we both swore on that wretched night, Reuben; but 'vengeance is mine, saith the Lord.'"

"True, aunt, and He chooses His own instruments. I and you are so chosen," answered Reuben. "His sin hath found him out. His punishment has come from those he most wronged."

"I fear it is sinfulness, Reuben," said the woman; "that we shall be judged for what you have done."

"I have no fear, aunt," replied Reuben. "I have thought night and day on the wickedness of the past, of the misery that man brought into your house and into mine. I have never had from my sight the thing we looked upon, and I could not have died anywhere with that wrong unavenged and as I had sworn to do it ——"

"And yet we pray, 'Forgive us our trespasses, as we forgive them that sin against us,'" said the woman. "Oh, Reuben; we cannot pray for our sins to be forgiven, and we shall perish in the wrath to come!"

"Aunt, you have been too much of late to those conventicles, as they are called, and have been frightened by their tales of fire and brimstone," said Reuben, doggedly. "We made a vow, and, as I remember, we prayed for death—ay worse than death, to ourselves—if we should be forsworn. I dare not brave that, aunt, and I have kept my oath. Where he loved he has been deceived. By her whom he loved he has had his heart bruised! And as she led him to break the promise by which he broke a heart as loving and as tender as her own, she lives a widowed wife and a sorrowing mother."

"Peace, Reuben!" cried the woman. "I cannot listen to such a story of the wicked thing we have done. As I look upon that sleeping innocent and know what misery we have worked its parents, I half resolve to seek Master Leyton, and on my knees confess the sin we have committed."

"It is lucky, then, that you will see Master Leyton no more. Here is the money for your charges, and in the morning a person will come for the child. Master Leyton leaves England to-morrow."

The woman let the money remain uncounted upon the table for some time, continuing to sigh and moan as though she were having a sharp contest with her conscience; but Reuben chinked the money bag, and the sound of the "incentive to evil," scared away the dame's good resolutions.

Leyton Hall was, as we have said, one of those moated manor houses which began early in Elizabeth's reign to take the place of the battlemented strongholds of the olden time. It stood on the spur of a lofty hill, on which grew a cluster of stately trees much older than the Hall itself. A park of some hundred acres stretched down to the river Dove, after that pleasant stream flowed through romantic Dove Dale. In one corner of the park stood the smaller dwelling called the Grange, which had usually been occupied by the elder sons of the Leytons, and was now occupied by Mistress Maud.

As Mistress Leyton, on her return home, caught the first sight of the noble Hall, a hundred pleasant fancies came into her mind. She pictured to herself the delight of Alice at seeing her again, and of the pleasure the child would feel at having a little playfellow like her cousin Walter brought home to share her sports, and in after time her studies.

Maud felt assured that Leyton would approve the promise she had made, and would find his pleasure, when the cruel war was ended, in training the pretty boy in manly exercises; and perhaps the cousins might in time to come grow to be lovers—such unions had been ere now, and Walter Gray would be no unworthy match for the heiress of Leyton Hall.

Unhappy Maud! her pleasant dreams were soon to be dispelled.

She had scarcely alighted at her door, when Dorothy, the nurse, met her, and wailing, "like one mourning the dead,' she fell upon her knees.

Maud, panic-stricken, had scarcely power to ask if her child were dead, and when assured that Alice was living, the revulsion of feeling was more than she could bear, and she sank down senseless. But why dwell upon every phase of grief shown by the bereaved mother?

At first she could not be made to comprehend what had occurred. Her husband had been there and taken away the child?—leaving no word, no line? Yes, Reuben had said he had been entrusted with some message for his mistress. Why was he not there to deliver it? He came after awhile, and gave Maud a scrap of paper—open, unsealed. The words written upon it almost blinded her as she read them—

" Miserable woman : Your infamy is known to me. We never meet again this side of the grave !—E. L."

Infamy! What did he mean? Never meet again? What did he mean? She had never wronged him even in thought. She loved him with her whole soul, as she had done since she had been his wife. Never meet again ! She could not understand the meaning of the words, and Reuben would not help her to a solution of the riddle.

At length, by the aid of Tabitha, she gained a clue to what the scrap of paper meant. Her bewildered brain could scarcely comprehend the new horror, and when it did so, it was but for a moment or two, and then a frenzy seized her, which only changed to settled insanity.

Tabitha had summoned such friends and connexions of the family as were within reach, and their counsel advised that Reuben should be dispatched in search of Leyton. But Tabitha earnestly objected to this proposal. She had, she knew not why, conceived a distrust of Reuben; and with a boldness which surprised her auditors, she did not hesitate to express her suspicions of Reuben's dishonesty to her mistress.

" No one word of pity has he spoken," said Tabitha ; "but with a cold sneer upon his ill-favoured face, he has sought to excuse the wickedness which has been done. ' No doubt our master had reason.' ' We can know nothing of the cause.' By my faith, I would not have that fellow's conscience for the king's crown."

What then was to be done? Many were ready to go in search of Leyton, but who could point out the trail they should follow? Tabitha at last bethought her of her uncle Magnus ; and believing that she could better manage matters with him than could the friends of her mistress, it was arranged that she should depart secretly to London and make inquiries.

But Jacob Magnus had been paid well to hold his peace on all that concerned Master Leyton ; and he prided himself on keeping his engagements, whether they were for good or evil. Tabitha, however, was not to be easily quieted, as she had discovered that her uncle and aunt had some knowledge of the matter in hand ; and at last she succeeded in gaining a clue to the whereabout of the woman who had had charge of Alice, and whom Reuben called aunt.

The woman, having left her old lodging, was traced with some difficulty by Tabitha and her old sweetheart, Thomas Handy—who, by-the-bye, had been long discarded by Tabitha for a smart serving-man, who, in his turn, had jilted her.

The woman occupied now a miserable room in the Mint, and was lying sick and penniless. So long as the money she had received from Leyton lasted, she had quieted her self-reproaches for her connivance at Reuben's wickedness ; but now—her money spent, chiefly in strong waters—she fancying death was at her bedside, became terrified, remembering the denunciations of evil-doers which she had heard in the conventicles, to which curiosity more than any worthier feeling had allured her. In this condition Tabitha fortunately found her, and partly by increasing her fears, and partly by a considerable bribe, the woman was brought to confession.

She could not say where Master Leyton had gone ; beyond seas she knew it was ; to the Barbadoes, she fancied. She had not seen him after his fight with one Master Cotterell.

" Why had he fought with him?"

"Ay, there was the wickedness of what had been done—she and Reuben. But she would make a clean breast of it, even if Reuben should come and kill her."

Her daughter Grace was a buxom lass, with a round form, and rosy cheeks, and hazel eyes. Reuben had courted her, and she had promised to marry him; but the young master of Leyton Hall came in her way, and an old story had to be told again. When her shame became known, Reuben abused her sadly, and poor Grace, betrayed and deserted, drowned herself. It was Reuben who had found and brought home the body of Grace; and, when the poor corpse lay with matted hair and bedrabbled clothes, lover and mother knelt beside it and swore a vow of vengeance. To accomplish this wicked vow, Reuben had obtained service at the Hall, to watch and watch until he could find a chance to strike a blow that should wound worse than the murderer's knife. And the woman told all that Reuben had done: how he had lied to his trusting master—what proofs he had given him that the wife was false—and what a terrible infliction had overtaken Leyton. Tabitha shuddered as she listened to this narrative and then, throwing down the money she had promised to the woman, hastened out into the street, and alarmed Thomas by her affrighted looks, fairly winding him by the rapid pace at which she traversed London Bridge and the streets which were between it and the Mermaid.

Tabitha returned into Derbyshire as soon as she could, and having recounted what she had learned, the friends of Maud consulted how they should proceed against the villain Reuben; but the law seemed to be powerless, and all personal retribution appeared so utterly inadequate to the crime, that the fellow was allowed to escape for the time.

He was not, however, to be long at his ease. The Parliamentary Sequestrators laid their hands on Leyton Hall, and Reuben, after a time, his crime being known, was shunned by all, and fled none knew whither. More than three years passed before Maud's reason was entirely restored, and then a gentle melancholy distinguished her. Her chief solace was in the affection of her nephew, Walter Gray.

CHAPTER V.

THE KING'S ROGUES.

LIVER CROMWELL was dead, and his son Richard proved but a feeble successor. The hopes of the royalists seemed to revive, the more especially as the people at large began to tire of the domination of the puritans, whose peculiar views of social life were strongly at variance with the natural joviality of the English character. The puritans had long put down the most favourite amusements of the people ; and the Lord of Misrule, May games, Plough Monday dances, church ales and wakes, were only heard of in the tales of old men and women. The puritans condemned all dancing in mixed company of the sexes, though some held that "men by themselves, and women by themselves," might dance without sin to recreate the mind oppressed with some great toil and labour.

Political reasons were also concurring to put an end to the Commonwealth, and more than one rising had taken place in favour of monarchy. As one of the consequences of the unsettled times, a number of loose characters—disbanded soldiers, ruined spendthrifts, and idle rufflers—were found in various parts of the country, living by their wits or their violences. Among other disreputable combinations, was one generally known as "The King's Rogues," although they assumed to be honest royalists, who had authority to collect any subsidies for the king's use from those loyal persons who were confiding enough to entrust money to them. Not far from Leyton Hall was a village long since fallen to decay, and at the time of our story occupied by a small community of agriculturists who prided themselves upon their loyalty to the king. On the outskirts of this village was a ruinous farmhouse, which no one cared to own, as there were scarcely two rooms in it which were habitable, and the roof had long since been scattered by the winds. The kitchen was tolerably wind and weather tight ; and there, on a March night, had assembled some dozen men, more or less bearing evidence of their claim to be ranked as King's Rogues. They were all armed with swords, and most of them wore the long buff boots with which we are familiar in portraits of horsemen of the period, though, sooth to say, they possessed but one sorry jade, grazing in the lane hard by. The lace and other tawdry with which some of their coats were tricked out were sadly tarnished and faded, and as the wearers were seen by the dim light of two candles, no honest man would have cared to be in their company.

They were jovial, however, although the great pitcher on the table was empty; and one, who seemed to be an authority, volunteered a song. The proposal was received with much applause, and the fellow roared out some doggerel which expressed his supreme contempt for all which pertained to roundheads and tub-thumpers.

When the applause which greeted the conclusion of the song had subsided, the thirsty vocalist looked into the empty pitcher, and then replaced it on the table with a deep sigh.

"Ha !" said the man—he was called Boardwine—"when the king gets his own again, we'll have no more of these beggars' revels, drinking small ale in bye-places. We shall have gold to spend, and rulers that honour good liquor."

"It's someway strange," observed a man who had suffered the loss of an eye either in battle or a brawl, "that we've heard nought of late from our friends in London."

"I doubt if they're true men," said Boardwine ; "I sent to one of them for the loan of a few pounds, and the niggardly cur returned for answer that he'd see me to the gallows ere he'd lend me a stiver. That was his answer after the sacrifices I have made in the royal cause !"

"What sacrifices hast thou made?" asked a villanous-looking fellow with a red cock's feather in a very battered beaver.

"What sacrifices !" replied Boardwine, with well-assumed surprise ; "dost not remember me a slim, sober lad, that could have crept into an eel skin—one that never knew anything stronger than the flavour of his grandmother's mead? And what am I now? A concentrated larder—a peripatetic beer-barrel!"

The group found so much humour in this speech of their comrade that they roared with laughter.

"But what hath the royal cause to do with that?" asked Cocktail.

"Why, thou art dull-witted for want of liquor," replied Boardwine. "Have I not advocated the king's cause in every ale-house in the county? Could I have done that without acquiring thirst? Could I thirst and not seek to allay it? Could I drink, and not feed upon the liquor?"

The argument was admitted to be conclusive, and Boardwine declared to be the most loyal subject that ever king had, and might look for his reward should the king get his own again, as the phrase went.

"Should!" roared Boardwine; "he will, and that ere long, I say. Men are tired of wearing their faces after the fashion of folk with the colic. The tavern is getting more relished than the conventicle, and your puritan ranter must out of his barrel, as it will soon be put to its right use again."

"I think you're right," said Cocktail.

"I am always right," replied Boardwine. "When have pipe and tabor been heard on Sundays until yesterday, even in this, the most loyal village in England? Has not crop-eared Zedekiah Waterwell, that keeps the public, set up a tent for the use of the market-folk who pass along?"

"All good signs," said Cocktail, whilst the others joined in chorus.

"That they are!" continued Boardwine. "The round-heads have had their day. Ho! for the cavaliers!" and then mimicking the drawl affected by the chosen, he added, "I know of vessels of gold and vessels of silver which shall assuredly be consigned to the melting-pot."

At this moment the door was opened, and a wretched looking man entered, bearing a small keg filled with ale, but which he said would be the last that Zedekiah would score against the fraternity.

"He has no more soul than a shotten herring!" cried Boardwine: "his true name is Dickory, which he forswore after he ran away from Worcester fight, and to pleasure his landlord, took on him to be called Zedekiah. But fill your stoups, lads, and I'll sing you another stave."

Boardwine had scarcely begun, when a loud knocking at the door stopped the harmony.

"See to the door, Reuben," said Boardwine. "We receive no stranger who has not the password of our order."

But before the wretched creature who had brought the liquor could reach the door, it was boldly opened by a man whose high steeple-crowned hat and closely-cropped hair proclaimed him of the opposite faction. The puritan stopped when he saw the group before him, and drawing himself up (as was the manner of his sect) he drawled, rather than said—

"Lo! is the bull parochial given to vocal ebullitions?" adding, as man after man rose up, "what! does one of the chosen affright the sons of recusant fathers?"

"Affright!" replied Boardwine, adding a fierce oath; "not a host of ye. But this is no place for spies and informers"

"Then shouldst thou stop the chinks in the wall, or the noise in thy throat, if thou wouldst not have men know thou art a friend of the man Charles Stuart. What if I seek a justice?"

"Men of my kidney," said Boardwine, "never give the law more chances than they can help, master, ——" But before the speaker could draw his long tuck from its scabbard, the puritan had tossed off his hat, and burst into a loud laugh. He was recognised instantly, and hailed as "Dick Hummall."

"Put up thy spit, bully lad, and give me welcome," said the new comer: and in a moment every man offered his stoup.

"Two hands—two cups," said Dick, taking the proffered beakers, and tasting first one and then the other.

"Small ale, as I am a sinner," said Dick. "Is this your welcome to a king's courier?"

"Gentlemen, gentlemen! I am ashamed of you," said Boardwine, holding out his hat. "Some of ye have purses, and yet I stand here like a beggar."

More than one of the group threw some small coin into the hat, and Boardwine, jingling the pieces together, said—

"Ha! that's music. Now, Reuben, rouse up, and fetch a gallon of double ale."

The wretched man approached to receive the money, and

so foul and woe-begone he seemed, that Hummall drew back instinctively. Reuben received the money, and shambled out of the room.

"Who is that fellow of 'shreds and patches?'" asked Hummall. "He has made free with some scarecrow's wardrobe. Who is he?"

"Old Reuben Studley," answered Boardwine. "Once as sharp-witted as a Newgate lawyer. He was steward to Captain Leyton, that fought so boldly at Naseby."

"Leyton, Leyton! Ah! I remember," said Hummall. "He lived at the Hall hard by? His wife had a roomy heart, and took in another lodger—she left her husband? I knew somewhat of her waiting-maid in aforetime."

"The same," replied Boardwine. "The father carried his daughter over seas, none knew where. The father died; and a stranger has but now taken possession of the old Hall. But tell me, how came you to discover us?"

"It is my wont to take unfrequented paths, as less likely to lead to the gallows!" answered Hummall. "As I passed by the end of the thicket here, I heard and recognised thy bull-like voice. But I've news from the king!"

A spontaneous hurrah was the rejoinder to this piece of information.

"The king, gentlemen—the king wants money," said Hummall.

"Call that news?" replied Boardwine. "Why, it's as old as the Protectorate!"

"True; but who'd pause now that the game turns in our favour?" said Hummall. "General Monk—Old George, as they call him—is known to be with us; so out with your canvas money-bags, and replenish the king's exchequer."

Boardwine drew forth the empty pockets of his slops, and said, "This comes of loyalty, Dick."

Hummall laughed, as he rejoined, "Think ye I would bleed the King's Rogues! If I wanted wool, I should not skin a wolf. Is there no loyal sheep left hereabouts that is worth the shearing?"

Before the question could be answered, Reuben returned with the ale; and its attractions silenced conversation for a time. Reuben, as was his wont, slunk away to the side of the fire, and seemed indifferent to all that was passing around him.

Boardwine, after a time, drew Hummall aside, and having lighted his pipe at the fire, said, in a low voice,—

"There is one lamb, Dick, that I have heard bleat the king's name; and he is still in his first fleece."

"Good."

"But honour amongst gentlemen—the lamb is mine own," said Boardwine.

"I understand you. Who is he?" asked Hummall.

"Young Walter Gray. His father fell at Marston Moor. He is nephew to Mistress Leyton, who lives, as you know, hard by at the Grange."

Reuben gave a start; but the motion was unnoticed by the speaker.

"This lad is the pet of his old aunt; and she hath lands," said Boardwine.

"Good again!" answered Hummall. "The precious metals come out of the earth."

"He must have credit also," observed Boardwine.

"Good again! Credit is a thing much needed by the king, and his poor rogues," replied Hummall.

"True. I know not the man who would trust me with a suit. Dost thou, Dick?" asked Boardwine, showing a formidable, ill-darned rent in his broadcloth breeches.

"I know but one," answered Dick, gravely.

"Name him, Dick, for the love of decency. Let me test his credulity," said Boardwine.

"I mean," replied Dick, pausing for a moment, "I mean the man who hath charge of the pillory."

"The jest is damnably out of place, Dick," answered Boardwine. "Thou art well clothed and well stocked with goldfinches—for I heard them sing in your pocket—and should spare those who have stood back and edge to the royal cause, when the wind finds entrance through many a cranny, and the colour of a Jacobus is almost forgotten."

Hummall made amends for his unseemly jest by quietly putting a gold piece into the hand of his offended comrade.

"And now friends," said Hummall, turning away from the fire, "I have not sought you for nothing. A little loyal bird—I would call it a kingfisher had it a song—a loyal bird, I say, has sung to me of gold and jewels to be had for the gathering. But we must be prudent; and, above all, I must not be suspected of holding converse with such sons of Belial as you, gentlemen. Let one of you meet me to-morrow in Dovedale, nigh to the great stone in mid-stream; they call it hereabouts, if I remember truly, the Pike Rock."

"I know it well," said Cocktail. "When a boy, I have taken many a lusty fi-h in that water."

"Well, then, to roost at once," said Hummall; "and sleep off the fat ale which now oppresses thee, and bring a clear head in the morning—nay, in the afternoon—if you can fast sober so long."

"I drink no more than my fellows," grumbled Cocktail; "an' if thou fearest to trust me, let another to the rendezvous. I have been trusted by those who carried a leading-staff, ay, and ridden with a trumpet to give credit to my message."

"And shalt again," said Hummall, laughing. "Let me have my jest when in free company. I have enough of long faces and vinegar phrases when I am one of the chosen."

Bidding his comrades "good-night," Hummall assumed the manners of the sectarians he resembled in garb, and forthwith took his way to the village.

Richard Hummall was a man of some importance, and made so by the times. He had formerly been a serving-man to one of Leyton's friends. It was then that he had entered into a flirtation with Tabitha, for no other reason than to extinguish the aspirations of the pious drawer, Thomas Handy. That triumph effected, Dick had proved faithless, and Tabitha had lost sight of him for years. Hummall had found better employment, as he considered, than that of a serving-man, and had become a sort of spy or agent of the royalist party. In this character Master Hummall contrived to keep a well-filled purse, thanks to the liberality of the king's partisans. He also, from time to time, supplied valuable information to those who were always watching to restore the monarchy. Richard Hummall was perfectly unscrupulous as to the means he employed to gain his ends. He could sacrifice friend or foe, and some information had reached him which he fancied he could make conducive to his own interest and to the "royal cause" (the phrase always on his lips), if he could establish friendly relations with Tabitha. He had heard, and he thought truly, that the newcomer at Leyton Hall had brought with him a vast amount of wealth in very portable materials; and from other sources of information, he was sure also that there was an easy way of obtaining access to the hall by means of a private door. He had such an opinion of Tabitha that he believed, if a secret way existed, she would have been certain to have used it, and—well, we shall see.

He had not thought of Reuben Studley—Reuben, who had fallen so low. Shunned, despised by all who had heard his story, the wretched man seemed spell-bound to the place where his guilt was known. He could not leave it; he would have been incapable of assigning a reason for his stay; but there was a vague feeling—it was not hope—that by some accident he might lighten the load weighing on his conscience, and perhaps be permitted to die peacefully.

CHAPTER VI.

REUBEN'S REMORSE.

THE information which Hummall had communicated to his associates was true in part. When Leyton, under the assumed name of Maybourne, left England, he remained a short time in Sicily, and then, in the course of the next year, took up his residence in Spain. By the influence of the Miltons with Cromwell and his ministers, the escheat of Leyton Hall was reversed on very favourable terms to the self-exiled royalist, whose motive for quitting England was supposed to have been purely political, and domestic cause was never suspected by his acquaintance, although surmised by his more intimate friends. Leyton (as we shall continue to call him) made some singularly successful ventures, and in the course of a few years had grown to be a man of great wealth, despite the terrible affliction of blindness.

Alice was instructed in all the refinements that money could obtain, but those great teachers—a mother's love, a mother's watchfulness, could not be purchased, and she imbibed some of the national peculiarities which distinguished the people amongst whom she had been nurtured. She had heard, from her earliest years, love spoken of as the great charm of woman's existence, and had come to associate that passion, which should be purity itself, with an indulgence in intrigue and coquetry. These errors were only parasites to her true woman's nature, but for a time they had their influence.

As time wore on, Leyton had a growing desire to return to

his native land, and yet it was difficult to overcome the repugnance he felt to recall his sorrows and dishonour where they were now forgotten. He had often doubted if his decision had been just towards Maud, but

> "Trifles light as air
> Are to the jealous confirmation strong
> As proofs of holy writ."

And he had allowed the trifling fact of Maud's reticence as to her knowledge of Sir Ralph Newberry, Cotterell's idle boasting and his sudden accession to wealth, to add increased importance to the fragment of the letter that had been given to him by Reuben.

But the love of country conquered at last; and collecting his wealth together in a form most convenient for its transmission, Leyton returned to the home of his fathers, but for a time retaining the appellation he had borne so long.

His chief attendant was a man whom he had rescued from the savage persecution to which his race was subject, and which the bigot Philip III. had instituted fifty years before. This Hafed was devoted to his master, owing him life and liberty, and he would have sacrificed both had occasion required him to do so. For Alice he entertained the same devotion, and a feeling which had all the attributes of a perfect love, except its hopes. She never moved abroad but Hafed followed her like her shadow. She never slept but the faithful Hafed kept watch near her.

One peculiarity of the man was his singular silence. He rarely spoke, and never but when the discharge of his duties rendered speech absolutely necessary. He as rarely smiled, as though he had some hidden sorrow ever oppressing him, and yet his swarthy and expressive face would suddenly beam with pleasure at any command—any word of commendation from Alice or her father.

Hafed was the only attendant whom Leyton brought with him to England; and when possession was taken of Leyton Hall—how sadly changed by time and neglect!—an old woman, a stranger to the neighbourhood, who had been found in possession, was retained as housekeeper. This arrangement was made by Leyton that he might avoid recognition; though few, alas! would have discovered in the sunburnt features and the long white beard of Master Maybourne, the once handsome lord of Leyton Hall.

So much premised, let us saunter, some month after Leyton's return, through the pleasant dale of the Dove, whose clear swift waters promise good sport to a young angler casting his fly with less care than a practised fisher should exercise. Ever and anon his eyes are turned to a fissure in the rocks, until weary with his lack of sport, he rests his rod upon the ground, and leans his head against the pliant wood. Presently he starts at what has met his gaze, and a glow like sunshine comes upon his face.

From the fissure in the rock have come a young girl and a swarthy follower. Both are attired in garments of a foreign fashion. They pause before they descend, as though the maiden hesitated from natural delicacy, but the youth—his name is Walter Gray—has cast down his rod and hastened to meet her.

It is difficult very difficult to trace the early foot-prints of first love; by what strange sympathy young hearts are drawn together; how they grow bold from fear, eloquent from silence, hopeful from what impedes, until "they love, and love for ever."

And so we must accept the knowledge that Walter and Alice had met before, and daily desired to meet again, nor seek to listen to the pretty talk which brought such pleasant smiles into both their handsome faces, until the time of parting came, and then their clasped hands parted reluctantly.

Though the swarthy face of Hafed grew dark almost to blackness, he had stood aloof, motionless, like a man carved out of the rock, and then followed without a word his young mistress through the subterraneous passage which led to the vaults of the hall.

"In the good old days," of which we sometimes hear the praises, when men burnt and sacked each other's dwellings, and valued life at the toss of a pike, or the thrust of a sword —a secret outlet was thought a necessary addition to houses of any importance. The exact position of such passages was known generally only to the owner of the house and his most confidential servants, and in order to preserve the knowledge of its whereabout, it was not unfrequently marked upon the ground plan of the building. Alice, in searching for some papers required by her father, had come upon the plan of Leyton Hall, and having made the discovery of a secret passage, girl-like, from curiosity, resolved to explore it.

Hafed was, of course, her attendant, and her delight was extreme when she found that, by its means, she could reach Dovedale readily. She had not met Walter Gray then, but when they had come to know each other, her Spanish proclivities made her think this secret way had been made for lovers.

Hummall had also heard that there was some secret means of access to Leyton Hall, and nothing deterred by his former ill-treatment of Tabitha, he resolved to get speech with her, and trust to the chapter of accidents to obtain the object he had in view.

As it was against Hummall's nature to go straight to his object, when he could find a crooked way, he determined to make his approaches in the disguise of one of the peddling men, who traversed the country to dispose of their wares.

Master Robin did not care to encumber himself with merchandise, and therefore, retaining somewhat of his puritanical seeming, he started for the Grange, with a few of the little books or tracts, then as plentiful as blackberries.

It was early morning when Hummall presented himself in the garden of Mistress Leyton's house. With a loud drawling voice he announced:—"Here's the choicest morsels of doctrine fresh from London; 'The Double Rowelled Spur for the Slow in Grace;' 'Limed Twigs to Catch Sinners Hopping,' and some others whose titles are unfitted for ears polite.

"This is the house," he thought; "and I could have been sworn on my missal that Tabitha would not have heard a pedlar's voice and kept within door. Mayhap the merchandise I have been crying hath no longer any charms for her. She was ever variable in her love and her religion." Then he bawled out: "Here! here! ladies, the newest patterns of coifs and farthingales, such as are worn on the court days of the Lady Mayoress of London, by the ladies of the wards within and without!" The bolts of the door were heard to be withdrawn, "Ha! ha!" thought Hummall, "the lure is right this time;" and Tabitha, in the full beauty of her three and thirtieth year, presented herself.

"What hast thou, Master Pedlar?" said Tabitha; "coifs and farthingales? Let me have sight of your pack."

"Daughter of foolishness," drawled Dick, "I did but cry such vanities to lure thee to me. I do but vend the goodly propoundings of worthy Simeon Bellowsgrowl and Ezekiah Leatherlungs."

"Then you have brought your pigs to a wrong market," replied Tabitha, angry at her disappointment. "We want none of their grunting here. I had enough and to spare of your sort sixteen years ago;" and Tabitha was about to close the door.

"Stay, maiden," said Hummall; "heaven hath made thee fair ——"

"I know it," answered Tabitha, sharply; "and I will show my gratitude by not spoiling a cheerful face, swallowing your puritanical vinegar." She was again retreating when Hummall said in a loud whisper, " Tabitha."

What could she do but turn and stare at the man?

"Tabitha, am I forgotten?" asked Hummall, in his natural voice. "Did the barber when he cropped my crown cut me from your remembrance?"

"Why, as I live," cried Tabitha, "it's Robin Hummall!"

"Yes, Tabitha, your own Robin. You should know these stockings, preserved for seventeen years. They're your own knitting." (A pure invention of the moment, be sure).

"If they be," replied Tabitha, "you left me to pay for the worsted; they cost me a groat a leg."

"Then I'm up to my knees in debt," said Hummall, with an impudent grin. "Tabitha, what does it matter? Let our fortunes be the same. One heart,—one pocket."

"That story won't do again, Robin," replied Tabitha, shaking her head. "One heart may be all very well, but next time I'm in love, we'll have each a pocket. But good-e'en, Robin, I have done with you."

"Done with me?" cried Robin, affecting surprise. "Lo! what a paradox is woman. She trusts herself to a man, and won't give him credit for eightpence."

"Two groats are not so easily come by," said Tabitha; "but lovers can be found on every hedge."

"How lightly women talk of their blessings," said Hummall. "Come, Tabitha, let's begin afresh. Let's be friends."

"Oh! I am friends enough," replied Tabitha, lingering rather at the door.

"When we were friends before, Tabitha, you always asked me to a stoup of ale. I'm still the same man, Tabitha. Dry as ever!"

Tabitha shook her head. "Robin, there is nothing but poison to thee at hand—small ale. Master Walter hath taken the key of the strong."

"Master Walter?" said Hummall, thoughtfully; "he is called thy mistress's nephew, and is bravely petted. Eh, Tabitha?"

"He is entertained as he deserves to be," replied Tabitha.

"Oh, nothing more?" answered Hummall, adding with a wicked leer, "Lovers grow on every hedge."

"I don't heed your gibe, Robin, not I!" replied Tabitha. "Master Walter is out of my reach. He's a fit mate for the new-comer's daughter at Leyton Hall."

"I have heard it said that the lady at the Hall is beautiful, and the father rich as Queen Sheba, and hath chests of gold and jewels brought from beyond seas," said Hummall.

"So 'tis rumoured at the village ale-house," replied Tabitha. "They say Master Maybourne keeps both door and window barred, and admits no one, so how it can be known what riches he hath within, I guess not."

As Tabitha said this, Hummall stole quietly towards the door, and leaning against the wall of the house, so that he could almost whisper into Tabitha's ear, said—

"Tabitha, shouldst like to be a lady?—to wear nothing but brocades as thick as deal boards, and brooches as large as wooden platters?"

"Should I not?" replied Tabitha, wondering what was Robin's meaning.

"To have six fat liverymen to wait on thee at table, and such a husband as your own Robin for every day in the week?"

"Hum! No," replied Tabitha, shaking her head; "with such a burthen as thee I would forego all the rest. I know you, Robin, and wouldn't trust thee again ——"

"Not for that?" asked Hummall, showing her a golden doubloon. "Take it." Tabitha did so, struck by the size and beauty of the coin. "I will make that pretty fellow five, if you will help me to a sight of those chests they speak of. There is a secret door—a passage—a somewhat—— and thou knowest it."

"Here, Robin," answered Tabitha, red with suppressed anger. "Take back your gold piece. I was a fool to think well enough of thee to handle it. A rogue in love is never honest in anything else."

As Hummall hesitated to take back the money, Tabitha threw it on the ground, saying, "I can't make the coin dirtier than it was, coming from thee. Go thy ways, Master Hummall; and be sure thy wife will take her last leave of thee at the gallows!" Having eased her mind somewhat by this parting prediction, Tabitha slammed the door in the face of her old admirer.

"Well," murmured Hummall, too used to rebuffs to be disturbed at what had passed. "An' if I marry, there's a promise of comfort at my end, if Tab's words come true. So," he continued, apostrophising the piece of gold, as he walked away from the house, "so thou'st turned traitor at last! I'll melt thee into small change, and drink thee to death. Chests of gold and jewels! Humph! if I know the King's Rogues, there is grist for his majesty's exchequer, and his poor servant, Rob Hummall."

Tabitha had baffled him; but when booty was to be had, Hummall would find a foil to it, if he took a month to hit it.

Tabitha had not spoken entirely "without her book," when she hinted at Walter's fitness to be Alce's suitor. A boy, who frequently attended upon Walter Gray, to carry his creel and landing-hook, had found his services dispensed with, and wondering wherefore, had ventured to keep watch upon his young master. The tale he told to Tabitha was so unlikely to be true that he gained little credence from the waiting-maid.

"I'd be swoored, Mistress Tabitha, she war a young 'ooman," said the boy, "tho' she war tricked out like our wenches at Christmastide, when they goes a mumming."

"You dreamt it, boy."

"I warn't a dreaming. I seed a black man wi' 'em, and he frighted me sorely; so I run'd away," said the boy.

Tabitha was quick-witted, and rather alive to her own interest, though in the main, a faithful servant to her mistress. She resolved, therefore, to say nothing of this conversation until she had sounded her young master, and perhaps made market of her silence.

It was long past mid-day when Walter Gray returned from fishing. He walked gazing on the ground, as though wearied by his day's labour. He paused at the entrance-gate, and almost said aloud—

"How strangely fate disposes of us!—that I should be in

love with this strange girl—I, who have always laughed at lovers!"

The young moraliser was at the mature age of nineteen!

"And yet," he continued, "I would forego the world, I fancy, for Alice Maybourne; and, for one smile of her sweet lips, brave all the jesters round the market-table."

There was a smack of love-sickness in the youngster's words. He called "Tabitha."

"Take in my rod and basket, please ye."

"Empty again!" said the waiting-woman, peeping into the creel. "Yesterday you had no better sport, Sir."

"The fish are cunning at this season," replied Walter, rather confused.

"Dear me," said Tabitha; "would nothing take the hook? Do any fish, Sir, bite at a ladybird?"

Walter felt the colour mount to his cheek at Tabitha's silly question, and he could only inquire—

"Where is my aunt?"

"In the orchard, Sir," replied Tabitha. "She has been asking for you—wondering why you forego your mid-day meal so often."

"So often," exclaimed Walter; "only to-day and yesterday."

"And the day before, Sir," added Tabitha. "I told my mistress there were wild cherries in the dale, which, mayhap, you gathered."

Walter turned his eyes quickly upon Tabitha; but that clever person looked simplicity itself. Having in some way satisfied herself from Walter's confusion—that there was a little more truth in the peasant boy's story than she had at first imagined, Tabitha carried the rod and basket into the house, leaving the detected lover to follow at his leisure.

"I wish I could take heart and tell my aunt of all that has chanced," thought Walter; "I would do so, but I fear to mention the Hall and bring back her old sorrow."

Thus musing, he entered the orchard where his aunt was seated, with a lace pillow on her lap, and plying with nimble fingers the rattling bobbins.

"So, Master Truant, you are home again," said Mistress Leyton, with a smile of welcome; "the capon would have grown cold had we waited dinner for thee."

"Pardon, dear aunt," replied Walter, with slight confusion, "but my sport made me forgetful of time and dinner."

"And yet Tabitha has but now told me that you came home with an empty basket," said Mistress Leyton.

"True, aunt; but—but I was ashamed of my bad sport, and sought to amend it;" Walter coloured slightly at this mild prevarication.

"Well, I'll not catechise thee further, Walter. Go in; you have outwearied thyself, silly boy! 'tis nearly sunset."

Walter gladly accepted his dismissal, and went into the house.

"Walter is ill at ease," thought Mistress Leyton. "Yet what disturbs him I cannot guess. Mayhap, he grows weary of a country life, and wants to see the town. 'Tis natural that he should do so, and I'll speak to him to-night."

The shades of evening deepened, and Tabitha, mindful of her mistress, had brought her a hood.

"Thanks, good girl," said Mistress Leyton, "I will go in;" but as she rose to do so, a wretched-looking creature came from behind a pleached hedge which crossed the garden and fell upon his knees. Mistress Leyton and Tabitha uttered a cry, but as the man appeared utterly prostrate, they did not move.

"He hath fainted, Tabitha; fetch him some water."

"No, no," said Reuben, for it was he, "a moment, and it will pass."

So changed was the man, that Mistress Leyton failed to recognise the voice, the features, of her deadliest enemy.

"Who art thou?" she asked, after a pause.

"A wretch to pity," replied Reuben; "black as my crime was, my punishment should be its atonement."

"What is your story—if it be one that I may hear?" asked Mistress Leyton, an undefined fear stealing upon her.

"A common one, Madam," answered the man in a deep, husky voice; "a wealthy libertine betrayed the woman I loved, and to avenge her wrong I blighted the peace of one as dear to him."

"Unhappy man!" said Mistress Leyton.

"Aye, mistress, most unhappy. By forged letters and wicked lies I made a husband believe his wife unfaithful."

"Reuben Studley!" exclaimed Mistress Leyton, stepping back and clinging to Tabitha.

"Yes, Madam!" cried Reuben, clasping his hands imploringly, "and my deep remorse has driven me almost mad. Do not curse me. See what a wretch I am!"

"Begone! begone!" exclaimed Mistress Leyton, "lest I lose all Christian patience and spurn you with my foot. Stand by me, Tabitha; my blood is chilled at sight of him!"

Reuben spoke not, but continued to clasp his hands and moan.

"What hast thou not done, thou man of lies? Torn wife from husband, a mother from her child; broken up home, sown hate where only love was, and made one life at least a living hell."

Tabitha became alarmed for her mistress, fearing that her excitement might produce ill consequences. But she would not be appeased.

"How durst thou look upon me, the widowed wife that thou hast made?"

"To save one dear to you, one ——"

"Peace! Let me not hear your voice! Never again approach me, or I will have you beaten from my gate."

"But for one moment hear me. Walter Gray ——"

Mistress Leyton made one step towards the cringing man, and raised her clenched hand as though to strike him.

"Does not that name blister thy serpent tongue! It should do so. Begone! thou hast poisoned the air about us. Begone!"

Tabitha again interposed, and at last succeeded in leading her mistress into the house.

"She will not hear me—she will not!" muttered Reuben, covering his face with his hands, and bending his head almost to his knees. "No, though I come to put my wretched life in peril to serve her kinsman."

Reuben rose up with difficulty,—either weak from hunger, or from the scene which had just been enacted,—and staggering like a drunken man, made his way from the orchard through a little wicket which opened on to a path leading to the river.

When Mistress Leyton had somewhat recovered, Tabitha went in search of Walter, but he was nowhere to be found.

CHAPTER VII.

THE TRYSTING PLACE.

HE sudden disappearance of Walter is easily explained. Seated in one of the bay-windows which opened on the park, Walter had made good progress with a substantial meal, as—let poets say what they will—love rarely interferes greatly with the appetite of the young, and Walter had fasted since early morning. He suddenly became aware of the presence of Hafed at the window. Opening the lattice instantly, Walter was surprised to receive a letter, evidently despatched in haste, as it was unsecured by either wax or silk. It contained but one line—

"Be in the dale at sunset."

Hafed, who spoke only Spanish, although he partially understood spoken English, inquired, by gesticulation, Walter's answer. Of course Walter intimated his readiness to obey; and Hafed, without either word or salutation, walked hastily away, concealing himself from observation by keeping within the shadow of a low wall which formed the boundary of the park.

Walter was at a loss to guess the cause for this unexpected summons from Alice. Had Hafed betrayed her to her father? Had some great sorrow come upon her? The reality could scarcely be more terrible than were his fears.

Taking his hat, which lay upon a chair beside him, he leaped lightly from the window and hastened to Dovedale, as the sun was already sinking behind the distant hills.

Before the lovers meet, it is necessary that we recount the

events which had occupied the time since they had parted from each other, happy as the "pleasant pain " of love could make them.

When Alice and her attendant had regained the Hall, she sat down near a window which commanded a view of the Grange, as it was the time when her father usually indulged in his *siesta*. She had sat thus for some time, when, looking round, she discovered that Hafed was still standing in the room, with his hands clasped before him, and his head inclined forward, as was his manner when testifying respect.

Alice was rather surprised, and addressing him in Spanish, gently dismissed him.

"Señora, may I speak to you?" asked Hafed, in the same language.

"Surely yes, Hafed," replied Alice. "Are you not my confidant—almost my only friend?"

"If to yield up my life could prove it, I would die to do so," said Hafed.

"And so I do believe. What would you say to me?"

"Knowing my devotion—knowing that I reckon nothing of pain, sorrow, life, to do you service—you must not be angry with your slave if he speak bold words—words that he would say to no other."

"Go on, Hafed," said Alice, guessing in part what she was about to hear.

"You know, Señora, from what misery, what degradation, your honoured father rescued me ; how, for many years I have been a witness to the helplessness which blindness brings. You know how he has trusted me, even to the care of his most precious treasure—you, his daughter."

Alice only answered by a movement of her head.

"Am I—am I proving faithful to my trust in what I see and know? Do I not deceive the blind confiding master by aiding such meetings as that of to-day and yesterday, and other days?"

"Yes, Hafed," replied Alice, rising up, and holding out her hand, which Hafed, kneeling, kissed. "Yes ; we are both unfaithful to the dearest father and the kindest master ; but I only am to blame. I have abused your devotion, and my father's confidence. Even now I was debating with myself how best to tell my father all that has been of late. I have no need to doubt his love or tenderness ; and yet I hesitate— somewhat because ——"

"You fear I shall have blame—perhaps reproaches. I deserve both, honoured lady; and I can bear. Speak—oh! speak at once."

"I will," said Alice; "I will, Hafed. There is no shame in what I have to tell. I love a worthy gentleman—of that I am assured by every word and thought he breathes. Yes, I will go at once to my father. Be not afraid, good Hafed, no harm shall come to you."

Hafed bowed low as Alice passed by him, and in that attitude remained for some time, as though he were engaged in deep reflection—perhaps in prayer.

When he aroused himself he walked straight to the door of the room where Alice was with her father. He placed his ear close to the panelling of the door; and the deep lines which came into his face gave indication that what reached him was giving him pain. At last he heard the sound of the silver whistle, which was his master's summons to him.

When Hafed entered the room, the sightless eyes of the blind man were raised upwards, and tears were falling fast upon his long and grizzled beard. Kneeling at his feet, her head lying on his lap, was Alice; but her father's hands were clasped about her head, as though she had confessed, and was forgiven.

Hafed scarcely entered the room, and then stood motionless.

In a few moments Leyton appeared to recover the command of his feelings; and turned his face towards the spot where stood his offending servant.

"Hafed," he said, "my daughter has told me all. Thy only fault to me is forgiven. Go—keep watch in the gallery. Let no one disturb us."

Hafed again bowed low, and, without speaking a word left the room. He did not listen again; he knew that his beloved mistress was forgiven, and for her he only cared.

"Come, put your arms about my neck, and kiss me," Leyton said, and was instantly obeyed. "Sit down beside me, and give me thy hand."

Alice obeyed.

"I have also a story to tell my child, and which I would have delayed until to-morrow, thy eighteenth birthday ——"

"Was this my birthplace?" asked Alice, eagerly; but such deep sorrow came into her father's face that she almost repented that she had asked the question.

"Yes," Leyton answered, with a sigh; "and it was for that reason—and one other—which made me come back to this dishonoured house. Alice, your first unfilial act has brought its fruit—none will know how bitter beside thyself and me."

"Oh, no; you have forgiven me," cried Alice, clasping her father's neck.

Leyton paused for a few moments, and then said—

"You have often asked me of your mother——" He paused again.

"Did she die here?" Alice asked, sadly.

"Would that she had!" exclaimed Leyton, "even when our love was at the newest. No, Alice, she did not die, though she is dead to me—to you—to all that should make life dear to woman."

"Oh, holy saints!" exclaimed Alice; "I dare not ask your meaning!"

"No; let us not give the deed its proper name," answered Leyton, pressing the hand of Alice until the pressure gave her pain. "Enough, she left me. I was away on duty with the queen in France. I came home—came here—where I had left all the hopes and happiness of my life. Gone! gone! She had fled—but had left me you. For that one act of mercy I have forgiven her the wrong she did me."

"Oh, father — dear, dear father!" and Alice sobbed aloud upon Leyton's neck.

"Be calm, my child; we never speak again upon this matter. But there is more to tell," said Leyton, with great effort.

"What? The proofs—the certainty you had of my mother's wickedness?"

"I had proofs enough: be sure of that. My state had become too poor; I was with a losing cause. A faithful servant brought me letters I could not question! I knew the man who had wronged me. He had not the boldness to deny his treachery. We fought, and he had died; but he blinded me."

Alice did not speak for some moments. She then asked, quietly—

"Did you not seek my mother?"

"No."

"Might it not have been a devilish lie coined to deceive you?" continued Alice; "or to revenge some wrong? It seems too monstrous that a wife and mother should have been bought with gold."

"I would have sworn she could not," said Leyton; "but I had such proofs——"

"I would have seen her," interrupted Alice. "I would have trusted to her love before appearances, though backed by every proof but her confession!"

"Child!"

"What if thou hast done my mother wrong, which, from the rashness with which you judged, seems more than probable? Is it now too late to do her justice?" asked Alice.

"Be silent, Alice," replied Leyton. "You speak because you love this Walter Gray."

"Indeed—indeed you wrong me!" said Alice. "If Walter Gray loves me, he will not forsake me for my mother's shame."

"Alice, you force me to the worst," replied Leyton. "You do not know how dear Walter Gray is to your mother—dearer, perhaps, than even you have been, although you were her first born."

Alice sprang to her feet, and holding back her hair with both her hands, stood as though terror-stricken. Leyton saw not this, and so continued—

"If you would seek your mother—if you would hear her tell her story—go with your Walter home. Mistress Leyton is your mother—is his."

A sickness followed by a sense of death, and Alice fell at her father's feet.

Leyton instantly summoned Hafed.

"I have killed her—I have killed my child!" he exclaimed, stretching out his hands. "Let me touch her! Oh, she is dead!"

Hafed drew a small dagger from its sheath and held the polished blade to the lips of his young mistress for a few moments.

"No, she breathes!"

"Thank God!" exclaimed Leyton; and then, covering his face with his hands, uttered more words of thankfulness.

It was some time before Alice recovered from the swoon which had overpowered her; and when, by the assistance of a woman-servant and Hafed, she had been conducted to her own chamber, she requested to be left alone, but desired the Moor to remain within call. She could not have defined clearly her reason for making this request, but Hafed was associated in her still confused brain with Walter Gray, and to him all her bewildered thoughts were directed as to a point where she was to find either wreck or rescue.

The terrible doubt of her mother's guilt—she refused to accept her father's condemnation as proof of it—made it imperative upon her to forego, and at once, all further interviews with Walter ; but she could not part from him without some explanation—she could not endure the thought that he would believe her fickle and changeable, or permit him to imagine that he had given her cause of offence.

After a time she saw the way to acquaint him with this painful termination to their short, sweet dream of love, but the shock she had just sustained prevented its immediate accomplishment. She had therefore written the one brief line which Hafed had conveyed to Walter.

The sun had set, and the young moon shone brightly over the dale of the Dove. The grey rocks, which rose like rugged walls on either side of the meandering river, picturesque at all times, now resembled some place in gnome-land, where silver held the place of stone, and every dewy leaf seemed to have a diamond covering. The gurgling water, foaming around the boulders and rugged stones which impeded its course, seemed also like liquid silver, except when it flowed past the shadows of projecting rocks and overhanging trees.

Walter leant against a large boulder on the edge of the stream, his eyes fixed upon the fissure in the rock, and which Alice had forbidden him to enter.

He was doomed to a long watch, as Alice had tried again and again to write what she desired to say to him, and at last only succeeded in producing a confused letter. Any other than a lover would have grown weary of his vigil, but Walter continued at his post until, by the course of the moon, he judged it to be nearly nine o'clock. His patience was to be rewarded, as a dim light shone in the opening in the rock, and presently the figure of the Moor stood out boldly in the moonlight. Walter made his presence known, and then Hafed, gliding like a cat among the loose rocks which lay scattered between them, descended to where Walter was standing, and gave him a letter which Alice had written. The Moor scarcely made any salutation, either on his approach or when he departed, and Walter was too much interested in the missive he had received to heed the messenger.

By the light of the moon, Walter read as follows—

"DEAR WALTER GRAY,—I would not lay aside my maiden modesty and so address thee, did I not know that I shall never see thee more—unless what I dare still to hope may prove to be the truth, and then I should be too happy to have made known my love for thee.

"I left thee this morning, Walter, without the consciousness of a sorrow; I write to thee steeped to my lips in misery. I have tried again and again to tell you whence this change has come, but the words, as I wrote them, seemed to turn to fire and blinded me. Walter, it is a sin to love as we have loved; but if a time should come when we may meet——I know not what I write—farewell!

"Farewell! A thousand words could not express more grief than that one—farewell! Keep the poor gift I send thee, for the sake of your most unhappy

"ALICE."

Walter had read the letter twice before he looked for Hafed to deliver the love-token it mentioned, but the Moor had disappeared, and the light from the fissure also.

Walter was about to go in the pursuit of Hafed, when he heard a voice call—

"Master Gray!"

Walter turned instantly, and was surprised to see a man—it was Robin Hummall—coming towards him.

Walter was in no humour to submit to an impertinence, and therefore he advanced to meet Hummall, saying—

"Who are you, Sir, that presumes to watch me?"

"Master Walter Gray, I am a man of peace," replied Hummall, with a nasal drawl.

"Thou art a prying knave," said Walter, "and it would be doing an act of right to cudgel thee for thy impertinence."

"Nay, Master Gray," answered Hummall, in his natural tone, "I have not borne sickness by sea, and hunger by land, to be paid with a cudgel for bringing thee the king's message."

"The king's message!" said Walter, with surprise. "What jest is this?"

"No jest, Sir," replied Hummall; "the king hath heard of thee as a likely young cock to fight in a battle royal."

"Indeed, Sir?"

"You doubt me!" replied Hummall. "All I ask of thee is, that you will meet some of the best men in this country within half an hour at Graseby Farm-house, ruin as it is, and you will give me credit for being less of a saint than I look."

Walter made no reply, but he thought, poor lover!—"If Alice be lost to me, any enterprise, however dangerous, will be welcome."

"Come, Sir," said Hummall, laying his hand lightly on Walter's shoulder, "don't let the pouting of a pretty wench make you suck in your cheeks like a blacksmith's bellows."

Walter turned round sharply, as though he resented Hummall's familiarity; but that worthy was not easily abashed, and he continued—

"Ah! that's the look for me. You'd stare misfortune out of countenance. Come, Master Gray, let us shake hands on this matter, and be friends."

"I must know more of thee before I cry 'yes' to that bargain," said Walter. "And is not that a man standing in the shadow of the Pike Rock?"

"Possibly," replied Hummall. "I have overstayed my appointment, and my friends may have come here to seek me."

Hummall then placed his fingers to his lips and blew a loud, shrill whistle. It was instantly answered, and some four or five men discovered themselves, to the surprise and pardonable alarm of Walter.

"We thought evil had come to thee, Robin," said Boardwine, "as Cocktail here repoited you had entered the dale an hour before sunset."

"You are honest fellows, *camaradoes*, and I thank ye for the care of me," replied Hummall; "but I have been recruiting for the king's service, I trust. Master Walter Gray ——"

"Robin! Robin!" said Boardwine, drawing Hummall aside, "that's my pretty little sheep, Robin; if thou hast sheared him, I'll have my half of the fleece."

"When did I wrong to a brother?" replied Hummall, in an undertone. "And now, Master Gray, these are the friends I told thee of—all deep in the king's confidence, and earnest workers in the king's cause—so much so that Crop-ears and Roundheads and other disloyal folk call us 'The King's Rogues.'"

"The King's Rogues!" repeated Walter, not favourably impressed by the appearance of the group.

"Yes, Master Gray," said Hummall, "and we are proud to be so distinguished. As we are to be friends, I hope, let me be plain with thee. As your privateers at sea, so we on land confiscate for the good of the king and the country—we being the country."

Walter remained silent.

"Now, these gentlemen and myself have heard that in Leyton Hall lie certain chests or caskets brimming with gold and jewels," said Hummall. "It would make too much stir to force admittance to this El Dorado, Master Gray; but as thou hast knowledge of the way to come and go quietly to this treasury which we claim in the king's name, we desire thy companionship."

"And dare you ask me to take part in such a robbery?" asked Walter, indignantly.

"No players' speeches, Master Gray," replied Hummall, insolently. "Are you with us?"

"No! a thousand times no!" exclaimed Walter.

The words were scarcely uttered when, at a signal from Hummall, Walter's head was covered with a cloak, his limbs strapped together, and in this powerless condition he was conscious of being borne away he knew not whither.

The gift for Walter which Alice had confided to Hafed was her miniature—one of those masterpieces of art, of which some examples have come down to us. The Moor, whose love for his mistress was only equalled by his jealousy of Walter, had learned from Alice that she and her lover were never likely to meet again; and as he looked upon the counterfeit face of the one he loved, he resolved to retain the picture. He had not, however, reached the Hall, before his better nature chided him for his unfaithfulness, and hurrying back he had hoped to have given the miniature to Walter. He arrived, however, only in time to witness the act of violence committed by the King's Rogues. Hafed's blood was roused by what he had seen, and he resolved to follow the assailants of Walter, and, if possible, effect his rescue.

As Hafed stole along, availing himself of every projecting

…ock or bush for the purpose of concealment, he came suddenly upon a man who was apparently engaged also in watching the retreating Rogues. Hafed was quickly on his defence, but the man he had surprised explained by action and a few plain words, which Hafed appeared to understand, that he had Walter's safety in view. This man was Reuben, and Hafed could not have met with a more determined helper.

The fellows who had seized Walter carried him with little difficulty to the dismantled farm-house where we first met them, and having reached the room usually appropriated to their meetings, the cloak was removed from Walter's head, and his limbs were unbound.

"You must pardon our rough courtesy, Master Gray," said Hummall, "but time presses, and we have much work to do before the morning."

"The gentleman cannot complain of his bearers," remarked Cocktail; "we carried him as tenderly as though he had been a babe in his long-coats. Our care is surely worth a bottle or two of double ale—eh, Master Gray?"

"Now that I know your honourable calling," said Walter, "I were a fool to hesitate. My purse, Sir," and he threw a leathern pouch containing a few pieces of money on the table.

The chink of the coin sounded like music to his captors, and more than one hand was extended to secure the bag. Boardwine, however, with the quickness of a hawk, threw himself upon the prize, exclaiming—

"Fie, gentlemen, fie! would you rob the exchequer?"

"Cease scrambling for such a petty quarry; you shall stoop to-night at true game," said Hummall; and then, turning to Walter, he continued, "How say ye, Master Gray; are you willing to do us the slight service we have need of from you? Show us the secret way to Leyton Hall?"

"You have had my answer," replied Walter.

"Then, gentlemen, we will trust to pick and crowbar. In the meantime, Master Gray, we will care for your safety until we can secure you a voyage to Holland."

"To Holland!" exclaimed Walter, alarmed for the first time.

"Ay, Sir—a rare place, where the land's half water and the men all breeches," said Hummall, with a coarse laugh.

"You will not commit such violence?"

"Yes; as the King's Rogues, we can afford to be liberal," said Hummall. "Common knaves would tighten your neck-band or open an artery; we send you to see the world gratis."

"You are bold villains!" said Walter.

"You flatter us," replied Hummall, with a bow. "Gentlemen, you will show Master Gray to the only spare chamber in this poor dwelling, and I will send you presently the best out of Zedekiah's cellar."

A lusty cheer was the answer to this address; and as soon as Hummall had left, Walter saw to his dismay that the spare chamber was beneath the floor of the room where he was, and that access to it was by a trap in the floor.

Walter felt that remonstrance would be vain; and scorning to show a white feather, he descended the steps when required to do so without a word, and then found himself in total darkness.

The villanous scheme which Hummall had concocted for robbing Leyton Hall had nearly been frustrated, for to his horror he found, on arriving at Waterwell's alehouse, that a party of mounted soldiers had halted there, and were likely to remain for the night.

Hummall instantly assumed his best puritanical manner and boldly mixed with the soldiers, saluting the cornet who commanded them.

"You march late, friend, dost thou not?" asked Hummall, carelessly.

"Yea," replied the cornet; "we had hoped to have reached Castleton to-night, but we missed the road. We are in pursuit of a band of desperadoes, of whom thou mayest have heard—the King's Rogues, as they are called."

"I have heard of the knaves," replied Robin. "Hath not the Council put a price upon their heads?"

"Yes," answered the cornet; "a hundred pound."

"For the lump?" asked Hummall.

The cornet bowed affirmatively.

"And you will abide the danger of the capture?"

"Assuredly," replied the cornet.

"Then I will as assuredly deliver them into thy hands."

"When?"

"At mid-day to-morrow, if the gold-finches of the Council

do sing in their cage," said Hummall, holding open the pocket of his doublet.

"Fear not for your reward, man," replied the cornet. "Where shall we meet?"

"Continue thy rout to Castleton," said Hummall. "There is a hostelry called 'The Miners,' where I will join thee at day-break. To remain here would alarm the country; so keep a still tongue, and ride forward."

The cornet soon marshalled his little troop, and acting in conformity with certain instructions given by Hummall, the march to Castleton was resumed.

Master Robin Hummall fairly laughed aloud when the last trooper rode from the door, and having ordered the liquor for his comrades, and a bottle of ale for his own drinking, he filled a small silver pipe with a pinch or two of real Trinidado, and smoked as though it were a calumet of peace.

"Ha!" thought Hummall, as he blew a wreath of smoke from between his lips, "this is picking pockets with both hands. He will march his men out of our way until I and my fellows have done our *devoirs* at Leyton Hall, and then my worthy friends, my King's Rogues, look to your necks. The Parliament gibbets will silence your scandals of *cavaliero* Robin, and put a cool hundred into his pocket." And so the cold-blooded knave smoked and ruminated.

Reuben and Hafed had seen all that had transpired between Walter and his captors, and had devised the best means which presented themselves for the deliverance of Walter Gray. Reuben knew how much the neighbouring peasants stood in fear of the desperate ruffians who had done the recent violence, and also how disinclined any would be to serve a cause which had his advocacy. Even Mistress Leyton would not permit him to approach her; but Providence had sent Hafed to aid in the rescue of Walter Grey.

CHAPTER VIII.

GONE!

THE unusual and continued absence of Walter occasioned considerable surprise and alarm to his aunt, who had been greatly disturbed also by her interview with Reuben.

"There is a bright moon," said Mistress Leyton to Tabitha, "and the boy knows every yard of ground, I have heard him say, for miles around."

"There is no fear of harm to Master Walter, Madam," replied Tabitha, "not more than many a youth hath encountered and come off scathless."

"What mean you, Tabitha?" asked the mistress.

Tabitha then repeated to her mistress all that she had heard from the boy, and also illustrated the narrative by describing how she had set word-traps to catch Master Walter's secret, if he had one. Tabitha pronounced that there was a lady in the case.

Mistress Leyton was puzzled and vexed. Who was this stranger who had become possessed, by the injustice of the times, of her husband's ancestral home?—who this girl, if indeed there were any cause for Tabitha's surmises? Her waiting-maid, she knew, was rather experienced in such matters, being, as Jacob Magnus had once described her, "a chicken of a forward hatch;" and it was the privilege of her class to know more of the secrets of a family than the head of it ever suspected.

"The youth is flesh and blood, Madam," said Tabitha,

"and thou wouldst not have him of ice or marble. If what Dickson says be true, and he kissed the maiden's hand at parting, be sure he will not rest until he hath tried the flavour of her lips."

"Tabitha," replied Mistress Leyton, "you are somewhat free spoken, and—gracious! was not there a noise at the window?"

Tabitha, after a moment's hesitation, withdrew the curtain, and then cried out, evidently greatly alarmed.

"What ails thee, girl!" asked Mistress Leyton.

"There is a black, evil-looking man—though, now I remember, such a one is said to be at the Hall," said Tabitha.

Mistress Leyton withdrew the curtain which Tabitha had closed again, and saw Hafed, who now tapped loudly at the window.

"Admit the man instantly," said Mistress Leyton; "doubtless he brings some news of Walter."

Tabitha would have delegated this duty to David, the man-servant, had not her curiosity overcome her fears; and opening the house door, she beckoned Hafed to follow her to her mistress.

The light of a large wax taper fell full on the face of Mistress Leyton as Hafed entered, and when he saw the still comely features of the lady, he started with evident surprise. He did not reflect upon the cause, but instantly endeavoured to convey the purport of his visit. As we have said, the Moor could understand the meaning of many English words, but could pronounce only a very few, and those with great difficulty.

"What are you seeking here at this hour?" asked Mistress Leyton. "Are you from the Hall?"

Hafed was greatly excited by his inability to convey what he desired to make known; until pointing to a portrait of Walter, and reiterating his name, gesticulating and working his expressive features, he contrived to inform Mistress Leyton that Walter was in danger.

Tabitha immediately summoned the serving-man, but could hardly speak for terror. David, having served in the king's army until the fatal day at Worcester, was always ready for a fray if one came in his way. He instantly divined that hard knocks were needed somewhere, and hastening to the homestead adjoining the garden, he blew on a great cow's horn a lusty blast, and aroused three or four farming men, much to their especial wonder.

"Bring thee flails and thee pitchforks, lads, Master Walter is in trouble. Stir thee, lads, stir thee," and in a few minutes David, armed with tuck and petronel, had marshalled his irregulars and was ready to march.

Hafed, who rarely carried other weapon than the dagger at his girdle, was also armed with a short sword belonging to Walter. Before he left the room he placed in Tabitha's hand the miniature of his young mistress, and pointing to the portrait of Walter, made the quick-witted waiting-maid understand that "the counterfeit presentiment" was to be given to her young master when he returned.

When the men had departed and Mistress Leyton had recovered somewhat from the alarm and excitement occasioned by Hafed's communication, Tabitha mentioned the charge she had received from Hafed.

"Here is the painting ——" but Tabitha paused, struck by the wonderful resemblance of the miniature to her mistress.

"Why do you stare so, girl?" asked Mistress Leyton; "give me the painting."

Tabitha obeyed; but no sooner had Mistress Leyton scanned the features than she uttered a loud cry, pressing her hand upon her forehead, as though some great overwhelming thought oppressed her brain.

"What is this!" she cried at length. "This face—it must be—here, girl, unclasp my neck-brooch?"

Mistress Leyton then took from her bosom the miniature of a child, and held it by the side of the one she had received from Tabitha.

"I cannot be deceived—I am sure I cannot! These are the features of my child; each infant beauty ripened by womanhood. Did he say her name?"

"No, Madam!" replied Tabitha, wondering at what she saw.

"But why do I ask a name?" exclaimed Mistress Leyton, kissing the portrait; "as though my love could be deceived; those eyes have looked upon me in my dreams—those lips kissed mine! Could they speak they would call me mother!"

Poor lady! she could endure bravely no longer, but yielding to her woman's weakness, wept convulsively.

Tabitha had had many sad experiences of her mistress's sudden attacks of acute suffering, and knowing that they must have their way, she let her weep unquestioned.

"To-morrow—to-morrow," Mistress Leyton said, "I will know the truth or falsehood of my surmise. I will to bed now, Tabitha—you shall wait the return of Walter. To-morrow I will go to Leyton Hall;" but to-morrow came and she was helpless to move or think. She was ill—very ill.

Hafed in the meantime led the little party, bent upon relieving Walter Gray, but it was nearly midnight before Graseby Farm-house was reached. The place was in perfect darkness, except where the moonlight stole through the casements and dilapidated roof. In the room where the desperadoes usually assembled there was still a few embers smouldering on the hearth, and as the apartment was used for "parlour, kitchen, and hall," there was the aroma of some savoury mess mingling with the odour of tobacco.

On the table among the *débris* of a coarse meal and drinking bout, was the remains of a large candle of tallow, such as were made by peasant women for domestic use. This was soon lighted, but no trace of Walter could be found. Hafed at last commenced searching the floor, and his quick eye soon detected the trap-door leading to the cellar, and upon which a heavy table had been placed.

"Young master's prison, I'd be sworn," said David. "Quick, lads. Shove away the table and up with the trap."

David then called aloud Walter's name, and was rejoiced to hear his young master reply:

"Hillo! David. I'm here in limbo, bound hand and foot, and nearly starved with cold and hunger."

The fellows by whom Walter had been kidnapped had taken effectual means to keep him prisoner, as his hands and feet were strapped together so artistically that there could be no doubt but the operator had had much personal experience.

Walter was much surprised to see Hafed among his liberators, but there was no time to waste in inquiries or conjectures.

Walter had gathered from what he had overheard, that the King's Rogues meditated an attack upon Leyton Hall, and that they must by this hour be at their dishonest work. David therefore knocked up some five or six persons, to whom he was known, in the adjacent village; but such was the terror inspired by the King's Rogues, that before the relieving party was half a mile on its way most of David's new allies had deserted.

But where was Reuben? Having satisfied himself that Hafed comprehended the danger to which Walter was exposed, and that the Moor could make himself intelligible to Walter's friends at the Grange, Reuben had started off in pursuit of the troopers, then on their way to Castleton. He knew that as the road was rough and circuitous, he might be fortunate enough to overtake them by crossing a moorland which lay between two lofty hills, which could only be traversed by one well acquainted with the almost undistinguishable track, and in this expectation he was not disappointed.

The Rogues, however, had gone straight to their work above an hour before, and would no doubt have secured their prize but from the appearance of lights moving about the Hall, until they became stationary in the two chambers of Alice and her father.

The absence of Hafed was inexplicable to his master, who, wearied at last, laid down on his couch without undressing, and was soon asleep.

Not so Alice, she knew the business on which Hafed had been despatched, and distracted herself with a hundred wild conjectures as to the cause of his detention. Had Walter been so much disturbed by what she had written, that he had by some angry word given offence to the fiery Moor? Had ill come to Walter, and did Hafed hesitate to meet her? Or had the faithful servant fallen a victim to his devotedness to his dear mistress?

Alice could not sleep, but she had dismissed her attendant to her chamber desiring to be aroused when Hafed returned. It was near midnight when Alice heard a noise, which was not a knocking or any other appeal for admission. As she listened, she fancied she could hear the hum of many voices, and then presently there came a crash, as though one of the lower windows had been opened by violence. Alice was a brave woman, and without any further hesitation she took the lamp burning upon her table and proceeded in the direction of the noise. It was useless, she thought, to disturb her blind father; and to rouse the domestics before discovering the necessity for so doing never occurred to her.

The room whence the noise had proceeded was the one usually occupied by her father, and therein was a large chest of oak, containing several small caskets—some clasped with steel or brass, and others merely of strong workmanship, secured by lock and key. Alice knew that more than one enclosed precious stones of great value, and that others were the depositories of bonds and deeds and similar documents.

As she approached the door she thought she heard the click of a flint and steel, as though someone were striking a light. No, she was not mistaken, and soon a strong stream of light came through the large keyhole of the door and played upon the wall opposite. The heart of Alice beat quickly, and she hesitated how to act. The door of the room she knew was locked, and the key hanging to her father's girdle. She listened at the door for a time, and heard the voices of men speaking in whispers. Now and then an angry oath reached her ear, and from the sounds which succeeded she fancied that someone was attempting to open the oak chest.

Alice was alarmed, and with all speed hastened to her father and aroused him. In a few rapid words she informed him of what she thought was in progress, and Leyton, blind as he was, resolved to know the cause of his daughter's fears.

Led by Alice, Leyton, having selected the proper key from the few which he carried, opened the door of his treasury, and was instantly surrounded by Hummall and his burglarious fellows.

"What means this intrusion, my masters?" said Leyton. "As I hear there are many of you, your purpose, I suppose, is easily divined?"

"There are enow of us, Master Maybourne, to overset any that this house holds," replied Hummall, "and we are disposed to deal fairly with you. Nay, mistress, you need not cling to your father so closely. We are cavaliers, and respect beauty."

"Ye are rogues and cut-throats," cried Leyton, "as you should know to your cost if I had but sight to guide my hand."

"Be not foul-lipped an' you desire to escape the gag and the strappado," said Hummall, fiercely. "Say us fairly, and we content ourselves with such loose matters as lie ready to our hands. Rouse us by ill words or threats of danger, and we know how to make still tongues, though it involve the opening of a vein or two."

"Do not provoke these men, father," said Alice. "Let them have what they seek, and begone."

"Well said, fair mistress," cried Cocktail; "and spare us the sweat and labour of forcing this d—ble piece of oak carpentry. A crow may peck at it till doomsday."

"The key of this chest, Master Maybourne," said Hummall, boldly.

Leyton replied by throwing his keys upon the floor.

"Unmannerly and foolish, Sir," said Hummall; "but for old recollections, I would make fair mistress pick them up again." But Cocktail had already secured the keys and was fitting them to the locks of the great chest.

When the lid was raised, the expectant thieves crowded round and stared with admiration at the accumulated caskets, all promising to contain a store of booty.

Alice and her father stood without speaking—almost breathless—the one from fear, the other from suppressed indignation.

What noise is that? Surely the tramp of men, unheard by the Rogues, now intent on the plunder they had secured.

Leyton's quick ear caught the sound also, and, pressing Alice closely to his side, whispered—"This may be a rescue."

Scarcely had he spoken the words when Hafed, followed by Walter and a dozen or more of the troopers, rushed into the room, to the consternation of the rogues, who saw instantly that they were over-matched, and at the mercy of their captors.

"Don't fire, gentlemen—don't strike!" cried Boardwine. "There is no use alarming young mistress here, and filling the house with the smell of villanous gunpowder. There lies my weapon;" and he cast his formidable-looking sword upon the floor.

"So, Master Walter Gray," said Hummall, recovering from his surprise, "you would not use your knowledge for our advantage, but in return for our foolish clemency in not giving thee thy quietus, thou hast shown the way to our destruction."

"Even so, rogue," replied Walter.

"Then let me die easy," said Hummall, as he discharged a petronel aimed at the breast of Walter Gray. There was a sharp cry and a heavy fall, a piercing scream from Alice, and then, when the smoke had cleared away, stretched on the floor lay Reuben Studley.

Yes, he had seen the direction of Hummall's aim, and, regardless of his life, he had thrown himself before Walter; and the smile upon his face implied a hope that his voluntary death might be accepted as some atonement for the wrongs he had done when living.

The shot had taken effect in the neck, and though the blood flowed freely, David, who took charge of the wounded man, did not consider it to be fatal—and the old campaigner professed to have some skill in surgery.

The parliament's troopers made short work with the King's Rogues. They strapped each of the rascals to the crupper of a horse, and in that manner set out for the town of Derby, where the rest of the regiment was lying. Spent and footsore were the rascals all when they reached the end of the journey.

There was soon a finish of these dishonest knaves. Some were sent to the Barbadoes, whilst others were drafted into the navy—a worse fate than that which had befallen their comrades, as to a man they had an unconquerable disrelish for water. Robin Hummall slipped his head out of a halter for a time by turning traitor to the king, for whom he had professed such devotion, and in whose name he had been guilty of such rogueries.

As soon as Walter was satisfied that Alice and her father were in the hands of friends, and in safety, he hastened to the Grange, knowing that his long absence must have been a source of great anxiety to his kind aunt.

There were lights burning in Mistress Leyton's room, and in that part of the building which Tabitha considered to be under her dominion.

Walter was soon heard and admitted by the drowsy waiting-woman, who—cross as drowsy people generally are—addressed Walter rather uncivilly.

"A pretty time of night, my young Sir, to be abroad, alarming the whole household, and almost frightening my good mistress to death."

"Has my aunt been so much concerned?" asked Walter.

"Of a truth has she!" said Tabitha, annoyed that her own disturbance did not seem to affect Walter one jot.

"Can I go to her?" asked Walter.

"What next will you ask?" replied Tabitha. "My mistress needs not to be disturbed further than she has been to-night already; and now—thanks to a posset I gave her an hour ago—she sleeps, though with troubled dreams."

"I will explain all to her in the morning," said Walter, making a show of retiring.

"And why not now?" asked Tabitha; "should my mistress wake it may be she would not sleep again without knowing what has detained you abroad."

"Then call me if she does, Tabitha, and I will come to her. Good-night," and Walter turned to go to his bed.

He paused at the door and asked, "Tabitha, didst thou ever hear speak of Reuben Studley?"

"Reuben Studley!" exclaimed Tabitha, in a low whisper; "that name must not be spoken in this house, or within hearing of thy aunt."

"Why so?"

"That were a story for my mistress only to confide to you, not for me," replied Tabitha. "As you value my mistress's health—and life perhaps—speak not that man's name to her."

"I will mind me of your caution, Tabitha," said Walter.

"But to me 'twere another guess sort of thing," said Tabitha; "what of him, Master Walter?"

"You shall know all anon, Tabitha. Good-night," answered Walter, and left the room.

"You have lost somewhat by your silence, young Sir," muttered Tabitha. "An' you had thought me worthy to have been in your secret, this pretty toy should have lain under thy pillow." Tabitha took the miniature of Alice from her pocket as she spoke, and placed it in an escritoir belonging to her mistress, and then retired to bed.

With the morning had come, a slight return of Mistress Leyton's old malady, and she sat in moody silence hour by hour, and then only talked of her lost child and her cruel husband. The physician who had attended her during her former attack again proved successful, but not until many days had passed. He had made effective use of the miniature, and when Mistress Leyton became convalescent, her chief solace appeared to be the contemplation of the semblance of her child. Yes! it was her child's features that she looked upon, and Walter had confirmed her in this conviction by mentioning the name of Alice, and would have made conjecture certain by going to Leyton Hall had not Mistress Leyton forbidden him.

"No, Walter," she said; "it is I alone who should claim my daughter. I have been long parted from her, and she believes because I was unworthy to be her mother. I will go and claim my right to be acknowledged an honourable woman and a chaste wife. When those concessions shall have been made, I will demand my child. I alone can do this."

Walter could but assent to this self-vindication, as it were, but he fretted and chafed at the tardiness of his aunt's recovery, which kept him—he was sure of that from his full acceptance as Alice's lover by her father—he was sure of that also—although he had now interrupted the happy course of their true love.

The sun shone brightly, and the wild-flowers by the wayside, and the young leaves on the hedge-boughs, had a look of peaceful thankfulness, strangely at variance with the agitating hopes and fears struggling in the brain of Mistress Leyton. Her jennet's head was towards the Hall, and her purpose was to win justice for herself, and acceptance for her nephew Walter.

Twenty years had passed since she rode a happy bride beneath the canopy formed by the stately trees which led to Leyton Hall. What joy then awaited her! Honour!— love; greeted her at every turn, and beneath yonder deserted roof she had known the crowning blessing of a woman's life when she became a mother. In those rooms, through whose dingy window-panes the sun can scarcely find its way, her darling child had made home Paradise! There she had lisped her father's name! There she had tottered from his knee to her mother's lap, and crowed with delight at the perilous achievement! Oh, why will those memories come and make her weep, when she should be "knit up in steel," to ask for justice—to claim the compensation due to her for all the wrong and suffering she had known so undeservedly!

Could she forgive the past?

Oh, yes! if she had borne a thousand times as much, so that her forgiveness would give her back her husband's love and trust, and the companionship of her child. She always remembered Alice as a child, never associating her with the passing time; and it was not until she saw the miniature that she had thought of Alice as a matured woman—a lovely reflex of herself when she had been young and happy. And thus, as she drew nearer and nearer to the place of trial, did Maud think of Alice.

Walter with heaving bosom and trembling hand struck the huge knocker on its bolt, and every blow beat on Maud's heart. No one answered the summons. Walter knocked again and rang a great bell which hung at a postern gate in the garden wall. The clang and clatter roused the rooks nestling in the great trees, and set them cawing and whirling round. Were they giving welcome to the true mistress of Leyton Hall? Or were they scaring her away again to endure the new-old-sorrow from which she was trying to escape?

At last the door was opened by an old man, whose scarred face declared his profession had been a perilous one, and that he bore the certificate of his deserving in his front.

"We have business with Master Maybourne," said Walter; "can we see him?"

"Not here," replied the man; "he left here more than a week agone."

"Left the Hall?" asked Walter, earnestly.

"Yea, Sir; he hath gone to London, but to what part of that growing city I know not," said the man. "He set off in much haste, and I and my dame are the only inmates, save a farming man and a boy."

Mistress Leyton would have fallen from her jennet had not David run to her assistance.

"What, ho!" cried the man. "Judith, a draught of water, quick. The lady is seized with faintness."

"Thanks, my good man!" said Maud, after she had tasted a little of the water. "And you—you know not where your master may be found, save that he has gone to London?"

"No, Madam," replied the man. "I served under him and the great Prince Rupert, and being too old for service, and on the wrong side for a pension ——"

"Thanks! here is a piece of silver. I will send to thee a few days hence, and if you can give me more tidings of where I may have speech of your master, I will reward thee well."

"I would I could serve thee, Madam," said the old man,

"but I fear me I shall know nothing more than at present; but as I hear you shall know."

Mistress Leyton and Walter turned away from the door of Leyton Hall, each with their own particular sorrow, and no word was spoken until they had reached the Grange.

"Do not go forth again to-night, Walter," said Mistress Leyton, holding up her cheek for Walter to kiss; "I want to talk with you about matters which concern us both nearly."

Walter promised to wait his aunt's pleasure; and as neither had appetite for their mid-day meal, they did not meet again until supper-time.

Mistress Leyton then told Walter what she believed to be her relationship to Alice and her father Maybourne, and of the wrong which she had been done to her by Leyton's unjust suspicions, and his hasty, unjustifiable condemnation. They had learned that he and her child were within the limits of one city, and she was resolved, if she knocked at every door, to find them out.

Would Walter take his part in this discovery?

Who could doubt his answer?

As soon as this interview with Mistress Leyton was over, David, to whose charge the care of Reuben had been confided, came to Walter and told him that the man was dying, and that neither priest nor presbyter could shrive him, he had said, until he had seen Walter.

Reuben presented a much less repulsive appearance now that he had been carefully tended for a few days. His matted locks had been combed, and his unkempt beard had been trimmed into order. There was also a solemn look of death in his face; and those who stood beside his couch felt into whose awful presence he was about to pass. Walter knew also that what others considered to have been a deed of impulsive bravery, was a determined act of atonement for a great sin committed, whose value the merciful Judge alone could estimate at its proper worth.

Reuben requested to be left with Walter for a few minutes; and when the other persons had withdrawn from the room, he said—

"Take your tablets, Sir, and write as I shall speak. The words must be few, but you will attest them, and men will believe what you say—perhaps believe me, now that I am dying."

Walter did not hesitate to do as Reuben requested, and with great effort the dying man confessed the villany he had practised upon Leyton, and the motive he had had in doing so. He then attempted to make his cross to his signature, which Walter had written, but the pen fell from his fingers; and murmuring "Forgive us our trespasses as we orgive them," Reuben Studley died.

CHAPTER IX.

WALTER AND TABITHA IN THE CITY.

THE abdication of Richard Cromwell gave renewed hopes to the royalists; and General Monk, after a perplexing reticence, having declared for the restoration of the king, Charles and the Dukes of Gloucester and Kent landed at Dover, and amidst the noisiest acclamations and the most frantic demonstrations of loyalty, made their way to London. The streets were strewed with flowers, and the houses decorated with banners, streamers, and tapestries. The conduits flowed with wine, and the Lord Mayor and Corporation, dressed out in all the splendour of the civic court, met the king. And so on to Whitehall, until the royal ears must have been deafened by the braying of trumpets and the shouting of the loyal citizens. No wonder that Charles, it is chronicled, said it had been clearly his own fault that he had remained so long in exile. "The king had got his own again," and we all know what the lessons of adversity had taught the man Charles Stuart.

The conspicuous part which Leyton had taken up to the fight at Naseby, and his marked recognition by the king and the gallant Prince Rupert, had rendered him very popular with the cavaliers, who did not fail to make his presence in London known to Rupert, who had lost sight of the comrade that had fought by his side through many a bloody day. Rupert had been apprised of Leyton's loss of sight at the time of its occurrence, and the misfortune excited the strongest sympathy in the breast of the gallant prince.

Leyton was sent for to Court at Rupert's instigation, and was most graciously received, but it was at the prince's lodgings in Whitehall that the blind cavalier had the greatest honour and influence. Many of the the losing faction, who feared to suffer the consequences of their adherence to the Commonwealth, sought the good offices of Leyton—a blind Poet among the number—and he had thus the satisfaction of returning many of the obligations which he had incurred to those who had served him when the sun was shining on the other side of the way. Leyton had therefore, after a time, to discard his assumed name of Maybourne, and again take part in the discharge of active duties which he had thought he had abandoned for ever.

The gratification which Leyton experienced from the restoration of the king, and the triumph of that cause for which he had endured so much, was sadly alloyed by his domestic sorrows. To the loss of sight he had been long resigned, and his grief at what he believed the cruel abandonment of his wife had yielded greatly to the assuaging influences of time, until recent events had renewed it in all its poignancy. It was even increased by a consciousness that Alice was a participator in his shame and sorrow, and of this he was made painfully aware by her altered manner and the absence of that cheerfulness which had often imparted its sunshine to his clouded mind.

With mutual consideration for each other, they had rarely spoken of the occurrences at the Hall, as Leyton could not disguise from himself the conviction that Alice did not coincide with him in the condemnation of her mother, and appeared to believe that he had too readily accepted the accusations of her detractors as proofs of her guilt. This conviction at times made him question the justness of his own conduct, and almost disposed him to institute new inquiries, the more so as Providence had brought them so strangely again together. But the settled belief of years could not be readily disturbed, and he dismissed the doubts which arose in his mind as the weak suggestions of the love he had borne to Maud, and which would not die out.

The very striking change in Alice's appearance — the cheeks which grew paler day by day—the eyes which so often gave evidence of some hidden sorrow—could not fail to attract the attention of those who, either from gratitude or sympathy, gathered about Leyton, seeking to alleviate the solitude of the blind man. At last Leyton heard from their lips of the existence of a change which he had long suspected and almost seen with the eyes of paternal love. He alone knew the cause, and how difficult it was of remedy.

"Time works wonders," however, and we must be content to wait patiently, and note the running of the sand in the old magician's glass.

The disappointment which Mistress Leyton had experienced by the departure of the inmates of the Hall was great indeed ; but she was so satisfied that her daughter and her husband were within reach of discovery, that the new difficulties which interposed made her only more resolute and brave. She determined to go at once to London, and by the help of such friends as still remained to her, endeavour to procure for herself that justice which had been denied so long, and effect her restoration to the honourable position of wife and mother, which she had never forfeited.

Walter was rejoiced to learn this determination on the part of his aunt. He strengthened it by the revelation of what had taken place between himself and Reuben Studley, and of which he had hitherto kept Mistress Leyton in ignorance, at the earnest solicitation of Tabitha, who feared to provoke a return of the distressing malady which seemed to be attendant on any mention of those perfidious scandals which had destroyed the happiness of Mistress Leyton's life. To Walter's gratification, however, the communication he had made to his aunt produced the most satisfactory results, as the fortuitous circumstances which had combined to bring the long-estranged together, and to wring from the wretched traducer a confession of his villany, inspired Mistress Leyton with a confidence that the truth was about to be acknowledged ? and the strong excitement which had recently possessed her changed to a stedfast patience, which promised to render the work which she had before her more certain of accomplishment.

The journey to London having been made, Walter, under the directions of his aunt, endeavoured to find out certain of the friends to whom the Leytons had been known in former years, but by whom they were doubtlessly forgotten, or remembered only to her disadvantage.

Time, indeed, had worked many changes, even in the old city itself. Houses had changed tenants, who had gone away and left no trace of their whereabout. New streets or clusters of houses had sprung up where green fields had been a few short years before. The population, despite the ravages of civil war, had increased and multiplied, and Walter was many days before he could gain any tidings of those whom he sought. Indeed, it was not until Tabitha had suggested the probability of her uncle Magnus being still alive—she had heard nothing of him for some years—and that she should accompany Walter on a visit to the Mermaid, that a clue was obtained to the family of the Newberrys, the oldest friends of Mistress Leyton.

It was nearly mid-day when Walter Gray and Tabitha left their lodging in Chancery-Lane to make their visit to the Mermaid. As they passed down Fleet-street, the impudent apprentices, standing at the doors of their masters' booths to solicit custom, did not fail to exercise their Cockney wit on them, as it must be confessed there was a rustical cut about Walter; and Tabitha, though London born, had lived so long in Derbyshire, that she had lost all trace of her city breeding.

"What do ye lack, gentles?" was the cry, as they passed on. "Napery for house-keeping, my noble bridegroom!" "Or," quoth another, "a gold ring that will wear out two husbands, and St. Bridget's is over the way, my pretty one." Neither Walter nor Tabitha heeded these gibes, but smiled and passed on until they came to the conduit which stood opposite Shoe-lane, and about which a small crowd was gathered, watching the angels placed on it to strike the hour of noon upon bells of brass.

Walter and Tabitha stopped also, and without knowing the cause of the crowd.

"What are the people looking at, master?" asked Walter of an elderly man, who seemed to be an artisan by his dress.

"The angels are going to strike the hour presently," answered the man. "It's worth the staying for; an' you have not seen it, Sir?"

"I have not," observed Walter.

"From the country, then, as I guess?" said the man. "You should not miss the sight, young master, as there is no such mechanical piece in the world as our conduit. See, the first angel raises his hammer!" and as the man ceased speaking, the figures struck upon the bells, and made solemn music, ending with twelve beats, to mark the meridian of the day.

Walter turned to thank the man who had so kindly directed his attention to this wonder of Fleet Street, but he was gone.

"Hast thou lost thy purse, master?" said a spurrier's 'prentice, running up to Walter from the opposite side of the street. "An' thou hast, the foist has gone down Shoe Lane."

"By my troth," exclaimed Walter, surprised, "but my leathern bag is gone!"

"I thought as much," said the 'prentice. "The man that stood beside thee is old Crookfinger, the most notorious setter, barnacle, and foist in the City."

"Then why did not you warn me sooner, master 'prentice?" asked Walter.

"And leave my master's wares to be filched by some of the rogues always at hand when the conduit's striking? I were as green as thou art, Master Cowmeadow, an' I did," replied the saucy lad, walking coolly away, and resuming his lusty calling of "What do ye lack? what do ye lack? Rupert-bits for runaways—sharp rowels for good horsemen —blunt jinglers for foot gentlemen! What do ye lack?"

"An' art sure thy purse is gone, Master Walter?" asked Tabitha, who had been favourably impressed by the honest look of the seeming artisan.

"No doubt on't. Let us walk on, or some of those malaperts will be gibing us. I see yon spurrier's lad is making merry, at my cost, with his neighbour, the cordwainer. What called he the fellow who robbed me?" asked Walter, walking towards Ludgate Hill.

"A barnacle, methinks, and a foist," replied Tabitha. "They be cant names for such thieves."

"Cant names?" said Walter.

"It was called, I remember, Pedlar's French; but why I know not," replied Tabitha, who had learned much from her whilom sweetheart, Robin Hummall.

They had passed through Ludgate, and were both gazing with admiration at the lofty spire of St. Paul's, and the vast edifice which had outlived so many ages—soon, alas! to be consumed, with all its memorials of the past, in the great fire which laid London in ashes.

"Halves! fair halves!" cried a man, making a dash at something lying on the footway, and close at the feet of Walter. "I don't know what luck has sent us," said the man, looking Walter full in the face, and smiling as he unrolled a small paper packet, which he had just picked up. "Be it great or small, thou shalt have thy share. Honest Joe, as men call me, never wronged man, woman, or child ; and—as I live by breath, it's a ring—a gold ring set about by precious stones ! What call they these?" and the man held the ring to Walter.

"They are called emeralds, if they be true stones," answered Walter.

"Emeralds, egad ! and stones of price !" said Honest Joe to himself, rather than to Walter. "Of what service are such baubles to me—a hardworking fellowship porter? My mates would only laugh at me did I wear such a gewgaw, master. A pretty piece of work, is't not, mistress?"

Tabitha could only reply in the affirmative.

"It be a lady's ring, I take it," said Honest Joe; "and would fit such a finger as thine, mistress. I know not the worth of the ring, but 'tis thine freely for twenty shillings."

Walter shook his head, saying, "I would that I could buy so good a bargain ; but a barnacle—a foist, I think you call him—hath eased me of my purse."

"Oh !" said Honest Joe, taking back his ring. "So, clapper-clawed already? I trust by a ben cull of my ken. Turn thy pockets inside out, master ; and save honest men from wasting their time upon thee. Shouldst be in Kent Street, or the Mint, Master Greenhorn, ask for Honest Joe ; I shall be main glad to see thee." And the fellow, laying his finger on the side of his nose, crossed the street, and took one of the lanes leading to the river.

"Good gracious !" exclaimed Tabitha. "I do believe, Master Walter, we have had another escape from plunder. I mind me to have heard of such fellows. They are called ring-droppers ; and had you bought his share you would have found the ring worthless glass and base metal."

"I mistrusted the knave from the first," replied Walter, somewhat piqued at Tabitha's remark. "I should not have parted with my money so readily. I would not have bought the ring but under a goldsmith's advice."

Tabitha was silent, as she was conscious of an inclination which she had felt to have taken the bait had the angler had a little more patience.

Tabitha and her young master soon reached Bread Street after this escape from the dummerer (as he was called in

Pedlar's French); and, to the waiting-woman's delight, the old picture of the Mermaid swung in its accustomed place, and still bore the name of Jacob Magnus. Yes, Jacob still kept house in Bread Street; and it said much for the strength of his constitution that he continued "to froth and lime" in the old hostel, and had not succumbed to the effects of his habitual intemperance and gross feeding.

Jacob was now about sixty-six, with a white beard, and something of a round belly. His bleared eyes and bloated face attested to the sensuality of his life; but many who had prophesied that Jacob was drinking himself to death had long since taken their last draught at the Mermaid; and were reposing in the neighbouring burial-ground of Bow. The seasoned toper had a long list of these prophets at his tongue's end; and often indulged in scornful laughter at the untimely taking-off of his old neighbours, who had been small drinkers. Mine host of the Mermaid had not escaped scot free from the troubles of the unsettled times which had passed since last we met him. Towards the close of Cromwell's life more than one plot had been discovered for the assassination of the Protector. Jacob had nearly realised his former homicidal supposition, and swung on his own sign-iron, as, when a conspiracy had been formed by certain wild apprentices, and other rash persons, to kill the Protector, fire houses, and slaughter roundheads, they had, unknown to Jacob, made the Mermaid their head-quarters. But Jacob had friends among the crop-ears of the city: some of whom not unfrequently were indebted to his Rhenish wine for a cheerful countenance and unsteady legs. Fearing possibly that Jacob might "peach" of their irregularities, or, perhaps, grateful for the good wine which had cheered their hearts, many of his neighbours readily endorsed his "supplication," and bore witness to his habitual abstinence from all political partisanship. Jacob, after a week's incarceration in the Fleet, was therefore permitted to return home, and again handle spigot. No man, it hath been said, but has some good in him; and Jacob, though a selfish sot, did not forget those who had stood by him in his peril. When, at the Restoration, the sudden loyalty of some of the citizens became excessively demonstrative, and would have laid hands on the goods and chattels, and personal liberty, of their more consistent neighbours, Jacob stood by them; and by using such influence as he possessed, with some of his cavalier customers, managed to keep his old friends in whole skins, and in quiet enjoyment of their worldly possessions.

Magnus was seated in a little room at the back of the tavern, compounding his morning draught of cock-my-cap (our topers of that day had as many names for their potations as are now found in a Yankee bar-room), and was not in the best humour at being disturbed "at his devotions," as he called his employment; but Tabitha, who had followed the tapster, was already in the room before Jacob could frame an excuse for a denial to his visitors.

"This is somewhat against the rule of the house," said Jacob. "This is my private sanctorum, and not a reception-room for unknown customers."

"But we are neither customers nor are we unknown to each other," replied Tabitha; "an' thou wilt look at me."

"I could have sworn that I had heard that voice for the last time, five years agone, when Mistress Magnus ran off the lees and made a morning's work for old Job Pickheart the sexton."

"An' hast thou forgotten me? Or is it that thy sight fails thee for want of thy morning glass?" asked Tabitha.

"Thou art comely," replied Jacob, "and has a smack of what my Jane was at thine age—yet —— By this light but it is so! Thou art such a woman as my niece Tabitha should have grown to."

"Thou hast guessed it, uncle," answered Tabitha; "I am Tabitha whom thou hast forgotten these fifteen years."

"Not so! Not so by every saint worth swearing by;" exclaimed Jacob. "Give me a buss as I give thee welcome —heartily, and like a true kinswoman."

Tabitha obeyed her uncle, and the smack of the kiss sounded like the crack of a carter's whip.

Walter had remained standing during the preceding colloquy, unnoticed by Jacob, but having established relationship with his niece, Jacob deigned to notice her companion.

"I give you good-day, Sir," said Jacob, resuming the compounding of his morning draught. "Be seated, Sir. prithee; I know not what liquor you affect of a morning, but you have only to give it a name. I would invite thee to a share of my brewage, but it is only fitted for a seasoned brain like mine own. What wilt have, Sir? Canary, Muscadel, Malmsey, or Hungary water?"

Walter chose Canary, as his morning's walk and its adventures had made a glass of wine acceptable.

"And now, Tabitha," said Magnus, when his own draught and Walter's had been placed on the table; "where hast thou been all these long years. Art married? and is this goodly youth thy husband or thy son?"

"Neither one nor t'other," replied Tabitha, colouring slightly, "but my young master, Master Walter Gray."

"Master Gray, I give you welcome," said Magnus, bowing respectfully; "although thy name is not familiar to me."

"Possibly that of my aunt may serve for my introduction, Mistress Leyton," replied Walter.

"Mistress Leyton! of course, I remember. An' hast thou never changed service, Tabitha?" asked Jacob; "thou didst not give promise of such constancy," adding, with a leer, "seeing how thou didst jilt that babe of grace, Thomas Handy."

Tabitha laughed as she replied, "Thomas was a good lad, I doubt not, but he came to tag his love speeches with scraps from conventicle sermons, and so I bade him good-morrow. As for my long service, more thanks for that to my dear good mistress than to my own merits."

"Thou hast deserved all the kindness ever shown to thee, Tabitha, for thy devotion to one who was so vilely belied and so sorely stricken," replied Walter. "Be assured, Master Magnus, a most faithful friend hath thy niece been to my poor aunt."

"By George! I am glad to hear thy praises so well sung, Tabitha; thou camest of a good strain that never forsook friend or fled foe, and I am glad thou has sought me out. It may not be the worse for thee, when other than malt-worms are busy with this old runlet; here's health to thee, Master Gray, and to thee, niece Tabitha," and Jacob took a deep draught of the contents of his tankard, as though to drown the unpleasant thought of the churchyard which he had conjured up.

"Now tell me what is the meaning of this visit; for though I may hope thy love for thine old uncle brought thee, Tabitha, to the Mermaid, I must opine Master Gray had other business with me?"

"You judge rightly, Master Magnus," replied Walter; and I will be brief in the telling of it. You no doubt remember the unhappy story of my aunt's desertion by her husband, Master Leyton."

"I have need to remember. Master Leyton," said Jacob, "seeing that the ward leet nearly pulled down my sign for a brawl he made here, and in which blood was made to flow, to my great scandal."

"You remember the cause of that brawl?" said Walter.

"Not clearly; I know 'twas about a woman, as most of our misadventures are," replied Jacob, laughing.

"It was no laughing matter, uncle," said Tabitha; "believe my word for that. The miserable boasting and saucy writing of a vain libertine drove Master Leyton beside his wits, and he believed the truest, lovingest wife that ever man had to be a wanton."

"Was't so?" asked Jacob, opening his eyes, and staring rather vacantly.

"Marry was it?" answered Tabitha. "The scurvy villain boasted of conquests he had never made, and dared to put his wicked desires on paper. These, by the cruel treachery of a trusted servant, were made known to Master Leyton, who, in the frenzy of jealousy, believed his wife disloyal."

"And was she not?" asked Jacob, softly.

"Was she not!" exclaimed Tabitha; "should I have given up my life to her if she had been? No; I know her to be most foully belied, and I saw the dreadful consequences of her unjust condemnation—madness, uncle—madness, and a melancholy that was worse than madness."

"Lord pardon us all!" said Jacob; "though I had no hand in the matter, I have often spoken lightly of her, poor lady. Well, what are you seeking with me?"

Walter then narrated — of course with the occasional assistance of Tabitha's ready tongue—all that had passed so lately; and that Walter had tried in vain to gain knowledge of any of Mistress Leyton's friends that might be living in London, and to whom her husband would also be known.

"Thou hast hit the right nail on the head, Walter Gray, in striking at the Mermaid," said Jacob, "and gladly will I serve thee to my uttermost. There is an old friend of the Leytons who hath been made a lieutenant of the city. He has been long a merchant, and hath preserved his love of a flask of the best Burgundy to be had between this and the vineyards that grow the divine liquor. Sir Ralph Newberry."

"Sir Ralph Newberry!" cried Tabitha; "the very man to do us service. He was the playmate of my mistress."

"There is another—well—acquaintance of the Leytons, who might do somewhat, did I clearly know the course you were sailing," said Magnus. "Master Leyton stands high in Court favour; and if Master Gray is seeking preferment, I doubt not but his uncle ——"

"Is he then in London?" asked Tabitha, earnestly.

"Yes; and daily, as I hear, at Prince Rupert's lodgings, in Whitehall. Have I guessed rightly?"

"No, Master Magnus," replied Walter; "and yet he holds possession of what I most covet on earth—next to my aunt's honourable acquittal, and her restoration to place and honour."

Walter then told Magnus the object of his aunt's visit to town—that she had resolved to see her husband, and by such evidence as she possessed convince him of the cruel wrong which had been done to her by him and by others.

Jacob sat very thoughtful for a few moments; and then, having drained his tankard, said—"I am unwise, mayhap, in meddling with matters which concern me not—losing the profit of a good customer, who drinks his five quarts a day of the rarest, but I have done some evil in my time, and I will hope that the good deed I intend may be put down against my score."

"What do you mean, uncle?" asked Tabitha.

"Suppose, and suppose, and suppose," replied Jacob, as though he hesitated to commit himself irrevocably to his good work, "I were to bring evidence of thy mistress's innocence into court, that even the jealous blackamoor they show at the 'Globe' would believe; what then?"

"I would call thee the best, the dearest, the honestest of men," replied Tabitha, giving Jacob a hearty kiss by way of instalment.

"Thou wouldst lie, then, Tabitha—lie most liberally," said Jacob; "but I will strive my best to do as I have said. Come thou and Master Gray thither to-morrow about noon, and I may have news to tell ye. In the meantime, seek Sir Ralph Newberry; say thou art my niece, and he will give thee sight of him. He lives hard by, in Milk Street; his sign is Walter Raleigh's Head, painted on a gold background—meaning the El Dorado which that noble voyager dreamed of.

Walter Gray having warmly expressed his thanks to Jacob, and Tabitha having kissed her uncle again, they took their leave, promising to be at the Mermaid on the morrow at the hour appointed.

CHAPTER X.

THE DEBAUCH.

T Tabitha's request, she again accompanied Walter to the Mermaid ; but as their experience of Fleet Street had been rather unsatisfactory, they decided to take the quieter road to the City down Old Bourne, and across the Fleet river to Snorer Hill—or Snow Hill, as it has been since named. The little gardens in front of the houses in Old Bourne were a pleasant exchange for the noisy, impudent 'prentices ; and Walter was congratulating Tabitha on the advantages of their selected route when a loud shout reached them, and looking down Old Bourne Hill, they saw a crowd of rabble come pouring out of Farringdon, and then make for the hill.

"What means yonder medley?" asked Walter of a staid old gentleman who was tending the flowers in his garden.

The old man looked in the direction indicated, and then said, carelessly, "A common sight enough to the dwellers in Old Bourne—a rogue on his way to the gallows at Tyburn. But step into my garden until the cart has passed, or the mob will take pleasure in spoiling two such decent people."

"Oh la ! 'a mercy !" exclaimed Tabitha, "that we should come to such a sorry sight. Prithee, Master Walter, accept of the gentleman's courtesy ;" and so saying, the terrified woman ran into the garden, followed by Walter.

Old Bourne was then the road to Tyburn tree, and so continued to be for many a year. Nearly opposite to where

Walter and Tabitha were placed was the George tavern, at whose door the unhappy culprits used to stop to drink, and to show off their bravado, as did clever Tom Clinch, to whom Swift has given an infamous immortality.*

The wretch in the cart, however, did not appear to have much of the bravo left in him, for, though he strove to smile and wag his head as if defying his fate, the ghastly pallor of his cheeks, and the occasional tremor which seized him, told the mortal agony which really possessed him. He took his draught, however, and when doing so, turned about to salute the gazers on all sides. The moment Walter caught a good sight of the man's features, he exclaimed—

"The scoundrel that headed the King's Rogues, and who would have taken my life at the Hall!" and turning to Tabitha as he spoke, he was surprised to find she had fallen on her knees, and appeared to be praying with great earnestness and volubility. As Walter did not feel justified in disturbing such a pious office, he looked again towards the cart which was moving on towards the gallows. The shout of the rabble dying away, Tabitha removed her hands from her face. Her large blue eyes were red with tears, and her comely face "as pale as a parsnip."

"Thou art a good girl," said the old man, "to pray for such a scoundrel as he, gone to his proper ending. A traitor to all who trusted him, and so mean a rogue that he beat a poor woman to death for her market pence."

Tabitha received these words of commendation "under false pretences," for the sight of Robin Hummall riding to Tyburn in the hangman's cart had a personal effect upon Tabitha, who remembered that she might have been the malefactor's wife, and lived for the rest of her life a hempen

---

* "As clever Tom Clinch while the rabble was bawling,
  Rode stately through Holborn to die in his calling,
  He stopped at the George for a bottle of sack,
  And promised to pay for it *as he came back*.
  His waistcoat and stockings and breeches were white,
  His cap had a new cherry ribbon to tie't;
  The maids to the doors and the balconies ran,
  And said, Lack-a-day, he's a proper young man."

The removal of the gallows from Tyburn to Newgate was due to the interference of the philanthropist Howard.

widow. In the fulness of her thankfulness for her deliverance, she had fallen on her knees and continued to repeat as much of the Book of Common Prayer and the Puritan Directory as she could remember, until Robin Hummall had passed out of her sight for ever.

Jacob Magnus had prepared a savoury and substantial refection for his visitors, and begged neither to stint of meat or liquor. Jacob excused himself from partaking of more than a slice or so of neat's tongue, for, in sooth, his past night's drinking had left him with a jaded appetite; but he found sustenance in the flagon—seeming, like a snipe, to live chiefly on suction.

"And now to business," said Jacob. "Yesterday I made bold to wait on Sir Ralph Newberry at his accompting-house, and was, I need scarcely say, honourably received. I told him what had passed between us, and for a time Sir Ralph appeared like one beside himself. 'I never doubted her!' said he, 'I never doubted her! and for that reason, Jacob'—he calls me Jacob at times—'and for that reason I have never questioned that'—well, he said—'Sot Cotterell. It would have been to do her wrong,'"

"Bless him!—bless him!" cried Tabitha; "Sir Ralph was always a true gentleman."

"He demanded your mistress's lodging—whose whereabout thou hadst fortunately given me—called to his head clerk, and bade him hasten to my lady and bid her be ready to go abroad. Then he counter-ordered, and said —'No; it would be late, and he would see Master Leyton first.' In fact, as I told thee, he was like one distraught."

"My good uncle, you will have done better work to-day than ever thou didst in thy life, if my poor lady gets justice through thy means," said Tabitha, putting her arms round Jacob's neck.

Walter also thanked Magnus for what he had done, and then added—

"You spoke of that villain, Cotterell. Is the fellow living?"

Jacob placed his finger on his lip, and pointed to a door which separated the sanctorum from the public drinking-room.

"He is there, Master Walter!—he is there. And—nay, stay where thou art, Sir, or you will ruin all," replied Jacob, checking Walter's movement towards the door. "You must not be rash, but wait the coming of Sir Ralph, who hath age and wisdom."

"It is a hard measure of patience to keep my hands from the villain's throat," said Walter. "Sir Ralph must drag the truth from him if his life comes with it."

"He will, no doubt on't," replied Magnus, soothingly. "Now, prithee, get thee home to Mistress Leyton, and bid her prepare to receive her old friend and his lady. Nay, be ruled by me; I promise thee your noble aunt shall have justice, and you a fitting revenge."

And so Jacob contrived at last to quiet Walter, and to despatch him and Tabitha back again to his aunt's lodgings.

"'Tis well he has gone, or there would have been letting of blood, which is a thing I abhor in my own house," thought Jacob. "Now I must go share either flask or flagon with Master Cotterell. It offends if I drink not with him."

Few who had known the smart, rattling Dick Cotterell of twenty years ago, would have recognised him in the bloated, blotched-faced man who sat apart in the public room of the Mermaid smoking his Trinidado out of a long silver pipe, occasionally, or rather frequently, moistening his lips by an application to a powerful compound of brandy and a strong Xeres wine, flavoured with cinnamon : it was called clamberhead. He had become what Newberry had named him, a confirmed sot. Immediately after his cowardly attack upon Leyton, he, to avoid the consequences of what could hardly be called a duello, flew to his estate in Wales, and lay there in hiding for more than twelve months. Having heard that Leyton had suddenly disappeared from society and his friends, Cotterell ventured to return to his old haunts, but found himself coldly treated by all his acquaintance, with the exception of a few miserable fellows, who were content to be his boon companions, and to participate in the debauch for which Cotterell was paymaster.

Sir Ralph Newberry had for a long time ceased his intimacy with Cotterell; but when they occasionally met—either in the street or at a tavern—a few words of courtesy were interchanged, and that was all. Newberry was out of England when the great trouble of the Leytons came upon them, and he had therefore only heard in part, and with the variations, additions, and subtractions to which a story is subjected in the course of long traversing about. Newberry had seen somewhat too much of the world to believe in the impossibility of the existence of faithless friends and wives; but he would never admit—not even to himself—that Maud Netherby had been untrue to herself or to her husband. When the busy tongues of censorious acquaintance condemned the absent woman, Newberry, true to his early faith in his boyish love, bravely asserted her innocence, and usually confounded her detractors, as none could support their insinuations to her discredit by one word of personal evidence.

Jacob Magnus could not have gone to a more earnest friend of the Leytons than Sir Ralph, who soon devised a plan by which it was hoped some of the great mischief of the past might be repaired. It was with this view that Magnus intruded his company on his half-tipsy guest.

"I trust, Master Cotterell, that thy liquor is to thy liking," said Magnus, pausing for a moment or two before he sat down in the large stuffed chair which he usually occupied when seated amongst his guests.

"It's villanously short of its fair measure of brandy," replied Cotterell; "and the Xeres smacks vilely of the pigskin which contained it. Not even two sticks of cinnamon can deceive me, Jacob. I know the true wine, and can measure the strength of good spirit by the tip of my tongue."

"Thou dost only jest, I know, Master Cotterell," replied Jacob, seating himself. "The wine and the spirit are fit tipple for an emperor; but your villanous tobacco, which, as the player says, 'is only fit to fill a man with smoke and embers,' leaves thy palate no true discernment."

"Thou liest, Silenus!" replied Dick; "the nicotian weed is a relish to good liquor—but call for thy glass, and help me to see this tankard to the end."

Jacob called for a drinking-glass; and as all liquor was alike to him, he soon aided Cotterell to finish the flagon.

"Let's have no more of that hell-broth!" said Cotterell, "but like a true friend, Jacob, be honest for one bout, and bring a bottle or two, an' thou canst, of veritable Canary."

"I will—I will, Master Cotterell—a wine above price, but thou cares tnot for that, I know;" and having retired to a private cellar, of which he alone kept the key, he returned shortly with a magnum bottle, and ordered the tapster to bring two of his Venice glasses to do honour to the wine.

"Here is liquid gold, Master Cotterell, and cold as an icicle—a draught to cool Dives' burning tongue if he could get it," said Jacob.

"Don't be—profane, Magnus," hiccuped Cotterell; "though I haven't been inside a church—save Paul's Walk—for these twenty years, I'll listen to no profanity. Come, pour out a glass of Dives—I mean the t'other—and let us see if thy boast is borne out by thy liquor."

"An' it be not, I'll empty the magnum at my own cost," said Jacob. "Ah! there's a posy! Smell it, smell it, my master! I always envy my corkscrew, because it tastes such liquor before me."

"By Bacchus and his pards! but thou has not lied!" said Cotterell. "It is rare wine!"

"I'm glad to hear thee say so," replied Jacob. "Those who have good wine like good drinkers: there is the best of the one, and thou art the best of the other."

"Don't flatter me, Jacob—don't flatter me; d——e! I hate flattery!" replied Cotterell. "I can take my *quantum sufficit*, or perhaps my *quantum pluribus*—is that dog-latin? —but there are better heads than mine that can beat me by a bottle, and say their criss-cross table without foundering. Fill my glass! What news is stirring?"

"I have not been abroad to-day," replied Jacob. "Our last night's rouse kept me late in bed. Yet stay, there was one here who had come from the Court, and had seen, at Prince Rupert's lodgings, who think ye?—old Master Leyton."

"Leyton!" exclaimed Cotterell; "I thought he had been dead long ago?"

"And so thought I, but he is alive, and a great man at Court, I'm told," replied Jacob, adding, after a pause, "Ifeekins! I am losing my head, for I had clean forgotten somewhat that may pleasure thee. My niece Tabitha—you remember Tabitha?"

Cotterell nodded his head.

"She hath been here and tells me thine old light-o'-love, Mistress Leyton, is in town!"

"Peace, raven, or I'll brain thee!" shouted Cotterell, seizing the bottle.

Jacob shrugged his shoulders, and then quietly raised his glass to his lips. It was well that no other guest was present; but as Jacob had discontinued his ordinary since his wife's decease, there was rarely much company at the Mermaid until after the business hours of the neighbouring citizens.

Cotterell sat silent for a time, and then rose to his feet, and paced with unsteady steps about the room.

"Friends have ruined wives and pinked husbands before now, and ruffled with the best," he muttered. "Why should I hide my head like a hunted ostrich, and grow maudlin—maudlin!"

Jacob did not interrupt the meditations he had provoked, but sat gazing at the empty fireplace.

After a time, Cotterell returned to his seat at the table, and filling his glass, drained it at a draught.

"What was wine made for, Magnus?" he asked, after a short pause.

"For good fellowship and good fellows," replied Jacob, quickly. "See how the bubbles on the top laugh till they burst! 'Tis pleasant to drink mirth by the pint."

"Dost think I drink for good fellowship!" asked Cotterell, with a sneer.

"Yes, truly," replied Jacob, "for I know thou hast a good fellow to drink with thee."

"Thou art a merry rogue, Magnus!" said Cotterell, sadly; "but I have always a companion that scoffs at song and jest, who watches the smile upon my lips only to drive it back into my heart."

"Master Cotterell—Master Cotterell!" exclaimed Jacob, "what playhouse rant is this! The wine hath disordered thy wits!"

"To what will this lead?" continued Cotterell, in a tipsy voice. "It hath made me a drunkard, and will drive me to beggary, and then will come more drink and then madness."

"'Fore George! don't prate such nonsense!" said Jacob. "Take another glass of wine."

"Wine! wine is to make men merry!" replied Cotterell. "Fetch me some brandy."

Jacob, who had great faith in the consolation of strong drinks, offered no opposition to Cotterell's unwise request, but produced a moderate-sized wicker-covered flask from his pocket, saying—

"At thy service, Master Cotterell. I always carry a small modicum of the best in case of colic, spasms, cough, cold, sprains, vertigo, or, in short, any and every disorder."

But Jacob jested to a dull ear, and Cotterell sat silent, ever and anon sipping at Jacob's flask, until it was empty.

The effect of the brandy soon became apparent in Cotterell's tipsy bearing.

"My familiar—my devil hath left me," he said, "and now let us toast bright eyes and cherry lips. I toast Mistress Magnus!"

"Ah!" replied Jacob, not caring to enter into any discussion. "*There* was an eye—blinking and winking like the fag end of a Christmas candle."

"By Venus and her pigeons, thou shalt not abuse Mistress Magnus! I'll make thee play Sir Pandarus of Troy, and light me by that good torch in thy face," and Cotterell made an ineffectual effort to rise.

"Touch not mine nose," replied Jacob, laughing. "It is of value, for it hath cost both time and money to bring it to this hue! What a marvel is it that pale drinks should paint the nose crimson!"

"None of thy tapster's farrago!" said Cotterell. "Where is fair Mistress Magnus?"

"Where she hath been silent for these five years past, and where I am in no haste to join her, good helpmate that she was," replied Jacob.

"By Jove, an' I had forgotten she had departed! I'm drunk, Jacob—no doubt on't—no doubt."

And either his potations or the conviction of his inebriety overpowering him, Master Richard Cotterell laid his head upon the table, and soon made known that he was asleep.

Jacob Magnus shook his head as he looked upon the sleeping sot, and muttered—

"I have managed this business vilely. I was to have drawn confession from him of the wrong he did to Mistress Leyton's fair fame, and I have made him incontinently drunk. He hath weaker brains than I had thought for, but for a certes men are degenerating."

Jacob soon disposed of what wine remained in the bottle, and then with steady foot and solemn face he retired into his sanctorum to sleep away what little obfuscation his debauch had produced.

When Walter returned to his aunt's lodgings, he found that she had been visited by Sir Ralph and Lady Newberry. What had taken place at the interview had produced a most consolatory effect on Mistress Leyton, as she had learned, almost for the first time, that there had been many amongst her friends who would not believe the calumnies uttered to her prejudice, but condemned the hasty decision of her husband, and his unnecessary desertion of his friends and position.

Both Sir Ralph and Lady Newberry had declared their determination to strive to the utmost to procure a reversal of Leyton's cruel sentence, and to obtain a restoration of the mother's rights and intercourse with her child. Fortunately, Major Fordyke, the brother of Lady Newberry, was in high favour with Prince Rupert, and had, she knew, served with Leyton. This unexpected combination of circumstances promised, it was augured, a favourable result, and the Newberrys left Mistress Leyton to go at once to Major Fordyke and take council as to the manner in which the Prince's influence could be used, in order to bring Leyton to a full and calm consideration of the events of the past.

Major Fordyke was luckily at his lodgings when the Newberrys called.

"This is a delicate matter to meddle in, dear sister," said the major, with a smile. "I know Leyton well, and can hardly believe but he must have had conclusive reasons for what he did. He is a cool-headed fellow, and would not have been readily deceived."

"You judge like all men—I mean like most men. Sir Ralph is as convinced of Mistress Leyton's innocence as I am," replied Lady Newberry.

"Ah, yes!" said the major; "but I fancy I have heard that Maud Netherby might have been Lady Newberry when she was ——"

"Eight years old," said Sir Ralph. "But, brother, this is no light matter, I assure thee. The happiness of more than one life depends upon the restitution of this poor lady to home and reputation."

"Well, I will do what I can to serve the lady, certainly," said Fordyke; "but I would rather ride through Brentford again than face Colonel Leyton on this business. However, thou hast my promise. When must I advance?"

"As soon as may be," replied his sister. "Every hour is one of misery to Mistress Leyton, which is now passed away from her husband."

"Look ye!" said Fordyke, as though struck with some sudden thought that looked promising. "It chanced that I was yesterday at Leyton's lodgings on business of his highness, and that done, our talk fell into ——No! I will keep my thought to myself in case I raise hopes which may not be realised. In the meantime, Sir Ralph, do you seek out the original sin—the serpent that destroyed the Paradise thou hast described at Leyton Hall. What name hath he?"

"Cotterell."

"Ay, Cotterell, and tell him I will measure swords with him if he doth not make instant confession that he hath belied your friend ——"

"The fellow's beneath a soldier's notice," replied Newberry. "I'll get a London 'prentice to club the life out of him if he refuse to sign his own villany. I have already set on a boon companion of his to draw out evidence."

"Good. Clara had better remain here," said Fordyke, "so that succour may be at hand should I need it. I shall look for thee to supper, Ralph, and if thou hast eloquence enough, bring Penelope—I mean thy poor client, with thee."

Newberry mounted his horse, followed by his serving-man, and rode back to the City. He dismissed his attendant when they had reached Cheapside, and walked down Bread Street to the Mermaid.

Jacob Magnus had barely slept off his mid-day debauch, when Newberry requested to see him.

"Well, Master Magnus," said Newberry, "hast thou made the rascal reveal ——"

Jacob laid his finger on his lip, and pointed to the still sleeping Cotterell.

"Is he sober enough, think ye, to understand me?" asked Newberry.

"I should say so, Sir Ralph; but have a care! He wakes up savage like, after such a debauch as he has had to-day."

"Oh, I fear him nothing!" replied Newberry; and then, going to Cotterell, shook him rather rudely by the shoulder. "Cotterell! Dick Cotterell!"

"Speak—I hear you!" answered the sot, without raising his head.

"Art awake and sober?"

"What's that to thee," replied Cotterell, raising his head, and looking fiercely at his questioner.

"Nay, I meant not to offend thee," said Newberry.

"But there was offence in thy question, Sir Ralph Newberry; and I bear not with that from any man!" replied Cotterell.

"I prithee, forgive whatever I said amiss. I have grave business with thee," said Newberry.

"I hate business," replied Cotterell, "especially at my tavern. What says the player, 'Shall I not take mine case in mine inn?' Well, what is't? Jacob, a cup of some of thy d—e drinks. I can't talk dry lipped."

Newberry (when the wine had been brought) proceeded with great consideration, and carefully selecting his words, so as to avoid giving his listener offence, to acquaint Cotterell with the purport of his visit, and was rendered rather hopeful of a satisfactory result, as Cotterell listened attentively and without any appearance of anger. He sat resting his elbows on the table, and holding his chin in one hand, his eyes stedfastly fixed upon the face of Newberry.

"And so you wish me to write myself down a villain, and confess to a rascality I was never guilty of?" asked Cotterell.

"Not guilty?"

"No; I never maligned Mistress Leyton. It was her own husband who accused and convicted her," said Cotterell.

"But you boasted ——"

"What of that? I did not accuse," said Cotterell. "I sign no lie against myself ——"

"You wrote to her?"

"I did; the letter was a folly. How Leyton drew such meaning from it I know not. You have my answer, I sign nothing. Where is Leyton to be found?" asked Cotterell, rising.

Newberry was so confounded by the turn the conversation had taken, that he could make no reply.

"No matter," said Cotterell, "I can hunt my own game. Magnus, my sword," and having received his weapon, Master Richard Cotterell marched out of the Mermaid.

When the Newberrys met at supper at Major Fordyke's, there seemed to have been little progress made towards the desired reconciliation of the Leytons.

Fordyke had interested Prince Rupert sufficiently to induce that good-natured person to go to Leyton's lodgings, and to enter somewhat on the painful subject of his domestic sorrow. But Leyton had stopped all discussion, by at once entreating the prince to forbear opening wounds which, if not closed altogether, yet had become deprived of their painfulness.

"But let not our defeat spoil our enjoyment," said the major; "and after supper I will tell thee of a plan of attack which presented itself to me some hours ago."

The expectation of some clever device to obtain the "consummation so devoutly to be wished," gave a zest to the supper.

CHAPTER XI., AND LAST.

MAUD'S INNOCENCE PROVED.

WHEN Sir Ralph Newberry visited Mistress Leyton on the morning after the failure of the prince's interview with her husband, and saw the look of hopeful expectancy in the poor lady's face, he could not find words to tell her of the ill-success of his mission. Mistress Leyton was quick-witted, and an expression of the deepest sorrow supplanted the look of hopefulness.

"Thou art silent, my friend," she said; "I need no words to tell me I am still thought guilty. I dare not repine. We are told that we are chastened for our good; but, looking back, I feel my faults so venial, that oftentimes the murmur rises to my lips."

"Leyton's obstinacy amounts to cruelty—to revenge," said Newberry.

"I do not feel it to be so," replied Mistress Maud; "I remember his kind, his loving nature, and know how clear to him must the proofs of my guilt have appeared, before he would have condemned me."

"'Tis strange! You still love him!"

"Love him? With all my soul! Did I not love him I should not care to wipe away the blot upon my fame; but for his sake—for my child's sake, I would brave a hundred deaths to prove I was not unworthy of his name and love!"

"But Leyton will not seek to be convinced that he has wronged you. Nor would he believe Walter's story; and

Studley's confession he would discredit, and tell us it had been obtained from him by threats or bribes."

"Dost think so?"

"I fear so. The villain Cotterell's word would be held as worthless as himself," said Newberry, sadly.

"There's one he would believe," replied Mistress Leyton.

"Who?"

"Me. If I could reach his ear, he would know there was truth in my words, and then let others testify."

"And what if he could be brought to hear thee? Could'st thou for a time command thyself to play a part that would demand a trial of all thy patience?"

"Yes, were it to thrust my hand into a fire and not cry out."

"Then endure a little longer and have hope. My wife will visit thee presently, and take thee into council. If I had found thee less constant, less resolute, thou should'st have been spared the risk of further pain. As I know thee now, thou hast a right to make a venture that may lead to a haven or end in an utter wreck. Wilt thou brave the peril?"

"I will, be it whatever it may, and promise to abide by any counsel you may give. My hand upon it."

Newberry took her hand, and pressing it to his lips, said,—

"Brave, much-wronged friend, I leave you with more hope than I have yet had in this unhappy business."

When Newberry had left, Maud strove to conjecture what was to be her trial; but it was not until the arrival of Lady Newberry that she understood the effort she was to be called upon to make for her exculpation.

Although the kindly interference of Prince Rupert had met with what might be considered a peremptory rebuff, Colonel Leyton showed no displeasure towards Major Fordyke, even if he had suspected him to have been the cause of the intrusion upon his domestic sorrows. On the contrary, he affected more than he had hitherto done, the society of the major, and received with evident pleasure the visits of Sir Ralph and Lady Newberry.

Alice, at first, was very reserved, if she was not positively rude in her reception of Lady Newberry's advances to intimacy; but as her conduct was generously attributed to her unhappy position, her new acquaintance continued her at entions, until at last Alice began to regard her, and to derive great solace from her disinterested friendship.

Lady Newberry had, of course, never questioned Alice on the cause of the melancholy which oppressed her, knowing, as she did, the story of her family; but by many indirect ways the new friend contrived to exhibit a consolatory sympathy, and to inspire a feeling of hope to which Alice had been long a stranger. The happy consequences of this intercourse became evident, in the return of healthful colour to the poor faded cheeks, and the old mirthfulness to the voice of Alice; and of this no one was sooner observant than the sightless father. He knew by the changed tone, and the cold pulseless hand, when the bitterness of sorrow had found its way into his darling's heart; and he also was the first to discern, in the altered music of her voice, that the sweetness of her youth had in part come back to her. He questioned his faithful Hafed as to the truth of his surmises, and received the fullest confirmation. Alice was the light of Leyton's home; and when a cloud came over her, the shadow fell upon all within reach of her influence.

"That dear Lady Newberry," said Alice; "she hath done me such marvellous good, that I have parted from my physician, who told me that his medicaments were no longer needed—I had found a better leech than he."

"May God bless her for her goodness," replied Leyton; and tears stole from his sightless eyes, for a thought had come into his mind that, had one proved true to him and to his child, there would have been no need to seek elsewhere for the companionship which they both required.

Lady Newberry was announced before the conversation proceeded, and that good lady saw that Leyton had been weeping, and could not refrain asking the cause.

"They were tears of thankfulness," said Alice, "I am sure, dear Lady Newberry. We had been speaking of thy great kindness to me, and acknowledging how much my restored health was due to it."

"I am fortunate in being the ministrant," replied Lady Newberry. "Any other person who could love you as I do, Alice, would have worked the same cure."

"Oh, no!"

"Oh, yes; is it to be wondered at that thou should'st be moped, and have the spleen, and vertigoes, and dolours, and a thousand other diseases of the fancy, seeing that thou hast no companionship but an old soldier and a heathen menial?"

"It need not be so," replied Leyton, quickly; "but Alice will not see my company."

"Old battered cavaliers who have nothing to talk of but their wounds and hair-breadth 'scapes, and camp rouses. I know them—noble, brave fellows, who have won the right to fight their battles o'er again; but hardly fit companions for a young maiden of nineteen.'

"I fear there is truth in what thou hast said," answered Leyton, sighing deeply.

"Now confess, Alice—am I not right? Dost not tire rather of thy solitude? Would'st not go abroad in the world, and have some one on whom to expend thy womanly sympathy? Say such an one as I am?"

"Oh! yes, yes!" cried Alice, embracing Lady Newberry. "I am so much happier when thou art with me, that I feel a sorrow when we bid 'good-bye,' although I hope that to-morrow will bring thee again."

"Dost hear, Colonel? I am quite right," said Lady Newberry. "Why not accept the knowledge, and act on't?"

"I hardly follow thy meaning,' replied Leyton.

"Plainly, sith thou asked me to advise thee, Alice needs companionship. I have, first, from my sympathy at her loneliness, and then from the love that has grown up for her, expended more time at thy lodgings than is compatible with my duties as a good housewife; and my husband's affairs have suffered somewhat."

"I am grieved that thy goodness to me ——"

"It was not for that I spoke, dear child, but to influence thy father to find a substitute for me," replied Lady Newberry.

"I guess your meaning," said Leyton. "You would have me find a fitting companion for Alice?"

"I would," replied Lady Newberry; "one who had experience to guide her, and qualities to interest her; an' such an one I know."

"That is fortunate," said Leyton.

"She is a poor gentlewoman—a distant kinswoman of my husband—without child or husband; but who has such rare qualities of mind and disposition that Alice would soon love her. Of that I feel assured. Her name is Mistress Stanley."

"You will add to your benefits, my dear lady," said

Leyton, "if thou wouldst undertake this business for me, an' it be convenient to thee, with the least delay."

"I will send for her to-morrow," replied Lady Newberry; "and, if I can, persuade her to undertake this pleasant duty."

The arrival of a gentleman allowed the two ladies to retire; and when they were alone Alice almost sank rather than sat down, and her tears flowed freely.

"Why art thou crying, dear child?" asked Lady Newberry.

It was some moments before Alice could speak.

"I have for the last few days," she said, "so longed to unburthen my full heart to thee that I have scarcely slept. I have held my peace because I thought I was betraying my father's secret; but our talk to-day has made me regardless of that consideration, and I must tell thee my secret."

"What if I know it already?" said Lady Newberry, pressing her arm closely around Alice, who still stood clasping the speaker's neck.

"What if I know of thy father's exile, and its cause?—that I know what the world hath said of thy mother? that thou hast given thy maiden heart to one who hath his part in this shameful story?"

Alice wept aloud.

"Be comforted, my dear one—be comforted. Look in my face, that thou mayst believe my words. Thou canst not see for those tears: let me dry them with my kerchief. Now look at me, and trust my words. I know thy mother to have been, and to be still, most loving, true, and loyal; that never, by word or deed, or thought, did she wrong to thy deceived father or to thee!"

Alice fell upon her knees, and, raising her clasped hands, spoke aloud the thanksgiving of her heart.

When she was calm enough to hear more, Lady Newberry said—

"Thy father is hard to win to reason. He judged rashly; he hath hardened his heart that it might not condemn him. But the truth shall prevail."

"Yes; it shall!" said Alice. "Where can I see my mother?"

"Here, in this house—here, in her place. But, to speak in the humour of the time, if we cannot treat, nor storm, we must mine and sap, Alice. Thy father is a stubborn foe to his own peace."

"When shall I see my mother?" asked Alice.

"Canst thou not guess?" asked Lady Newberry.

"Yes, when I see ——"

"Mistress Stanley! Thou seest we have been plotting! Thou canst now meet thy mother without wounding her sensitive love by the least show of distrust. And now that thou knowest how deep I am in all thy secrets, hast thou no word for a poor youth who is nigh dead with love-sickness?"

Alice's face became crimson; but after a moment of maidenly confusion she took a flower from her bosom, and gave it to Lady Newberry. That clever diplomatist, having received the flower with a smile, and kissed the burning cheek of the fair donor, took her departure.

The gentleman who had been announced was, like Leyton, blind also. He, too, had had his share of domestic sorrows, and knowing Leyton's story in part, had often of late, when they had met, spoken magic words of sympathy. It was his gift to utter "thoughts that live and words that burn." He had called to thank Leyton for his kindly interference in his behalf with the restored king, and when Charles the Second did the noblest act of his ignoble reign by leaving undisturbed his great antagonist — he who had sung of Paradise!

The two friends had talked of their domestic griefs, and one had said—"How small—how insignificant were all our wretched squabbles, although they made up the chiefest sorrows of our lives."

Leyton thought of his words—thought of the strange and unexpected interview with his old and loved commander— thought of all which had happened at Leyton Hall, until he felt the foreshadowing of some coming event which was to bring him in collision with his old sorrows. On the following morning Leyton, attended by Hafed, had gone to take his daily exercise in the Park of St. James—then being planted and beautified—and afterwards to attend a morning council at the lodgings of Prince Rupert. There were many cavalier friends, who had suffered in the king's cause, to be served and considered, as well as many who stood in danger from their disloyalty, but who had claims upon the victorious party for services rendered to the cavaliers in their hour of adversity.

It was during Leyton's absence that Lady Newberry

arrived at his lodgings, accompanied by a lady whom she desired to be announced as Mistress Stanley. Whilst the servant was placing chairs—oh, how tardily!—two hearts were beating tumultuously, and were only relieved by the flood of happy tears which came to the relief of mother and daughter as they stood locked in each other's arms. Happy! —happy Maud! her child had called her mother, and by her embraces acquitted her of all dishonour!

Happy, happy Alice? The vacancy in the heart, which a mother only can fill, was now overflowing with filial love, and the terrible affliction which had threatened to destroy the happiness of her young life had passed away, never to return!

It were vain to attempt to describe the incidents—the outpourings of those two long pent-up hearts; the linked hands would not part—the loving eyes would not look away, except when the lips, grown silent from excess of happiness, were pressed again and again upon each other.

All Maud's sorrows were for a time forgotten, and she no longer doubted that her husband was to be restored to her.

It was late in the day when Leyton returned. He had gone to his own room to rest awhile, as was his wont, having dined abroad, and it was not until the evening that he requested to be visited by the new-comer, Mistress Stanley.

Leyton was seated, reclining, in a large chair, the light of two wax tapers falling on his face, when Maud, his wife, looked on him after seventeen years of cruel separation. The auburn locks had become nearly white; the bright, intelligent eyes were closed and sightless; the stalwart form was that of an aged man. And yet the old love was stronger in her heart, and but for the restraint she had promised to observe, she would have clasped her arms about him, nor loosed her hold until he had pronounced her guiltless. As it was, she stood holding her hands upon her forehead and trembling as though an ague had seized her.

Had not Leyton been blind, he would have wondered at the group which stood at the entrance of his room. His daughter Alice and his daughter's friend supporting a woman, whose agitation was almost beyond control. He would have recognised, no doubt, a faded face, which had once appeared to him the most beautiful of all he had ever looked upon. But he was blind, and knew not who was near him. At last he heard a voice, and asked—

"Is Mistress Stanley here?"

"Yes, Sir," was the scarce audible reply.

Only two brief words, and Leyton sat up in his chair! Had his ear caught some old familiar music?

"Our kind friend," said Leyton, with some effort, "our kind friend, Lady Newberry, hath told thee, no doubt, all the duties to be required of thee."

"Yes, Sir."

Leyton paused again before he spoke, —

"You are now, as I grieve to hear, childless, but we should not sorrow for the young. The flowers of Paradise spring from the graves of children. My daughter hath had a greater loss—her mother."

"Indeed, Sir! I thought her mother still lived."

"Not to her—not to me!" said Leyton, excited. "She died, long years ago, the worst of deaths. For the adulation of a villain she left all that was her home."

"That is very horrible; and was it proved?"

"Ay, Madam, beyond the scepticism of my love."

"Dare I ask your proofs, Sir? I, too, have suffered."

Leyton turned his sightless eyes towards the speaker before he answered.

"I do not brook such questioning often, Madam; but you—yes, I had proofs. I had brought to me the letter which proposed her flight."

"That was no proof of her guilt."

"But with it her answer, showing a preconception of the villain's purpose, and her fear of detection by her husband."

"Impossible!" exclaimed Mistress Leyton, aghast almost at what she had heard.

"So I had thought once; but I read the words—read them now, for they are ever present to my mind," said Leyton, clasping his hands upon his forehead.

"Some omitted word, some word added, must have changed her meaning. It was a fragment, which expressed nothing, perhaps, but which you weighed against the unchanged love of years."

"Who speaks to me?" said Leyton, starting up.

"The messenger of truth, Colonel Leyton. Thou hast bruised her whom thou hadst sworn to cherish. The selfishness of your pride made thee condemn the innocent unheard. The world's opinion was more to thee than thy wife; and for false honour thou hast sacrificed thyself and her."

"Who speaks to me? Why will none answer?" cried Leyton, extending his hands, as though to touch the speaker.

"One who can prove thou hast been unjust."

"Who art thou? Think that I am blind, and tell me who thou art."

"Maud, thy wife!" and she fell upon her knees at Leyton's feet, "who knows her solemn protestation of her innocence will not be unbelieved; who vows, before the God who holds her life in his hand, that never hath she done thee wrong, or forfeited her just claim to be thy honoured wife."

Leyton shook violently, and tried to cry out, but could not.

"Am I believed? Or art thou the only one who sets my word at naught?"

"Walter Gray!" Leyton said, with effort.

"My sister's child—the unhappy cause of much that hath happed between us. My sister sent for me—conscious that she was about to die—thou wert away in France, I thought—I went to Constance, and received, as her last gift and that of her noble husband, their only child, Walter Gray."

"No, no! I cannot—cannot have been so unjust!" murmured Leyton.

"Shall I bring other proofs than my own word? Walter hath Reuben Studley's dying confession. How for revenge for a wrong you did him years agone, he abused your ear—led you to believe the letters you have trusted to were evidences of my guilt. The man Cotterell lives!"

Leyton groaned with suppressed agony.

"I am not believed!" said Mistress Leyton, rising up. "'Tis well I am prepared with witnesses ——"

Newberry and Walter entered the room, followed by Cotterell, who had evidently been qualifying himself for the occasion by strong drink.

"Walter," said Mistress Leyton, "give me that paper which the villain Studley signed. Whose eyes will you trust to read it, Leyton?"

"Give it to me!—give it to me!" said Leyton, extending his outstretched hands.

"Not till it's truth's acknowledged. It is in part my sentence to life or death!" said Mistress Leyton, now roused into indignation. "Stand forward, fellow. I speak to you, Richard Cotterell."

"No! let him not look upon me. Drive him from the house!" cried Leyton.

" Oh, well! an' I care not to stay," said Cotterell, doggedly. "Thou wouldst not hear me years ago when I should have told thee the same tale as now. Mistress Leyton treated me as became your wife; she spurned me from her ——"

But as his voice seemed to excite Leyton, Walter and Newberry removed Cotterell from the room.

" Has that villain gone?" asked Leyton.

"He hath. What then?" asked Mistress Leyton.

" For mercy's sake, speak not to me in anger. I am so utterly oppressed by the deep sense of all the wrong I have done to thee, my poor injured Maud ——"

" No more—no more!" exclaimed his wife, clasping her arms about his neck. She kissed his cheek, and then swooned upon his breast.

Before the autumn had passed, wreaths of pale blue smoke curling from the chimneys of Leyton Hall proclaimed that its long-deserted rooms were again to be full of life. The old hedges of yew which had grown wild and shapeless were again clipped into rounded verdant walls, and here and there diversified by fantastic forms which would have puzzled a modern student of natural history. The pleasaunces and lawns, long resigned to rank vegetation, were mown again, and made to the tread soft as a three-piled carpet. The terrace walk was shaven smooth or in part strewed with broken spar, and on the boundary-wall a stately peacock stalked in the full pride of his gorgeous plumage, at times disturbing his neighbours, the rooks, by his discordant cries.

When the winter sun shone on the terrace walk, a blind man leaning fondly on a lady's arm, went to and fro, seeing with her eyes what otherwise would have been lost to him. Guests came and went—the Newberrys amongst them every year—and Alice Leyton and Walter Gray would sometimes form their escort through the park, to return at foot-pace, gazing in each other's faces, and holding "sweet converse" together. Poor men and women came and went also, returning happier for the dole they had received at the old Hall. When Christmastide came round, there were light, music, and seasonable revelry within, and two lovers led the dance for four successive years, and then they married, and for other years they still led the dance.

Tabitha—Mistress Tabitha now—was housekeeper, as any would have known who had seen the burnished bunch of keys hanging at her side. Jacob Magnus, when he died, left her all that the Mermaid had left him. Colonel Leyton's bailiff, John Hoskins, sought to win what little heart Tabitha had left; but though John was a thriving man, and had a pretty home, Tabitha, remembering what sorrows of her dear mistress she had witnessed, could not leave the sight of her new daily happiness—not to mention Mistress Tabitha's two cosy rooms, her well-spread table, and "brief authority." No, Tabitha could not abandon all these; and so she refused John Hoskins, who was not much disturbed by his rejection, seeing that in a month he married the pretty dairymaid.

Hafed was still the constant attendant of the colonel, and had contrived, by Tabitha's assistance, to speak a *lingua franca* which the good-natured housekeeper pretended to understand.

It matters little what is the end of Master Richard Cotterell, so long as he clings to his old vices. And Cotterell did so—drinking! drinking! but never being able to drown the memory of the past.

Any who may have felt an interest in our story will look in vain to find a trace of Leyton Hall or the neighbouring village of Rockley. Nor will they find in pleasant Dovedale the secret way to the old Hall, although it may be conjectured where its entrance was; but it can only be conjecture.

Gentle reader! we kiss your hand, and thank you for your patience.

HEARTS ARE TRUMPS.

A DRAMATIC STORY.

CHAPTER I.

THE TEMPTER.

THERE are few more happy retreats from the perplexities and disappointments of this uncertain life, than a well-appointed London Tavern, and the White Post in —— Street was, twenty years ago, pre-eminently cosy. Near to one of the most fashionable streets of the day, it was frequented by persons of limited means, but whose social position made them excellent judges of the *cuisine* of the White Posts; and their patronage gave assurance that no inferior gastronomy was permitted to obtain there. The exclusiveness of a club was necessarily wanting, and the society to be met there could not fail to be alloyed by some of the black sheep of what is called "the fashionable world," but who, from their external appearance and correct behaviour, rendered detection difficult, even by those whose experience of mankind had been long and general. No disparagement this to the White Posts, for

"Where the palace where foul things intrude not?"

A constant visitor was Mr. Robert Ruby; a man of

gentlemanly bearing, although somewhat of an ancient dandy, being apparently between fifty and sixty years of age. His clothes were cut with scrupulous regard to his fine figure, and he wore a full-curled brown wig (once known as a George the Fourth), a purple cravat, and kid gloves of a delicate lemon colour. His Wellington boots were faultless in their polish and fit, whilst his Stanhope hat was black and glossy as a raven. He usually dined alone, and seemed to have a limited acquaintance for a man who resided so much in London, and who evidently had his time at his own disposal. He was by no means averse to the society of strangers, and made himself particularly agreeable to those whom he felt disposed to entertain.

He was not altogether unknown to a few of the most respectable frequenters of the White Posts, and who would sometimes recognise him by a slight bow, but rarely courted a closer intimacy. The personal friends that now and then dined with him appeared to be equally respectable and unrecognised. He was a liberal guest and paymaster, and consequently stood high in the good opinion of James, the waiter.

But why envelope Mr. Ruby in a cloud of mystery? His pursuits and character were well known to many a ruined spendthrift and thoughtless scapegrace about town, and who recognised in the seeming gentleman the professed blackleg and proprietor of more than one gaming-house in the bye streets of St. James'.

His gains were known to have been considerable, and he was reckoned in the play-world a man of honour, exact in the fulfilment of his engagements, and punctual in the payment of his debts.

There were stories of kind actions done by old Bob Ruby, and many more of clever knavery and successful speculation on the turf and at the gaming-table. None knew more than this; none knew his origin or his family connexions, or whither he went for days altogether, always alone and secretly. By-and-by we shall learn his story.

The London season was over, and the White Posts had lost many of its accustomed visitors; but Mr. Ruby was seated in his favourite corner, at dinner, with a young man whose acquaintance he had made the preceding day. The only other occupant of the room was a vulgar, cunning looking person, soberly dressed, and whose time appeared of great value, as he eat rapidly, and devoured the newspaper at the same time ; now taking a mouthful of food, and now a paragraph of information. A blue bag lay on a chair beside him, and declared him to be a member of the legal profession,—" A gentleman, etc.," by Act of Parliament, and nothing else. Ever and anon he threw a furtive glance at Ruby and his young companion, and a faint smile played like a jack-o'-lantern, for a moment, over his rugged features. Mr. Goad evidently knew Mr. Ruby.

When Mr. Goad was in the act of paying his bill, taking exception to every item, a gentleman entered the room and made his way to the table at which the grumbling lawyer was seated. There was something remarkably striking in the appearance of the new comer. He appeared to be about thirty years of age, although his hair was nearly white, except his moustache, and that was dark brown. His bearing was soldierly, and he had the easy confidence of a man accustomed to society. He had recognised Ruby also, but no sign of intimacy passed between them.

"Ah ! Captain Wagstaff," said Goad, "how do you do? You're used to these places—I'm not—just glance over that bill, and tell me if the charges are not disgraceful?"

" Not in the least," replied Wagstaff, scarcely regarding the proffered paper, " for the White Posts. Sit down, Goad, and have a glass of wine."

" No wine for me ! Never take wine at these places. I've already paid two shillings and ninepence, and owe the waiter his penny," answered Goad.

"Pshaw ! the wine is my affair," said Wagstaff, and this liberal assurance overcame the lawyer's objection.

When the waiter had placed the wine upon the table, the captain observed in a low whisper to Goad :—" Ruby is at the opposite table, I see, and wishes to remain unnoticed."

" So I discovered !" replied Goad. "What a dear old dove he looks ! As a humbug, that man is unapproachable."

" Hush !" said Wagstaff. " I fancy he wants me to hear what he is saying."

" I think you said you were from Shrewsbury, and this your first visit to London?" remarked Ruby to his young companion.

"Yes. My father held some odd opinions ; amongst others, that London was little better than a city of the plague, infected by all the vices to which youth is prone."

"A pardonable superstition in a *wealthy* country squire," said Ruby, with a marked emphasis on the pecuniary adjective.

The young man coloured very slightly as he replied, "He was not a squire, although a rich man."

"A trader," said Ruby, again smiling; "a more useful member of society. It is to trade, Sir, that England owes her greatness and prosperity." And Ruby, making a slight bow, raised his glass to his lips. The young man accepted the compliment, with a look of pleasure, and his tempter continued:—

"Have you many friends in London?"

"Scarcely any, except my late father's business connexions," was the reply.

"Then I rejoice to have met you," said Ruby; "there is my card, I generally dine here, and shall have much pleasure in showing you any civilities in my power."

"You are very kind," answered the young man, giving Ruby a card bearing the name of Charles Wilmot. "I am leaving home for a few days to visit an aged relative near London. On my return I hope to renew our acquaintance."

"Were you at the Derby this year?" said Ruby, carelessly, after a short pause in the conversation.

"Yes," replied Wilmot, "though I take but little interest in horse racing, as I never bet."

"And I but seldom," said Ruby, holding up his glass to the light. "I lay a few pounds now and then to increase my interest in the race, just as one takes an olive to enhance one's zest for the wine."

"Ah, that is pardonable gambling," observed Wilmot; "but, to make a trade of betting, to live by the simplicity ——"

"Oh, shameful!" interrupted Ruby, "and there really seems something cruel in converting an innocent amusement into a very doubtful kind of traffic. Will you take any more wine?"

"Not unless you wish," replied Wilmot.

"Then we will walk together. Waiter! the bill!"

Wilmot proposed to pay for both.

"By no means," said Ruby, smiling and shaking his head reprovingly. "Let me warn you against such generous folly. You will find too many ready to accept your hospitality, and laugh at your simplicity. I speak plainly, because I mean honestly."

"I will not forget the lesson," answered Wilmot as he and his dangerous acquaintance left the room, the latter regarding Wagstaff and Goad as utter strangers. We shall see.

Wagstaff struck his closed hand upon the table, to give vent to his pent-up feelings of admiration.

"A lesser genius," he exclaimed, when the waiter followed "the parting guests,"—"a lesser genius would have taken the pot luck; but he has more confidence in Fortune, than to sell her favours for a mess of pottage!"

"Beautiful! his coolness would send the mercury to freezing-point in the dog days," added Goad. "What a witness he would make to swear to imaginary facts!"

"He's an honour to our profession," continued Wagstaff. "Card or die never ruffled him. I've seen him set a hand for a thousand, and never winked when the thrower nicked him."

"I honour him, Wagstaff!" said Goad. "I feel that my first floor contains a glory when that man is in it. Ah! it was a lucky thing for me when you and Ruby converted my humble dwelling into a private pigeon-house"—and the ugly lawyer chuckled at his own miserable joke. "Dear me," he continued, after looking at his watch. "Six o'clock, and I ought to be at Reigate on professional business."

"Reigate! Professional business!" remarked Wagstaff, his eyes twinkling as he spoke. "What have you in that bag? Not a fiddle?"

"A fiddle! No, Sir; mine are legal instruments," said Goad, showing a bundle of papers.

"I beg pardon," continued Wagstaff, laughing heartily—not at the lawyer's joke, however, but at some mental picture which presented itself.

"I must tell you what tickles me, Goad. The day before yesterday I went to Reigate, and, as I was sitting in the parlour of the little inn near the station, a loutish fellow came in and asked "if I was Mr. Fillet, the dancing-master from London?" I don't know what made me answer 'Yes,' but I did so, and learned that a young and pretty girl, wanting instruction in the polka, had written to one of the London advertising dancing-masters to come down to Reigate. I can play a little, so I got the lout to borrow a fiddle from the barber, and I had the honour of giving a first lesson to the prettiest pair of ankles I ever saw in my life. This evening I am again engaged."

"Captain Wagstaff," said Goad, draining the decanter, "I always thought arms was not your *forte*. You see it's legs, evidently legs."

The two friends laughed in concert, and then, Wagstaff having paid for the wine, they went on their way to Reigate.

CHAPTER II.

"WHEN GREEK MEETS GREEK."

HERE was not a household with any pretension to respectability in Reigate, but was in a flutter. Every female of the industrious population that could wield a needle was secured at fabulous prices; and so much business was rushing in and out of the four principal drapers' shops, that Ludgate Hill would have been envious, had it run down to Reigate by rail. Several secret embassies had been despatched to London, and parcels of formidable bulk were known to have been delivered in various directions in and about the town of Reigate. In fact, there was to be an Autumn race meeting, and the stewards, being young men and gallant, had announced that a race ball would conclude the week's amusements. A committee had been formed of the leading residents, and great care was being taken to make the matter as respectable as possible.

A short distance out of the town stood the neatest of cottages, nearly overshadowed by a grand old oak tree, which gave a name to the little dwelling. The occupants were scarcely known, living as they did, a most secluded life; and their servants, not being natives of the locality, little could be learned concerning them by their more curious neighbours. Two female domestics and a man-servant indicated the possession of competency, and their neat pony equipage spoke well for the taste and judgment of those who had selected it. The mistress of the cottage was an elderly lady, who might have been the mother of the beautiful young creature her companion, but for a certain deference always observable in her bearing towards her. The relation they bore to each other will be explained by what follows.

"What a time Joseph is gone, Mrs. Millar!" said the younger lady (her name was Mary Grey), her beautiful face hidden among the flowers clustered round the open window.

"Really, Mary," replied the lady addressed, "I repent of having given way to this foolish whim of yours. I am afraid your father would not approve of your attending this race ball."

"Nay, dear Milly," said Mary, leaving her seat at the window, and placing her arms round the elder's neck, "my father will approve of anything to which you assent. You know how seldom he visits us—how completely he leaves me to your control. I am now twenty and have not even seen a ball. Think of that, dear Milly! Before you were my age, I have no doubt, you had seen a hundred. Remember I am young and foolish, if you will, but I do sometimes think I am like my little canary—I've a very nice cage, but it often looks sadly like a prison."

"Well, we must talk about it," answered Mrs. Millar, who was evidently not proof against the music of Mary's voice, and which continued—

"We have talked enough about it already, dear Milly, and I am sure you are too kind, and love me too much, to deprive me of this innocent pleasure. Recollect how often I've heard you tell stories of your young days, the pleasant companions you had then, the gay scenes you visited, the pretty dresses you wore, the merry parties you shared—whilst I never see anyone but you, except now and then my dear, dear father." She clasped her hands together as she said this, and gazed earnestly at the portrait of a grey-haired man, whose benignant eyes seemed to return the look of love then turned towards them.

"Very true, Mary," replied Mrs. Millar, with a deep sigh; "you must get very tired of me."

"No! no! not tired, dear Milly," said Mary, kissing the calm, passionless face of the speaker, "but *you* look dull enough sometimes; and then I think, Ah, Milly is recalling the times when she was young, as I am; when she was not shut up in this pretty prison, as I am, but went abroad into the happy world, and shared its happiness, as I do not."

"Very true, Mary," answered Mrs. Millar, evidently giving way at every word; "I do sometimes wish that you could have more society."

"I know you do! I know you do!" exclaimed Mary, "and therefore you have sent Joseph for those ball tickets, and you intend taking me for once—only for once—to a dance, or why did you send to Mr. Fillet, the London dancing master, to come down and teach me the polka, which I know already—almost?" and humming a once popular air, she danced round the room, until the bewildered Mrs. Millar exclaimed—

"Oh, Mary, Mary! you make me do wrong in spite of myself! But mind, not a word in any of your letters to your father. I don't like deceit, but I would rather tell him of this silly matter myself."

"You shall do just as you please," said Mary, giving Mrs. Millar such a hearty kiss, that Joe Martin, coming up the garden, was startled by the report.

Joseph, or Joe Martin, was one of those useful compounds of footman, groom, and gardener, which now and then are found in small families. His father was a Sussex man, he believed, and his mother a Yorkshire woman, so no wonder that Joe was a sharp fellow enough.

He came into his present service with a very feeble character, but had proved honest, sober, and industrious, during the three years he had served Mrs. Millar and her pretty ward. For Miss Grey, Joe entertained a feeling that would have been called love, had he been equal in position to his mistress; and it is difficult to find any other name for the sensation which had place in the bosom of this serving man.

He felt for her loneliness, and considered it part of his duty to be ready to do battle positively and figuratively, whenever she required a defender. He had laid a lance in rest for her that very afternoon.

"Well, Joseph, have you got the tickets?" said Mary, as the messenger approached the porch of the cottage.

"Why, no, Miss, I've not quite got 'em," replied Joe, with some slight confusion of manner.

"Not quite?" said Mary; "what do you mean by that?"

"Why you see, Miss," replied Joe: "I sent Mrs. Millar's note to the committee, as were sitting at the Blue Lion, and arter waiting about half an 'our, I war tould to walk upstairs. 'Pray,' says Mr. Committee, 'who be Mrs. Millar? I suppose she be respectable?' 'Of course,' says I. 'She keeps a footman, gardener, and groom,' though I didn't own that the three individuals were inside this striped waistcoat."

"Well, and what did the fellow say then?" asked Mrs. Millar, with her head erect and her bosom swelling with indignation.

"'Why I ask,' says Mr. Committee, 'is, because it's not usual for ladies to come unattended to a public ball.'"

"True!" gasped Mrs. Millar, "I had forgotten that."

"'Nor be they comin' unattended, Sir,' says I; 'there be a gentleman comin' wi' them,' meaning myseen, Miss, tho' I didn't tell them he'd sit in the tap-room till the ball were over."

"Really!" said Mrs. Millar, "I think we must not go."

One glance at Mary, and Joe replied, "O, but you must, Ma'am, now! 'cos he has promised to send the tickets tomorrow, and told me to get a pint of ale, and put it down to Committee—which I did, in course."

"Oh, Joseph! I am so much obliged to you," said Mary, "and there's a bright new shilling for you; but mind our visit to the ball is to be quite a secret. Is it not, Mrs. Millar? Mr. Fillet will be here directly, so I'll go at once and change my walking shoes, and be ready for my lesson." And then, once more embracing Mrs. Millar, and humming the lively air, as she had done before, she danced out of the room, leaving her elderly companion perplexed and silent.

Joe Martin kept the bright shilling in his hand, mentally boring a hole through it, and adding it to the steel watch-key and seal given to him by one whom he loved in his rough way very dearly. "Things are looking up a bit wi' me at last," thought Joe. "For five years I've been slippin' down in the world as though it were greased all over; but this week folk have been takin' my pocket for a money box. First of all there was Mr. Fillet, the dancing master, dropping half-a-crown, beside another for the lend of the barber's fiddle. If he be a regular perfessional gentleman, I'm another, that's certain. Then to-day comes up a smart young chap and says: 'Do you live at Oak Cottage?' 'Yes,' says I, 'I does.' 'Are your ladies going to the ball?' says he. 'Yes,' they be,' says I. 'Thankee,' says he; and so he drops a crown. I've a good mind to go up to Lun'non and open a shop in opposition to the Bank of England." Joe was chuckling at his own pleasant thoughts, when Mr. Fillet, otherwise Captain Wagstaff, turned the corner of the lane.

"The ladies at home, Joe?" said Wagstaff.

"Yes, Sir!"—and Joe opened the garden gate.

Wagstaff paused, and looking Joe full in the face, said abruptly:—

"Joe, will you answer me a question for half-a-crown?"

"That depends on the question," replied Joe.

"Well said, Joe. You're sharp for a native. Now tell me who's your mistress?"

"Mrs. Millar. Half-a-crown," replied Joe, holding out his horny hand.

"Sharp again, Joseph," said Wagstaff; "there's the money; and now my boy, who's the young lady?"

"Be that question half-a-crown too?"

Wagstaff shook his head. "Oh!" continued Joe, "because the answer be."

Wagstaff was not the man to be offended, either at the familiarity or cupidity of Mr. Martin, so giving Joe some loose silver, he said:—

"Come, I'll trust to your generosity—so tell me, has she any money?"

Joe's doubts concerning Mr. Fillet were strengthened; but he replied:—

"Lots; she gave me a shilling just now."

"And her name?" asked Wagstaff.

"Miss Grey."

"An orphan?" said Wagstaff.

"Only half an orphan," replied Joe, "her father's living, he is a commercial traveller, a bagman, and so if you want to know any more you must ask my missus."

"Why, Joe," said Wagstaff, "you're as close as an oyster."

"Yes, I be close for a native," answered Joe; giving Wagstaff a look that brought the red blood into that gentleman's brazen face.

As Wagstaff entered the cottage, Joe thought he would keep his eye on Mr. Double Shuffle, as he called him, and resolved what he would do if his suspicions proved to be correct.

Joe having constituted himself the dragon of this Reigate Hesperides, made his way to the stable, and having fed the ponies, sat down on the corn-bin, prepared to do battle at a moment's notice. The sound of the fiddle was quite audible where he sat, and Joe, after drumming for awhile with the heels of his boots on the sides of the chest, became sufficiently inspired to perform a sort of saraband in an empty stall of the stable.

"Very well, indeed, Sir, very well indeed!" said our acquaintance of the White Post, Mr. Goad, peeping in at the stable door; "you'd have made your fortune if dancing bears hadn't gone out of fashion."

"I am sorry they has," replied Joe, who was rarely at loss for an answer, "'cos I could have given you a job as my leader."

"Oh!" said Goad, not relishing the implied compliment. "Witty as well as saltatory, Mr. MARTIN." He emphasised the name in the knowing manner assumed by pettifogging attorneys, when trying to catch a witness.

"Mr. Martin?" echoed Joe, somewhat startled by the inquiry.

"Yes, that's your name, is it not, Sir?" asked Mr. Goad, screwing his mouth on one side and cocking his eye.

"Well, I never said it wasn't!" replied Joe, evidently puzzled a little.

"Born at Balcombe in Sussex, once servant to Mrs. Barker," continued Goad, referring to a brief-like bundle of papers. "Right, I believe?"

"Why, if you know all about it, it's no use axing of me," replied Joe, fencing the question, without a doubt.

"One morning, June the 16th, 1851, a silver spoon was missing; June 17th, you were ditto. Eh!" said Goad, screwing his mouth and cocking his eye again, only much harder than before.

"But I didn't steal it, master," exclaimed Joe, dashing his hand down upon the corn-bin. "As I've breath, I didn't! For five years I've been mucking about the country for fear of that spoon, tho' I know'd no more of it than an unborn baby."

Goad continued to scan his brief, without heeding apparently a word of Joe's defence.

"You committed suicide, I believe!" asked Goad.

"I did," answered Joe.

"In a letter addressed to Mrs. Barker, a circumstance which haunted Mrs. Barker to her dying day," remarked

Goad, folding up his brief and depositing it in a capacious blue bag, partly filled with other papers.

"Then why did she accuse me of taking her spoon? That's haunted me, I can tell you, master," said Joe, his lip quivering and his cheek flushing with excitement.

"Joseph Martin ——" Goad paused, and tightened the strings of his blue bag, whilst he kept his eye fixed upon Joe—"Joseph, I am going to present you with 6s. 8d."

Joe could hardly believe his ears.

"Listen. Mrs. Barker is dead, consequently you have nothing to fear on account of the spoon, and that opinion is equal to 6s. 8d."

"Six and eightpence!" cried Joe. "Six hundred pounds! for now I can hold up my head again like a man."

"And so you shall, if you'll be guided by me," said Goad. "Your fellow-servant at that time was named Susan Fletcher. Could you identify her?"

"No," answered Joe; "for she were innocent, I'll swear."

Goad smiled at Joe's application of the word "identify," and then said, "I know her to be innocent. What I meant was, should you know her again?"

"Know her!" exclaimed Joe; "know her! I should think so, from ten thousand!" for Susan had given him the steel watch-chain years ago.

"Then I can put ten pounds in your pocket, Martin," said Goad. "This is my card, that's my name and address;" they were printed in a fat smudgy type, and had a suspicious appearance; "and if you will be at my house by twelve o'clock to-morrow, you shall have ten pounds."

"Hem! master!" replied Joe, his confidence in himself perfectly restored, "this is all very well;" and he turned Goad's card about, as though he were examining a bad shilling; "but I don't see any promise to pay on this."

"Those who catch you asleep must get up remarkably early, eh, Mr. Martin?" said Goad. "To show you that I'm in earnest, there's half the money;" and from the recess of an enormous black bill-case the lawyer produced a new bank-note.

Joe received it without a moment's hesitation, and folding it up very carefully (having first looked at the water mark), placed it, with much deliberation, in his watch-fob.

"I may expect you to-morrow now, I conclude," said

Goad, with a horrible contortion of features, which he intended for an ingenuous smile.

"I'll be there to a minute, master, rely on it, if only to look after the twin brother of this chap," answered Joe, slapping his pocket.

"Then good-day, Joe," said Mr. Goad, throwing his blue bag over his shoulder, and quitting the stable.

"Good-day, Sir," replied Joe, touching his forelock, "and I wish myself many happy returns of it, for it'- the best I've seen for many a hanny dominer."

CHAPTER III.

THE PROMISE.

CAPTAIN WAGSTAFF, in his assumed character of dancing-master, was earnestly engaged with his fair pupil, and the notes of the fiddle were now exchanged for those of the piano, elicited by no very skilful hand, as Mrs. Millar, it must be confessed, had a very indifferent ear for time and tune. The fact was, Wagstaff, with reckless impudence, had induced the old lady to play whilst he danced the figure with the unsuspecting Mary. The innocent girl was much perplexed when her brazen instructor encircled her waist with his arm, and held her small hand within his own, occasionally increasing the pressure in a way which at length alarmed and annoyed her. Wagstaff's boldness increasing with the excitement of the dance, he pressed, almost impalpably, his lips upon her fingers. The outrage made Mary's face crimson, and she instantly disengaged herself from the insolent offender.

"I shall dance no more, Sir," she said, seeking protection at Mrs. Millar's side. "Take your fee, Sir, at once, and go; I shall dance no more."

Wagstaff was silenced and confounded for a moment. "I have gone too far," thought he. "It is lucky that I am not dependent on my present profession for a living. Bah! I am not to be put down by a chit like that."

Whilst Wagstaff was fumbling with his fiddle case, Mary briefly conveyed to Mrs. Millar what had occurred, and that feeble-minded but very proper lady instantly bristled up like a Friesland hen.

"There is your fee, Mr. Fillet," said she indignantly; "we will not trouble you to ca l again."

"Not the least trouble," stammered Wagstaff, more abashed than he had been for years — "not the least trouble, I assure you. I attend several families of distinction in the neighbourhood, and shall have the greatest pleasure in completing Miss Mary's education gratis, Ma'am, gratis!" and the bold *roué*, blushing like a rustic novice, turned to go, as Joe Martin appeared at the door in great haste, and announced that "Master" had arrived. In a moment Mary was on her way to the garden-gate to meet her father.

"Oh, dear me! what shall we do?" said Mrs. Millar, conscious that she had not acted quite right in admitting Mr. Fillet, to whom she was now compelled to appeal. "Will you oblige me, Sir, by going out this way?" and she opened a door which led into the little stable-yard.

"With pleasure, Ma'am," replied Wagstaff, who saw, from Mrs. Millar's confusion, that something was wrong, and, with the meanness of such a man, determined to profit by his advantage; and so he added, "Then, I may call upon you again?"

"Oh, yes—no, Sir—pray go! pray go! or I am ruined!" exclaimed the terrified old lady.

Wagstaff turned to go the way he had been desired, as Mary and her father stood midway on the garden walk, the loving daughter's head resting on the bosom of the loving father. His hat had fallen to the ground, and his grey hair shone like threads of silver in the sun. Wagstaff started, and for a moment appeared lost in wonder.

"Is that the master of this house?" he asked at length, almost in a whisper.

"Yes, it be," said Joe Martin, "and he won't want to see you;" adding, "why don't ye go when you're tould?" and, without further parley, he pushed the astonished Wagstaff into the stable yard.

Mr. Grey was a fine, hale man of about fifty-five. His hair, white and spare, revealed a broad, intelligent-looking forehead. His eye was bright and restless, and his smile had less of mirthfulness than a pleasant satisfaction. He was dressed with scrupulous neatness. A black coat and waistcoat, grey trousers, and short gaiters, seemed to mark the staid man of business; and the full white cravat and large shirt frill indicated that their wearer was not given to change with the fashion of the day.

"And so you are glad to see me?" said Mr. Grey.

"Indeed! indeed, I am!" replied Mary, kissing him again and again. "Why, what a long journey you have had this time! It is five weeks since you left us. I am sure commercial travellers ought to be well paid."

"And I am so, dearest," said her father. "In another month I trust to have done work for the rest of my life."

"And then, father, we shall never be separated?"

"Hum!" said Ruby, with a sad smile. "I would not pledge you to that bargain, in case, Polly, some worthy fellow should ask you to keep house for him."

"La, father!" replied Mary, "how silly you talk!"

"Not so, darling! It would gladden my heart to see you, whom I cherish beyond all else in the world, married to some honest man who would love you as you deserve to be. In the game of life, Mary, HEARTS ARE THE BEST TRUMPS," said the old man, with a sigh.

"I want no one to love me but you," rejoined Mary; "no one!"

"Nonsense! nonsense!" said her father. "Do you think that I, who have been deprived by toil and anxiety of the happiness of your childhood, do not look forward to my darling's darlings creeping about my knees, speaking to me words in which there is no mistrust, and leading me to forget the selfishness of men in the confiding simplicity of children?"

He kissed her; for his tone had been very sad, and there were tears in Mary's eyes.

"Now let us be merry! Merry? zounds, we will be happy as the day is long, before the year is out. In the morning you shall make my breakfast; then, in summer, we will sit in the porch, and you shall read the paper to me, the state of the odds, the ——"

"The *what*, father?" asked Mary.

"The—the state of the country," answered Ruby, a slight flush tinting his face; "and then we will ramble in the green lanes and hear the merry birds sing as they used to do, when I was a happy boy—happy and innocent," he muttered.

The last words did not reach Mary's ear, and she continued :—

"On winter evenings, father, we will sit around the fire, and you shall tell me stories of what you have seen and done." Ruby started, as though he had been pricked by a sharp sword. "And then sometimes, just now and then, you shall take me to London."

"No! not to London," said Ruby vehemently, and rising from the rustic seat, on which he had been resting. "Once free, I never set foot again within that dreadful city."

Mary was alarmed and surprised at her father's violence. When he perceived the effect his words had produced, he laughed aloud, and said :—

"And so, I have frightened you by my earnestness; I only meant to say, that in London, everybody is miserable, if they would only own it. Real happiness cannot exist in a city—there is too much to excite envy and discontent. Don't think that fine feathers make fine birds—gay attire is vanity's mourning for a dead heart. No, no! we'll live in the country, my child, and enjoy Nature, before man has tried to improve it. Come, let us go in. I declare, this sniff of country air has made me anxious for my supper." And so, leaning on his daughter's arm, the loving father and the innocent girl passed out of the little garden.

How treacherous are outward appearances! Few would have recognised in Mr. Grey the professed gambler, Robert Ruby. It was he, however.

Nineteen years before the time of our story, a dying woman lay in a prettily decorated room of a small villa in the suburbs of London. The hired nurse was sleeping in a chair beside the bed, and, in a cot near her, an infant was asleep also. The clocks of the surrounding churches struck three; and the booming of the bells seemed to strike upon the heart of the poor sufferer; for she pressed her hand upon her side, and tried to raise herself from her pillow. Vainly, vainly! for the hand of death held her down.

"Nurse!" she said—so feebly that it was strange that the sleeping woman was aroused by her voice—"Nurse, open the window, please, and see if Robert is in the street."

"My dear Ma'am! I will do so if you wish it; but it is only three o'clock, and Mr. Grey seldom favours us with his company so early," replied the nurse, with a sneer.

'Hark!" said the sick woman, "I am sure I hear his

footstep! Yes! that *is* his step, I am certain. He stops—I hear him opening the door. Nurse, do not let him go to his own room without seeing me, for I feel to-night will be my last."

"Oh, nonsense, Ma'am," replied the nurse. "You'll see many more nights and days too, if you'd leave off fretting about"—she went out on the landing—"this brute of a husband."

Mr. Grey received his wife's message, and said—

"How could Mary imagine that I should have passed her door without seeing her?"

He entered the room as he was speaking, and then went to the bed and bent over his sick wife. She put her arms around his neck, and clasping her hands together, pressed his face closely to her own, kissing him.

"Robert, sit down, dear; and nurse, lease pleave us together for a few minutes."

The sick woman's orders were obeyed.

"Robert, husband, dear, dear husband,' the invalid began; "I am so glad you have returned, for in another hour I should not have had power to tell you all that is resting on my heart. Don't speak, dear, but listen to me once and for ever. Robert, four months ago I learned—*how* must be the only secret I ever hid from you—the dreadful trade you follow. Hush! I know all."

Grey could not look longer at her pallid face, but turned away his head, still holding her feverish hand in his.

"Robert, forgive what I am about to say (for I do not speak to reproach you), but for the sake of our child—of that sleeping angel by your side. Kiss me, Robert, dear, and then I will go on. And now hear what I have to say, and treasure up my words in your heart. I shall not live to see another night such as this has been, and such as many have been before—watching, watching the whole night through—but watching patiently so long as I believed that you were not—that you were not ——" She could not utter the words which rested on her tongue.

"You guess what I would say; press my hand if I need not recall the past. Ah! well! Robert, you have told me that you have striven with the fatal love of play, and yielded; though you knew it had reduced a noble gentleman down, down to a knavish trickster, and broken the heart that loved you—loved you too well to know of your dishonour, and live.

I do not ask you to promise again to abandon your wretched pursuit. Ah, yes! you would promise, as you have done before; but where I am going the truth is known, and perhaps the angels know it also. Robert, dear husband—dearer at my death than ever—only promise this—promise that our child shall be kept apart from your wicked life, that she shall have another home than yours, where no knowledge of her father's crime can ever reach her; for children learn and remember strange matters often. Promise this; perform this; and in His own good time, perhaps—perhaps—oh, promise!"

Exhausted by her effort, her head fell upon her shoulder; and when her wretched husband, wretched every way, uttered the words, "I promise, Mary," her spirit passed away as she was smiling.

The unconscious babe so left and cared for was Mary Grey.

CHAPTER IV

JOE AND SUSAN

IN one of the streets leading out of St. James's Street resided Mr. Goad. There was a dingy look about the place that made the passer-by, who regarded it, melancholy for the moment, and those who contemplated it from the opposite side of the way, strongly of opinion that it was a human spider's web from attic to parlour. We except the kitchen, because a cheerful voice might now and then be heard singing some old country ditty in the depths of the area, and a bright buxom face might also be seen looking up to the sky through the well-cleaned kitchen windows. The owner of cheerful voice and buxom face was no other than Susan Fletcher, to whom Mr. Goad had referred in the preceding chapter, and who was now engaged in ironing at the window. Susan, as she pursued her work, appeared to be full of thought; and as story tellers have strange privileges, we will put the substance of her lucubrations into words.

"Dear me!" she thought; "what a dreadful thing it is to have such an easy place as I have. I like work—downright hard work!" and here she emphasised her expression by banging the iron down upon the table—"but here I have nothing to do but cook my own dinner, and keep the place tidy. Mr. Goad never dines at home, the boy sweeps out the office, and Mr. Ruby, the lodger up-stairs, hires a charwoman to do his work. And yet what pains Mr. Goad took to find me out. There's something very mysterious about it —very!" and Susan, leaving the iron to cool, folded her hands and sat down on the table. But only for a moment, as she started from her seat, her rosy face changing to the hue of death; and all because a passer-by sang, in a loud rough way,—

> "It was as young Coddlins, ear-ly one morn,
> Went whistling along thro' the fieldes of corn."

"Oh! if ghosts had ever been known to sing," said Susan, half aloud, "I could have sworn that that was Joe's voice!" And the singer, repassing, sang on,—

> "And then she smil-ed, like to any doove,
> And did consent, all for to be his loove."

"It must be Joe," cried Susan, running to the window— "yet it can't be he, 'cos he committed suicide—and yet, there ne is, nodding his head—and—coming down the area steps!"

It was Joe in the flesh, sure enough, as no one would have doubted who heard the five or six hearty kisses he gave Susan's glowing cheeks, and justified the conclusion at which she arrived, that her old lover was not dead after all.

"No, Susey," said Joe, "mine was only a case of suspended animation. As Mrs. Barker would have it that I had stolen that spoon, I thought I'd better die and bury mysen', than be taken up and transported. But it's all right now, Mr. Goad says, and he gave me ten pounds to come to London, and make mysen' genteel and conspicuous, and I think I've done it." Joe was perfectly right; he had done it, by the purchase of the gaudiest of waistcoats, the brightest of green coats, and a breast pin of remarkable splendour, its brilliancy mitigated, however, by the satin stock into which it was inserted. He fairly dazzled Susan's eyes as she gazed upon him, with the admiration of a woman's first love. When she had satisfied her eyes, she naturally inquired the reason for Mr. Goad's extraordinary liberality.

"I'm come up to 'dentify you," replied Joe; and seeing poor Susan turn pale at the announcement, he added also, " He means nought to harm you, Susey, but he's got some scheme in his head, and his head's as long as the Thames Tunnel, which I saw yesterday. However, you can get through *that*, if you've luck and patience." This pleasant announcement and beautiful metaphor re-assured Susan, and so, having turned the various articles airing on the clothes-horse before the fire, she invited Joe to take some refreshment, announcing, with commendable independence, that she was on board wages, and kept her own larder.

"Well, I'll not say no," answered Joe, "for somehow or t'other, whatever I want beside, I never want an appetite."

"That's a small bit of cheese, Joey," said Susan, as she placed a section of a Dutch Bolus on the table. "I don't have much at a time, as I've nobody to help me eat it."—(Artful Susan.)

"That's a melancholy thing to say," observed Joe, taking Susan's plump hand in his own, "but it's very easy to remedy it. It's my belief that men and women are like gloves—they're no use except in pairs."

"O Joe!" exclaimed Susan, "you always was so poetical; it's as good as a valentine to hear you talk."

"Much better," said Joe, "because I speak sincere and honest. I don't tell you my heart's a roasting on the altar of love. No,—but I says I have saved £15 10s., and am able to take care of a horse, look after a garden, and wait at table. Them's arguments as sound like getting a livelihood," and the orator ventured to put his arm round the substantial waist of his auditor.

"And I'm not without a penny," said Susan, with pardonable pride. "I've got £12, besides a tea-caddy and a pair of silver sugar-tongs."

"Come!" cried Joe, "this is courting in earnest" (and we quite agree with him). "I'll speak to my old missus in the country, and if she don't forbid the banns, I'll ——"

The voice of Mr. Goad, calling Susan, brought Joe's protestation to an untimely end, and caused him to inquire with much earnestness—

"Will he come down here?"

"Very likely," replied Susan.

"Then hide me somewhere," said Joe. "He promised me another £5 if I wouldn't come after you. Where's this go?" pointing to a door.

"You can't go there; that leads up to the lodger's room. There, go behind the clothes-horse."

Joe obeyed, but the bright, blazing fire made him remark that he should be done as brown as a gipsy if Goad stopped long.

Susan resumed her work, although her iron was not half so hot as poor Joe was destined to be, and Mr. Goad entered the kitchen, carrying with him his blue bag, from which he was supposed never to part, not even when a-bed.

"Ah, Susan!" said Mr. Goad, in the cheeriest of tones, "busy, busy, as usual! You are a good girl, and an excellent servant."

"Thank you, Sir," answered Susan, modestly; "I've not much to do to prove that."

"Oh, yes! oh, yes!" said Goad. "Susan, sit down; I want to talk to you."

"Going to sit down and talk!" thought Joe; "if they do, I shall want basting."

Susan, however, did as she was bid; for she was too flustered to think of the fiery ordeal to which Joe was subjected.

"Susan," said Mr. Goad, "what I am about to say to you may appear strange, but you must only blame your own pretty face." A fresh supply of coals could not have warmed Joe more than those few words of Mr. Goad.

"How old are you, Susan?" asked the master.

"Three and twenty," faltered the maid.

"Next grass," thought Joe; for he knew her age to an hour almost.

"And still single!" continued Mr. Goad, with a ludicrous expression of astonishment. His voice fell to a whisper, as he added, "You must not continue so. You have known me some time; I am not ill-tempered, not ill-looking" (Joe differed in opinion). "I have a good position in society, and can make you a lady. I am a man of few words; will you marry me?" An entire chaldron of inflammable emotions blazed within the bosom of Joe Martin.

"You marry me, Sir!" asked Susan, rising from her chair, and looking wildly towards the clothes-horse, as though she expected her tortured lover to burst from his purgatory. "I'm only a servant. I—I should make you ashamed of my want of manners and learning."

"No, no!" exclaimed Goad. "I will have you instructed. You shall be my pride! my glory! A four-wheeled chaise! a boy in livery! your own mistress! a perpetual Sunday out!" How long he would have continued in this incoherent strain, or whether he would have ever come to a conclusion, we know not, had not Trotter, the office boy, run down the stairs to announce that "Mr. Ruby wanted to speak to Mr. Goad;" and was terribly frightened when his master seized him by the collar, and exclaimed, "Miscreant! how dare you intrude at such a moment?"

"Because Mr. Ruby sent me," replied the boy; "he's in the front office, and in a great hurry."

Mr. Ruby was not a client to be neglected, and so, fortunately for Joe Martin, Mr. Goad followed Trotter to the office, promising to return immediately.

"He's just gone in time!" exclaimed the half-roasted Joe, rushing from his concealment. "Just in time; I couldn't have stood it any longer. What with a raging fire behind me, and a burning rage within me, I should have blazed out in a minute. Well, Susan Fletcher!" he added, as loud as he could bawl, "what do you mean to do?"

"La, Joe!" answered Susan; "don't shout at me in that way!"

"Don't shout! I understand. You want to pick a quarrel with me!" cried Joe, jealousy giving him a poke up.

"I want no such thing," said Susan. "There go and take a walk in the area, and cool yourself, do. I'm sure I was never more surprised in my life."

"What's his motive?" asked Joe. "What's he want to marry you for?"

Well, Susan might have excused him for that presumption.

"Ah, here's his bag of combustibles!"—Goad had really left his bag upon the table, and Joe did not hesitate to inspect its contents.

"What's this?—a newspaper—the *Times;* and here's a 'vertisement scored round with ink, and your name, 'Susan Fletcher.'"

"My name?"

"Yes."

And Joe read as follows:—

IF SUSAN FLETCHER, formerly servant to Mrs. Barker, will apply to Mr. Goad, Solicitor, she will hear of something to her advantage.

"It was through seeing that in the paper that I came here," said Susan.

Joe dived again into the bag, and brought out "The Will of Jane Barker, widow."

"Mother Barker's Will," exclaimed Joe. "I see it now, she's left you a legacy." As he spoke, he loosened the red tape tied round the paper, and, having cast his eyes over the contents, read out to the astonished Susan:—

"'And I, Jane Barker, having done a great wrong to Susan Fletcher, by accusing her of robbery, and thereby destroying her character, do hereby will and bequeath to her one thousand pounds."

Susan could only exclaim "Joe!" and then fall, solidly, on to a chair.

"Don't faint now, wait till I have done," said Joe, "for here's some'ut about me : 'Also the sum of ten pounds, for a tombstone for Joseph Martin, who unfortunately killed himself from the same cause. Had he been living, I would also have provided for him.' There's an ungrateful old woman! Why didn't she leave it to my executors, and I'd have proved as my own next o' kin?"

"This accounts for Mr. Goad's wish to marry me," said Susan. "What shall I do, Joe?"

"Do!" replied Joe, who ought to have been a verger in the temple of Themis. "Do! Let me take these papers to a lawyer, whilst you pack up your box, and be ready to leave this place to-night. Now you're an heiress, you bean't safe a moment. Goad's just the man to hire ruffians, and carry you off in the middle of the night, and marry you with a pistol at your head! You're not safe till you're Mrs. Joe Martin."

This advice was so much in accordance with Susan's own inclination (when did a woman ever doubt the man she loved? and Susan had long loved Joe), that she promised to pack up forthwith, and entreated Joe to return directly, in case anything dreadful should happen.

Joe, taking the will and the newspaper, and giving Susan a kiss, for which Mr. Goad would gladly have paid 6s. 8d., he bade her call murder, if her master ventured to speak to her, and give him in charge to the police. Joe then hastened away to consult with the landlord of the public-house where he had passed the night, as to obtaining the legal assistance he required.

CHAPTER V.

A PROPOSAL OF MARRIAGE.

MR. Ruby had not waited for Goad in the office, but gone to his own apartments, whither the latter followed him. The rooms which Ruby occupied opened into each other, and were divided by curtains instead of doors. In the front one there was a larger loo-table than is usually found in similar lodgings, and the back room had four card-tables, on which were placed lamps with green shades.

Without exchanging the usual salutations, Ruby at once asked Goad if he had seen Captain Wagstaff, and was told that he would be with them presently.

"Remember," said Ruby, "to-day he is to appear as your friend, or young Wilmot will wonder, as we have often seen the captain about town, that I did not introduce him." So it was evident that the old hawk and the young pigeon had been much together.

"You have ordered dinner at seven?" said Ruby.

"Yes, Sir, and I flatter myself that you will approve of my catering. I have explained to Wagstaff the object of our meeting, and he is delighted. I hope you will find me an apt pupil."

"I do not doubt it," answered Ruby. "I fancy your conscience is as elastic as my own."

"It is india-rubber, Sir," said Goad, with a chuckle. "Conscience was only intended for man in his primitive condition, and is not adapted to a high state of civilisation."

"Perhaps so," observed Ruby, thoughtfully; and then asked, "Any letter for Mr. Grey?"

"No, Sir," said Goad, smiling wickedly; "I have not seen that crow-quill hand these six days."

Ruby walked to the window, and was silent. "What can be the reason Mary has not written to me?" he thought. "I must steal an hour to-morrow, and visit her. Can she be ill? No; to-day I must not think of her."

At that moment Trotter announced Captain Wagstaff, and Goad retired to prosecute his love affair in the kitchen. Susan was not there, however; so taking his blue bag from the table, he returned to his other avocations in the office.

"Ah, Wagstaff!" said Ruby, shaking that worthy by the hand, "it seems an age since we met."

"It is more than a fortnight," Wagstaff replied, laughing; "but great occasions require great sacrifices."

"True," said Ruby, "and I have had that in hand which will repay us for our privations. I have ascertained by a shilling and Doctors' Commons that young Wilmot is entitled to twenty thousand pounds, although at present he is not over-burdened with ready money."

"So much the better," said Wagstaff, "he will be the easier involved, and then, like a limed bird, the more he struggles to get free, the more embarrassed he will become."

Ruby paused for a minute, and then said—

"I am sorry for him. Somehow or the other, the fellow has obtained a hold upon me, for which I cannot account."

Wagstaff was somewhat surprised at this observation from his old confederate, and could only observe in reply, "But business is business, you know."

"True," answered Ruby, shaking off any momentary compunction; "true, we play the game of life in little. Ignorance puts down the stake, and experience wins it. Goad has told you our plans for to night. Wilmot must not be alarmed by too great a loss."

Wagstaff agreed with this suggestion.

"Well," continued Ruby, "what have you been doing since we parted?"

"Very little that has been profitable," replied Wagstaff, "I have passed"—and he fixed his eye upon Ruby as he spoke—"I have passed most of my time at Reigate."

Ruby had been standing at the window, looking out upon

the street. He now turned round suddenly, and almost exclaimed—

"Reigate?"

"A charming spot," said Wagstaff, not appearing to notice Ruby's voice or manner; "do you know it?"

"Why, yes," replied Ruby, turning his face again to the street. "I have been there."

"I have a remarkable love of nature," continued Wagstaff, lighting a cigar, "human nature particularly; and the women of Reigate are models for a Canova."

Ruby affected to laugh, as he said, "And so—and so you have been love-making, I presume?"

"Why, yes—slightly," answered Wagstaff. "As you turn down the lane—but you don't know Reigate?"

"I do—yes, I do!" said Ruby, a vague terror stealing over him.

"Well, then, perhaps you remember," continued Wagstaff, coolly puffing his cigar, as he went on—"perhaps you remember a pretty little place called Oak Cottage" (Ruby started), "and which contains two inmates, a middle-aged lady, and a charming creature just ripening into womanhood?"

Ruby instantly faced Wagstaff. "What of her?" was all he could utter.

Wagstaff broke into a loud laugh, whilst Ruby could scarcely keep himself from falling. "Ha, ha, Sir Reynard, have I found your earth at last? By Jove! I envy you your good fortune. I saw you—looking as though fresh from Exeter Hall—creep into that bower of roses. Be not ashamed, man! You have an excellent excuse for your folly. I saw her rush into your arms, and ——"

"Stop!" said Ruby, almost choking with emotion. "If you have seen this, you have misapprehended what you saw. She is my daughter."

Wagstaff shook his head, despite the terrible earnestness of Ruby.

"I swear it—my daughter. I have often stood your friend, Fred; now stand you mine. Never speak of what you saw. That girl is dearer to me than life. A light word must not be coupled with her name."

"And she your daughter!" said Wagstaff, now convinced that Ruby was speaking the truth.

"I know your thoughts!" continued Ruby. "You wonder

that one so good, so pure, should be the child of Robert Ruby. She knows not what I am. She has been kept apart, as spotless as when her mother died, and left her to my care."

The hardened gambler sat down, and covered his face with his hands, the tears welling through his fingers.

It was now Wagstaff's turn to walk to the window. For a few moments the distress of his old confederate touched him; and then his thoughts took a selfish direction, and he considered how he might turn this knowledge to his own advantage. "Ruby is rich," he thought, "and will be richer. The girl is pretty and good. What if I were to marry her?"

Ruby had sustained his double character too many years to be long over-mastered by his feelings; and so, joining Wagstaff at the window, he laid one hand upon his shoulder, and offered the other, saying—

"You *will* keep my secret, eh, Fred? and if so, count upon me as a friend in any emergency."

Wagstaff took the proffered hand, and replied, "Ruby, I am as dumb as an oyster—but—did it ever occur to you that, should anything happen to you, your daughter would be in a deuce of a fix?"

"Often! often!" said Ruby; "and I shudder when I think so."

"Then why don't you find her a husband?" asked Wagstaff. "That never occurred to you, eh? Let me find her one."

Ruby turned away impatiently, saying, "No! no! let us talk on some other subject."

"Well, but you don't know the man I would propose," said Wagstaff.

"Mary married to such as we are," muttered Ruby; "I would rather see her in her grave."

"Ruby!" continued Wagstaff, "are you attending to me? The man I would propose is no other than Fred Wagstaff."

Ruby faced his questioner, and his eyes glared like those of a roused tiger. Wagstaff did not notice him, but went on:—

"I'm the only fellow I know worthy of her—I'll keep her like a lady. You know I stand as well as any man in the ring. I'm pretty fairly off. I'm partner in two houses in

St. James's, and half owner of the best horse of the day. Come! say done, and I'll call you father-in-law in a week."

Ruby walked up to Wagstaff, and looking him steadily in the face said, in a tone scarcely above a whisper, "You marry my child!—you, that I know by every name that honest men use to designate a scoundrel!"

"Hallo!" cried Wagstaff.

Ruby heeded him not, but went on:—"Gambler! blackleg! cheat!—and dare you propose to make my innocent Mary your wife? You are mad!"

"Well!" said the astonished Wagstaff, "this is cool! And pray what is Mr. Ruby, that I should bring disgrace upon him?"

"What am I? Doubly the knave I have described you to be. You cannot paint me blacker than I know myself to be; but Mary has been kept in ignorance of my evil life. She does not even know me by the name of Ruby! No! Wagstaff! no! it is not such as you must call my Mary wife."

"Indeed!" said Wagstaff.

"Yes, indeed!" retorted Ruby.

Wagstaff's face became almost black with anger, as the old man walked from room to room, and it was some minutes before either could master the evil spirits which had taken possession of them. Ruby was the first to do so.

"Forget this meeting, Wagstaff," he said. "Come! let us be friends. We have a golden game to play to-night, and must be cool and confident. Forget what has passed! Forget it!" and exhausted by this conflict of passion and feeling he threw himself upon the sofa.

Wagstaff made no reply; but lighting another cigar, smoked in silence. "Forget it!" he thought. "Not whilst I've breath in my body. 'Cheat! gambler! blackleg!'—those are words to be forgotten!—and from him too! If his girl were an angel he couldn't think more of her."

The fiend in his bad heart spoke louder.

"If I could hit him through her! that would be a revenge." He referred to his watch. "Twelve o'clock, and we don't dine till seven." He rose up and looked at his old confederate in many a nefarious scheme, crouched upon the sofa, and felt more remorseless. "Forget this meeting? No! old boy, we'll play double or quits, if I live!"

The man thus silently apostrophised lay motionless, as though asleep.

"Well! good-day, Ruby," said Wagstaff, aloud; "we meet at dinner."

A voice unlike that of the bold gamester, for it was as soft as a woman's, answered—"Good day—forget this quarrel;" yet it was Robert Ruby that spoke.

CHAPTER VI.

THE EXPOSURE.

THE soft south wind stole through the flowers in the windows, which kept out the mid-day sun from the little parlour of Oak Cottage, wherein were seated Mrs. Millar and Mary Grey, in peaceful contrast to the scene we have just described. Mrs. Millar was sewing, whilst opposite to her sat Mary, reading one of those never-tiring volumes of Walter Scott. Suddenly she paused, although there was nothing in the passage which she had just read to justify her evident emotion. Even dear, dull Mrs. Millar observed the sudden change, and said :—

"Are you not well, Mary?"

"Dear Milly, you must excuse me," replied her ward. "I cannot read this morning; my mind is ill at ease. I know not why it should be so, but for this last week I have felt so unhappy."

"Ever since that Race Ball. Eh, Mary?" said Mrs. Millar. "I have observed it with much uneasiness, and blamed myself for taking you there."

"Oh, do not say that, dear Milly," replied Mary; "I never spent such a happy night in all my life. The music was so exhilarating, the dancing so exciting, and Mr. Wilmot so kind and attentive ——"

"That you have never had him out of your head since," interposed Mrs. Millar.

Mary instantly fell upon her knees, and hid her face in Mrs. Millar's lap, saying, in the sweetest tone—

"Oh Milly!"

"I am right, then?" asked that perplexed lady.

"I fear so, indeed," replied Mary, slowly raising her beautiful eyes to the face of her questioner. "Every day on some pretext or other, he has visited us, until I have learned to watch for his coming—to feel that in his presence only I am happy."

"Good gracious, Mary!" exclaimed Mrs. Millar; "I had no idea you were in love. We must put a stop to this."

"I know not how, dear Milly," said Mary, with a sad smile; "I strive to banish him from my thoughts, but neither my flowers nor my books have power to do so."

"Oh, you must, Mary!" exclaimed Mrs. Millar; "I wouldn't have you in love without your father's consent for the world. You must forget him."

"Must!" and Mary sighed as she spoke. "What an easy word to speak! What a difficult one to obey! You have loved, Milly; I am sure you have, and must remember how impossible compliance with such a command would have been then."

Mrs. Millar was driven into a corner, so she said—

"That's quite a different matter. Very true, I did love, dearly love, poor John Millar, but ——"

"And, therefore, you will counsel me, dear Milly. You will speak to me as a friend—as a woman, and not as a schoolmistress? You will let me talk to you of him?"

"No, no!" said Mrs. Millar, the tears trickling down her cheek.

"Ah, yes!" cried Mary, trusting those watery witnesses of Mrs. Millar's sympathy, rather than her spoken words. "You will; for my heart is so full at times, that silence is painful to me, and I long to tell you all I feel and hope."

"Don't talk to me in that way," said Mrs. Millar, fairly breaking down. "You will make me do as you like, in spite of myself. And, as I live, here comes Mr. Wilmot! Bother the fellow!"

Mary was on her feet in an instant. A moment's glance at the looking-glass, and then her book was resumed. Oh, foolish Mary?

Wilmot was soon at the door, his fine face glowing with his walk in the warm sun. He carried a fly-rod in his hand, his creel was slung at his back; and a more dangerous fellow, where maidens' hearts were to be had, could hardly be found in broad England—much less in Reigate.

Mrs. Millar intended to have received him in the porch, but, staying to arrange her cap, he was already in the room.

"I am fortunate, indeed," he said, "to find you at home this lovely day. I trust you and Miss Grey are well?"

"Quite well! quite well, I thank you," replied Mrs. Millar, terribly nervous, whilst Mary said nothing, but smiled him a smile that was worth a whole dictionary of words.

"I have killed a brace of trout this morning," said Wilmot, "and venture to ask permission to leave them here."

Mrs. Millar felt she must defend her position at once, or be carried by storm; so, giving a short cough, to rally her retreating spirits, she said with much emphasis—

"Really, Mr. Wilmot, I must decline your politeness, and indeed, to be plain with you——"

She paused for a moment, and Wilmot thrust in,—

"Am I so unhappy as to have given you offence?"

"No, Mr. Wilmot, not offence; but your calling so frequently, your attentions——"

"I acknowledge my intrusions, and plead for forgiveness. If you deny me the pleasure of visiting you, you will inflict pain upon me beyond endurance;" and he certainly looked most wretched.

Mary did not speak, but her face expressed clearly the distress she felt, and Mrs. Millar knew she was upbraiding her for her cruelty.

Wilmot saw his advantage, and recognised his ally.

"If I dared hope that Miss Grey were not offended," said the wily wooer; "that she does not desire my absence———"

Unconsciously, almost, Mary answered what appeared to be a question addressed directly to herself.

"I—I do not, Sir; but Mrs. Millar thinks—thinks——"

"That I have some unworthy motive in desiring your regard?" said Wilmot.

"No, Sir; I don't care about your motive," answered Mrs. Millar, almost driven distracted. "I believe you, Sir, to be a good, kind young man."

"Then do not discard me," urged Wilmot. "Do not think the interest I feel for that lady is less earnest because of its sudden growth."

"What shall I do? What shall I do?" cried Mrs. Millar, wringing her hands.

Wilmot felt he had no right to give pain by his further importunity.

"Pardon me," he said, "I see that I distress you. I am wrong to do so. Must I say farewell?"

"No!" exclaimed Mary, involuntarily, adding immediately—"excuse me if I seem bold, but I am not used to dissemble what I feel, and why should I hesitate to confess my gratitude for all your kindness?"

"Mary!" cried Mrs. Millar, "you shock, you alarm me!"

"Why, dear Madam?" asked Mary, her beautiful face and neck suffused by the effort she was making. "Mr. Wilmot knows how ignorant I am of the world, and the world's ways, and will pardon what may be my unmannerly sincerity."

"I will imitate your frankness," said Wilmot, exultingly, "and say how much my happiness depends on your favour."

Mrs. Millar grew more alarmed, expecting to see her ward carried off bodily.

"I can't allow any more of this!" she exclaimed, "without the knowledge of your father."

"True, dear Milly," said Mary; "I thank you for recalling me to my duty. Without my father's permission, Mr. Wilmot, we must not meet again.

"Then let me see him," replied Wilmot. "Let me satisfy him that I am some way worthy to aspire to the happiness I covet."

"Mr. Wilmot!" exclaimed Mrs. Millar, tears trickling down her face. "You are a man! If I do seem harsh and tyrannical, it's quite against my nature. Mary, let Mr. Wilmot see your father."

"Yes," said Mary, blushing again, as she asked "where?"

"At his place in town," answered Mrs. Millar. "His letters are sent to his lawyer, Mr. Goad, in Chudleigh Street, St. James's."

"Indeed!" said Wilmot. "I have a friend living at Mr. Goad's, and if you will entrust me with your letter, I may obtain an interview this evening."

"I will, Mr. Wilmot," replied Mary; "and upon the result of that interview depends our future—friendship. You promise that?"

"I do."

"In a few minutes my letter will be ready. Mrs. Millar will give it to you."

Wilmot advanced towards Mary as she rose to leave the room, but Mrs. Millar seemed to think matters had proceeded far enough, and led Mary away.

Wilmot stood gazing at the closed doorway through which she had passed, as though he believed she would come again to wish him good-speed on the errand which might concern all their future lives; but she came not. Strange that he should know so near a connexion of Mr. Grey as his confidential lawyer, and that he should be going to his house that night to meet Mr. Ruby for the last time; for, despite his apparent disinterested civility, Wilmot mistrusted his friend of the White Posts.

Mrs. Millar soon returned with Mary's letter, which she gave to Wilmot, a letter that was to exercise such powerful influence on the fate of nearly all the personages of this story.

When Wilmot left the cottage, Mary returned to the little parlour, and watched him from behind her flowers, as he passed down the garden walk, and then up the lane. She saw him look back many times, as though he felt the influence of her presence, and could not depart. He was gone at last.

Mary had never been so happy before. She knew not why, but perhaps she was conscious that she had overcome a pleasant temptation, and discharged her duty to her beloved father.

Wilmot had been gone half-an-hour, when Mrs. Millar was startled, whilst gathering flowers in the garden, by the advent of "that odious Mr. Fillet," as she and Mary now designated Captain Wagstaff. Mrs. Millar saw him coming down the lane, and instantly sought shelter in the house. Unfortunately, Joe Martin was away, as we know; and therefore she felt that Mary and herself were entirely at the mercy of the impudent dancing-master. With his easy *nonchalant* manner, Wagstaff followed Mrs. Millar into the cottage; and, though neither of the ladies made the least sign of friendly recognition, he was perfectly unabashed, and said, smiling impudently,—

"Ah, ladies! You see I have not forgotten my engagement."

Mrs. Millar was determined to close the interview at once, and so replied with an energy most unusual,—

"Mr. Fillet, I can but express my surprise that you should intrude yourself here. As a dancing-master we received you —as a dancing-master we paid you."

"There it is, Madam," said the imperturbable Wagstaff,

"there it is! I am desirous of putting myself right with you. That young lady has created an interest ——"

"Do not insult me, Sir," said Mary, her beautiful eyes brilliant with indignation.

"I should do so had I no other credentials to your favourable consideration than a fiddle; but I have imposed upon you," said Wagstaff. "You have hitherto known me but as Mr. Fillet, a cutter of capers, but I am Captain Wagstaff of Her Majesty's Service."

"In either character," replied Mary, "your presence here is an intrusion. No honourable man descends to practise deception. I am surprised you are not abashed at your own meanness."

"Hey-day," said Wagstaff, rather taken aback by Mary's plain speaking. "I see you are your father's daughter. You have all the spirit of 'Old Ruby.'"

"My father's name is Grey, Sir," replied Mary.

"*Alias* Ruby," said Wagstaff, his anger rising at the contemptuous tone and look of Mary. "I know him well—better than you do. A fortnight ago he entered this house as I left it."

"Yes, I remember he did so," replied Mary, very coolly. "You now know that I am the daughter of an honourable man, who will not allow me to be insulted with impunity."

"An honourable man?" cried Wagstaff, forcing a laugh. "Ha! ha! Old Bob Ruby—the gambler, blackleg, cheat!"

"What, Sir?" exclaimed Mary. "You do not know my father."

Wagstaff's face assumed the devilish appearance it had worn in the morning during his quarrel with Ruby, as he almost hissed out,—

"When next you see your father, ask him if I have maligned him? Ask him if he knows Fred Wagstaff, the confederate in many of his clever schemes. This very day he told me you were ignorant of his real name and character. He has used bitter words to me—as bitter as those which have but now fallen from your own lips. A worm will turn when trodden on. You both have spurned me on the strength of your presumed goodness. Ask him if what I have said be true—'No honourable man would practise deception.' If he be one he will tell you, as he but lately told me, that he is known by every name that honest men despise."

Wagstaff's brutal harangue was brought to a close by Mary

falling senseless to the ground, and Mrs. Millar thrusting him from the room, as she exclaimed,—

"Coward! Leave my house! Coward, coward!"

Wagstaff took his way to the lane, Mrs. Millar's words ringing in his ears long after he left the garden.

Mary soon recovered, and looking wildly around, asked, like one who had seen some frightful object—"Is he gone?"

"Yes, dear," replied Mrs. Millar. "Villain that he is!"

"Oh, what has he done? what has he done?" cried Mary, hiding her face in her hands. "Left me with distrust of my own father;" then checking herself, she rose up, and wiping the tears from her eyes, continued, "Oh, wicked girl that I am, to doubt one so kind, so loving, on the word of such a villain. 'Gambler! cheat!' the words sound in my ears as though uttered by a thousand tongues. I cannot rest here, dear Milly, we will go to London at once and see my father."

"My dear child," said Mrs. Millar, alarmed at the earnestness of Mary's voice and manner, "wait till to-morrow."

"It is useless to dissuade me," replied Mary; "either go with me, or I go alone. Did I remain here, I should not see another day with unshaken reason. Are you decided? Do we go together?"

"Yes, Mary, yes!" said the bewildered Mrs. Millar. "This all comes of that plaguy ball; I wish that fellow's legs had been in a man-trap before they had brought him to this house."

Before her lamentation was ended, Mary had left the room, and Mrs. Millar felt convinced that there was nothing to be done but to prepare for a journey to London instantly.

CHAPTER VII.

THE DENOUEMENT.

MR. GOAD had been too busily occupied about many matters to renew his love-suit in the kitchen, and had just descended again to his office, after washing his face and hands, combing his hair, and putting on a clean cravat, in fact, having, as he considered, dressed for dinner, when Mr. Wilmot presented himself, the clock in the office chiming the half-hour.

"You are rather before your time, are you not?" said Goad, after the usual salutations; "we do not dine until seven."

"I am so," replied Wilmot; "but I have a little matter of business to transact with you before dinner."

"Business!" said Goad. "Delighted to be of service, I assure you;" and he opened a diary lying upon his table, in which he instantly wrote :—Charles Wilmot, Esq.—Consultation. "Nothing like being particular, Sir."

"I have a letter," said Wilmot, "for a client of yours, Mr. Grey."

"Mr. Grey!" echoed Goad, with a look of astonishment.

"It is addressed to your care," continued Wilmot, not observing the effect his words had upon Goad; "and for very particular reasons I am desirous of knowing Mr. Grey."

"And for very particular reasons I am not desirous you should know Mr. Grey," thought Goad, though he bowed, as expressing the pleasure he should feel in introducing them to each other.

"If you will procure me an early interview, I should esteem it an obligation."

"An obligation?" repeated Goad, not knowing what to say.

Wilmot misunderstood his hesitation, and added, "to be charged for accordingly."

Goad bowed and smiled, and proceeded with the entry in his diary, saying, "Really, I would oblige you if I could, but Mr. Grey is a commercial traveller." (He paused to watch the effect of this assertion). "However, your letter shall be forwarded to him."

It was evident that Wilmot did not suspect that Ruby and the person he had named were the same (to the great relief of Mr. Goad), for Wilmot requested permission to write a few lines to inclose with Mary's letter, and was shown into the inner office for that purpose.

Goad knew the letter Wilmot had given him was from the unknown correspondent of Ruby, and he thought, "How lucky this note fell into my hands! It is the neat little crowquill character that old Ruby receives with such pleasure. Had he had this to-day, our pigeon might have escaped plucking; for, after one of these epistles, Ruby is as soft as a woman." He placed Mary's note in his waistcoat pocket.

Joe Martin had not been idle all this time. By the aid of his landlord he had found a legal adviser, and placed Mrs. Barker's will in safe keeping. According to his promise, he had hastened back to Susan, and arranged with that terrified young person to take advantage of Mr. Goad's dinner engagement and leave the house that very evening. The newly-united lovers had had, what Joe called, "a dish of tea and a bout of courting," and Susan's large box stood ready corded to be conveyed up the area steps as soon as the evening closed in. Joe had gone into the street to reconnoitre, when, to his great amazement, he saw Mrs. Millar and Mary pause before the house he had just quitted. Mrs. Millar appeared in a state of more than her usual trepidation, and he could see that the face of his young mistress was pale and full of sorrow.

"This is the house, dear Milly," said Mary, with constrained firmness; "knock, and ask for my father."

"Oh, dear me!" replied Mrs. Millar, the tears streaming down her cheeks; "I daren t, Mary! I daren't! My courage has failed me all the way we came, and if Mr. Grey should open the door, I should faint."

"Then I will," said Mary. "Here is a bell with 'Office' written beneath it; is that the one I should ring?"

"Mrs. Millar could only sob out, 'Yes! Yes!'"

"Come, Milly," said Mary, very kindly, "remember I depend upon you for support. I know not what trial is in store for me."

She rang the bell, and the church clock of St. James struck eight. No one came to the door. She rang again. The door was now opened by Trotter, the office boy, wearing, however, a suit of buttons.

"Did you ring?" he asked, rudely.

"Yes."

"Well, it's after office hours; you ought to know that," said Trotter. "What do you want?"

"I wish to see Mr. Grey," replied Mary, the words almost inarticulate from her emotion.

"He don't live here, Ma'am," said Trotter; "we know nothing of him. We only take in his letters;" and, the upstairs bell ringing at that moment, the boy shut the door.

Mary turned to Mrs. Millar, who had almost performed the threatened fainting. "What does this mean? Not know him? There is some frightful mystery!" and the poor girl clung to the iron railing for support.

Joe Martin instantly crossed the road, and Mrs. Millar's exclamation of surprise and delight aroused poor Mary. Without waiting to ask a question, nay, without even feeling any surprise at this fortuitous appearance of her servant, she said,—

"Joseph, you find me in sad trouble, with no one to advise, to aid me. I want, nay, must find my father immediately. I have no clue to his London residence but at this place. They deny that he lives here."

"That I believe to be true enough, Miss, 'cos Susan Fletcher, that I knows, lives in the kitchen. Mr. Goad lives in the offices, and the upper rooms belong to a Mr. Ruby."

"Ruby!" Mary almost screamed the word—"Ruby was the name!"

Joe started at the voice of his young mistress, as she continued,—

"How do you know this?"

Joe told her how he had acquired his knowledge.

"I must see this Susan Fletcher," said Mary, "instantly! instantly!" and she seized Joe's arm so tightly that he almost cried out.

In a few moments the whole party was in the kitchen, to Susan's great astonishment.

"You live in this house," said Mary; "you know its inmates? There is a Mr. Ruby, is there not?"

"Yes, Miss," replied Susan, drawing nearer to Joe as her natural protector; "a gay old gentleman as keeps a deal of company, and sits up very late of nights."

"Oh, should that man's tale be true!" cried Mary. "Can you place me anywhere to see Mr. Ruby unobserved?"

Susan was frightened and confused, but Joe spoke out, "Yes, Susan, you can; there's this staircase that goes to the lodger's room, you told me."

Susan was still too frightened to reply until Mary took her hand between her own, and said, "More than my life depends upon my seeing Mr. Ruby this night. Do not refuse to help me, and I will never forget your kindness." Joe Martin then told Susan who her suppliant was, and urged her to comply with the wish of his mistress. So it was arranged that Susan should go up-stairs and see how the desired reconnoissance could be effected. Two weary hours passed away, and Mary's dreadful doubts remained unsatisfied, as Trotter was continually busy about the landing.

Let us precede Mary, should she, indeed, be admitted to a knowledge of her father's wickedness.

At one of the card-tables, lighted by a single lamp, whose green shade left the players' faces in shadow, were seated young Wilmot and Wagstaff. The night was yet young, but the play had evidently been some time in operation, and, from the conversation, it seemed that Wilmot had been the winner. Ruby and Goad were, apparently, careless lookers on, although the former made bets of some amount with Wagstaff, and had shared in the good fortune of the young dupe. Goad endeavoured to imitate the *sang-froid* of Ruby, but with indifferent success, and kept continually fumbling in his pockets, taking snuff, and rubbing his fingers through his bushy hair. During these nervous manipulations, Mary's note escaped from his waistcoat-pocket, and, falling to the ground, remained there some time, until it attracted the attention of Trotter, who was employed in supplying the players with wine.

"Luck's with me this time," said Wagstaff, the game having terminated in his favour.

"I am glad you are a winner at last," remarked Wilmot. "I dislike having all the advantage, I fear the fairness of my play may be suspected."

Such a possibility was scouted by the whole party. A heavy sum was now at stake, and from Ruby's compressed lips, it was evident a change in the play was intended. The game was in progress when Trotter handed, on a salver, Mary's note to Ruby.

"Don't bring me letters now," said Ruby, peevishly; "to-morrow," and he waved the boy away.

"I found it on the carpet, Sir," replied Trotter. "It is addressed to Mr. Grey."

Ruby instantly took the letter, and his hitherto calm face flushed and twitched, as he recognised the handwriting of his daughter. He rose and went to a light on the sideboard. "Her letter found in this room!" he thought. He broke the seal hastily, and read as follows—

"MY DEAREST FATHER,—

"The bearer of this letter is Mr. Charles Wilmot" —(a blow could not have made him recoil more. It was some moments before he could read further.) "He will explain all. I have met him frequently of late, and his kindness has been so marked, that I knew not until to-day how deeply he had interested me." (Ruby filled a large goblet with claret, and drained it at a draught.) "Now, convinced to what my fault has led, I hasten to ask forgiveness for myself, and your favour for Wilmot."

He read the letter, word for word again, being almost in a stupor, and was only roused by hearing Wagstaff say—

"Let us give over for to-night. I am winning more than I care to do."

"I can afford my losings—luck may turn again, and if not, no matter!"

He looked to the players, and could see that the stakes were large, and Wilmot greatly excited.

"If it be that she love this man," he thought, "what have I done? Excited in him the lust of play; that fatal passion which soons grows master over all."—"Again," Wagstaff was heard—"I will not play longer. The cards are dead against you."

"Luck's all, my dear fellow," said Wilmot; "if I complain not of losing, surely you need not grumble at winning."

"The deadly poison works," thought Ruby. "To-night his losses are great, or Wagstaff would not fence his play. Then will come the consequence of injury—a desire for retaliation. The downward course is easy, and Mary loves him! He must be rescued!" With great effort, Ruby recovered his usual calmness of manner, and joined the players as Wagstaff exclaimed:—"Encore! You see you cannot win; you have already lost a thousand pounds."

"What's that?" replied Wilmot, flushed with the excitement of the play and the wine he had unconsciously drank during the game. "I've twenty more to back them. Come!"

"Perhaps a change of players," said Ruby, calmly, "may equalise the game? I'll take the hand."

Wagstaff insisted upon Ruby's proposal being accepted, and the game proceeded. Wagstaff had already won more than had been intended at this initiatory meeting. Wilmot's whole fortune was the quarry of the gamesters, and they feared to alarm him prematurely; but Wagstaff had so much reliance upon the judgment of Ruby in conducting such disgraceful raids, that he did not hesitate to accept a large bet offered by Wilmot.

Wagstaff, as he sat watching the play, felt his sleeve cautiously pulled by Goad, who then motioned him to the sideboard.

"I've dropped a letter addressed to Mr. Grey somewhere," said Goad.

"Oh —— the letter," replied Wagstaff, annoyed at being disturbed for such a cause; "mind the play. Ruby never failed to plant a card when he wanted it."

"I tell you, if the old boy gets that letter now," said Goad, "it will be fatal to us."

"Mine!" exclaimed Wilmot.

"I've lost," said Ruby, coolly.

"That letter's done it," whispered Goad to Wagstaff, who boiling with rage, cried out—

"Sold! by heavens! You're playing false!"

Wilmot, supposing the words addressed to himself, sprang

to his feet, and in a loud tone demanded who dare accuse him of playing false?

"Silence, poor gull!" said Wagstaff, beside himself with passion; "it was not to you I spoke, but to that old knave there!" and he shook his fist in Ruby's face.

In a moment Ruby had his confederate by the throat, and so powerful was his grasp, that Wagstaff shrunk within it.

"Unsay that word! Unsay it, or I'll strangle you!"

Ruby slightly relaxed his hold, and enabled Wagstaff to speak.

"Never, Ruby! You have sold us, like a selfish rogue, for the sake of that girl at Reigate."

"Silence!" cried Ruby, "if you would not die in my hands."

Some word that Wagstaff muttered infuriated Ruby still more, and Wilmot and Goad were on the point of interfering when Ruby loosed his hold, threw his hands up in the air, and staggered from his foe. One word had wrought the change. Mary had said, "Father!"

Yes, she had entered the room at last, hearing the noise of the struggle, and the angry voices, to behold the one she sought in Robert Ruby the gambler! Did that stay her? No; in a moment her arms were around his neck, and her wondering face turned up towards his.

"What brought you here, Mary?" he said.

"I came because he told me what—I could not believe," replied Mary.

"He? Wilmot?"

"No; he with whom I saw you struggling," said Mary, her tears falling fast; "and it is true, it is true!"

"What did he tell you, Mary? That I was a gambler?" Ruby's voice was hoarse and low.

"I cannot tell you what he said you were," replied Mary, hiding her face in her hands.

"Ah, you turn from me!" cried Ruby. "You, the child for whom I have lived this life of scorn—for whom I have spent the night in feverish excitement, and the day in wearying thought—you now despise me! But it is just!—it is just!" He staggered to a chair. Mary tried to go to him, but could not.

"Do not leave me, Mary," he said, after a moment's pause: "do not leave your father desolate — despised.

Think! think how I must love you, when upon my knees I pray you not to leave me!"

He had risen, and was about to kneel at her feet, when Mary pressed him to her bosom, and said—

"Leave you! Kneel to me! No! here is your place, dear father!"

Although Ruby and Mary remained silently locked in each other's arms for some moments, neither of the other three men spoke a word. Even Wagstaff was moved by what he saw, and reproached himself for his vindictiveness.

Mary was the first to speak.

"Now, father," she said, "let us quit this hateful place. Let us go home."

"Home!" exclaimed Ruby. "Ah, that peaceful dream has gone for ever!"

"Not so!" said Mary. "Knowing what the past has been, my love shall be more active in the future, we will never part again."

"No, no!" cried Ruby, covering his face. "My cunning plans are blown into the air; I can never look in your dear face again as I have done, Mary."

"Yes, father," she replied, "yes, for you will find no change—none."

"I must! I must!" said Ruby. "I shall see there no filial love, only filial duty, for I have robbed myself of honour; I shall see there the settled sorrow of your widowed heart, for I have robbed you of him you loved."

"No, Sir!" exclaimed Wilmot, unable to keep silence longer.

"You still here?" said Mary. "It would have been kinder to have left us."

"When you were in this great sorrow?" replied Wilmot. "No! I loved you for your goodness, and every trial proves your greater worth. If you dare trust my love, and to my care confide your future happiness ——"

Mary interrupted him.

"I would have trusted you—believe that of me, but what has passed makes my course of duty certain. My father and I cannot part—never."

"Yes, yes!" said Ruby, convulsively; "I will quit England."

"Not without me, father," replied Mary. "Long years of love have yet to be repaid. Farewell!"

She held forth her hand to Wilmot; he took it and pressed it to his heart.

"I cannot part from you—cannot lose you, Mary, for such a cause. Have I been blameless? No! Without temptation I was a gambler."

"And would have been ruined," cried Wagstaff, "but for Ruby!"

"I own it," continued Wilmot. "You hear how much I owe your father. Let not a false pride mislead you ——"

"Pride, Wilmot?" said Mary, interrupting him. "I have no pride now."

"No," said Ruby, "your father has humbled you too much."

Mary drew her father's face to hers, and asked pardon for her thoughtless words, and again urged him to go away.

Wilmot felt that he could not let them go alone, and, therefore, made bold by his love, prayed her not to reject him.

Ruby at length spoke.

"Mary," he said, "have I still a claim upon your love? Accept his generous offer, and let me not think I have destroyed your happiness."

Can you doubt her answer? It was not given in words. One loving look, one gentle pressure, made Wilmot happy.

Goad was utterly dumbfounded by the course affairs had taken, and was disposed to claim a share in the *dénouement*, much having turned upon the letter which he had lost so opportunely; but reflecting that he had not altogether consulted his new client's interest in the matter, he prudently dispensed with gratitude, and contented himself with his prospective bill of costs.

Not so Wagstaff. The scene he had witnessed had penetrated the hardened crust about his heart, and he could not help saying to his old confederate—

"Ruby, I am sorry for what I have done in this affair. You revoked, and I played the knave. Wilmot, I wish you joy of your treasure, there. Rely on it, HEARTS ARE TRUMPS after all. Good-night."

"One moment, Captain Wagstaff," said Wilmot. "If you would quit the dreadful trade you follow ——"

"It is too late, Wilmot," he replied. "Thanks! but the rattle of the dice-box would always lure me to it."

"But what will be the end?" asked Wilmot.

"The usual one, I suppose—first the gaol, then the madhouse or the hospital; but it's too late. Good-night."

And so the gamester went away, to fulfil, in a few short years, the destiny he had foretold as awaiting him.

Before the world was quite a year older, two happy pairs in whom we have an interest had stood, at different times, before the altar of Reigate Church, and formed afterwards one household in a distant part of England. Need we say that we refer to Mr. and Mrs. Wilmot, and their faithful and obedient servants, Mr. and Mrs. Martin! for Joe was their farm-bailiff, and Susan housekeeper, until certain interesting events occurred, which rendered a separate residence desirable.

With Ruby's closing years come many painful remembrances. Let us hope he uses his chastenings wisely. If so, there may be good in store for him, made sweeter by the bitterness of the past.

MIND YOUR OWN BUSINESS.

A DRAMATIC STORY.

CHAPTER I.

THE OLD BEECH TREE.

T was the middle of October. The fields had yielded up their harvests, and the plough had been again busy, but the country had acquired a new beauty from the change which had come over the forest trees and untrimmed hedgerows.

The beech was clothed in golden leaves, which almost glittered in the sun, harmonising with the rich brown of the oak and yellow of the elm, contrasting pleasantly with the tender green of the ash and the more sombre hue of the larch. The graceful ferns, now dry and sapless, mingled their many shades of colour with those of the hornbeam, quickset, and brambles in the hedgerows which bordered a green lane leading to a pretty village some miles from ——. It was morning, and despite the thick autumn covering of hedges and underwood, the hounds were abroad, the occasional whoop of the huntsman and the cry of the pack directing the eye to an adjacent copse, where might be seen the red coats of the horsemen glancing through the close-set trees, until, with a joyous cheer the whole field streamed away in hot pursuit of the chase. The village could be seen here and there through the trees, and the light cloud of smoke which hung over it was a cheerful addition to the scene. A snug, red-brick cottage was also visible, and its trim garden and well-cared-for fences assured the passer-by that no idle man kept house there.

Mr. Oddiman was one of the busiest men in the neighbourhood, although of no profession, and possessed of ample means, to which must be added a benevolent heart. The poor had in him an active friend—and for the matter of that —the rich also, for no service was too irksome for the goodnatured Mr. Oddiman. There were some people ill-natured enough to call him a busy-body, and to instance occasions when, but for his friendly interference, matters would have arrived at a satisfactory conclusion much sooner than they did, and to declare that sometimes no difficulties would have arisen had he been content to "mind his own business." We confess to sharing in those opinions, and the tale we have to tell will be our justification.

The green lane of which we spoke was about half a mile in length, and at the end farthest from the village stood a cluster of beeches crowning a gentle slope descending to a bright swift stream which turned the wheels of a mill, and formed altogether as pretty a subject for a picture as Arthur Mowbray or any other landscape-painter could desire.

We will tell you at once all we know of Arthur Mowbray, the young artist who is now striving to transfer to his canvas the scene we have attempted to indicate. He had been left an orphan at a very early age, and his education and nurture had devolved upon a kind-hearted blundering uncle, a captain in the merchant-service, who, dying after making a bungling will, left Arthur dependent upon the liberality of his cousin Orgrave, to whom all the old captain's property reverted. Notwithstanding his cousin's earnest reasoning to prove that the will was not a true expression of the old man's intention, and that therefore Arthur had no right to have any delicacy in accepting the annuity paid to him, yet he still felt his dependence, and determined to free himself from it as soon as possible. With this intention, he had cultivated sedulously for some time the practice of an art which had been a favourite amusement with him from his boyhood, and his improvement had been commensurate with his industry. In his rambles "in pursuit of the picturesque," he had wandered to Dawley, and struck with the beauty of the surrounding scenery, had taken up his quarters in the house of the village blacksmith. At the end of a fortnight he fell sick, cold and fever prostrated him, and he would probably have died for want of nursing, had not the doctor, whilst smoking his evening pipe with Mr. Morrison, the schoolmaster, mentioned his case and excited the sympathy of the tender-hearted dominie and his two pretty daughters. The invalid was forthwith visited, and afterwards nursed and cared for, as though a father's and sisters' love watched over him. Mowbray's recovery was slow, notwithstanding all the care of his new-found friends, and his removal for a time from the rough lodging at the blacksmith's to the prettiest of chambers, hung with the whitest of dimity, and fragrant from the freshest and sweetest of flowers that the school-master's garden could supply. As strength came back again, the day was shortened by pleasant rambles or agreeable employment in the evening, made almost too brief by the gentle influences which converted the school-house into home.

When Mowbray was well enough to resume work, he returned to his old lodgings, for the blacksmith and his wife had shown him all the kindness within their knowledge or capacity. It was not, however, an easy matter to reconcile himself to the change, and he found it necessary to seek the school-master's society almost as much as when he was his guest. With what result?

The day on which our story opens was almost as warm as the latter summer, and Mowbray was engaged as we have described him. Three times had he painted in that grand old beech, and each time with diminished effect. It was evident his mind was not in his work, and ever and anon he kept glancing down the green lane, when his eyes should have been fixed on the object before him. In his half-finished picture there was seated at the foot of the tree the figure of a young girl. The face had been worked upon with great care and skill. It was evidently a portrait, and for a landscape painter excellently done. The church-clock struck eleven, and as the last stroke fell upon the bell, a young girl stepped into the lane from a hidden footpath, which led to Mr. Morrison's school-house.

"Ah!" said Mowbray, half aloud, "as punctual as the sun;" and rising from his seat upon a felled tree, he hastened to meet Marian Morrison.

"How kind, how very kind you are, Marian," he said.

"I am too happy to be of service to you, Mr. Mowbray," she replied; "and you tell me your time is wasted if I am not here to sit for you."

"Indeed, it is so, Marian," replied Mowbray, his face flushing as he spoke; "my thoughts are ever with you, and when you are away I only daub at random."

"How foolishly you talk," said Marian, colouring deeply. "Where shall I sit? Where I did yesterday?"

"No, Marian; sit here beside me on this tree;" and he held out his hand to her, but she refused to take it.

"No, Mr. Mowbray, where I sat yesterday, or I return," replied Marian.

"Do as you will," said Mowbray; "and I will look at you as a child gazes upon space and thinks it heaven."

"Such silly compliments displease me," replied Marian, "and make me blame myself for listening so often to you."

Mowbray laid down his *palette*, as he said: "Marian, now it is you who are unkind. You must believe I love you, or why do I remain here, spell-bound as it were, asking only the happiness of your companionship, the blessing of your presence?"

Marian rose and said, "How wrongly I have acted!"

"Wrongly;" exclaimed Mowbray, "it is ordained that all should love!"

"I must not listen to you," said Marian, turning to go, "and if you regard me ——"

"If I regard you!" exclaimed Mowbray, taking her hand and pressing it passionately to his lips.

"Well, if you love me," said Marian, her face one rosy blush; "if you love me let it not be a secret from my father. I know these meetings to be wrong, and wrong knowingly pursued will assuredly bring its punishment."

"To-morrow he shall know all, dear Marian."

"To-morrow! Why not to-day?" she asked.

"You will laugh at me if I confess the reason," said Mowbray, smiling. "I am by nature so bashful, so cowardly, —perhaps that is the better word,—that I need the day to nerve me for the encounter."

"Surely, you do not fear my father?" asked Marian, smiling in her turn.

"Fear him!" replied Mowbray, "Fear him! dear, good old man! who gave me welcome as a stranger, and made me an honoured guest when I was ill and lonely. No; but think what I am about to ask—his dearest treasure."

"You forget I have a sister," said Marian.

"True, I had forgotten all but you."

"Here she is to remind you of her existence," said Marian, as her almost counterpart came towards them. "I told her I was coming here. Resume your work, Arthur; my father must be the first to know our secret."

Fanny Morrison accepted her sister's presence as a matter-of-course, and proceeded at once to examine Mowbray's canvas.

"How beautiful!' she exclaimed. "What a transparent sky, and the light upon those pollards is excellent!"

"Confess, Miss Fanny, you paint," said Mowbray.

"Oh, dear, no! but I admire pictures, especially of places which I have known, and this one is very dear to me, as it is associated with my poor dear mother. You remember, Marian?"

"Yes, it was a favourite walk of dear mother," replied Marian, looking down upon the ground as though some thought of wrong-doing rose up in her mind.

Fanny did not observe the expression of her sister's face, so much interested was she in the picture.

"How very like this is to Marian," she said, clapping her hands with the pleasure of the discovery. "Just her expression when she is very pleased and interested."

"I am glad you think so!" exclaimed Mowbray, with undisguised delight. "Praise to a poor artist is very welcome."

"It is deserved, in my poor opinion. Why, what is there to blush at, dear sister?" asked Fanny. "You are pleased and interested sometimes, and I know who would prize that picture very much."

"Who? pray, tell me who?" said Mowbray earnestly.

"Do you see that pretty old-fashioned house yonder," and Fanny pointed to an old Manor-house, half-hidden among the stately elms which grew around it. "The owner of that house is Mr. Verdon, a great admirer of my sister!"

"Fanny!" exclaimed Marian, her face reddening with anger.

"Why, you know I am telling the truth," replied Fanny; "I have not said that you admire him, though I hope some day to be able to do so."

"Mr. Verdon will always be indifferent to me," said Marian.

"No! no, dear sister—a handsome man, well educated, good tempered, and prosperous, is not likely to be treated with indifference," replied Fanny, laughing. "May I ask Mr. Verdon to see your picture?"

"Thank you," answered Mowbray, his manner indicating embarrassment, if not displeasure; "I see no use in giving him that trouble, as I intend this sketch, when finished, as a present to your father."

"Oh! how pleased he will be!" said Fanny, "for he doats upon his children, and should—mind I only say *should*—Marian leave us for the pretty home yonder, this faithful likeness will still seem to make her present amongst us."

Fanny's careless talk silenced Mowbray; and Marian, with a woman's quickness, read her sister's thought, and so she said:

"If you will release me, Mr. Mowbray, I and my sister will leave you."

He could but thank her for the time she had already devoted to him; and Fanny, too unskilled in lovers' stratagems to understand the truth, placed her arm around her neck, and bidding Mowbray good day, and inviting him to their cottage in the evening, went homewards.

Mowbray gazed after them until they had left the green lane for the footpath through the copse, and long after; his mind full of Mr. Verdon, of whom he had heard for the first time as an admirer of his beloved Marian.

At length he resumed his work, but his progress was slow and unsatisfactory, as Marian's face at times filled all his canvas, or Mr. Verdon's old Manor-house attracted his eye in place of the grand old beech. He was roused from this unsatisfactory dreaming by the crash of timber, as a well-mounted horseman leaped the hedge into the green lane, and then rode quietly towards the spot where Mowbray was seated. The painter started, as he evidently recognised the new comer, and it was also clear that, for reasons of his own, he wished to avoid an interview. Not so the rider, who stopped his horse, and having regarded Mowbray's work for a few moments, said coolly: "What have you got there, a picture? I'm very partial to painting;" and then dismounting, stood at the painter's shoulder. "Oh! a landscape, eh? Not a bad subject. The sky's too blue, and the grass too green. What's the price?"

"It is not for sale," replied Mowbray, curtly.

"I beg pardon. Am I addressing an amateur?" asked the horseman, and then exclaimed, as Mowbray turned his face towards him, "What! by Lord Harry, it's Arthur Mowbray!"

"Yes, Ernest Orgrave," replied Arthur, holding out his hand, "I am your poor cousin."

"I'm devilish glad to see you," said Orgrave, taking the proffered hand coolly; and speaking in a tone that indicated anything but enthusiastic delight at the meeting, adding, "How long have you been a dauber of pigments?"

"Painting has been long an amusement to me. I am now practising it as a profession," replied Mowbray.

"A what?" asked Orgrave, surprised. "Why, you are not about to turn artist?"

"Why not, Sir? Painting is an art which has ennobled kings, and added to a nation's glory."

"Oh! if you're going to talk fine," said Orgrave, "I've done. Profession, ha! ha! Why you told me lately that the allowance I make you was sufficient."

"A sufficient obligation!" replied Mowbray, colouring deeply. "I am desirous to relieve you of a charge you have so kindly undertaken, and to free myself from dependence."

"Nonsense, Arthur!" said Orgrave. "Our uncle's bungling will made me sole inheritor, and I cannot do less than provide for you in some way. I daresay you were surprised to see me here? I was staying some five miles off, and hearing that the hounds met at Dawley, I thought I'd have a run, and possibly look up a connection of ours, Mrs. Frazer—Tom Frazer's widow.—You knew Tom Frazer?"

"No," replied Mowbray; "I always understood his reputation to be none of the best."

"I believe not," said Orgrave, "nor his wife's either."

"Under those circumstances I never thought it desirable to make their acquaintance."

"Oh, there! there!" cried Orgrave, "don't be moral. If a man were to consider the characters of his acquaintance he would soon be a hermit. I'm content to know anybody who don't bore me or spoil my dinner, be he rogue or honest fellow."

"Such indiscriminate liberality seems both unwise and unjust," remarked Mowbray.

"Very likely," said Orgrave, "but there would be no society without it. There, I know what you are going to say, something about virtue being its own reward—an admirable provision of nature; virtue don't require, and therefore don't receive, any acknowledgment. "Well, this Mrs. Frazer has lately committed matrimony;" and here the speaker broke into a loud laugh, which continued so long that Mowbray inquired the cause of his merriment.

"Why," said Orgrave after some effort to speak, "she married a fellow named Smith, who turned out to have been servant to one Bangalore—an Indian something or other. The old fellow died of a surfeit of mangoes, and left his footman the greater part of his money. Mrs. Frazer, not knowing what he had been, and being as poor as Job, though as proud as Juno, married the ex-flunkey, and they are now living in this neighbourhood."

"They call themselves Smythe, and live not a mile from Dawley," said Mowbray.

"So I heard," replied Orgrave. "I hear the flunkey is gloriously vulgar, and that his wife writhes at his *gaucheries*. So pack up your pigments and let us call on them. I want something to excite me."

"You must excuse me, cousin," said Mowbray; "I have no wish to make an acquaintance that would either pain or annoy me."

"Oh, bother!" cried Orgrave. "You always were so infernally sensitive—I'm not. I make a rule to find amusement, when, where, and how I can; and after all I lead a melancholy life, yet I live well and do nothing."

The conversation of the cousins was interrupted by the sudden, the almost supernatural appearance of Mr. Oddiman, who had, unperceived, joined the party.

"Good-morning, Mr. Mowbray," said the urbane old gentleman, bowing with the air of a courtier. "Delighted to see you in this part of the country, Mr. Orgrave."

Orgrave returned the bow, and then said, "Much obliged, I am sure. Some friend of yours, Arthur?"

"Yes, gentlemen, an old friend," replied Mr. Oddiman, "for I recollect your grandfather, Mr. Orgrave, making my first pair of leather breeches. He was a capital tailor and a very worthy man."

He was quite right. Orgrave's grandfather had been a tailor and a very worthy man, and his grandson, not in the least disconcerted by the reminder, merely observed, "Oh, ho! you're an eccentric, I see."

"Well, I suppose I am," said Oddiman, "for my notions of right and wrong seem sadly at variance with those which obtain at the present day. You and I now should be at odds about most things."

"Possibly," replied Orgrave. "Pray, how do you know anything of me?"

"By report, Sir; only by report," said Oddiman, "and that lady declares"—here the old gentleman bowed very politely —"declares that you are a most accomplished libertine, and that your cousin, Mr. Mowbray, is but little better."

"You seem to have been strangely misinformed, Mr. Oddiman," interposed Mowbray.

"You think so?" replied the old man, his tone, manner, look, assuming a seriousness, quite unusual with him, as he pointed to Marian's portrait. "What is this? The portrait of a young and simple girl, almost a child, the life of an old man's heart. Is it well to employ the leisure riches have given you, to use the advantages education has bestowed, to lure a guileless creature into ruin?"

"You do me injustice!" exclaimed Mowbray. "I—I—" he hesitated, he felt to explain his own conduct Marian must suffer, and Oddiman formed an unfavourable opinion of his silence.

"The lie sticks in his throat," thought he.

Orgrave silently enjoyed the scene; and, removing his hat, approached Mr. Oddiman with an expression of respect, and said:—

"I am most desirous of standing well in the opinion of one who has such gratifying recollections of my grandfather, the breeches' maker, and as some atonement for my cousin's folly, will you allow me to contribute a guinea to the Dorcas club, of which you are doubtless the president."

Oddiman saw the insult intended, and exclaimed, "Do you mean that I am an old woman, you impertinent puppy?"

"What!" said Orgrave, "don't like being quizzed, old boy? You wince as though I had pricked you with one of my grandfather's needles."

Mowbray endeavoured to pacify the enraged old gentleman, but without effect; and the two cousins at length withdrew, as Mr. Oddiman sat himself upon the fallen tree, and in a few minutes recovered his wonted equanimity.

"What a fool I was," he thought, "to be put out of temper by those profligates—I'll thwart those fellows yet."

He took from his pocket a small silver whistle which he blew, and in a few moments a man whom he called Weazle came from behind a clump of alders where he had been evidently keeping watch.

"Weazle," said Oddiman, "keep you constantly on the track of those fellows."

"I have done so on Mr. Mowbray all the morning; I've been behind those alders these two hours. Mr. Mowbray is certainly in love with Miss Marian."

"In love!" exclaimed Oddiman. "Weazle, you are a donkey! He knows no more of love than that gate-post. You would believe his fine words, as that poor silly girl will, if I don't open her eyes to the character of that fellow."

"Well, Sir," said Weazle, "you *will* have your own way, but it's my opinion you'll be spoiling a good match if you meddle in the matter."

"Meddle, Sir! What do you mean by meddle?" exclaimed Oddiman. "I never do anything, but from the best intentions. Meddle! that's a very unpleasant word, Weazle, and don't use it again, don't!"

"I shall," said Weazle to himself, "for he's always making some mess with his good intentions. I wish he would mind his own business."

Mr. Oddiman was out of humour with himself somewhat, and with his attendant more, and so he paced rapidly down the lane towards the village, followed at a respectful distance by Weazle.

CHAPTER II.

MR. ODDIMAN'S INTERFERENCE.

IT is unnecessary for the purposes of our story to recount the wooing of Mr. and Mrs. Smythe, into whose country house we will now intrude ourselves. Such a *mésalliance* would have been impossible, had not Mrs. Frazer been a woman of vulgar tastes and extravagant habits, and utterly incapable of self-exertion, when the death of her husband, Tom Frazer, a scampish fellow, left her penniless. She made Mr. Smith's acquaintance, or Mr. Smythe, as she chose to spell his name, in a Liverpool coach, and finding him possessed of considerable wealth, and most desirous of sharing it with any personable lady who would have him, Widow Frazer brought herself to swallow all Mr. Smith's deficiencies, and married him clandestinely, having secured to herself a settlement of sufficient amount to insure her against future penury.

The married life of the Smythes was not an enviable one—constant recriminations, constant breezes; and we will drop in upon them whilst one is in full blow.

"I didn't say wixen!" said Mr. Smythe.

"You did, Sir!" replied the lady. "You said I was a *wixen*. The word is bad enough with a *v*, but vulgarised by a *w*, it's not to be borne."

"Fiddle-de-dee!" cried Smythe. "I only meant you was werry aggrawating."

"Werry aggrawating! there it is again."

"Well, how you go on," said the perplexed husband, "as though w was to do nothing but look at the other letters of the alphabet. You wasn't so perticalar ——"

" *Particular*, if you please, Mr. Smythe."

"*I say* perticaler," retorted Mr. Smythe, " perticaler once on a time, Mrs. S."

" I wish to goodness I had been," replied the irritated lady. " What made me so blind to your defects, I can't think."

" Oh, but I can ! " said Smythe, " you had my jinture in your eye."

" Jointure—pray say jointure," cried Mrs. Smythe.

" I object, Ma'am ! " replied Smythe ; " do you think everybody learned to spell out of your dixinary ? What I mean by jinture is the ten thousand pounds I was fool enough to settle upon you when we was married."

" *We was*. Ah ! I sold myself, I own it. I sold myself for that miserable sum," said Mrs. Smythe.

" Miserable sum ! " exclaimed her husband. " Egad, do you know anybody who would buy you at half price ? "

" Brute ! " exclaimed the lady. " You will want to take me to Smithfield some day with a halter round my neck." The thought was too horrible to sustain in an upright position, and so the fair speaker threw herself upon the sofa and affected to weep.

" Mrs. Smythe," said the husband, " that's not fair of you to cry. What *is* the matter with you ? Haven't you everything you wish for ? A handsome house, splendid furniture, a footman in livery, a first-rate wehicle, besides a pony chay."

" Wehicle ! pony chay ! " groaned the lady on the sofa.

" I'm sure them's enough, considering the few wisitors we have. You won't let me see my old friends, and your old friends won't see you."

" No," exclaimed Mrs. Smythe, looking up like a tigress from her lair. " I've sacrificed them all for you ! "

" And the jinture," added Smythe. " You knowed what I was before you married me."

" No I did not ;" said the lady flatly. " You never told me you had been a footman."

" Because you only inquired whether my property was freehold or funded. I'm not ashamed of having worn plush."

" No, that is evident, quite evident," said the lady, " or you would not be continually instructing the servant in his duties."

" Well, I own that's wrong," replied Smythe ; " but when I see a fellow waiting at table as though he was lion's pro-wider in a menaggerie, my blood biles, regularly biles. You shouldn't be too hard upon me, because, you see, I've been a little took in."

"What! by me, Sir?" The tigress sat upright, as though ready for a spring.

"Well, to be plain, yes, by you," replied Smythe. "I married you to get into genteel society. You told me a great deal about your grand relations; now the only one I've seen is your brother, and the sight of him cost me five-hundred pounds."

The tigress sprang to her feet, and said, "How mean of you to mention such a trifle! Frederick, I am sure, will always consider the money as a loan."

"That's what I'm afraid of," retorted Smythe. "I'd forgive him if he'd return it. As for the rest of your family, they seem to be *non est inwentus*."

"To be what, Sir?"

"That's Latin," said Smythe, "and means they're not inwented."

"And can *you* taunt me with the desertion of my friends?" cried Mrs. Smythe, the tigress evidently let loose. "You for whom I have become thus isolated! Can *you* blame me because, in seeking to—in seeking to ——"

"To provide for your old age," said Smythe, supplying the conclusion of the sentence.

"No, Sir! In seeking to find a protector I have left myself without a friend. But that shall be remedied. I will have one conversable being about me. I intend to engage a companion!"

"Well, that's nothing to me," said Smythe; "but you ought to give her remarkable high wages."

This connubial skirmish was interrupted by the servant presenting a card to Mrs. Smythe, who instantly exclaimed with great delight, "What! my cousin Orgrave, the member for Puddleton. Tell him I'm dressing, Rusty, and will be with him directly;" and the obedient servant carried the fib to the drawing-room.

Mrs. Smythe's manner changed altogether; and, approaching her wondering husband, she purred rather than said, "Now, my dear John, will you oblige me for once in your life?"

"Well, your ciwility's so uncommon," replied Smythe, "that I will."

"There's a dear man! So now promise me that you'll stay here until my cousin Orgrave has left the house. Don't ask why, but promise me, and I know if you do so, nothing will make you break your word."

"Well; but why?" said Smythe. "Why do you wish me to be inwisible? Are you ashamed of me?"

"Ashamed of you? How can you say such a thing, dear John? No; the fact is Mr. Orgrave is notorious for his borrowing propensities; and, knowing your good nature, I would not have you led into making him advances," purred Mrs. Smythe.

"Say no more. I promise," said her cautious husband, adding, "Don't ask him to dinner, because I'm uncommon soft after wine."

"I'll dismiss him directly, my dear," replied the lady, leaving the room.

When the door was closed, Mrs. Smythe shook her closed fist at her unconscious John, and muttered between her really fine teeth, "If I can only get Orgrave to countenance me in London, I'll find some escape from this domestic purgatory."

Mr. Smythe was looking at his honest vulgar face in the glass—which wore a self-satisfied smile, as he reflected that, though his wife was a bit of a tartar, she was cousin to a member of Parliament—no small distinction in the eyes of John Smythe—when Rusty announced Mr. Oddiman, who, not doubting a favourable reception, had followed the servant into the room.

Rusty had no sooner retired, than Oddiman astonished Mr. Smythe by asking abruptly :—

"You have a visitor here, have you not?"

"Yes," replied Smythe; "my cousin Mr. Orgrave, the member for Puddleton."

"Your cousin?" asked Oddiman.

"Yes. I took him along with Mrs. Smythe. I was to find money and she was to find relations, though I've never seen this one."

"I thought not!" exclaimed Oddiman. "Are you a man of strong nerves?—no disease of the heart? Can you bear a shock?"

Smythe having assured him that he believed himself to be "a heligable life for an assurance office," Oddiman confided to him his bad opinion of Orgrave, declaring his belief that

Mrs. Smythe's cousin was not to be trusted in any man's house, and that he was the worst of robbers.

"And our plate, all new, and plenty of it," said Smythe. "Besides, there's my emerald brooch ——"

"That's not what I mean," replied Oddiman. "To abandon metaphor, Orgrave is the greatest rake about town."

"O, I can trust Mrs. Smythe," said her husband, laughing; "her natural ferocity isn't so easily subdued."

"I'm delighted to hear it," said Oddiman; "and I shall be glad to make the acquaintance of Mrs. Smythe."

"Sir, she'll be delighted to know you or anybody else," replied Smythe, "though we go to London next week; and her ladyship's on the look-out for a companion. Hark! there's the drawing-room bell. I've capital ears for bells."

And John puzzled Mr. Oddiman exceedingly, by laughing heartily at his old professional accomplishment.

As Mr. Oddiman took his way homeward after his introduction to the lady of the house, he thought that Marian Morrison would be better away from home for a time, and that it would be a capital arrangement to procure her the appointment of companion to Mrs. Smythe; and full of this idea, he walked briskly towards the little school-house of Mr. Morrison.

He had been preceded by Mr. Verdon, of whom Fanny had spoken so favourably—not too favourably, however—for Mr. Verdon was a general favourite all the country round, and as fine an example of a thorough English yeoman as you would find look England through. He had taken his old friend Mr. Morrison somewhat by surprise, in calling upon a day when the Dawley hounds were out, he being a keen sportsman and one of the boldest riders in the hunt; and this feeling was not diminished when Verdon after much hesitation, declared the object of his visit to be nothing less than to propose to become the suitor of Marian Morrison. The old schoolmaster had known Verdon from his youth upwards, and held him in great esteem, and such a proposal could not be other than most acceptable.

"Have you ever spoken to Marian?" asked Mr. Morrison.

"Never directly," replied Verdon, "but with Fanny often. She has been my counsellor, my comforter when hope would have left me."

Fanny entered the room as he spoke, and soon learned the purport of his visit, and replied in answer to her father's inquiry, that she had often spoken to Marian of Mr. Verdon, and had told her how kind, how generous he ever seemed to be, and what a happy girl she was to be esteemed by one who had the praise of all.

"Your friendship has been too liberal in its advocacy, dear Fanny," replied Verdon.

"Oh, no," said Fanny. "Have we not known each other from our childhood, and could I be silent when I learned how much you loved my sister?"

Why did Fanny sigh as she said this?

"And what has Marian said?" inquired her father.

"Little at any time, and less of late; but this is hardly fair to Marian. Mr. Verdon knows how to woo, and would not win without it."

"Indeed, I would not," answered Verdon. "Her hand must be the free-will offering of her heart, or I will be a hopeless man without it—yet I wish you to speak to her, for, should I have deceived myself, I would spare her the pain of telling me the truth."

And so it was arranged that Marian should be questioned by her father, and that Verdon should return within an hour and learn his fate in love.

"It is not without some regret that I undertake this task," said Morrison. "To ask my child to love another—to become the sharer of another home than mine—to leave me! It seems an anticipation of the grave! But he is a generous fellow."

"Oh! did you know how generous!" said Fanny, her eyes sparkling, and her cheeks glowing as she spoke. "How long he has loved Marian, and yet forborne to seek this interview, knowing how your life is bound up in your children. How he has trained his mind to the same tastes as Marian's, read the books I've told him of, studied the same subjects that we have done at home, but with a result far better, investing all things with a charm peculiarly his own."

"Hey-day, Fanny!" said Mr. Morrison, smiling, "one would think that you yourself loved Mr. Verdon."

Her father did not see how this idle speech had driven the roses from his daughter's face, and how her swelling heart almost choked the words she strove to utter.

"No, no! he is my sister's lover. I see Marian yonder in the garden, father, and here is Mr. Oddiman to keep me company while you go to her."

It was impossible for Fanny to conceal her emotion, whatever the cause, from such a quick-sighted busybody as Mr. Oddiman; and as that gentleman had just encountered Mr. Verdon in a very confused and perturbed condition, he did not hesitate to put this and that together, and say to poor Fanny—

"Ha, ha! Sly, sly, both of you, but I'm sly too. I was young myself once, but my heart was burnt to a cinder. So you won't tell me what Mr. Verdon has been here for? then I shall guess. He has been proposing to some one."

"Yes," replied Fanny, almost mechanically, "to my sister."

"To your sister!" exclaimed Oddiman, "What a monopolist that girl is! I thought it was to you."

"Oh no!" replied Fanny, sitting down quietly on a chair. "It is an old attachment, one of years. My father is with her in the garden."

"Then a word from me may perhaps clench the business;" said Oddiman; but Fanny caught his hand, saying, "Stay, I think you had better leave them together, my sister should be unbiassed in her decision;" adding after a pause, and with a deep sigh, "Should she not?"

Oddiman was bothered. Fanny's emotion perplexed him. His cognisance of Mowbray's proceedings in the morning weighed upon him like a guilty knowledge which made him *particeps criminis* against the family peace, and he could not refrain exclaiming as Morrison and Marian entered the cottage, "Well, I know all. Does she consent?"

As Mr. Oddiman was a privileged intruder, Morrison replied:—

"She asks until to-morrow to decide."

"Why until to-morrow?" said Oddiman. "The acceptance of such a suitor as Mr. Verdon should not require much consideration; unless, indeed, there is somebody else in the case. Eh, Miss Marian?"

The look which accompanied this inquiry, instantly satisfied the conscious Marian that her secret love for Mowbray was known, and she said at once, "Father, I will see Mr. Verdon to-day."

Fanny started up from her chair, but instantly recovering her self-possession, went to her sister and kissed her fervently.

"Bravo!" cried Oddiman. "Marian, you are a good, sensible, dutiful girl;" and the thought striking him at that moment, that he would pop off to Mowbray's lodgings and give him his *quietus* by letting him know Marian's decision in favour of Verdon, the well meaning busybody almost ran out of the house, doing a little unintentional mischief on his way by making one personage of our story supremely happy by the few words he uttered in passing.

That person was Verdon, who entered the little schoolroom radiant with joy and love.

"I have just seen Mr. Oddiman," he said, "and he has told me of the happiness which awaits me. Marian! dear Marian, you do not reject the love I offer you."

Marian hid her face on her sister's bosom.

"You know not," continued Verdon, "how long that love has been pent up within my heart—how it has been my torment and my joy." Each word he uttered went like fire to one listener's brain.

"Speak to me, dear Marian; confirm these blessed tidings."

Taking Marian's hand, he would have pressed it to his lips, but with a strong effort she withdrew it as Arthur Mowbray entered the room, his face like snow, his eyes like fire. He said: "It is too true what I have heard. You have deceived me."

"No, Arthur, no!" and in a moment Marian was in his arms.

"What does this mean?" asked the astonished father.

"Before you, Sir," replied Mowbray, "I feel like a guilty man. I have won your daughter's love unworthily because secretly. To-morrow would have made you acquainted with my presumption."

"Is this true, Marian?"—the daughter made no sign—no answer. "And you have deceived me—me, your doating father!" He raised his hands as he spoke, and as though some evil thought struggled for utterance, but Fanny clasped him round the neck and said, "Oh! father, judge her not too harshly. Love grows not with our will. It springs up in the heart like wayside flowers, sown by the hand of Heaven. Forgive my sister."

The appeal was not made in vain.

"My friend—Verdon—what can I say to you?" Morrison, the tears flowing from his eyes.

Verdon had hitherto remained almost motionless. He now went to Marian's side, and in a gentle voice, almost in a whisper, asked her—

"Marian, do you love him?"

"Yes," she answered. He took her hands in his, and gazing at her stedfastly for a moment, let them fall gently, and left the room.

CHAPTER III.

CONTENTMENT.

YEAR and some months had passed away, and many changes had taken place in the little town of Dawley. Mr. Oddiman had made interest with Mrs. Smythe on Fanny Morrison's behalf, and obtained for her the companion's situation with that lady; and for many months—ever since Marian's marriage with Arthur Mowbray—Fanny had been in London.

Poor Verdon had not waited to hear the wedding peal that would have told him she whom he had loved so long was lost to him for ever. No, he had gone away, none knew whither for some time, until news reached Dawley that he was in London, leading a life of reckless gaiety, seeking the foolish man's refuge from his sorrows—the short forgetfulness of dissipation.

Mowbray and his wife occupied a small cottage at the end of the village, which had recently received a new inmate, whose christening was made the occasion of a whole holiday to Mr. Morrison's scholars now, when we resume our story.

Mowbray had followed his delightful art with much success, but purchasers were few and his gains very small. He had an annuity still from Mr. Orgrave, which a less liberal hand would have found sufficient for moderate wants.

In a pretty arbour in their little garden were seated Mowbray, Marian, and her father, the rustic table furnished with two bottles of home-made wine, rosy apples, and brown-coated pears.

"Cowslip! Currant!" said Mowbray, reading the labels

upon the wine. "Is there nothing but sickly 'home-made' for our libations?"

"Contemning grandmother's wine, I declare!" exclaimed Marian, laughing as she spoke.

"The most generous draught the Dawley Arms could furnish would be unworthy the toast I give: 'Our child!'" and Arthur, as he spoke, gently put aside, almost untasted, the glass which Marian had filled for him.

"He is really serious!" said Marian, her mother's joy fading from her face.

"Not he!" replied Mr. Morrison. "The perfume of the cowslip still haunts the wine; and it was in the spring-time he first met you, Marian."

"I am an ungrateful fellow not to have remembered that;" said Mowbray, draining his glass. "Nectar! Nectar! worthy Olympian Jove!"

"Let me be Hebe, then," said Marian, "and fill your glass again, in remembrance of the absent,—dear sister Fanny. I often think she must recall her pleasant country life now that she is pent up in smoky London."

The toast was drunk; and Mr. Morrison reminding them that he had promised Fanny a letter, left the husband and wife together. Mowbray sat silently gazing upon the ground for some time, until roused by Marian offering a penny for his thoughts.

"They are yours, dearest; for I was thinking we could endure to be a little richer."

"What, again, Arthur?" said Marian, somewhat reproachfully.

"Yes!" he answered; "I blush to own that at times when I compare our lot with that of others less deserving, I think that fate has dealt somewhat hardly with us."

"How this discontented spirit grieves me," said Marian, rising and placing her arms about his neck. "We are not poor, and need not be, so long as we make our wants subservient to our means. We were not nursed in luxury ——" she paused, and then added, "I mean that I was not."

"Go on, Marian; go on," said Mowbray, "and make me own myself the ingrate that I am; but still remember that, from my earliest years, I have had scarcely a wish ungratified."

"I do not remember that!" she replied: "I know and feel what you have sacrificed for your love of me."

"Never think that, dearest! Believe that all the blessings of my life are multiplied a hundred-fold since you have shared them with me. I poor! I'll never think so again, dear wife!" rising and walking towards the cottage. "We will envy no one. My selfishness has made me forgetful and ungrateful. I would not now exchange our pretty cottage for a king's house, Marian!"

"Think what it will become, Arthur," said Marian, her face radiant with her love,—"Think! when every spot is hallowed by our children's feet, and every room has some legend of domestic joy."

"How it grows in beauty!" he continued. "What brocade, though of silk and gold, could equal those modest curtains? What perfumes vie with these fragrant flowers? Not rich with such a wife—such a clever wife, who, like a fairy, has changed almost a hovel to an Aladdin's palace! Some day you shall teach me the spell which works such wonders."

"One word declares it," replied Marian,—"Contentment."

"Contentment!" he repeated. "I'll take a walk and school myself—contentment! I'll get that word by heart; at least I'll try." So, kissing Marian's cheek, he smiled and took his way to the green lane where we first found him at his artist-work.

Marian turned thoughtfully to the little arbour, and tears trembled in her eyes. "Why do I not tell him all?" she murmured. "Did he know how much we owe to Fanny's generosity, his pride would make him more careful of our means. Dear Fanny, how many an anxious hour have you spared me!" How, we have soon to learn.

CHAPTER IV.

MEDDLING AGAIN.

SEVENTY years ago, in Dean Street, London, was a coffee-house much frequented by men about town, and many distinguished artists and writers of the day. We remember it in later times, when it had been long deserted, its hangings time-worn, and dingy with the dust of years. The spacious coffee-room had many tables, bright enough to reflect the taper brass candlestick which stood in the centre of each, supporting the smallest of dips. When we entered this old-world coffee-room, the only occupant was an enormous buck rabbit, hopping about its sanded floor, as though the ghosts of departed guests had scared away all human visitors. Seventy years ago at one of its tables sat Mr. Verdon, sleeping, a decanter partly filled with wine before him. His deep, stertorous sleep told how his waking hours had been employed, and it scarcely needed Weazle's story to Mr. Oddiman, as they sat in a distant corner of the room, to tell how Verdon's life was being wasted.

"There is not a place of riot in this great London where Mr. Verdon is not known," whispered Weazle. "I found him at a faro table, in the neighbourhood of Ranelagh, followed him to this tavern, and took up my abode here as you desired me."

"Weazle, you're a treasure," said Oddiman. "I believe you would find out the longitude of a lawyer's conscience, if it had any. Have you delivered my letter to Mrs. Smythe?"

"I have, Sir," replied Weazle; "and I hear Mr. Orgrave dines there frequently."

"That's my doings," said Oddiman, his face beaming with satisfaction. "Arthur Mowbray desires to keep his marriage a secret from Mr. Orgrave. Why? I guess why, and introduced Fanny Morrison to Mrs. Smythe, in order that Orgrave may see and admire her, and so more readily excuse his cousin's marriage with her counterpart. That is what I call diplomacy."

"And so do I," replied Weazle; "for you seem to have made a terrible mess of what was a very plain case before."

"What do you mean by a mess, Sir?" exclaimed Oddiman, in a great pet.

Weazle did not care for his anger a jot, and so went on.

"I mean simply this, Sir. Mr. Mowbray's sole motive in concealing his marriage is to avoid persons for whom he has no regard, and whose curiosity might induce them to visit him."

"I don't believe it. He is dependent on Mr. Orgrave. He fears his displeasure."

"I don't believe that," said Weazle; "but let that be as it may, there's worse mischief done."

"What, you old owl?" asked Oddiman. "Speak, and don't look so mysterious."

"Then Mrs. Smythe's house is not a fit place for Miss Morrison," replied Weazle, in the most remorseless manner.

Oddiman started back, and fairly gasped for a few moments. He then said—

"That's false, Weazle, emphatically false."

"It's not, Sir," replied the unflinching servitor. "Miss Fanny is likely to suffer in reputation; and, in fact, you have made another mess of it, I'm certain."

Oddiman almost wept, for he had great faith in Weazle's opinions and honesty.

"What an unhappy goose I am," he said, "I did it with best intentions. I do believe I broke Verdon's heart by giving him a dose of hope by mistake when I ought to have administered nothing but despair. What shall I do, Weazle?"

"Take the girl away at once! Mrs. Smythe, in her desire to get into society, has made the acquaintance of people of very doubtful character; and, mark me, if Mr. Orgrave meets Miss Morrison, you will regret it," said the comforting Weazle.

"She must be got away, that's certain. Her father shall write to her directly. Book me a place in the coach to-night. I'll go home. I wish I could mind my own business; it would be so much better for me, wouldn't it, Weazle?" said poor Oddiman.

"Yes, Sir, and for other people also," replied the scarifier. "I've told you so a hundred times. You had better remain here, Sir, whilst I go and make preparations for taking you into the country;" and Oddiman felt someway comforted when he saw the back of his very faithful servant.

Poor Oddiman; he saw that he had been making good and bad matters worse by his meddling. He would not willingly have harmed a fly, and now he thought he was crushing his fellow creatures in swarms, from the very best intentions. He was constitutionally meddlesome, and couldn't help it. And so he set himself to work to devise some plan for the rescue of Verdon, who now gave indications of awaking.

"Poor fellow," thought Oddiman. "Never came home until three to-day. Out all night, I hear. Gone to sleep in his chair, having attempted vainly to keep himself awake by drinking brandy."

As these reflections passed through the old gentleman's mind, a waiter went to Verdon and roused him from his heavy slumber.

"Well! what's the matter?" said he, scarcely conscious. "More brandy, Robert!"

"Not at present, Sir," replied the waiter. "'Tis near four o'clock, and you are engaged out to dinner at five."

"Where? I forget where," said the half-drunken man.

"In Wimpole Street, at Mrs. Smythe's. You promised Captain Fowler to call for him, and told me to remind you of it," answered the waiter.

"Did I? Well, if I have promised, put out my things to dress. There is some brandy left, is there not?"

"Really, Sir," said the waiter, hesitating, "don't you think ——"

"Give it!" said Verdon, in a loud voice. "I am capable of regulating my own actions. Now leave me." With a shaking hand the glass was filled, but before he could raise it to his lips, Mr. Oddiman had addressed him by name.

Verdon put down the glass; and, muddled as he was,

instantly recognised his old friend, and held out his hand, saying,—

"And what brings you to London?"

"I've the misfortune to be an executor to a deceased brother-in-law, an attorney. To-morrow, I am going back to Dawley. You remember Dawley?" asked Oddiman.

"Why should I have forgotten it, Sir?"

"Well—why—it is so long since we have seen you there, and you have been so much in the gay world," said Oddiman.

"You have heard that at Dawley, have you?" asked Verdon, with a tipsy sneer. "Well, Sir, and what do they say to it? Some, I suppose, prophecy my ruin, and compute the bargains they may get in my broad acres. Some, I suppose, laugh at me for a fool, who had his heart broken for the love of a coquette; or, am I, like better men, forgotten by all who used to call me friend?"

"Indeed, Sir, you do the lady an injustice."

"What lady?" said Verdon, fiercely. "Mrs. Mowbray? I can speak her name—I have heard it too often, sleeping and waking, in the midst of riot, in the silence of a sick man's room. May she be happy, is all my prayer!"

"I am sure it is! I am sure it is!" acquiesced Oddiman, "and for yourself ——"

"For myself," interrupted Verdon, "there is nothing but forgetfulness! I seek it everywhere, and sometimes find it; sometimes among the base I strive to forget her excellence! Sometimes with wine, though that betrays me now and then, and makes my misery madness." He leaned his head upon the table and sobbed audibly.

"Of course! of course!" said Oddiman, consolingly. "Now, my dear friend, listen to a little good advice. Give up this rackety life. You are killing yourself by inches, and cheating the coroner. You'll die, Sir—you'll die very soon."

"Is there nothing to be feared worse than death?" asked Verdon, raising his bleared eyes to Oddiman's face.

"Yes!" answered he, emphatically. "Yes! strait waistcoats, and you will be wearing one. Now be persuaded by me, let me take you a place in the mail this very night; go down amongst neighbours and friends ——"

"To be the laughing-stock of all!" interrupted Verdon; "to have my heart wrung and wrung again by every scene I looked on! To think that here I have listened to her voice

—here watched for the first sight of her. Man! man! you know not what you do when you talk thus to me!"—and he walked about the room with his head thrown back, and his face buried in his hands.

Oddiman became alarmed at the effect of his eloquence, and said: "Oh! Mr. Verdon, don't go on so. If you knew how you were loved and pitied!"

"Pitied!" cried Verdon, striding up to his would-be comforter. "Pitied! Here I can escape that humiliation. In the world of pleasure, who cares if you have griefs so that you wear a mask of happiness? Add but your share of mirth unto the present, your past or future is alike unheeded. Henceforth be that my world. My heart shall ache no more;" and with a player's strut he left the room.

"Oh! good gracious!" sighed Oddiman. "Now I've set him off worse than ever! He'll go and drink a quantity of wine, get taken up by the watch, and have no one to bail him. I won't go by the mail to-night. Oh! if I could but mind my own business. But I can't! I can't!" So paying his bill, and bribing the waiter to keep a careful watch for the next four-and-twenty hours on Mr. Verdon, the miserable goodhearted meddler went in pursuit of Weazle.

CHAPTER V.

MR. SMYTHE'S NATURAL ELEMENT.

MRS. SMYTHE had secured for the London season a ready-furnished house in Wimpole Street, and had gathered about her, by the assistance of Mr. Orgrave, a very shady set of people, whose reputations, although not decidedly bad, were of such an equivocal character as to approximate very closely to it.

Fanny Morrison was herself too innocent to discern the true position of those who formed the general society at Mrs. Smythe's table; and Mr. Smythe, who had really good instincts, was too ignorant and ill-bred to detect the true metal from the false. He had been absent from home for some days, and was not expected to return until the ensuing week; and Mrs. Smythe had sought to relieve her solitude by giving profuse dinners, little suppers, and card parties. To more than one of these gatherings, Verdon had been invited through the introduction of a Captain Fowler, a man about town, and supposed to be on half-pay. He had a vulgar, brazen woman for a wife, who might have been anything down to a camp follower. He never presented her.

Fanny was sitting in her own room, when the parlour maid knocked at the door, and afterwards announced that Miss Morrison's company was requested in the drawing-room after dinner, adding,—

"Ah, Miss, anybody but me would wonder why you should sit moping in your own room instead of going to the gentry down-stairs; but I don't, our visitors ain't the sort of people for you—they're a queer lot, depend upon it."

"Hush, Jane!" said Fanny, checking this criticism of Mrs. Smythe's friends.

"Why should I hush, Miss?" asked Jane. "I gave warning a month ago, and my time's up to-morrow. The servant next door tells me we're the talk of the neighbourhood; and if I were you, I'd give warning too. Character's everything to a poor girl, and I suppose you young ladies can't do without it?"

"To speak the truth, Jane," replied Fanny, greatly moved by what she had just heard, "I am not happy here; your kindness has been a great comfort to me, I assure you. I have had strong reasons—very strong reasons—for continuing here."

"So I should think," said Jane, "or you never could put up with Mrs. Smythe's bounce. I couldn't, so I gave a month. See what a lot is dining down-stairs!"

"We are not to judge of what Mrs. Smythe pleases to consider right," said Fanny, holding up her hand reprovingly. "Will you be kind enough to have this letter posted to-night? Be careful, for it contains a bank-note."

"Ah, Miss, that's it!" observed the humble friend. "Whenever I see these letters to Mrs. Mowbray—these, I mean with money in them—I always says to myself, that's why Miss Morrison stands it; she has somebody as wants her assistance, and ——"

"Quite true, Jane," interrupted Fanny. "It is for the sake of others that I have remained here; but in a very short time I hope to be able to return to my own dear, quiet home." She did not dare to trust her thoughts in that direction, and so she went at once to the drawing-room.

She seated herself at a harpsichord, and played a familiar air: her heart would guide her fingers, and in a few moments the faces she loved the most, looked at her from the music page. She was roused from her happy reverie by Mr. Orgrave, who had entered the room unknown to her.

"Pray play on, Madam!" he said; and Fanny, blushing, rose in some trepidation. "Nay, I must retire if you consider my presence objectionable; but our friends below are getting too boisterous for my weak nerves."

Fanny said something about the absence of Mrs. Smythe, for Orgrave's bold *roué* gaze confused her.

"She will be here shortly," he replied; "though it is a great relief to have the advantage of Mrs. Smythe's absence occasionally. I am sure you must find that vain and foolish woman a bore now and then."

"Mrs. Smythe is my employer," said Fanny, with a frown, anxious to close the conversation. But Orgrave was not easily abashed or silenced, and so he answered,—

"More shame of Fortune to make her so! How can you waste your attractions—your accomplishments, on such a woman as Mrs. Smythe, when this drudgery might be exchanged for a life of ease and elegance?"

There are some words better unspoken, some evil thoughts and deeds better unrecorded, and those by which Orgrave offended Fanny's modest nature among the number.

"At length I guess your meaning, Sir," she said. "I should have thought my position would have protected me from insult."

"Nay, Madam, stay!"

"Not a moment, Sir. This is the last time I will ever exchange a word with you!" and with all the tragic grace of an insulted woman, she passed by Orgrave and left the room.

Orgrave looked in the glass, arranged his wig and steinkirk, and muttering—"Mrs. Smythe was deceived," made a horrible grimace, and returned to the party in the dining-room.

The candles up-stairs had been lighted some time, but the ladies had not thought fit to leave the dinner-table, when Mr. Smythe, unobserved by any of his household, stood, calise in hand, reflected in the pier-glass in his drawing-room.

"Well!" he said, half aloud. "Well! I suppose I am at home, though it seems that one of the 'Rabian Nights' Entertainments was going on here. I thought the house was a-fire from the outside. It's very lucky I'm not above going down a arey, or I mightn't have got in. I might have walked off with the plate basket if I'd been in that line, and it hadn't been my own property. I suppose I may take the liberty of ringing the bell, if it's only to find out if I am master!" Suiting the action to the word, he startled Rusty, in his pantry, then finishing some of the "bottoms" of Mr. Smythe's choice old Parson's port.

"I never heard missus and the ladies go up-stairs," he thought, as he hopped up two steps at a time, so vigorous had been Mr. Smythe's tug at the bell-rope.

Rusty could scarcely believe his eyes when he saw his master.

"What! you here, Sir."

"Yes!" answered Smythe; "I'm here without an invitation.—What's going on below?"

"Missus has got a dinner party," answered Rusty, smiling, as he always enjoyed the family battles, and he knew this event would be considered a *casus belli.*

"There's six on 'em! Sir—Mrs. Grasper, Mrs. Tricksey, Mr. Orgrave ——"

"Mr. Orgrave!" cried Smythe. "Well, that is cool, considering that a week ago I opened the door to him myself, and told him I was not at home. If that wasn't a dead cut I should like to know what is; who else is there?"

"There's Mr. Verdon, a friend of Captain Fowler."

"Oh! he brings a friend, does he? I suppose he'll be billeting his troop, if he's got one, on us next. They've been working the wine pretty well."

"Yes, Sir, they has," said Rusty, with great glee; "four of champagne, three of hock, and they've just got their second magnum of port."

"There, that'll do!" said Smythe, fearing to hear any further particulars, "there's the ladies coming up—take them things to my dressing-room, and don't say I'm here. I must put a stopper to those goings on."

The ladies were so much amused by something they had heard at parting, and laughed so violently, that they neither saw nor heard Mr. Smythe, until Mrs. Smythe having declared Cousin Orgrave was a very dangerous fellow, the whole party were astounded by the appearance of the master of the house in the midst of them.

"A very dangerous fellow, ladies; but you like him all the better for that!"

"Why, Mr. Smythe?" said his wife, as soon as she could speak; "I did not know you had returned."

"I didn't suppose you did, and it looks werry like an unexpected pleasure," he replied. "It's as well I did return, seeing what is going on here."

"What is going on, Sir? I have a party!"

"Five parties, you mean, and one party that I particularly requested you to cut—Mr. Orgrave. Besides, these good ladies," he continued—turning to Mrs. Grasper, and her friend Mrs. Tricksey—"these good ladies have been here quite often enough."

The persons addressed were so astounded that the powder left their heads in little clouds.

"Mr. Smythe!" exclaimed his wife, "how can you proceed in this way before my friends?"

"Because I won't say nothing behind their backs I won't say to their faces. I want 'em to understand that I don't want 'em here."

It required all Mrs. Smythe's persuasive eloquence to soothe her irritated friends, and induce them to remain; assuring them that she would not have invited them, had she anticipated her husband would have been present.

"Well, that's a compliment to my respectability, and I thank you for it!" bawled out the plain-spoken Smythe, and then adding in a quieter tone, "I suppose all this comes out of your jinture?—because I'm not going to make a set of people conwivial for whom I don't care a button!"

"I shall not condescend to answer you," replied the indignant lady. "I suppose you will show some respect for the decencies of society, and meet our guests at least with the appearance of a gentleman!"

"Oh! you want me to dress, do you?" asked Smythe. "I suppose the dinner would disagree with them unless I waited on 'em in my best clothes? Werry well—just ring the bell, my dear, and tell Rusty to bring me up some hot water."

There was a wicked smile on John Smythe's face, as he left the room, that boded no good to somebody.

Mrs. Smythe had to endure the condolence of her friends at being allied to such a brute, and the only extenuation she offered for her folly in marrying him, was a certain parchment which secured to her ten thousand pounds.

The gentlemen now joined the party up-stairs. They were all more or less flushed with the wine they had drunk: Verdon the most, for his previous debauch. Fanny, who had been summoned again to the drawing-room, did not recognise him at first, and when she did so, her fingers almost refused to do their office at the harpsichord.

"How changed! how changed!" she thought. "How strong must have been the love that could so revenge itself."

Fortunately, none heeded her playing, and so her faulty performance was of no moment. It was well that it was so, for her mind was occupied by thoughts of Verdon, and her fingers at times strayed over the keys at random.

Two of the ladies, with Fowler and Verdon, were seated at cards, while Mrs. Smythe and Orgrave engaged in conversation. The latter were sufficiently near to Fanny, and spoke so loudly that she must have heard much that they said, had her mind been less occupied. One speech of Orgrave's did reach her ears, and startled her by its reference to herself.

"A schoolman at Cambridge's daughter!" said Orgrave, repeating something he had just been told; "then she knows the world only from books? I thought so from a tragedy speech she made to me just now. She seems to be rather struck with that sot Verdon."

Fanny's heart almost stopped, from a vague fear of danger to herself, and the knowledge of what Verdon had become.

"Does he deserve that name," she thought, as her earliest playmate stood before her mental vision in all the brightness of his glad boyhood and the nobleness of his young manhood. Her reverie was to be rudely broken; for Verdon, overpowered by the heat and the wine he had taken, rose and staggered from the room a drunken man, the loud laughter of his recent friends ringing in his ears as he went out into the street.

In a few minutes afterwards, Fanny, closely muffled, was on her way to Mr. Oddiman's lodgings.

Mrs. Smythe was invited to take the vacant hand.

"One moment," she said, "I must see where my bear of a husband is."

Her anxiety was instantly relieved, for that somewhat eccentric gentleman "put in an appearance," dressed in a full suit of his own livery.

"Here I am?" he exclaimed, "at yours and the company's service."

"You wretch!" screamed his wife; "you're in livery!"

"My natural element, as I call it," replied Smythe. "I seem to occupy such a rum position in this house that I thought I'd dress according. Is there anything I can do for anybody? Oh! nothing?" continued Smythe, not the least disturbed by the general silence, "you don't mind eating the footman's dinners and drinking the footman's wine, but you're ashamed to own the crystal."

"The what?" asked Orgrave, in surprise.

"The crystal when he's not a butterfly," replied Smythe.

"Ignorant booby," said Orgrave, turning to Mrs. Smythe,

"good-evening, my dear cousin;" and he left the room, followed by Fowler and the ladies.

Mrs. Smythe was a limited Pythoness. She could, with the greatest pleasure, have shaken her low-minded husband out of his livery.

"What am I to understand by this? Why am I to be thus degraded? How dare you appear in that odious dress?"

"To remind you, Ma'am," he replied coolly, provokingly cool, "that I ain't forgotten what I was, if you have. I ain't going to be ruined because you want to play the fine lady. You've heard of people standing in white sheets with candles in their hands. Now, once a quarter I mean to appear in full livery."

"You do?" screamed the lady.

"I do, in full canonicals, as a sort of penance."

Mrs. Smythe did not wait for the concluding insult, but said—

"Then from this hour we live apart."

"Well," said Smythe, when his lady had left him to his own reflection, "live apart? Well, upon mature reflection, I don't think that's an event that will send me to an early grave."

Mr. Smythe then went to the dining-room, and having satisfied himself that Rusty had deposited the remainders in the sideboard, retired to rest.

CHAPTER VI.

RECLAMATION.

R. ODDIMAN, perhaps fortunately, was not at home when Fanny reached his lodgings, but the invaluable Weazle no sooner heard her story than he set out for the Dean Street coffee-house, accompanied by Fanny. Verdon had already arrived, and was in a small room adjoining the coffee-room—Weazle guessed how occupied, and so he asked the mistress of the house to receive his fair companion for a short time. The landlady was a tender-hearted woman, and seeing at once poor Fanny's distress, induced her by a few womanly words to tell her the cause of her sorrow.

Weazle had been welcomed by the more than half-drunken Verdon, who had had recourse to his treacherous ally, strong maddening drink.

"And so," he said, "you mean to stay with me, eh? and not leave me to the consolation of brandy and the society of some night-house."

"Even so, Sir; I wish to save you from a morning of self-condemnation," replied Weazle.

Verdon repeated the words "self-condemnation;" and then added, "as though more brandy would not drown conscience? No matter, 'twas kindly meant, very kindly." As Verdon raised the glass of steaming punch to his lips, Weazle laid his hand gently upon the toper's arm, and said—

"Nay, Mr. Verdon, no more."

The action incensed Verdon greatly, and he exclaimed

with tipsy ferocity, "Take away your hand—no man controls my actions." He drained the glass; and, Weazle, thinking it useless to let Fanny see him in this painful condition, rose to take his departure.

Verdon, however, seized his arm, and said, "No! no! you shall not go; sit down five minutes, till the bowl is finished, it is long since I have seen a Dawley man." Then, turning away his bleared and drowsy eyes, he seemed to reflect for a few moments. "Ah!" he said, with a deep sigh, "I often fancy I am walking the old stubbles with brave old Ponto—man never shot to a better dog. There he is at my feet, looking up into my face, and beating the ground with his tail. Good dog! good dog!" He sat a few moments waving his head to and fro, one of life's saddest sights—a self-made idiot.

"Ah! Sir," Weazle said at length, "it would do many a heart good to have you at Dawley again."

"And they shall see me there again, but not yet—not yet! I'll be as I have been, the first in the field. Why should I not? I can hunt hounds as well as ride to them! I know the cry of every hound in the pack, in cover or out. Hark, to him! that's old Rattler's challenge! View the varmint steal away! The hounds come streaming from the wood, some topping the hedge, others creeping through gaps and holes! Yoicks! Yoicks! The best place to the best man!" and waving his hand above his head, poor Verdon led the chase again.

"Old scenes, old friends," thought Weazle, "may have yet a hold upon him. Miss Fanny was right—I will bring her to him;" and, unnoticed by Verdon, he left the room.

Pushing aside the bowl and glass, Verdon rested his head between his hands and seemed lost in thought.

"Go home again," he muttered. "Why not?—why should a faithless woman make me an outcast? Go home?—Never!—Never! Better the madness of the gaming-house, the hell of drinking, than that! than that! It will soon end."

Weazle had returned silently with Fanny, who closed her eyes and clung to her companion's arm, the moment she saw the wreck before her.

"You are alarmed?" said Weazle.

"No;" she replied, "but I was not prepared for this—he must be rescued—speak to him."

Weazle obeyed her by telling him there was another friend from Dawley.

"He's welcome too!" Verdon replied, but when his eyes fell on Fanny's face, he started, and then stared at her vacantly.

"Mr. Verdon," she said, "no doubt you are surprised to see me here, and at such a time. Do you not know me?"

"Yes, I know you," he answered, covering his face with his hands, and resting his head upon the table.

"You once called me your friend—your almost sister. May I still speak to you fearlessly, truly, as I have before spoken?"

Verdon muttered "Yes," without raising his head.

"You once loved my sister, Verdon."

"Once, ay once! and who believed it?"

"I did!" replied Fanny, "You would then have died to prove that love."

"I *am* dying," cried Verdon, still with his face hidden on his hands, and his head bowed down, "I am dying, and how? Ah! how?"

"Then, Verdon, to have saved her but a moment's pain what would you not have done? But now each day you show yourself regardless of her peace, and strive by acts, unworthy of yourself, to wound her gentle spirit."

"Not so!" cried Verdon, looking up at last—"Fanny, not so! I have debased myself that she should think I was never worthy of her love, and so saved her from the self-reproach she must otherwise have felt, for she did love me once; *you* know that!"

"I once believed so!" replied Fanny, blushing deeply as she added, "I now know we were deceived. Oh, Verdon, did you know all—as one day you may, you would forgive me for so misleading you. Oh, spare me! spare my sister the dreadful thought that we have been your ruin. Come home again. Resume your place among those who honour you."

"No more, Fanny," he answered, "leave me; I am not worth your thought or care. Deceived by my hopes, I have played the coward and fled to excess, when I should have borne with patience! Oh, so debased, how dare I claim my place again!"

"Think only of the past as of some disease which robbed you for a time of reason—the delirium over, recovery will be speedy—Verdon, there are a thousand means to work your cure!" and Fanny, made bold by her holy purpose, took Verdon's feverish hand.

"I know of none," he said.

"None? Are there no poor, with pinching wants, to seek and succour? No ignorant to teach? No kindly offices to be done between friend and friend?"

"But I have lost all right to such high duties!" replied Verdon, with tears upon his cheeks. "Who would not taunt me with my vices, and call me hypocrite?"

"None, Verdon, none!" urged Fanny. "Go home again, and redeem the loss both rich and poor sustained when your dear father died. Let not the loiterers in our churchyard say, when standing by your parents' grave, their son despised the legacy they left him in their virtues."

"I would! I would! but it is too late! too late!"

"Never too late to quit an evil course, to seek the good and find it!"

Verdon clasped the speaker's hand between his own, and pressed it to his burning lips.

"You will return?" she said. "You will."

"I will! I will! Fanny, you have saved the prodigal!" and, clinging to her as though she were his better angel, he would not let her go until sleep overpowered him.

CHAPTER VII.

THE RETURN HOME.

OWARDS the close of a calm summer's evening, two riders, master and man servant, mounted the hill that overlooked the village of Dawley. No sooner had the former caught sight of the grey church tower embedded in the midst of a grove of fine old elms, about whose tops the rooks kept constant motion, than he stopped his impatient horse, and for a few minutes shaded his eyes with his hand.

"I cannot go on," said Verdon, for it was he, dismounting at the little inn which stood midway down the hill. When in the parlour he wrote a few lines on a leaf of his note-book, and dispatched them to Mr. Oddiman.

The landlady had instantly recognised Verdon, changed as he was by the dissipation of the last few months, but learning that he wished to remain undisturbed and unrecognised for a short time, she respectfully curtsied and left him alone.

Verdon could see his own home from the bow-window of the inn, and he was moved almost to tears.

"Only two years! only two years!" he thought. "No more have passed since I was honoured, if not loved, by rich and poor, and now I fear to enter my own home lest the spirits of the dead should rise up and upbraid me with my folly, my shame."

He turned away from the window as though he could not pursue the train of thought which led him to the past. "I think I should never have returned here but for Fanny—dear, noble girl; but when she spoke to me, my happier life appeared to come again, and made me loathe the guilty present."

He was roused by the noise of wheels, followed by Oddiman's voice, and the entrance of the good old busybody.

"How kind of you to come to me at once. The morning would have been time enough," said Verdon.

"Couldn't help it," replied Oddiman; "I knew it was no use going to bed without seeing you. I should have lain awake all night, kicking off the clothes, wondering what you had to say to me, and why you had halted here when the door of the old hall is gaping to receive you, and my little house is cracking its walls with vexation, that you didn't think it worthy to receive you and your valise."

"I am sure I should have been welcomed," said Verdon, shaking Oddiman warmly by the hand; "but,—you will laugh at me perhaps,—when the old church appeared in sight, the recollections of my follies made me sick at heart, and I had not courage to go on. Mr. Oddiman, when last we met, I treated you somewhat rudely."

"No, no! not for a man who had breakfasted upon brandy!" observed Oddiman, smiling.

"You must forgive me, Sir, I was then a fool—a madman!" said Verdon.

"Not quite so bad as that," replied Oddiman, "though with a little perseverance there is no knowing what you might have become. But no man is wise at all times, and it gives me great pleasure to think that I have been the humble means of bringing you to your senses."

"It is not to you, my dear friend, that I owe my deliverance," answered Verdon, "it is to Fanny Morrison. She sought me out when many would have shunned me; but, strong in her own purity, she feared not for herself. She only saw in the degraded man, the once honoured friend and playmate of her childhood. When I reflect upon the past, I hate myself. What must that gentle girl believe me?—and what others also? But I have come to make atonement. You told me, as Fanny did also, that Mrs. Mowbray had been made unhappy by my conduct. You must obtain permission for me to visit her. I know not why, but, since the recovery of my reason, I feel as though my love for her had gone, and that I can meet her again without emotion."

"So much the better," said Oddiman. "We're all alike. Twenty years ago I had the love-fever myself; couldn't eat, lost flesh till my bones rattled in my clothes like dominoes in a bag. The flame within me produced a settled thirst, I drank to allay it, and I am sorry to say gave the watch and the justices a great deal of trouble, for which I humbly beg their pardon. You see I am now hale, merry, and heart-whole; you'll be the same. But tell me, Verdon—did you meet Fanny at Mrs. Smythe's?"

"No, thank heaven!" said Verdon, with great earnestness, "not at that wicked woman's house. Dear Fanny, I should not have had courage to see her again, even had I known where to find her."

"Why, at Mrs. Smythe's, in Wimpole Street," gasped Oddiman. "I sent her there as a companion."

"You alarm me!" cried Verdon. "That is no place for Fanny Morrison. She must return home instantly. To-morrow I will care for that."

"Bless you, Mr. Verdon, bless you! I suspect I have made another unintentional mess of it. Get me out of this difficulty, and I will reform; I will mind my own business. For three days I have lived upon suction. If you are a guilty creature, what am I? You were only ruining yourself, now I am ruining all my friends and their relations. Not a word to Weazle, if you please. What a ride home I should have if he knew all. You go to the old hall to-night?"

"Yes," replied Verdon, "and will call upon you early in the morning."

When Oddiman had departed, Verdon's thoughts returned to Fanny instantly. "She the companion of that woman! To have been a witness, perhaps, of that disgraceful brawl; and yet to seek me out. It seems as though Providence had linked our fates together, and she should be my better angel —'Your friend and comforter;' yes, those were her words. Strange that I should remember them, yet they are ever sounding in my ears like pleasant music."

As soon as the night had come, Verdon returned to his long deserted home. Let none disturb the loneliness of his chamber, nor the meditations of a repentant man.

CHAPTER VIII.

MR. SMYTHE'S NEWS.

TWO empty egg-shells, the well-picked bone of a mutton cutlet, and an empty silver tankard, declared that Mr. Oddiman had made an excellent breakfast, without reckoning the cup of bohea now steaming before him.

"That is the first meal I have made these three days—ever since my return from London," said Oddiman to his faithful Weazle. "Why old lawyer Crimpem should have made me his executor, I am at a loss to guess."

"Because he was your brother-in-law, Sir, and knew how partial you are to meddle in other people's business."

"Weazle!" said his master, "that is unkind, very unkind. You know the state of mind I am in consequent upon Miss Morrison's position. You know I have tried for these three days to muster up courage to see her father, and now when I was recovering my equanimity a very little, you knock me down like a nine-pin. You know my moral corn, and like a tight shoe, will pinch me. I was about to confide to you a great secret, Weazle, something concerning that packet of Crimpem's which you gave me the other morning, but I'll be silent."

"As you please, Sir," said Weazle, "I hate secrets."

As he finished speaking, the down mail from London stopped opposite the garden gate and deposited no other than Mr. John Smythe and his very limited valise.

"Good gracious!" cried Oddiman, "what's the meaning of this? Why has he come here? House on fire, perhaps, and everybody burned."

"Well, matters was not quite so bad as that," Mr. Smythe said, "though two things have brought him down, first my own business, and second somebody else's."

Oddiman foreboded mischief.

"First my own," continued Mr. Smythe; "I followed your advice, I sneaked into the house, and blowed up all the women."

Weazle looked significantly at his master, who blushed up to his wig.

"I put on my old livery and came down among them, like King Log in the fable-books. It settled Mrs. Smythe."

"Settled her? What do you mean?" asked Oddiman, aghast.

"Oh, it's not manslaughter!" replied Smythe, laughing, "but I've lost my encumbrance. We're separated. I'm now a sort of pinchbeck widower. It's true I can't marry again, and I'm very glad of it."

Weazle looked at his master once more, but the old busybody only frowned, and inquired what had brought Smythe to Dawley.

"Why, you see," he replied, "as Mrs. S. only married me for what she could get, I know she will get as much as she can. Now there's a good many moveables about our country house, and she's been a little too sharp for me in London. The silver tea-service has wanished, and I hadn't time to count the spoons. I shouldn't have done it but for you, though; Mrs. S.'s friends was queer 'uns—werry queer 'uns."

"Why, surely, no one could be injured by Mrs. Smythe's friends?" asked Oddiman, more alarmed for Fanny.

"I don't know," replied Smythe. "Judging by the change which has took place in myself, I think evil communications does corrupt good manners; and—if I hadn't nigh forgot it!—Miss Morrison's bolted with that rake-helly fellow, Mr. Orgrave."

Poor Oddiman staggered to a chair, and could only exclaim "Impossible!"

"Not with a woman!—nothing's unpossible with them," rejoined Smythe. "I heard him tell her our house wasn't worthy to hold such a angel—I heard ——"

"Then why didn't you knock him down?" exclaimed Oddiman.

"Thank you," said Smythe. "I once got such a thrashing from a coal-heaver that I've forswore the noble art of self-defence ever since. Yes—she left us; and as you placed her with my good lady, I thought it right to let you know how Miss had behaved."

"Oh, what a meddling ass I am!" exclaimed Oddiman. "What a load of misery I have harnessed to myself! but I'll bear my burthen patiently. I'll go to Mr. Morrison, though he'll look upon me as the destroyer of his child, and curse me accordingly. But I'll go—I'll go!"

"Do so, Sir," said Weazle; "but assure him of Miss Fanny's innocence—I'll be bail for that."

"I never felt so wretched in my life," remarked Oddiman, despondingly. "May I ask your company, Mr. Smythe, as far as Mr. Morrison's?"

"Why, I think I'd rather not," replied Smythe. "I want to get on to my place, and Mr. Veazle's used to your lamentations."

So master and man set forth at once on their melancholy mission, whilst Smythe regarded them with evident satisfaction at the course he had taken.

"I daresay," he thought; "I was not going to walk a mile and a half with that walley o' tears. When some people are miserable, they're never happy except in company. Now, when I'm in the dumps, I hate to have anybody a-nigh me. I always takes a corkscrew and shuts myself in the wine-cellar."

CHAPTER IX.

"I SHALL 'MIND MY OWN BUSINESS.'"

RTHUR MOWBRAY'S was the most perfect of cottages. His own good taste had helped to make it so, and Marian's busy fingers had completed the rest.

She was now at work at some embroidery, for which it was difficult to assign a use in the lowly home she occupied. Fletcher, a faithful servant of her husband's family, had just returned from a visit to Dawley, where she had been to pay certain tradesmen's bills, and one bright guinea lay upon the table.

"Well, Fletcher, all paid at last, I suppose," said Marian, "and this is all that is left of dear Fanny's ten-pound note— Forty pounds? Yes, forty pounds I owe her."

"Ah! Madam," remarked Fletcher, "I am sure my dear master would be grieved at heart did he know the sacrifices which are made for him. He will never forgive me when he knows all, as he must do some day."

"But he must not know," replied Marian, smiling as she spoke. "He is progressing so rapidly in his art that he will soon realise large sums for his pictures."

Arthur's cheery voice was heard singing in the garden; and, in a minute after, Marian was in his arms. He had been away on a sketching tour, and had returned. he said, with a score of scenes, so that she would praise his industry, if not his progress. When she had relieved him of his knapsack and sketching-stool, he took her face between his hands with the intent to kiss her for her attention, but as the light fell upon it, he started and exclaimed, "Marian! dear girl, what has happened? You are not looking well; not half so well as when I left you!"

"Oh, indeed I am; but the pleasure of seeing you has agitated me," replied the wife.

"No; you look careworn. Fletcher, tell me," said Mowbray. "You will not conceal anything from me?"

"Oh, Sir! Oh, Madam! I must speak," replied the one so appealed to. "When you are away, she slaves and slaves until her health is failing; denies herself the commonest needful things, to make your means sufficient for the luxuries she thinks necessary to you. This embroidery is the work of hours that should have been given to sleep. Miss Fanny, too, has often sent her money."

"Fanny!" exclaimed Mowbray, his face reddening as he spoke. "Oh, my dear wife, to what humiliation has my thoughtlessness exposed you?"

"No, no," said Marian, "nurse has over-stated all."

"Marian," replied her husband, "I read the confirmation of her story in your face. But this shall end. What your love has purchased for me shall be treasured in my heart for ever, but henceforth I will be prodigal no more!" and so, both thanking the good and faithful servant who had restored confidence between them, they went forth into the garden to talk over their plans for the future.

That evening, when seated side by side, examining the sketches Arthur had brought home, a knock was heard as though given by a feeble hand—Marian went to the door, and on opening it received in her arms her fainting sister, Fanny. Meanly dressed, travel-stained, and wearied to exhaustion, she hardly recognised the one she loved so dearly, and whose name but now had been upon her tongue.

As soon as Fanny was restored, and able to converse, she told the story of wrongs suffered, and of perils braved and overcome.

She told of Orgrave's wicked wooing as already known to us; but by Mrs. Smythe's connivance more cruelly pursued. How, fearing to remain, she had sought protection with Fowler's wife, but found her more depraved, and only escaped insult by the aid of the servant Jane, who had lent her money and clothes, the better to avoid pursuit. How she had travelled on foot, and, by the aid of the carrier's waggon, down to her native Dawley, where she hoped to wear out her life.

"My trials," she said, in reply to her sister's recognition of the good she had conferred on her, "my trials have not been without their recompense, I feel I have rescued one from a mistaken course, whose welfare should be dear to all, Mr. Verdon."

"Have you seen him?" asked Marian, eagerly.

"Yes, designing men for their own bad purposes had drawn him into great excesses," replied her sister. "It was my happy lot to save him. That thought is now my greatest happiness. In the midst of riot he listened to my voice. At my bidding he left his evil course, and when I told him how much there was for noble minds to strive for, how much for gentle natures to love and foster, he pressed my hand to his lips and blessed me. Oh! Marian! to have saved him from ruin is to have earned the right to be most happy!" Her face grew radiant as she spoke, and her large dark eyes glistened with tears.

No wonder that Marian said, "Fanny, you love him! You have loved him long, and he must be a dullard, indeed, if he thinks not the same."

"Oh, no!" cried Fanny, "let me not think that! Let me not believe that I have confessed to him a love that he must spurn. Oh! he will despise me."

"Not so, dear sister—his nature is too generous."

"True, I will trust to that!" murmured Fanny, as she laid her head upon her sister's bosom and wept.

Was it joy or sorrow?

Not vainly did she trust to Verdon's generous nature. At his first interview with Mrs. Mowbray, he had been startled by something she said to him, and he pondered on her words until he saw the light.

"Are you sure," said Marian, "that you did not invest me with the graces of another? We seldom met. Was it my mind that charmed you? We seldom conversed together. Were my tastes known to you, except by one who reverenced your own? Are you sure that it was me you loved? Could my voice have been heard, when your reason was the slave to passion and intemperance. Whose voice had the power?"

Verdon at last could answer these questions with his heart. What but love could have had courage for his rescue? What but love could have reclaimed the profligate and found an eloquence to win him back to peace and honour.

And so Verdon and Fanny's tale of love is told, and they became plighted to each other.

It was on the very morning that those two hearts had found a resting-place, that the inmates of Mowbray's cottage were surprised at the advent of Mr. Orgrave and Mr. Oddiman.

Orgrave entered without announcement, and paused, as no one spoke, all regarding him with mute surprise, whilst Oddiman remained standing in the doorway.

"I'm afraid I disturb you, Mr. Mowbray," said Orgrave. "Why is this my reception beneath the roof I provide for you? Has Mr. Verdon been excusing his own follies at my expense?"

Fanny had given a letter to Verdon the moment she had seen Orgrave approach. As soon as he had read it, he looked at Orgrave and said: "Hypocrite! mean and cowardly! What answer do you make to your own letter to the wretch who is the pander to your vices?"

Orgrave was confused, and could only stammer out: "So, Miss Morrison condescends to open a letter addressed to another. Fie! fie!"

"Mr. Orgrave," said Mowbray, "henceforth we meet as strangers."

"We do!" exclaimed Orgrave, turning to go. "Ungrateful fool, that I have kept from beggary, starve!"

"Stop, Mr. Orgrave," said Mr. Oddiman, as Weazle, breathless with running, placed a parchment in his hand. "One minute will suffice. Did you know Crimpem—Lawyer Crimpem?"

Orgrave's face blanched, as he answered: "Yes, Sir. What of him?"

"He was a cunning rogue, Sir. He once took two thousand pounds to destroy your bond to your uncle; but his conscience would't let him do it. I have the honour to be Mr. Crimpen's executor. Read, Weazle—there!" and he pointed to a paragraph written on the parchment.

Weazle read: "When I am dead, and insensible to praise or censure, I will do justice ——"

"He couldn't afford it while living," said Oddiman, "so he does it by a *post-obit*."

"Then follows," continued Weazle, speaking very slowly, "the copy of an agreement to destroy a bond for eight thousand pounds, given by you, Mr. Orgrave, to your uncle."

"And which bond," said Oddiman, "was made a free gift to my young friend here, Arthur Mowbray. Here is the bond properly endorsed and signed. Crimpem did not destroy it, for which *requiescat in pace.*"

"This must be explained," said Orgrave.

"Shall we send for a constable to assist us in the inquiry?" asked Oddiman. "Perhaps not—you shall be furnished with our account of interest, deducting the yearly allowance received by Mr. Mowbray, and possibly a residence on the Continent may enable you to retrench and discharge the same."

The detected knave had no word to answer.

Let us draw a veil over this painful picture, and hasten to a happier scene, where all was honest love and cheerful hope.

Poor Oddiman was the only one whose happiness was momentarily interfered with, as it was proved that, had he been contented to "mind his own business," he would have discovered the bond three weeks earlier, and so have saved much distress to most of his dearest friends. He profited, however, by the lesson, for when Mr. Smythe dashed in to seek his aid, saying—

"Oh, here you are, Mr. Oddiman; I want you again. Mrs. Smythe has come down after me, and she's a-going it, playing at nine-pins with all the chancy wases, and using the celestial globe for a skittle-ball. Now I want you to interfere."

Mr. Oddiman replied—

"Not I, Mr. Smythe, that is a branch of diplomacy I have given up. With quarrels foreign and domestic I have nothing more to do. Henceforth, if I can, I shall 'mind my own business.'"

THE TALKING SHELL.

A TALE FOR THE YOUNG.

CHAPTER I.

THE STORY OF THE PEARL.

LAURA was very beautiful. She had been called so from the hour she was born. All who sought to win the favour of her wealthy mother were never tired of praising the blue eyes and rosy lips, the round arms and delicate fingers, of the baby beauty; but, though all were lavish of their admiration, Laura's mother thought they never praised enough, for the eyes of maternal pride could discover a thousand graces which were hidden from the cold scrutiny of fawning flatterers and interested dependents. As Laura grew in years, there were many cruel enough to tell her that her lovely face and graceful figure were alone sufficient to command the esteem and respect of all, and that she had only to consult her own desire in all things to be perfectly happy. The mother of Laura was equally to blame; for, instead of teaching her to consider the cultivation of her mind and the regulation of her disposition as the chief duties of her life, she was for ever employed in designing some new dress or ornament, which in reality served only to disguise the natural graces of the child, and had the effect of encouraging the growth of one of the most fatal passions—vanity. At fourteen Laura was frequently quite ridiculous; for she knew that she was much admired, and every day she became desirous of attracting more attention; and in order to do so she threw herself into unnatural attitudes, and made all kinds of simpering grimaces, which she foolishly thought graceful and becoming. Those who had flattered her began now to suffer the consequences of their own wickedness; for Laura never having been taught that it is our duty to be kind and gentle to all our fellow-creatures, used her servants very harshly, and indulged in violent passions whenever they, through mistake or carelessness, gave her offence. Laura, though much attached to her mother, treated her with scarcely more consideration than she did her servants; for her wilfulness had obtained complete mastery over her affection. Bitterly indeed did the poor mother reproach herself; for too late she saw the mischief she had done, and the good which she had neglected.

A few weeks before Laura's fifteenth birthday her uncle, a merchant, returned from a long voyage in the Indian Seas. He was proud also of Laura's beauty, and had brought home some rich stuffs and valuable ornaments for his pretty niece, who kissed him a hundred times, and called him the best and dearest of uncles. Among other presents was one of a single pearl, and this, either from its rarity, or the interest she had felt in her uncle's narration of its capture by the pearl-diver, was an especial favourite with Laura. It came from the celebrated pearl-fishery at Condalchy, on the coast of Ceylon, and the poor diver who brought it from the bottom of the sea died from the exertion used to obtain it. Laura would sit before her looking-glass an hour at a time, placing the pearl sometimes in her hair, or round her neck, or hanging the precious toy upon her lovely forehead. She had been thus engaged on a sultry afternoon until she grew weary of the pastime, and, throwing herself upon a sofa, took one of several beautiful Shells which her uncle had brought also from the Indian Seas. She was still thinking of her pearl, which she intended to wear upon her approaching birthday, and wondering what everybody would say, when, unconsciously, she placed the Shell to her ear—and lo! there was a sound like the murmuring of the sea. This was the first time she had heard the sounds, though she remembered to have read a book of poetry where it was said of a shell :—

> Place its polished lips unto your ear,
>   And it remembers its august abodes,
>   And murmurs as the ocean murmurs there.

Laura was delighted with her discovery, and continued listening to the Shell, and thinking of her pearl, until she become unconscious of everything else around her. Presently she heard the voice within the Shell speak her name. Yes! again it said, " Laura!" She felt neither alarmed nor surprised, for she had listened to it so long that she had become familiar with the wonder.

"Well, pretty Shell," inquired Laura, "what do you want with me?"

"Are you not pleased that I can talk to you?" said the Shell.

"Oh! very pleased," replied Laura, "for I grew dreadfully weary of being alone so much, and the people about me never speak of anything but my beauty. I am tired of hearing them."

"Ha! Are you sure of that?" said the Shell; "you forget how often I have seen you before yonder looking-glass, and heard you say to yourself, 'Well, I certainly am very handsome.'"

"Oh! I never said that," exclaimed Laura.

"But you have often thought so," replied the Shell, calmly, "and I have the power of hearing your thoughts."

"Indeed!" said Laura, a little frightened.

"You have often thought that for the world you would not have Caroline's merry pug nose, because some one has praised your own, which is straight; and that you would almost rather die than have Julia's gentle grey eyes, because your own are blue."

"Well, I own it," said Laura, in a very little pet; "I should hate to have a pug nose, and I'm very glad that my eyes are not grey. I can't help being beautiful, and I know I am."

"There is beauty in all things which God has made," replied the Shell.

"What! beauty in all things?" exclaimed Laura. "What! in spiders, and beetles, and—and—red hair?"

"Yes, in all, did you know how to seek for it," answered the Shell. "The time may come when you will do so. At present you are too much engaged with your own prettiness to see how others equal or excel you."

"Equal me! excel me!" thought Laura.

But the Spirit in the Shell heard her, and said, "You will not believe me now; you are too vain. You think that your beauty will command always the admiration of those you wish to captivate, and that the consciousness and exercise of that power will make you happy. Gentleness, affection, self-sacrifice, and kindness are unknown to you, because they have been unsought."

"You are very rude," said Laura. "Pray, do all shells talk, like you?" asked Laura.

"No; but I am endowed with this power to benefit you," said the Shell. "I am to tell you the 'Story of a Pearl,' the sister of the one you wear upon your wrist."

"Indeed!" cried Laura. "Had my lovely pearl a sister?"

"Listen," said the Shell.

THE STORY OF THE PEARL.

"The Pearl whose story I am about to narrate to you was of the ancient family of the Aviculæ Margahretta, one of the most renowned in the dominions of the Sea King. It had been predicted ages ago that the children of the Aviculæ should be very beautiful, and, as such, be liable to many dangers and temptations. The founder of the race was wise and prudent, and he therefore petitioned the King of the Sea to hide the exceeding beauty of his children under an exterior of the rudest form and most unattractive colour. Aviculæ was a great favourite with the Ruler of the Waters, and his petition was instantly granted by his royal master. The form which Aviculæ selected was that of an oyster."

"What!" exclaimed Laura, "was my lovely pearl ever an oyster?"

"Even so," continued the Shell; "and it is the same upon the earth as in the waters: a rude exterior oftentimes conceals the most precious qualities. For many years the Aviculæ lived in peace and honour in their rocky home under the sea which is called the Gulf of Manaar. One day a Cingalese, who lived upon the Island of Lions, was dis‑
‑ng to his youthful bride, Otaly, his expertness as a diver

in the same bright waters beneath which the Aviculæ had flourished so long ; and to assure his companion, who sat upon the beach, that he had descended to the bottom of the sea, he brought up in his hand what he thought was a stone, and with a shout of triumph hurled his prize to the shore. And the hapless Aviculæ (for such it was) striking the sharp point of a rock, was violently rent asunder.

"The diver stretched himself upon the beach nearly exhausted by his exertions, whilst Otaly proceeded to examine the novel thing which her husband had gathered from the sea. Struck with the beautiful colours of the opened shells, she scooped a hole in the sand, filling it with water, carefully washing away the particles in which the hitherto concealed pearl had been imbedded. She ran in ecstasy to her husband with the beauteous thing she had discovered, and clapped her hands with delight as she beheld the pleasure and wonder with which he regarded it.

"When they returned to the hut, Otaly soon succeeded in fastening her sea-gem (as she called it) to a fillet of red berries, which she bound upon her dark forehead, and then hastened to the bright stream in which she was accustomed to admire herself. Again and again she clapped her hands, for she had never seen anything so beautiful as the white pearl her husband had brought from beneath the great waters.

"The fatal gift of beauty to the Aviculæ was now discovered, and the evils which the founder of the family foresaw were about to visit them ; for the fame of Otaly's new ornament had reached even the ears of the King, the great Hijaya. By his command fifty of the most expert divers were ordered to descend into the sea, and search for the rude shells which contained such treasures. From that time unto the present, thirty days in every year the children of the earth make war upon the descendants of Aviculæ, and numbers are carried away from their home beneath the waters to become the slaves of human avarice and vanity.

"At the time of one of these incursions the sister of your favourite pearl was seven years old, being the age at which the daughters of the Aviculæ Margahretta arrived at maturity. She was known to be very beautiful, and she herself was aware of her own claims to admiration ; and so constantly did this knowledge occupy her thoughts that she grew dissatisfied with the seclusion in which she lived, and longed to be taken from her quiet home beneath the waters to the world of earth, where so many of her ancestors had been carried by the pearl-divers. She knew not what her lot would be in the new world which she desired to visit, but she felt sure that some great distinction awaited her, for those who sought with such labour to obtain her kindred must set a high value upon one so beautiful as she was.

"For twenty days the divers had ravaged the country of the Aviculæ, and had carried off numbers of the inhabitants; but she, who desired so much to become a captive, had hitherto escaped. She was lamenting what she considered her hard fate, when she felt herself torn from her native rock, and was sensible that she was being borne towards the surface of the sea. Oh how happy she thought herself in the fulfilment of her wishes! In her joy she forgot all those she had ever known or loved, and though she was but a few minutes on her passage from the bottom of the sea to the upper air, she grew impatient at the delay. At length she was drawn from the water. In a moment she was oppressed by a feeling of suffocation, which was only increased when she was tumbled with a dozen others into the bottom of a boat. What would she have given for a draught of the pleasant sea which she had so lately left, the sea which she had so lately despised, and whose soothing murmurs she was never to hear again—never!"

The Shell paused for a moment, and Laura heard it sigh deeply. Poor Shell! The sea had been its birthplace, and it knew that it should never see it more. After a pause the Shell continued:—

"The boat into which the unhappy Aviculæ was thrown contained twenty men, besides a tindal or pilot. Ten of the men were rowers and ten were divers. Of these latter, five had just been drawn up from the sea, each laden with his captives. The same number were preparing to go down as soon as the large stones of red granite which had aided their fellows to descend should be hauled up by the ropes, to which they were attached. This was soon done, and each of the fresh divers holding a net between the toes of his left foot, and the rope, to which the stone is fastened by the toes of his right foot, plunged into the sea. In about two minutes a signal was given to the men in the boat, that the purpose of the divers was accomplished, and they were drawn up again, as their fellows had been before them, the nets filled with the spoils of the deep waters. It was now noon, and a breeze blowing across the sea warned the fishers to return. Presently a noise like thunder came booming over the waters. It was the gun which told the return of the boat to land. Upon the shore were many of the rude huts and tents, with each a bazaar, or shop, before it, surrounded by thousands of people of different colours, countries, castes, and occupations. The sea was covered by a multitude of boats, all returning from the same pursuit as that which contained the poor Pearl. As they severally touched the shore their anxious owners ran to meet them, and hailed with loud acclamations the number of captives with which each was laden. The unhappy Aviculæ were thrown roughly into baskets, and carried away to holes or pits dug in the ground, and there placed upon coarse mats; alas! to linger and to die. Then, how the vain Pearl lamented her folly, and thought more and more lovingly of her own home beneath the waters!

"The Pearl now only desired to die in peace.

"But this was not to be. The moon arose, and again the gun was heard booming over the sea. The breeze was blowing gently from the land, and the whole fleet of boats and their crews of divers and rowers put off to renew their ravages in the deep. But the poor Aviculæ was past all physical pain; yet the power to feel and to remember was strangely preserved to her, for what purpose you will learn as I proceed with her story.

"After a short lapse of time the Aviculæ were taken from the pits in which they had been buried, and carefully examined by their captors, to discover their value. The Pearl whose story I am relating far exceeded in beauty all others which the fishers had obtained, and a hundred merchants contended for the possession of her. For days she was exhibited by her master, who seemed never to tire of praising her form and colour, until she almost forgot her past sufferings in the admiration which she excited. At length a merchant was found to give the large sum required for her purchase; and by her new possessor the pearl was carried to England, and confided to the care of a skilful artisan, who made for her a delicate framework of gold, attached to a chain of the same precious metal. When the Pearl found herself thus arrayed, all her former pride returned, and she no longer regretted her rocky home beneath the sea.

"The merchant himself was childless, but he had a niece he loved very dearly, named Adeleve ; and it was for her that he had bought the Pearl, and had it placed in its costly setting. Adeleve was very beautiful ; and, like the vain Aviculæ, she knew it, and was satisfied to be only beautiful. You can judge how proud she was of her uncle's gift, and what use she made of it. Adeleve had an idol."

"What ! an idol like the ugly Joss in the drawing-room?" said Laura.

"Do not interrupt me," continued the Shell. "This idol was enclosed in a shrine, which was made of the clearest crystal, and a glittering substance resembling the purest silver. But although the shrine was very curious, the idol was still more wonderful, for its features, which were remarkably beautiful, would change their expression twenty times a day, and yet always bore a strong resemblance to those of Adeleve. In fact, it was almost like herself.

"Adeleve was never so happy as when she was decorating this image, either with flowers, or gems, or golden ornaments ; and as soon as she received her uncle's costly gift she hastened to the shrine, and hung the pearl upon the forehead of her idol. The figure smiled, while an expression of great delight beamed from its eyes, and Adeleve thought it had never looked so beautiful. Hour by hour would she stand and gaze upon the object of her adoration, neglecting for its worship her studies and her duties.

"It was not always that the idol smiled ; for, at times when Adeleve had been using violent words and indulging in angry passions, it would assume a strange forbidding look which was perfectly frightful, and Adeleve would turn away from it, and weep with vexation. These angry moods were of such constant occurrence that it was wonderful the idol preserved its beauty or that Adeleve retained a servant to wait upon her ; and it was only by large bribes that the dependents of her mother consented to submit to the treatment which they received. Even the Pearl, though proud of being the slave of such a lovely mistress, was oftened ashamed of the scenes of violence and waywardness which it was compelled to witness.

"Adeleve had but one friend, her cousin, Mary Merton ; for her early playmates had grown tired of her caprices, and annoyed by her passionate disposition; but Mary Merton bore patiently with her cousin's ill-humours, and only remembered her acts of kindness towards her; though she, from her gentleness, was more exposed than anyone else to be treated slightingly by the young beauty.

Mary was a year older than Adeleve, and could lay no claims to any personal attractions. Her features were irregular, and her eyes of no decided colour, but there was ever an expression of gentleness and good nature in her face, which more than made amends for the absence of beauty. She was always dressed very plainly, and seldom wore any other ornament than a flower or a bow of gay-coloured ribbon, thus presenting a marked contrast to her more wealthy and beautiful cousin; but her mind and disposition had been carefully trained, and all who knew Mary Merton loved her. Even Adeleve did so, as much as her own self-love would allow her to esteem another; but she never failed to draw unfavourable comparisons between her own personal advantages and the plainness of Mary.

Then Adeleve would wonder that her cousin should be always happy and contented, when even she, whom everyone praised and admired, was so frequently annoyed and dissatisfied. As she had never been taught to consider the feelings of others when she desired her own gratification, she one day asked Mary if she did not wish that she were beautiful?

"'Not I,' replied Mary, laughing merrily; 'for not even Fortunatus's wishing-cap would make me so. Mamma would have nothing to tease me about if I had not a pug nose, and we often laugh heartily because papa will not admit that it is like his own. Many and many a kiss has my poor little pug gained for me because it has been made a jest of.'

"Adeleve thought these were strange reasons to make any one satisfied with a pug nose. She wondered what could reconcile her to her straight flaxen hair.

"'But surely you would like hair that would curl, Mary?' asked the beauty.

"'Well, if it would always curl,' replied her merry cousin; 'but you know I like to have the wind blowing about my temples when I am gathering wild-flowers in the fields; or when my good spirits run away with me, how sadly I am disposed to be a romp. My straight hair never gives me any trouble then; and I often hear merry-hearted girls like myself confess that they would gladly do as I do but for fear of disturbing their ringlets. No, Adeleve; I am quite contented to have straight hair, since it allows me o enjoy the good spirits with which God has blessed me.'

"Adeleve pitied her poor cousin; thinking in her own ignorance how much she had to regret. It was with this conviction that, one day when they were together in her dressing-room, Adeleve proposed to her cousin to accept one of the beautiful dresses which her uncle, the merchant, had given to her.

"'You are very kind, dear Adeleve,' said Mary; 'but I cannot accept your pretty dress. It is quite suited to you; but this muslin frock, with its bright cherry-coloured bows, is more fitted to me and to my station. You forget that papa is not so rich as your mamma.'

"What has that to do with it?' asked Adeleve, a little angry at the rejection of her offer. 'What has that to do with it?'

"'Much, my dear cousin,' replied Mary, with a smile; 'much more than you may think. I should be obliged to tell everybody this dress is a present from my cousin Adeleve, or papa would be thought to be extravagant and foolish to buy me such an expensive material. Besides, I have sisters.'

"'Surely they would not be censured for your appearance,' said Adeleve.

"'No, dear cousin,' replied Mary; 'but it would be wrong of me to incur the chance of giving them pain; and I might do so by appearing so much more splendidly dressed than themselves.'

"Well, they might be annoyed, for what I should care,' said Adeleve; 'I wouldn't dress myself a fright to please anybody.'

"'I hope I am not quite a fright," replied Mary, with a laugh; 'and I deny myself nothing in refusing what you so kindly offer; yet I would do much to please you.'

"'Well, you do that, I must acknowledge,' said Adeleve; 'and why, I am at a loss to discover.'

"Because there is great pleasure in pleasing others,' replied Mary.

"'What! when it is to your own inconvenience,' exclaimed Adeleve.

"'Yes, my dear cousin,' answered Mary. 'The little

sacrifice we make increases the pleasure of doing a service; and without some self-denial we deserve no thanks, although we may receive them.'

"'No thanks would pay me for a personal inconvenience, said Adeleve; "I mean to consult my own pleasure in all things—let others do as they please.'

"'You must not do so if you wish to be happy,' replied Mary. 'We are all dependent upon each other, dear cousin, from the highest to the lowest. It is our interest as well as our duty to remember this. The love and kind offices of others are necessary to our own happiness; and, therefore, we should be always gentle, loving, and ready to do good.'

"'What a capital parson you would make, to be sure!' said Adeleve, evidently displeased.

"'I only repeat what mamma has told me,' answered Mary; 'I am sure you would be happier if you thought so too, Adeleve.'

"'I am quite happy, thank you,' answered the beauty, tossing her pretty head; 'and I think you had better go down to the drawing-room whilst I am dressed, for I should not like my maid to hear such very strange ideas.'

" Mary left the room, and Adeleve sat herself down before the shrine which held her idol. The face of the image looked angry and perplexed; and the Pearl was very sorrowful, for she remembered the time when she had forgotten all she had loved and known in her selfish joy at being taken from her home beneath the waters."

CHAPTER II.

CONTINUATION OF THE STORY OF THE PEARL.

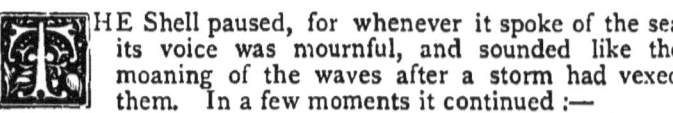HE Shell paused, for whenever it spoke of the sea its voice was mournful, and sounded like the moaning of the waves after a storm had vexed them. In a few moments it continued :—

"Adeleve was now twenty-one. She had passed the last three years in the pursuit of pleasure, and a more fervent devotion to her idol. Her beauty had gained her many admirers, but the Pearl (who, like myself, had the power of understanding human thoughts) had seen how her vanity and frivolity had made her an object of ridicule. She was, however, about to be married to one as vain and frivolous as herself, and whom she only valued for his wealth and position in society. She thought that his riches would give her more opportunities for display, and that she would be envied for the grandeur of her house and the splendour of her equipages. She knew that he was proud of her beauty, and would deny her nothing that could set it off to the greatest advantage; and for this she had consented to pass her life as the companion of a foolish coxcomb.

" Her wedding was to be the grandest of the season, and numbers were invited to see how splendidly she was to be attired, and how beautiful she would look. Her cousin had been married, a year before, to the curate (whose name was Merton also) of a small parish in the country, and it was with some difficulty that Adeleve could be persuaded by her mother to invite Mary to be present at her marriage, fearing that the simplicity of her early friend and her husband might detract from the splendour of the scene. It was well for Adeleve that she did so.

The church was crowded with persons to witness the ceremony, and not a few gratified the vanity of Adeleve by their exclamations at the beauty both of her person and her bridal dress. Her happiness, however, was to experience some alloy (as even at the altar her vanity had sought to gratify itself); for the church dignitary who was to have read the marriage service was taken suddenly ill, and the poor country curate, Mary's husband, had to officiate in his stead.

"The wedding party returned from the church to a sumptuous breakfast, at which were present a hundred people who cared nothing for Adeleve, and for whom she cared as little. The only persons, besides her mother, who felt any concern for the future welfare of the bride, were Mary and her husband. But Adeleve treated them with marked neglect, as though she were ashamed to own relationship with two such homely people; but they felt no resentment at such conduct, for their own goodness made them ready to excuse any forgetfulness of themselves; and they returned to their own quiet village without envy of the splendour they had seen, or anger at the vain and selfish girl who had forgotten what was due to the only friend of her wayward youth.

"The Pearl, too, had received her meed of praise on that day, for she had heard the thoughts of many upon her beauty; and, in her gratitude to the mistress who had obtained for her such an opportunity to be admired, she heeded not the selfishness and vanity which she saw in the mind of Adeleve. She felt how ashamed she should have been had an unsightly oyster claimed kindred with her, when a hundred tongues were lavish in the praises of her loveliness. Poor silly Pearl! She knew not what was in store for her.

"And Adeleve's image seemed in its crystal shrine as though it could never again own a vexed or angry look. Alas, it was a deceitful idol!

"Time passed on, and with it Adeleve's wedded life. Her home had no charms for her, except when it afforded her the opportunities of displaying her wealth and beauty before people whom she thought envied and admired her. As she grew older she became more greedy of flattery, and those interested in pleasing her paid the most fulsome compliments, which her vanity made her believe were the honest expressions of their thoughts. When there were none to flatter she was petulant with all about her; and as her husband was very frequently exposed to her bad temper, she soon grew distasteful to him, and he avoided her society as much as possible. For this she cared but little, as he had long ceased to administer to her vanity, except by allowing her the means to dress extravagantly, and give grand entertainments. When she was not employed with these frivolities she was very miserable, for she had not provided her mind with any other resources of pleasure, or cultivated her disposition to find delight in acts of kindness and benevolence, whereby her leisure and her wealth might have been made blessings to herself and others. She felt that no one really loved her; for, as she had lived for herself alone, all her friends repaid her selfishness and indifference. When this feeling was strongest in her mind she would sometimes weep very bitterly, not with sorrow at her past folly in neglecting the opportunities she had had, but with vexation at her want of influence over others. At those times she seldom visited her idol, but when she did so she saw the image with red and swollen eyes, and its dark eyebrows contracted together, making its pallid cheeks look more sorrowful. Then would she turn away from it in haste, and laugh disdainfully, as though she sought to deceive herself into the belief that her annoyance was not real. The poor Pearl, who knew the truth, was now doomed to suffer greatly; for, though she did not love her mistress, she could not witness these exhibitions of human weakness without a desire to escape from them, and she often sighed, how vainly! for her peaceful home beneath the deep waters."

Again the Shell paused, for it was thinking of the sea which it loved so well.

"Adeleve had been married about four years when two events occurred which materially affected her. One was nothing less than the appearance of a new beauty, called Laura."

"My name!" cried the listening girl.

"There are many so called," continued the Shell. "The Laura of whom I speak was not only as lovely as Adeleve, but she was some years her junior. Her beauty, however, was her least claim to admiration."

"Her least claim!" exclaimed the surprised listener.

"At present you will not believe me," said the Shell; "nevertheless, I speak truly when I say that her beauty was her least claim to the admiration of those who knew her. She had been trained by good and wise parents, who had sought to store her mind with the knowledge of kindness and truth—and well had she repaid their care. Gentle to all, she was obeyed with an alacrity that proved it was a pleasure to consult the least of her wishes. Mindful of the duty she owed to those beneath her, the poor had reason hourly to bless her care of them. Grateful for the love which was shown towards her, she sought to evince her own affectionate regard for all those who were worthy of esteem. No selfish thought occupied her mind; but her greatest pleasure was in consulting the happiness of others. Richly was she rewarded; for, though she sometimes met with an ill return, she knew from many kindly acts how much others sought to show their gratitude. She had read much and was thus enabled to converse on subjects of which Adelaide knew nothing. She was also a proficient in minor accomplishments, and sang well but naturally, and played with taste and feeling. Against such a rival Adeleve's claims to admiration were small indeed, and great was her mortification when she found herself deserted for the new beauty.

"The wicked thoughts which filled the mind of Adeleve made the Pearl tremble as she hung around the neck of her enraged mistress, and gladly would she have been the unregarded pebble upon the the shore of Manaar.

"When Adeleve returned home she flew to her idol for comfort in her distress; for she believed that so long as that continued beautiful she herself should command the admiration which she coveted. The image was ghastly pale, and looked more angry than ever she had beheld it. Its eyes seemed like sparks of fire, and its features were painfully rigid.

Adeleve turned away in terror, and, leaning her arms upon the marble slab above the fireplace, she hid her face in her hands. In a moment her dress was in flames. The light gauze had been drawn into the fire; but Adeleve was unconscious of her danger till roused by a sense of pain. Her cries brought assistance, but not until the fire had injured her severely. For many days her recovery was doubtful, and fever rendered her insensible. There was one who watched her day and night, and bore patiently the restlessness of the sufferer, and seemed never to tire of her painful office. That one was Mary. As soon as she heard of the accident to Adeleve she came to her instantly, for she judged rightly that her cousin would have no attendant but hired nurses. How could it be otherwise?—she never sought the goodwill of any, and she had made her dependents fear her. Though money could procure the services of many, the untiring care of one who loved her could not be purchased. Therefore Mary came to be her nurse. It was many weeks before Adeleve could leave her bed, and for the first time in her life she knew the feeling of gratitude. Again and again she thanked Mary for her care and tenderness, without which she felt she never could have recovered. She remembered that Mary had said to her years before, 'We are all dependent upon each other;' nor could she forget how she had scoffed at the saying.

"When Mary returned to her home, Adeleve felt a loneliness she had never known before, for no one came to fill her cousin's place. No! She had but one friend, and she was gone.

"As strength returned, Adeleve's old vanity came back also. The shrine which contained her idol had been removed from her chamber, as the surgeon, knowing the influence it had over her, had feared the effect it might produce. She now desired that the shrine should be restored to its place, and as her attendants did not care to dispute her orders, her command was obeyed. When she was left alone she anxiously approached the object which contained her idol. She looked, and fainted instantly, for the image had a bright red scar upon its cheek, and she knew that she resembled it. When consciousness returned, her rage was fearful. Instead of thanking the goodness which had preserved her life, she upbraided all who had ministered to her recovery, accusing them as the authors of her misfortune.

"Wretched Adeleve! the beauty for which she had sacrificed so much, was hers no longer."

CHAPTER III.

"REMEMBER."

"WE will talk no more at present of Adeleve," said the Shell, "as I have much to tell you of Mary Merton.

"The village where she lived was in a secluded part of the country. The old grey church and modest parsonage stood upon the brow of a hill, from which you might see large tracts of meadow land, spotted over with cattle of various kinds, and here and there patches of cornfields. A bright river ran like a band of silver through the vale, turning in its course a couple of water-mills, whose noise was pleasant to hear, as it told of human life and industry. In the distance was a large wood, which, stretching right and left, seemed to shut out the rest of the world from this pleasant valley. The village itself was composed almost entirely of cottages, the female inhabitants of which gained a living by making pillow-lace. It was a pretty sight to see the cottagers—some very young, some very old—seated at the doors of their humble homes, each with a round pillow in her lap, throwing about the bobbins, which rattled merrily under the busy fingers of the workers. Twice a week in the summer time they would assemble in the parsonage orchard, and form a circle round Mrs. Merton, who read to them whilst they pursued their labour. In the winter time they all met in the school-room, on half-holidays, for the same purpose, and thus there grew up between the parson's wife and the parishioners a regard and love for each other that produced the happiest results. Mrs. Merton used her influence over her poorer friends to make them cleanly and provident housewives, whilst she derived a great amount of happiness from the affectionate regard which all professed for her.

"Soon after Mrs. Merton came to live at Cherryvale, one of the cottagers brought from the neighbouring market-town where she had been to sell her lace, two very young children, of whom she had undertaken the care. The eldest, a boy, was named Edward, and the other was called Rose. They had lost both father and mother six months before, and their grandfather, being a commercial traveller, and much away from home, had thought it better to send the children into the country, as their health was very delicate. Mrs. Morley, to whose charge they were confided, was a well-meaning woman enough, but, being very ignorant of everything except making lace, to which employment she devoted all the time she could spare from her household duties, little Edward and Rose were left very much to take care of themselves. They were so attached to each other that if they were separated for a few minutes their anxiety was instantly perceptible. If the day were fine, as soon as they had finished their breakfast of bread and milk, they would take each other's hands and walk away to some quiet hedge-bank or corner of a field, and, making themselves toys of broken crockery or wild-flowers, amuse each other for hours. Sometimes they would stroll down the green lanes—but ever hand-in-hand—watching with childish wonder the birds flying from hedge to hedge ; or Edward would gather twigs of May-blossom or blackberries for himself and Rose—for what one had the other must share always. They seldom played with the children in the village, and when they did so, Rose and Edward would be sure to sit beside each other, and very soon become silent spectators of the sport, whatever it might be. Not that they were sulky or ill-tempered children, but they seemed to be of such timid natures that they were happiest when alone. They never laughed as merry children laugh : but they would often look at each other, and smile, and were very happy in their quiet, gentle way. It was impossible for them to escape the notice of Mrs. Merton, who endeavoured to form an intimacy with the two orphans ; but, kind as she ever was, and a general favourite with little people, it was some time before she could overcome the shyness of Rose and Edward.

"'Do you not like me?' said Mrs. Merton, after trying in vain to make the children cheerful.

"'Oh, yes,' replied Edward. 'You talk to us as mamma used to do.'

"'And you loved your mamma?" said Mrs. Merton.

"'The children looked at each other; and then, speaking together, said, 'Yes, yes! very much.'

"'And is that why you are not merrier?' asked Mrs. Merton.

"'I don't know,' answered the boy; 'but mamma was ill so long, and we were left alone so long; and nurse always told us to be very quiet'—and again he looked in his little sister's face for a moment, and then kissed her.

[Ah? dear ones; you who have happy homes, without one absent face! be good and grateful, and believe in the love which seeks to guide you!]

"Mrs. Merton now understood why the children were so fond of solitude and being always together, and endeavoured more and more to make them love her. It is seldom that kindness and gentleness fail to make an impression on the young; and very soon Edward and Rose came to the parsonage every day; and, though they loved each other as ever, seemed happier when Mrs. Merton was with them. When they were quite at their ease with her, Mrs. Merton taught them to read and write, and both Edward and Rose proved apt scholars, and progressed very rapidly. Mr. Merton also took great interest in them; and, as he had no children of his own, proposed that they should live entirely at the parsonage. Their grandfather readily gave his consent, and for some years Edward and Rose lived very happily with their kind friends, repaying the care bestowed upon them by affection and diligence. At the end of this time Mrs. Merton had a severe illness. For some days it was thought that she would not recover, and when she did so it was only partially, for she could no longer walk about, but was obliged to be drawn in a garden-chair, propped up by pillows. Edward would let no one perform this duty but himself, and Rose never left the poor invalid except when rest was absolutely needful for her.

"It was at this period when Adeleve, neglected and forgotten by all her former admirers and acquaintance (for she was without *true* friends), thought often of the kindness of her cousin Mary, and resolved to visit Cherryvale, in order to be near the only one upon whose attentions she could rely. It was not that her misfortune had alienated those whom she used to call her friends ; but, finding that she no longer attracted admiration, she had become more overbearing and captious in her manners and conduct, until every one avoided her. Her time was chiefly employed about her idol, upon which she bestowed increased attention—dressing it in the richest materials, and employing every art to hide the scar upon its forehead and the seams upon its face, occasionally believing that she had concealed its blemishes, but learning, often very painfully, that she had deceived herself. Her anger would then return and render her so ridiculous that those who were once disposed to pity her regarded her with contempt.

"The poor Pearl knew all this too well, and lamented that its own beauty should have made it a witness of her humiliation.

"When Adeleve arrived at Cherryvale she was grieved to see the change which illness had made in Mary Merton ; but, feeble and suffering as she found her cousin, Mary's kindness and gentleness were unchanged.

"'You are very welcome, dear Adeleve,' said she, 'though I am afraid you will find me a wearisome companion after the gay friends you have left behind you.'

"'I have no friends,' replied Adeleve. 'I do not believe in friendship.'

"'You must be sceptical no longer, Adeleve,' said Mary, 'for here are two who daily prove to me that there are true friends to be found by those who have sought them. You must know these, my friends, Rose and Edward.'

"Adeleve looked at the two persons referred to, and then, turning to Mary, said, 'Are these your only friends?'

"'I think not, dear Adeleve,' replied Mary ; 'I hope I know, I have many more. But, for a long time, Edward and Rose have been my constant attendants. Unwearied by my restlessness when in pain, watchful of every want—and those who are sick have many—denying themselves every enjoyment but that which they derive from their affectionate care of me. Are not those friends?'

"'Indeed, they are !' said Adeleve. 'But you were always fortunate ;I had never any one to care for me. Once, indeed, I had many to flatter me and profess an admiration which they could not have felt, or I should not be abandoned by all, as I am now,'

"'Not by all, dear Adeleve,' said Mary, and she held out her thin white hand.

"'Well, not by you,' replied Adeleve, 'or I should not have sought you. But even you I find ill and in more need of consolation than in a condition to bestow it upon me.'

"'I think not, Adcleve,' said Mary. 'True, I am sorely afflicted, but I am resigned to bear my affliction. 'I remember how much happiness I have enjoyed, and how little I deserved it. I feel, too, that the trifling good which I have sown has produced a most abundant harvest in the affection which now seeks to soothe my suffering.'

"'Did I not say you were fortunate?' exclaimed Adeleve. 'Where are those whom I have feasted and entertained? The dependents whom I have fed and rewarded? All, all have deserted me.'

"'Are they alone to blame?' But Mary could not tell her unhappy cousin that she had consulted only her own selfish enjoyment in all which she had done, and that those of whom she complained had understood her motive.

"'I know what you would say, replied Adeleve, colouring deeply—'that I have lived for myself alone. I remember well the sermon you once preached to me—that we are all dependant upon others. But I have no right to be dependant. I have wealth, I had beauty, but now what am I? But for that dreadful accident I should have been admired and followed still.'

"'Ah, dear cousin,' said Mary, 'our chastenings are for our good, if we could only understand them so. Your beauty was a fatal gift to you, and you have lost it that you may gain a better nature.'

"'I have lost it to be made miserable,' exclaimed Adeleve; 'and I would that I were dead.'

"'If that wish were sincere it would be impious,' said Mary. 'I do not desire to die, although my life is of hourly suffering, for I have still duties which I can perform. But you have health to enjoy the world of beauty which is around you, wealth to assist the needy—not by the careless giving of alms, but by encouraging the deserving, by lending succour to the sick and aged, whose labour is done. and who now ask for a little rest before they die ; to seek out the ignorant and teach them good and truth, and thus win friends whose testimony will outlive the grave.'

"Rose, who was sitting by the side of the couch, took Mrs. Merton's hand and laid her cheek upon it. The invalid looked at Adeleve and smiled, as though to call her attention to this simple evidence of the affection of the child. Adeleve observed it without any emotion, but the time came when she remembered it.

"As Mrs. Merton became daily more infirm, her cousin found her visit very irksome to herself, and soon made an excuse to leave Cherryvale. She never spoke to Mary again, for a few weeks after her departure Mrs. Merton died. There were many mourners in Cherryvale, for Mary's goodness had won for her the love of all."

"Oh, yes, I love her," said Laura, when the Shell ceased to speak. "Poor Edward and Rose, what became of them?"

"They remembered the example of the one they loved, and lived to imitate her virtues," answered the Shell. "But we must follow Adeleve."

"I don't care what becomes of her," said Laura; "a vain, selfish creature."

"Yet her story, I hope, may be of use to you," replied the Shell. "Listen a little longer.

"Adeleve had taken more than ordinary pains to dress herself, and was lost in contemplation of her beloved idol when the letter announcing Mary's death was put into her hands by her servant. She paused a moment before breaking the black seal, for she anticipated the news contained in the letter. When she heard how peacefully Mary had died—how she had remembered Adeleve in almost her latest prayer—and how the grief of those to whom she had been so dear was tempered by the belief that she was now beyond the chance of change or sorrow—Adeleve was deeply touched, and for the first time for many years, she wept tears of earnest, unselfish grief.

"And lo! her idol was weeping also!

"As she looked stedfastly upon it—thinking how *she* should die—how *she* should be mourned and remembered—a mist overspread the shrine, and she saw (or fancied that she saw) the face of her idol change to that of Mary). Pale and transparent as the purest alabaster the face appeared, and wore an expression of such heavenly peacefulness that Adeleve thought she looked upon a sleeping angel. Gradually it passed away, and the seared and painted features of the idol were again before her. Oh, how hideous it now appeared! How ghastly the living image, compared with the shadow of the dead!

"Adeleve rose up, and hastily removed her dress and ornaments, casting them heedlessly on the floor, as though they hurt her body. The Pearl rested upon her forehead, but even that was taken off and thrown carelessly away, and, as it fell, the fire received it !

"The cruel fire" (and the Shell trembled in the hand of Laura), "the enemy of all things that dwell beneath the sea, closed round the poor Aviculæ and calcined her to dust."

The voice in the Shell was silenced ; and Laura thought she heard a deep sigh, like the sound the sea makes upon the beach when the waves are quiet, and mourning for the wrongs which they have done to brave ships and their drowned crews.

"And Adeleve ?" asked Laura, after a short pause.

"She sought and found a better nature ; and lived to believe the sermon Mary once preached to her," answered the Shell.

"And the shrine, and the idol? What became of them?" said Laura.

"The shrine was her LOOKING-GLASS, and her idol was HERSELF—only herself," replied the Shell. "Like you she was very beautiful ; like you ——"

"Oh do not say that I am like Adeleve, dear Shell ! Do not say that ! Let me be like the Laura of whom you spoke ! Whenever you see me growing vain and selfish, and careless of my duties to others, murmur in my ear, 'Remember Adeleve ! Remember Laura !'"

"That must not be," said the Shell ; "I have spoken for the last time. It has been permitted me to tell you the story of the Pearl : it is for you to remember."

"And I will," cried Laura, "I will, dear Shell. Oh, how can I thank you enough ?"

"Would you, then, do even me a kindness?" asked the Shell.

"Yes, yes !" exclaimed Laura. "Anything you require of me I will do."

"Then return me to the sea—anywhere in the sea—so that I may rest again in the cool, green waves of my beloved ocean !" exclaimed the Shell.

"I promise that you shall," said Laura—"soon, very soon."

And, in a voice as musical as the rippling of a little brook, the Shell murmured "Remember !"

FLOWERS AND THORNS.

THE last lottery to be drawn in England was announced. Those old enough to remember that event will not fail to recall the golden promises made to stimulate the public to speculation, and prizes of £5,000, £10,000, and £20,000, seemed to be within the reach of all who had the courage to invest a few paltry pounds in the wheel of fortune. The lottery was the general subject of conversation at most social gatherings in town and country, and the epidemic—for so it might be called—had spread to the market-tables round and about Little Grabley; but few of the careful, penny-saving farmers were taken with the tempting baits, although four of the small tradesmen of the village clubbed together to buy "a sixteenth," and then fell into a state of painful perturbation, which lasted until the day of drawing declared the club a winner of a share in a prize of £5, amounting exactly to six shillings and threepence. The loudest declaimer against the folly of sending good money on such an errand was Farmer Gathercole—old Sam Gathercole, as he was called; but, as he could neither read nor write, his opinion went for little, as it was concluded that he was necessarily ignorant of the great advantages to be obtained by the investment. He was known to have scraped—yes, scraped — a few pounds together by great industry and skilful management of his little farm of about a hundred acres, and no one blamed him for being careful of what he had gathered together. Besides, he had no one to care for besides himself and his little nephew, Jabez Coulterson—a good-tempered, handsome boy of twelve years, who was kept as ignorant as his uncle of the great mysteries of reading and writing, for the satisfactory reason that, as Sam Gathercole had done very well without those accomplishments, Jabez couldn't do better than follow his uncle's example. His neighbour, Mr. Grainger, did all he could in a friendly way to get Jabez sent to school, as the boy was a great favourite with all at Islip Farm (some seven or eight hundred acres), which Mr. Grainger cultivated, and, in consequence, generally had "a voice potential as the Duke's" in the parish of Little Grabley; but old Sam was fond of showing his independence, and would not change his treatment of the boy Jabez.

Farmer Gathercole had been to London shortly before the drawing of the last great lottery, and there was a marked change in him from that time, as he was very fidgetty at home, and more vehement in his condemnation of the lottery at the market-table and elsewhere. The day after the drawing he was at the Courtnay Arms, where a newspaper was taken in, half-an-hour before the arrival of the coach which brought the paper from London, and appeared to be strangely perplexed when, in answer to his inquiry of "What number has won?" the landlord read out the list of prizes and the numbers which had gained them. From that day Sam Gathercole never mentioned the lottery to anyone in Little Grabley.

He had his own reasons for this reticence, and you shall know them. Like many other ignorant men, Farmer Gathercole was sly and suspicious, hardly caring to let his left hand know what his right hand did. He was very fond of money, working hard and honestly to obtain it, and he was greatly tempted to try his luck at the wheel of fortune, but, fearing to be laughed at if he should lose, or be pestered by needy neighbours if he should win, he cunningly descried the means whereby he resolved to obtain riches if he could.

Having sent two of his best beasts to Smithfield Market, he invested the money they brought in a lottery ticket, and was fortunate enough to win one of the great prizes. For ten long years he kept the secret of his good fortune, neither spending more nor labouring less, but remaining content with the enjoyment of knowing what a rich man he should die, and surprise all the people of Little Grabley.

When he died, his will was the wonder and talk of the county, and none ever surmised that the thirty odd thousand pounds which Samuel Gathercole bequeathed his only relative, Jabez Coulterson, had come, mainly, out of the wheel of fortune. Nor was this the only surprise which agitated the minds of the Little Grableyans—Mr. Grainger, having engaged in a Chancery suit, became bankrupt, saving out of the wreck of his property barely enough to take Gathercole's farm when it became vacant by old Sam's death. Neighbours said it would be a sad change for Miss Daisy, who had been brought up like a lady, playing "the piany," some believed, though it was confessed that she had been often seen in the kitchen making pastry, or pickling and preserving, as a farmer's daughter ought to have done.

Mr. Jabez Coulterson did not forget his kind friends of Islip Farm now that he had become rich and they poor. No ; and he would have offered help if he had known how to set about it ; but it seemed so strange that Mr. Grainger, for whom he had always entertained such respectful admiration, should be in a position to accept assistance from him that he had not the courage to obey the dictates of his kind heart. Mr. Grainger, too, was far too proud a man to trespass upon the pocket of his friend, however full it might be, and the more so as far as Jabez was concerned, as he had made Mr. Grainger adviser and confidential friend.

Jabez did not suspect for some time that he had another reason for visiting the old farm than a desire to have Grainger's advice and counsel ; but when his poor friend had pressed him to seek instruction—book learning, Jabez called it—the good young man tried to follow the suggestion, but found his mind so occupied with other thoughts than a desire to be acquainted with big A and bouncing B that he gave up the pursuit of knowledge in despair.

The truth was, he had fallen over head and ears in love with Daisy Grainger, and, sooth to say, she, estimating the good qualities of Jabez, had, despite his want of culture and his money, conceived a great liking for Jabez. We say despite his money, for that really stood in the way for a long time between her own desire and the confession of her love, as she feared that it might be thought, perhaps, by him, that she had listened to the jingling of his money-bags and not to the promptings of her own heart.

We do not care to dwell upon the wooing of Jabez and Daisy, as it is with an incident of their married life we desire to point the moral and adorn our tale.

Mr. and Mrs. Jabez Coulterson occupied one of the prettiest residences in the neighbourhood of Little Grabley. It had attached to it quite a model homestead and about fifty acres of land, which afforded amusement and employment to its proprietors. Jabez also rented the shooting over some five hundred acres adjoining, as he was fond of his gun, and he could follow the sport without bringing himself much into contact with the neighbouring gentry, his education and former position making him diffident and embarrassed in the presence of strangers. His household consisted of Patty, his uncle's old housekeeper, two or three maid-servants, a gardener, a groom, and a sort of odd man who looked after the little farm in conjunction with Mr. Coulterson.

A frequent visitor was a cousin of Mr. Coulterson—Miss Millicent Grainger—whose chief aim at present seemed to be the very natural one of securing as good a husband as she could for a pretty face, a good temper, cheerful disposition, and three thousand pounds.

One fine December morning she was sitting in the dining-room of Lazy Hall (as Jabez had named his house) looking vacantly at the ceiling—the while the kitten was playing with the ball of worsted which Milly ought to have been knitting into socks — and might have continued in her reverie for some time longer, had not old Patty entered the room to make an inquiry, and who had had to speak twice before she could attract the attention of the young lady.

"Good gracious, Patty! how you made me jump!" said Miss Milly.

"So I see, Miss," replied Patty (who was quite a privileged person, and said whatever she pleased to everyone in Lazy Hall); "and as you know how fond I be of you all, you won't take it amiss if I speak a bit of my mind to you." Patty then went on to say that she was sure something was going wrong with Miss Milly, as she was always day-dreaming—always, ever since the London gentleman, a Mr. Fortescue, had called some five days before; and concluded by declaring that Miss Milly "went moping about like a hen with the croup."

Milly affected to laugh at this homely simile, and declared that Patty was an old goose for having such nonsense in her head. Mr. Fortescue was a friend of Mr. Coulterson—a friend he had met in London; but upon this declaration Patty joined issue, as Jabez had only been in London one fortnight in all his life. This little controversy was ended by the report of two gunshots near the house and the loud laughter of Mr. Coulterson, or Jabez, as we elect to call him.

Milly gave a little scream, and then ran to the window.

"Why, I do believe, Patty, that Mrs. Coulterson has been letting off a gun; she has one in her hand, and she and Jabez are laughing," said Milly.

"I shouldn't wonder" replied Patty, "for missus humours Jabez—I mean master—in everything, and she is a good wife to do so. They'll be wanting lunch, I take it, as we doesn't have dinner till I've now you're here, Miss Milly." So saying, Patty left the room as Daisy knocked at the French window for admission.

Milly withdrew the bolt, and was terrified into running to the further side of the room, when Daisy asked her to take charge of the gun she was carrying.

"It's not loaded, silly one," said Daisy. "I have just discharged both barrels."

"You, Daisy? Never!" cried Milly.

"Indeed, I have," said Daisy; "Jabez showed me how to hold the gun, and seemed so pleased at the idea of my discharging it that I fired both barrels at his hat, which he had thrown up, and hit it too, Milly."

Jabez had never witnessed such a good joke, he declared; the crown of his hat had been riddled by the shot, and he now entered the house, laughing immoderately, and bearing in his hand Daisy's target.

"How could you have been so silly as to let me do it?" asked Daisy, smiling at sight of her handiwork.

"Do it?" replied Jabez, "why, if it had been my Sunday one I shouldn't ha' cared. Daisy, I am proud of you, that I am. The first time of handlin' a gun, and you've riddled him finely. Next season I'll take out a license for three, and we'll go shoot every day together."

"Well, not quite that, Jabez," said Daisy. "Now and

then, and without the license. Oh! here's lunch brought in by Patty herself, who, knowing how you like bacon, has provided a delicious piece. Eh, Patty?"

Before the old servant could reply, Jabez had taken her face between his hands, saying, "Bless your ould wrinkles! If it was only Christmas time, and the misletoe up, I'd give thee a kiss, I would."

"Don't wait for the misletoe, Jabez," said Daisy; "I sha'n't be jealous."

"Thee won't," cried Jabez, kissing Patty; "take that, old girl; and not the first by the score."

No, nor by many a score; for, when Jabez was left an orphan, Patty had supplied almost the place of a mother to the curly-headed boy adopted by Farmer Gathercole.

Jabez was desirous, very desirous, to improve himself in all things; so, as he said, that his wife should not be always ashamed of her ploughman husband; but Daisy had a very unpromising pupil, and old habits took a long time to eradicate. As lunch proceeded, Jabez cut a slice of bacon, and placing it upon a piece of bread as he had been accustomed to in former days, began to eat it, to the horror of Miss Milly, who nudged Daisy, and begged her to tell him not to be so vulgar.

Daisy shook her head. Milly's mode of correction was not Daisy's. "She never made Jabez ashamed of himself," she said afterwards; "I always make him ashamed of me." And, in practical illustration of her theory, she cut a piece of bacon and bread as Jabez had done, and commenced preparations for eating it. Jabez saw what she was doing, and, taking the hint, transferred his "hunk," as he called it, to a plate, without saying a word, and Daisy as silently followed his example. And then their eyes met, and it was plain that the scholar understood his lesson.

As soon as luncheon was over, Milly relapsed into one of her reveries, and Daisy, perceiving her thus occupied, said, rather maliciously for such a good-natured person, "Has Mr. Fortescue been here this morning, cousin?"

Poor Milly fairly jumped at being thus addressed, and blushed, and stammerd so, in her endeavour to appear unconcerned, that Jabez laughed outright.

"How ridiculous you are, Jabez!" said Milly. "Mr. Fortescue comes here to see you."

"See me! Come, that is a good 'un," replied Jabez.

"Why, when I went up to London about my fortune I met Mr. Fortescue at my lawyer's. He was civil enough when he heard what uncle had left me; but one day I see him in Hyde Park, lolling over the rails; and being precious lonely for want of some one to speak to, I walked up to him and nods, but he cocked up his eye at the clouds, and never so much as said good-morning."

"Then why did you ask him here?" said Daisy.

"Always return good for evil. I see him leaning over a gate, yawning, and then whistlin', and then throwin' stones in the horse-pond—feeling, thinks I, just as I did in London. So I took compassion on him, and says, 'How do, Sir?' He didn't cock his eye up in the clouds then, I can tell 'ee; but nigh shook my arm out of joint, he was so glad of a friend. What could I do but ask him home to a bit and a sup?"

"And we have made ourselves so agreeable that he has found occasion to repeat his visits five times in five days. Eh, Milly?" said Daisy, with a knowing look, which drove the blushing girl from the room.

Jabez had been married nearly twelve months, and during that time had been Daisy's pupil, striving very diligently to acquire such knowledge as she could impart to him; and whilst they were thus engaged Mr. Fortescue was announced.

Mr. Fortescue was evidently a man about town, and, being now rusticating for reasons best known to himself, had selected Little Grabley as a covert less likely to be drawn by the sheriff's pack than any other with which he was acquainted. His introduction to Lazy Hall was therefore an opportunity to be improved, and he availed himself of it to the full, especially when he heard from one of the servants that Miss Milly was worth ever so many thousand pounds, and perfectly disengaged.

When Mr. Fortescue's metropolitan difficulties were arranged, the country became intolerable to him, and therefore he endeavoured to tempt the household of Lazy Hall to visit London, but was met by a flat refusal from Jabez.

"You must be more amenable, my dear Coulterson; you must, indeed," said Fortescue. "Mrs. Coulterson and Miss Milly would produce a sensation in town."

Jabez expressed a very strong opinion on that point, and vowed "that he hated London, and that nothing on earth should take him there if he could help it;' declaring "that Rotten-row was not worth a turn in his straw-yard; and that it was all very well for those who had been reared among brick and mortar, sniffing nothing but coal smoke, to like the hard paving-stones and stifling streets; but for him, who had rolled upon daisies until he was old enough to walk upon them, he'd have no more of London."

Miss Milly, of course, sided with Mr. Fortescue, saying that it was cruel to Daisy to mew her up in the country all her life, and never know what real pleasure was; but Daisy came to her husband's aid, and declared that she was always happy—always; and if she ever had a momentary wish to visit London (which she remembered only as a child), she thought of all the good they had at home, and was contented.

Jabez rewarded her eloquence with such a hearty smack that it made Mr. Fortescue wink at the explosion.

When Mr. Fortescue returned to town he set his wicked wits to work to accomplish the object he had at heart— namely, to obtain possession of Milly's little fortune. He was a thoroughly bad fellow, and perfectly unscrupulous wherever his interest appeared to be concerned. Having ascertained that Coulterson's lawyer, Mr. Winch, would be absent from London for a fortnight, at least, Fortescue sent a letter in that gentleman's name, therein requesting Jabez to come to London, as a difficulty had arisen about the transfer of some property, and an appeal must be made to a Master in Chancery. A clerk in Mr. Winch's office was paid to assist in this scheme, and to keep Jabez in play, should he bite and take the hook.

This letter came like a bombshell into Lazy Hall, as Jabez, among a number of good qualities, had rather a violent temper, and for some half-hour or so he raved like a madman. He wouldn't go! They should bring Master Chancery down to Lazy Hall. He wouldn't go up to London so near Christmas time, when he had made up his mind to invite all his old neighbours and friends to a great feast on Christmas Eve. What did he pay a lawyer for? He wouldn't go, not he! But when Daisy told him that it was his duty to attend to his own business, adding, when that argument appeared to fail, "Now that he *must* go to London, Jabez, I don't mind confessing—though I have never said this before, because you were opposed to it—that I should like to see London again; and now that you know how much pleasure you will give your wife, you will not feel this business such a trouble, will you?"

"And you wish to go, Daisy?" said Jabez, making a very lugubrious face, "to leave our dear little home, where we seemed never to want anything more than one another to be happy? Oh! how happy I ha' been, Daisy, thinkin' that you cared for nought that these four walls didn't hold, and that you was content to be the teacher, the guide, of the poor man who, tho' no scholar, yet learned to love you more than all the world contains. Oh, Daisy! I shall now feel that you long to live for somethin' more nor me—me who loves you so."

Daisy threw her arms round his neck, saying, "Jabez! dear Jabez! I cannot bear this, I cannot."

"Well, then, say you won't go. Say you don't wish to leave home, and you ain't tired of our home—your husband."

Daisy took his hands and looked him tenderly in the face before she replied—

"When I married you, Jabez, it was not until after a long wooing. Folk thought it was your home and your money which made me yours at last. It was not so. I saw all the goodness of your heart, and loved you for it. Since we have been man and wife, what day has not made me love you more, my dear, good husband?"

"Then all's right again, dear Daisy," said Jabez, rubbing his eyes with the knuckles of both hands.

"Yes; I will stay here whilst you go to London," replied Daisy, "for you must go, as the person who gives you this new trouble—read the postscript to Mr. Winch's letter—assails the fair fame of your mother."

"Says aught agin my mother!" cried Jabez, snatching the letter, which had hitherto been read only by Daisy; "I'll make the fellow eat his words." And he began spelling the postscript, as Jabez was not a proficient in reading "written hand."

"That's enough," he continued. "Pack up, Daisy dear; we'll go at once. I don't fear London now, with its plays and operas, carriage folk and fine gentlemen. Cousin Milly, you'll go with us, wont 'ee? And Patty. Tell Patty to pack up as well, Daisy."

Mrs. Coulterson was too anxious for Jabez to answer Mr. Winch's summons not to avail herself of this decision instantly, and Milly was so delighted that she clapped her hands and ran out of the room to commence preparations for the journey. The day after the next, Jabez, with a heavy heart, permitted himself to be driven from Lazy Hall, in company of his household, on his way to London.

Mr. Winch's dishonest clerk (to whom Jabez had been requested to address his reply) and Mr. Fortescue were at the station waiting to receive the Coultersons on their arrival in London, and this considerate attention was very gratifying to one of the party at least. Mr. Fortescue had heard from Mr. Winch (so he said) of Mr. Coulterson's visit, and knowing that he could not come alone, had ventured to engage (subject to approval) some apartments for them in the house of a person of respectability; and thither the whole party proceeded, Mr. Fortescue kindly accompanying them.

The rooms were gaily furnished, being rather tawdry than elegant; and there was a boldness about the landlady which would have been offensive to persons accustomed to good society; but Jabez and Co. accepted it as best London manners, and acknowledged their own inferiority.

Mrs. Beauchamp let lodgings and dealt in left-off wardrobes of the nobility and gentry, giving the very best prices for court, evening, and other dresses, laces, and jewellery. Mrs. Beauchamp and Mr. Fortescue had been acquainted for many, many years. The knowledge which they had of certain questionable proceedings connected with each other made them what they were pleased to call friends; and the Coultersons were therefore to be enmeshed for their mutual advantage, and in less than a week from the time of their arrival the victimisation had commenced.

Mr. Winch's clerk had called on the day succeeding the arrival of the Coultersons in London to say that his principal had been most unexpectedly called to Jersey on business of the greatest importance, but his return to town should be instantly announced; and an order had been taken out "to stay proceedings." Poor innocent Jabez received this statement as truth; and, indeed, like many other nervous people, was rather glad to have his introduction to Master Chancery delayed.

Mr. Fortescue promised to prevent time hanging heavy on the hands of his country friends, and he therefore took them to the theatres and operas in the evenings, and for pleasant drives in the mornings—at the expense of Jabez, of course. Miss Milly never thought of that, but believed Mr. Fortescue to be one of the kindest of friends, the most agreeable of gentlemen.

One afternoon the ladies pleaded fatigue as an excuse for remaining at home in the evening, and Mr. Fortescue therefore availed himself of the favourable opportunity of taking Jabez away to dinner. We have neither space nor inclination to record how that evening was passed at Mr. Fortescue's chambers, in Lyon's Inn; but Jabez lay late in bed the next morning—long after Daisy and Milly had gone for a little shopping; and when he came to breakfast he actually asked for soda-water.

Patty guessed the cause of Jabez's incapacity to enjoy his breakfast, and shook her head when he looked up at her, very ruefully.

"Oh, Patty!" said Jabez, "I be very badly; never, old gal, take Bashaw'd lobster and champagne for supper—never!"

"It is not likely I shall be asked," replied Patty; "I never takes only bread and cheese. Ah! Jabez, Sir, I shall be glad to get back again to the country."

"And so shall I," said Jabez. "We've been here above a fortnight, and I'm sick on it. Mine's an early-to-bed constitution, and late hours don't agree with it. Where's Daisy—Mrs. Coulterson?"

"She and Miss Milly's gone out shopping," replied Patty. "They're going to this Christmas-tree party to-night at my lady's."

"Oh, Lor! I'd forgot that," said Jabez. "I wish Mr. Fortescue hadn't asked 'em; but they seemed so pleased to go, I couldn't say nay. It's a real lady's, Patty, and there's to be a Christmas-tree—something from Jarminy; and I've paid Mrs. Beauchamp's milliner a mint o' money for Prince of Wales's feathers for Daisy's head, and—and what's that stuff that sounds like sneeze?—Tissue! tissue! that's it."

"Bless her!" continued Jabez, after a short pause, "she might eat gold if she could do it; but she doesn't seem to have the light heart she had, since she came to this Babylonish captivity, as rector says."

"You're right, Jabez—master, I mean," said Patty.

"No, call me Jabez. When I ain't well I like to be spoke kind to," replied Mr. Coulterson.

"Well, then, Jabez," said Patty, leaning her two hands on the table, and speaking almost in a whisper, "I don't like the goings on in this house; I don't like Mrs. Beauchamp."

"Not she?" said Jabez, in surprise; "why she's hand and glove with all the nobility and gentry in London."

"You mean she's second-hand," replied Patty, making her only attempt at a joke during a long life, "and with lady's-maids, not ladies. I picked up her card, and read it."

Jabez did so also, to his utter confusion, and then exclaimed, "Why, if she ain't been dressing out Daisy second-hand! That won't do."

"Hush, Jabez," said Patty, again whispering; "best keep quiet, and get away. Missus needn't know nothing till we gets back, and then we can all laugh together. Miss Milly and she has set their hearts on this Christmas-tree, so you must let 'em go; but you ha' done with that Mr. Fortescue; he means no good to you or any o' us women either."

Jabez jumped up and clenched his fist, but Patty stopped any ebullition of temper by boldly placing her hand on his mouth and hurrying him into his bed-room, leaving him there, as Mr. Fortescue knocked at the door, according to his morning custom.

Mrs. Beauchamp came with him into the room which Jabez had just quitted, saying, "The Coultersons are out, the ladies some time, and the gentleman just this moment, I fancy. You'll kill that poor fellow, Forty. You see what a sufferer he has been this morning," pointing to the breakfast-table.

Jabez, finding his shaving-water cold, had opened his bed-room door with the intention of obtaining a fresh supply from the urn just as Mrs. Beauchamp made this reference to him; and, as the two friends then sat down upon the sofa for a chat, Mr. Coulterson showed his normal want of manners by listening to what they said. Fortescue laughed, and said something about having bled the bumpkin freely, and then be presented Mrs. Beauchamp with a crisp bank-note, which that lady received without any hesitation.

From what Jabez could hear, Fortescue seemed to be praising Daisy's beauty and simplicity, and then some allusion was made to Milly. Again they spoke of Daisy; and then, Mrs. Beauchamp having mentioned some word which sounded to Jabez like Pollygamousus, made a short exclamation, which reached the ears of the speakers.

Mrs. Beauchamp having pointed with her thumb to the

door of Jabez's room, the two friends rose and quietly withdrew.

Jabez got on very badly with his shaving, and, before he had quite finished that irritating operation, he sought a dictionary, and looked up the word "poly-gamy."

The meaning of that terrible word set Jabez in a fever, and half-shaven and carelessly dressed, he went out into the street, without knowing why he did so.

"I begin to think there's some dreadful plot at work," thought Jabez, after a time. "Why did he mix up Daisy's name with that ugly word? Oh, if his villany could succeed it would make me a staring lunatic! No! I shouldn't fear nothing! Daisy's too good, too true-hearted. But why should I let her be tempted? That's wrong o' me, downright wrong, and it sha'n't be. Lawyer or no lawyer, we goes back to Lazy Hall to-morrow."

He continued to ramble about for more than two hours, and when he returned Patty opened the door, her face so full of settled wonder that Jabez was frightened, his mind still occupied with Daisy.

"What's the matter, Patty? Speak out, will 'ee?" said Jabez.

"Oh, Jabez Coulterson!" said Patty, leaning against the wall, " I have just come from thy wife ——"

"Well! well!"

"And there she be, looking like the pictur of a queen upon her throne!"

"Be that all? You turned my blood to ice with your silly face," said Jabez, going up-stairs, followed by Patty.

"And so she's been trying on her finery, eh?" asked Jabez. "An' she looks grand, do she? and beautiful in her fine feathers and di'monds? She'll not want them when we get home agen, think ye, but be content wi' her pretty silk gown and simple bonnet?"

"Oh, surely she will," replied Patty, as Daisy, dressed in a very elegant toilet from Mrs. Beauchamp's milliner, entered the room. She certainly looked very handsome, and her cheeks were rather more rosy than usual, as Mrs. Beauchamp had offended her during the process of dressing by speaking somewhat disparagingly of Jabez, and hinting that the preceding evening had been spent at cards and the bottle.

Mrs. Beauchamp had been earning Mr. Fortescue's money.

"If Mr. Coulterson," Daisy had said, "has been so misled as to be guilty of follies and vices to which he was until lately a stranger, his wife is the last person who should be told of them."

But her anger had vanished when she presented herself to the astonished Jabez, who sat gazing at her silently for some minutes.

"No word of admiration?" asked Daisy, at length. "Are you not pleased to see me?"

"Yes, yes—very pleased," replied Jabez.

"You little thought, when you came courting the poor farmer's daughter, that you would ever see her dressed as I am now, Jabez, and all by your bounty."

"Don't talk so, Daisy," said Jabez, "I pray o' you, don't. If all I've got could make you happy, I'd give it freely, but ——"

"Surely you don't object to what I have done?" asked Daisy—"have I done wrong?"

"No, no," answered Jabez, "but mine's such a greedy heart I can't bear thee to like aught I can't share. Go! have thy night of glory! You've a loving heart still, Daisy, that nothing can change, haven't you? Nothing can change?"

"Nothing!" replied Daisy, emphatically.

Jabez rose up, and kissed his pretty wife, who then left the room to disrobe until the evening.

Poor Jabez was sorely troubled by what he had overheard, and he thought over it until he concluded that Fortescue was a villain, that Mrs. Beauchamp was as bad as he, and that both had combined in some plot against the peace of Daisy and himself. He was not wrong.

Jabez therefore stole down-stairs to Mrs. Beauchamp's room, and found the lady alone. Without waiting to be invited, he sat down at the table at which she had been writing, and said, bluntly,—

"Mrs. Beauchamp, you be what's called a woman o' the world. Don't deny it, because I want you to be so. I am a new scholar in the same school; but I've learned my few lessons thoroughly and well."

"What do you mean, Sir?" asked Mrs. Beauchamp.

"This—I ha' seen that most of the world is guided by lust o' pleasure and lust o' money."

Mrs. Beauchamp nodded her head affirmatively.

"You like money; you've sold a good deal for money besides left off wardrobes. Don't start! I bean't angry at that discovery, and won't taunt you wi' my bargain; but you've sold a little bit of your conscience now and then, and I want to buy some of the same commodity that you've sold Mr. Fortescue."

Mrs. Beauchamp was a cool card, and she nodded her head again.

"Time's short, so I'll be plain wi' you," said Jabez. "For his money you have undertook to do some'ut — say with Milly, or say wi' some one else. You see I guess pretty true, so your plot must fail."

"What plot, Sir?" asked Mrs. Beauchamp, very coolly.

"Now, no more secrets atwixt us," replied Jabez. "There's one hundred pounds; take it. Now hear what I say. He can't pay you to do them wrong as I will to save 'em. Make a clean breast to me, and I'll pay you more. What's he mean; what's he seeking?"

"Well, Mr. Coulterson," replied Mrs. Beauchamp, after a few moments' reflection, "you are so very liberal that I should be wrong not to answer you. I think—in fact I know—that Mr. Fortescue admires your ladies very much."

"What! both—both on 'em, perhaps?"

"Well, I fancy so; but Miss Grainger is in most danger," replied Mrs. Beauchamp, coolly, pleasantly, as though she were telling the young lady's fortune; "but, if you will undertake to make this one hundred two, I will prevent any injury——"

"Houd up your hand," said Jabez, interrupting Mrs. Beauchamp; and then, striking his own against the hand of the lady, as though he were making a market bargain, he added, "Done! Bought and sold; and now to deliver!"

"Very well, I will take your word," said Mrs. Beauchamp. "Mr. Fortescue certainly admires Mrs. Coulterson, and for that reason, among others, he has led you into dissipation; but his design is to marry Miss Grainger, if he can obtain her money, and then desert her."

"The scoundrel!" cried Jabez.

"He is not scrupulous, certainly," said Mrs. Beauchamp. "I fancy that Miss Grainger would be a consenting party; but Fortescue is married—a wretched match, made years ago; and his wife has been living away some years, under an arrangement, in Brussels. He would risk the discovery, as his fortunes at present are very desperate."

"Well ; and Mrs. Coulterson?" asked Jabez.

"Oh ! I think nothing of her flirtation with Fortescue," said Mrs. Beauchamp, artfully. "Pretty women know their influence, and use it."

"Yes, yes," said Jabez, gazing vacantly ; "and she is pretty. Mrs. Beauchamp, I'll be as good as my word ; oh, yes ! and keep your seeret, and better than my word if——" He paused.

"I understand you, Sir," replied Mrs. Beauchamp, "and be sure I will be your friend."

Jabez thanked her, poor fellow ! and then went out again, saying that he should dine abroad, as he was going once more to seek Mr. Winch, the long-absent lawyer.

Daisy and Milly were dressed for the party, and Jabez had not returned. Daisy was sitting alone in the drawing-room, when Fortescue was announced. He stood for a few moments in silent admiration, as it were, of the beautiful woman seated before him, and then, in a most respectful tone said :—

"How very beautiful you look ! I could not have believed that dress would have improved you so much."

Daisy felt a strange alarm at this address, and when he at length proceeded to use still stronger phrases of admiration, her woman's pride was aroused, and she rose to ring the bell. Fortescue would have prevented her, but she looked at him defiantly, and said :—

"Sir ; more than once lately you have addressed me in language the meaning of which I did not dare to suspect. You have now presumed to make your previous expressions intelligible. Be pleased to leave me ; " and she rang the bell violently.

Fortescue tried to excuse what he had said, but Daisy refused to hear him or to see him again except in the presence of her husband, if he dare stay to meet Jabez.

Mr. Fortescue, abashed and confused, was obliged to leave the house, to the terrible consternation and disappointment of Milly, who would not believe Daisy's interpretation of her admirer's conduct, and she and her cousin parted angrily.

Daisy tore from her head the feathers, and shook her hair free of its bandages, as though her brain were oppressed by them, and then sat down and hid her face as Jabez returned and entered the room.

"So the day's turned out showery, and there's thunder about," he thought; "Milly crying below, and Mrs. Beauchamp looks like a fiery furnace. Well, Daisy," he said, aloud.

"Oh, Jabez, my dear, dear husband!" cried Daisy, running to him and embracing him passionately.

"What! thee's been in the wars, I see," said Jabez, in a strange, cold voice. "I heard somewhat of it down-stairs. It's all as well that disappointments and troubles should come by degrees. You've had yourn; I've had mine."

"Oh! nothing serious, I hope, dear Jabez?"

"That's as may be, thanks to your friend, Mr. Fortescue," replied Jabez. "I've found out the plot some o' you had to get me up to London."

"Plot?" asked Daisy. "I in a plot?"

"I said some o' ye. Mr. Fortescue, perhaps—perhaps Milly. Mr. Winch never wanted me. It's all a trick to get here. Well, here I am."

"Jabez, you frighten me," said Daisy. "Your manner, tone, look—are all changed. What has happened?"

"They've been making a fine gentleman o' me," replied Jabez, sternly; "takin' me to a gamin' house—giving me wine, and what not; and I've lost my money. There be many wicked things done in this great city. Why shouldn't I ha' my part? You would come to London, all o' ye, tho' I warned you what would happen."

"Oh, Jabez, Jabez!" said Daisy, "you are concealing something from me. What is it? What has happened? Let us go home to-morrow!"

"*You* can—*you* can if so please you," replied Jabez. "I don't go till I've had my revenge, or till I am ruined right out."

"Oh, Jabez! What are you saying?"

"But not you, Daisy. I cared for that when I made you my wife. You can live like a lady, no matter what comes o' me."

"What have you said, Jabez; what have you said?" cried Daisy, the tears falling fast, "the only unkind words you ever spoke to me. Leave you? Leave you if you were ruined? Oh, how cruel!"

"Cruel!" Jabez paused. "Then you — then Mr. Fortescue"—he could not, he dared not say more.

Daisy flushed very red as she replied—"Mr. Fortescue is a villain. He has dared to address me ——"

Jabez stopped her by taking both her hands and looking her in the face. He only looked a few moments and then pressed her to his bosom. "I know how you answered him, my wife—my true wife!"

Daisy, when composed enough, told Jabez all that had passed, and then Milly was summoned; but she still contended that Daisy had misunderstood Fortescue, and confessed that he had addressed herself as a suitor.

"Poor child!" said Jabez. "If you care for him I am sorry, Milly. You shall have the truth out o' him. Write him a note and ask him to see you in the morning—here, alone like." And after some further discussion, a note was written and sent to Fortescue.

The next morning Jabez was in great good spirits, and one or two sly looks passed between him and Patty, much to Daisy's wonder.

It was arranged that Milly should receive Fortescue alone at first; but scarcely had that person been introduced, when Jabez and Daisy joined the party. Fortescue started, and said, "I understood, Miss Grainger, that you desired to see me alone."

"You must excuse what I have done," said Milly, "but I have brought you here for your own sake—to remove from my cousin's mind that ——"

Jabez couldn't keep quiet—"That you're a bad man—a scoundrel, in fact. You have addressed Cousin Milly as a suitor—a regular, honourable suitor."

"I have. Why should I not?" asked Fortescue, boldly.

"Because the law o' England won't let a man marry two women, both on 'em alive. You've a wife already."

Fortescue fairly staggered at this assertion, and watched with intense interest Jabez proceed to the adjoining room, whence he led forth a trembling woman, closely veiled, who would have fallen had not Jabez placed her in a chair.

"This lady calls herself Mrs. Fortescue," said Jabez, but the confounded trickster could not conceal his own secret, and Fortescue exclaimed,—

"My wife in England! Woman, you shall repent this violation of our contract." And repeating this declaration with the addition of an oath, he left the house.

Poor Milly was terribly distressed; but Daisy strove to

comfort her by congratulating her on the escape she had had from such a wicked man.

"Well," said Jabez, "I think we have had enough o' London for some time, and 'arn't drawed many prizes off Lady Thingamee's Christmas-tree, so we'll home, all on us, and this poor crittur shall make one of our party."

Daisy was astonished at this proposition, but ceased to be so when Jabez pulled off the veil and discovered old Patty.

"So you see," said Jabez, "there's not much harm done, after all," laughing heartily.

"But your losses?" said Daisy, with an arch look.

"Not a flea-bite, lass. I've only been shamming. Shamming to lose my fortune—shamming about going to ruin—shamming to have found Mrs. Fortescue."

"And the drinking?" said Daisy, shaking her head and smiling.

"Well, there war a little truth in that; but, once home at Lazy Hall, I'll do—what do they call it?—penance; but not till Christmas-tide is over, for we'll have a frolic when we get back."

And Jabez kept his word, and holly and holly-berries sparkled in every window of Lazy Hall, and in the barn, where old friends and neighbours had been invited to make merry. Jabez had reared a Christmas-tree, upon every bough of which hung substantial prizes of good worsted-work, or packets of tea or tobacco, and not one of them without a bright half-crown hidden within; in gratitude, so Jabez and Daisy said, that they had gathered from the London Christmas tree nothing which they had carried home with any lasting regret.

WHAT CAME OF KILLING A RICH UNCLE ONE CHRISTMAS TIME.

BE it understood, good reader, if you require confirmatory evidence of the truth of all the facts of this Christmas story, we at once declare our inability to satisfy you; neither will we tell you how they came to our knowledge. We have not invented them, be assured of that, although we have decked them out in holly and mistletoe, and other Christmas associations, as befitting the season when all are making due preparation to bear part in the general festival of peace and good-will instituted eighteen hundred and sixty-six years ago.

Now to our story.

CHAPTER I.

"YOU ARE SO PRETTY."

"DANCE with me, Letty Green?" said George Poynter to a pretty girl with blue eyes, and "hair that shamed the morn."

Her ample ball-dress was of the purest white muslin, fastened at the sleeves and round the waist with blue ribbon—bluer than her eyes.

"Yes," answered Letty, "I want to dance with you."

And the music striking up, the young couple made the most of it, to the occasional derangement of less determined terpsichoreans.

The dance at an end, Letty tried to smooth her golden curls into order with her little hands, and then, opening her pretty blue eyes to their full, said,—

"George Poynter, I should like some orange."

"Yes, Letty," said the young gentleman addressed; "and there's lemonade, and negus, and such a sponge-cake!"

Letty thought that sponge-cake and lemonade would be more acceptable than orange *pur et simple*, and her partner fought his way bravely through the crowd surrounding the refreshment-table, and returned with the desired delicacies.

"I like dancing with you better than any one, Letty,' said George to his pretty partner.

"Do you? Why?" replied Letty, her voice rather obstructed by the sponge-cake.

"I think it is because I like you—you are so pretty," replied the young gallant.

"You mustn't say that, or mamma will scold you, George. She scolds every one who tells me I am pretty," said the young lady.

But the words had been spoken, and from that night until the end of the Christmas holidays George and Letty said they were sweethearts.

CHAPTER II.

THE PONY-RIDING ARRANGEMENT.

SOME four or five years had passed, and Letty Green and her mamma were sitting together under the verandah of their pretty cottage, working, and talking of a pleasant day they had spent at Mr. Poynter's, when Master George came in, he said, to bid them good-bye, as he was returning to school on the following morning.

"And I want to ask you a favour, Mrs. Green, and Letty a favour," said George, colouring slightly.

Mrs. Green would grant it, of course, and so would Letty, if she could.

"I want Letty to ride Rufus, my pony, whilst I am at school. Papa has no use for it, and it carries a lady beautifully."

"But to accept this proposal would give so much trouble."

"Not in the least. Tom—that's our groom—says it won't, and papa says it won't, and I say the same; so please say you'll use the pony. Straps, the harness-maker, will lend a side-saddle."

Mrs. Green accepted George's offer, as Letty was rather fragile, and pony-riding had been declared to be good for her; but Mrs. Green's income would not allow of the expense, she said. There were people who called Mrs. Green a mean woman, and hinted that she loved money better than her child.

George Poynter went to school very cheery, because he had made such a capital arrangement about his pony, and he often thought, when the weather was fine, of Rufus, and wondered if Letty were riding him. George had not forgotten, perhaps, that years—years ago, he and Letty had called themselves sweethearts.

CHAPTER III.

SWEETHEARTS.

MORE years had passed, and brought their changes. George and Letty were alone together in a small book-room in Mrs. Green's house, the windows opening to the garden. George was attired in deep mourning, and there were strips of black ribbon here and there on Letty's white dress. They had been talking of death and sorrow until both had become silent. After a time Letty took George's hand, and said,—

"Dear George, you must strive to meet your great affliction with a brave spirit—indeed, you must."

"I have—I do strive," replied George, looking away from Letty; "but remember what has come to me. Two years ago my mother died. A year ago that villain Jackson ruined my father—broke his heart—killed him. Oh, Letty! what have I done to deserve this? What can I do?"

"Trust still to the Father of the fatherless," replied Letty. "We do not know why great afflictions are permitted to overtake us, any more than we can tell why great good comes to us when we least expect or deserve it, dear George. You are young, clever, good, and have many friends, and one—who is more than a friend."

She raised George's hand to her lips when she had said this (they were true sweethearts now), and he—what could he do but press her to his bosom, and kiss her cheek, burning with blushes?

Mrs. Green had been walking in the garden, evidently busy with her thoughts. She had stopped near the book-room window, near enough to hear what the sweethearts were saying to each other, and she appeared to be made more thoughtful by what she heard.

When Mr. Poynter was a thriving merchant, Mrs. Green had been more than a consenting party to her daughter's acceptance of George Poynter's attentions—indeed, she had by several indirect means encouraged the young people to think lovingly of each other. But now matters were changed. Master George, as he was generally called, had neither houses nor lands, nor had he "ships gone to a far country," and Mrs. Green was perplexed how to act. She knew that Letty loved her first sweetheart, and would perhaps love him more now that he was poor. Girls are very perverse sometimes, and will not see with their mothers's eyes, which look upon love only with respect when the little gentleman has a good wardrobe and a balance at his banker's. Mrs. Green therefore was perplexed when she heard what the sweethearts had said to each other, and conjectured how they were "signing and sealing" some loving contract, when silence prevailed in the little book-room.

Mrs. Green was relieved from her perplexity more agreeably than she deserved to have been, as George Poynter called the next day, bringing with him a letter from his uncle, rich old Silas Cheeseman, promising to provide for his only sister's only son, and hinting that George might by good conduct look to be heir to all his thrifty savings.

Silas was a bachelor, having been blighted in his youth. He then took to loving money, and had been a most successful wooer, as those clever people who know everybody's business but their own declared old Silas Cheeseman to be worth his hundred thousand pounds—"more or less, as the case might be."

Uncle Silas had also procured a situation for George in the neighbouring town of St. Gnats—merely a probationary situation—as clerk to a timber merchant who was under pecuniary obligations to Silas. All this was very cheering, and very kind of Uncle Silas, although Mr. Bawk, the timber-merchant, was indelicate enough to surmise that George was placed in his establishment as a spy, to watch the interests of his uncle. George would have scorned such a position for all Uncle Silas had to give or to leave behind him.

CHAPTER IV.

MISS BEADLE'S MARRIAGE.

EFORE we pass on to the events of the next few years, we will introduce Chauncey Gibbs, a friend of George Poynter, of whom we have yet made no mention.

Chauncey—his patronym of Gibbs was rarely mentioned—Chauncey was a good-natured, good-for-nothing, unsettled, amusing fellow, who contrived to live a gipsy kind of life on two hundred a year, stedfastly refusing to encumber himself with any employment or to incur responsibilities more (to quote Chauncey) than his hat would cover. He was a native of St. Gnats, and known to everybody in the town, but he had no regular abiding place, as he chose to wander at will; and George Poynter would not have been surprised to have received one of Chauncey's brief letters dated from London, Paris, Vienna, or Pekin. He mostly affected England, however, and London especially in the winter. When money was scarce, Chauncey walked—when he was in funds he availed himself of any cheap conveyance which offered, sometimes never inquiring its destination, but making himself equally at home wherever he was stranded. At Christmas time he always returned to St. Gnats, and was a welcome guest at many hospitable tables in that thriving town, making his head-quarters, however, with his old friend and school chum, George Poynter. He had written to announce his return to St. Gnats for the Christmas approaching the end of the two years which had intervened since George Poynter had assumed the stool of office at Mr. Dawk's, and supplies of tobacco and bitter beer were already secured for the welcome, expected guest.

Chauncey had a favourite lounge in London, a tobacconist's in an out-of-the-way street in the neighbourhood of St. Mary Axe.

The proprietor was a beadle, or some official of that character, to one of the companies, and the tobacco business was conducted during the early part of the day by the beadle's wife and daughter. It was Chauncey's pleasure to sit on a snuff-tub in front of the counter and smoke, in turn, all the varieties of tobacco sold at the beadle's, beguiling the time, also, with animated conversations with the daughter, whose powers of repartee were more ready than refined. It is not our intention to chronicle more than Chauncey's parting interview, and what came of it, as slang from a woman's lips is our abhorrence.

Chauncey was about to leave the shop after one of his long sittings, when the younger lady said—

"You won't see me again, I expect, Mr. Chauncey; I'm going to be married."

"*You* married!" exclaimed Chauncey, as though such an event had been the most unlikely thing that could have happened.

"Yes, me; why not, I should like to know?" asked the lady, a little piqued.

"I am sure I envy the happy man," replied Chauncey. "It's not the Scotchman at the shop door, is it?"

"Well, I'm sure!" said the young lady, and without another word she bounced into the little parlour at the back of the shop.

"Now you've regularly offended Becky," said Mrs. Beadle, "and such old friends as you was—and she to be married to-morrow, and so respectable."

"Well, I'm glad to hear that," said Chauncey. "Where's the wedding to be? I'll buy a bundle of watercresses, and strew her way into church as an apology for my rudeness."

"Oh! she won't want no apology from you—she knows what you are, Mr. Chauncey; but she's to be married at ten to-morrow, at St. Mary Axe's, but we don't want it spoke of, as the bridegroom's nervous," said Mrs. Beadle in a whisper.

"I'll be there in time," replied Chauncey. "I suppose her father will give her away—in full costume, cocked hat, staff, and all that?"

"He will do all things that is proper, Mr. Chauncey," said Mrs. Beadle, with much dignity; and Becky at that moment calling "Mother!" in rather an hysterical tone, Chauncey was allowed to find his way out of the shop as he pleased.

On the following morning Chauncey was at the church of St. Mary Axe a quarter of an hour before the time appointed for the ceremony which was to unite Miss Beadle and somebody to their lives' end.

A hale old gentleman between sixty and seventy, perhaps, was the next arrival. Having made some very confidential communication to the old pew-opener, he was conducted, evidently in great trepidation, to the vestry, and there immured until the arrival of the tobacconist and family—but without the emblematical Scotchman. Chauncey concluded, therefore, that Miss Beadle had captivated the old gentleman now awaiting his doom in the condemned cell called the vestry.

The beadle was in *mufti*, but his costume still partook of the splendour of his office, and a canary-coloured waistcoat with glittering buttons of ruby glass rendered him somewhat conspicuous even in the gloom of St. Mary Axe. His general expression and bearing was that of a tempered indignation, as though he were about to consent to the infliction of some injury which he could avoid if he pleased. A word, a look, might have provoked him to have torn the licence from the parson's hands, and to have dragged his daughter from the altar. He was therefore allowed to walk up the aisle unmolested.

Mrs. Beadle was very lively on her entrance into the church—more lively, perhaps, than black tea and the occasion warranted; but whatever had been the stimulating cause of her cheerfulness, it ran in plenteous drops from her eyes as she approached the altar, and must have been exhausted entirely by the end of the ceremony. Niobe weeping for her children would have been a dry nurse compared with Mrs. Beadle.

Miss Beadle was resigned, as became her to be at thirty-one. With closed eyes and drooping head she leaned upon her mother's arm, until, with pardonable confusion, she released her hand to put up her parasol as she drew near the altar. Chauncey rushed to her relief, and with some difficulty possessed himself of the encumbrance; and as there were no attendant bridesmaids, the impudent fellow attached himself to the wedding party, to be, as he said, "generally useful and to pick up the pieces."

The ceremony proceeded with all proper solemnity, but there was some association with the name of one of the contracting parties which made Chauncey fairly start, and then determine to witness the signing of the certificate, to satisfy a doubt which had suddenly entered his mind.

The wedding party retired to the vestry when "amazement" had ended the ceremony, and proceeded to sign the registers attesting the union which had just been solemnised. Mr. Chauncey Gibbs, being, as he said, a friend of the family, signed also, and there read—what had better be revealed in the next chapter.

CHAPTER V.

FINANCIAL.

ANY one had only to have walked down the High Street of St. Gnats to have known that Christmas was at hand. The grocers' windows were overrunning with lusciousness; the butchers' shops were so choke full of beef and mutton that the butchers themselves would have to cut their way out into the street; the poulterers had laid in such stocks of turkeys, geese and chickens, that Mr. Babbage's calculating machine could alone have computed them—mere human intellect would have failed. The window frames of the houses seemed sprouting with holly and the "ivy green," and no doubt but mistletoe hung, kiss provoking, within.

Mrs. Green had made every room in her cottage an anagram of her name, as it was holly-decked everywhere. Nor was the sacred bough forgotten—" on the young people's account," she said, " though Letty and George had long ceased to want an excuse for a kiss." All promised a merry Christmas time to come, but promises, we know, are not always realised.

George Poynter was waiting the arrival of his friend Chauncey Gibbs. A glorious fire blazed within the grate; the table was spread to welcome the coming guest, for whose delectation a faultless rumpsteak pie was browning in the oven. The train, punctual to its time, was heard screaming into the station close by, and, in a few minutes after, the two friends were together.

If you are hungry, it is tantalising to listen to the parti

culars of a dinner you are not to share; if you are sated, you are bored by the recapitulation of dainties you care not to touch, and therefore we will allow the friends to take their meal in peace. Neither will we join their after-revel, when two or three old cronies came in and made a night of it, until George and Chauncey sought their beds fairly tired out with jollity.

When breakfast was over the next morning, and Chauncey found that George had excused himself from attendance at the timber-yard, he said—

"I am glad you can give the morning to me, as I have some news for you that may, perhaps, surprise and annoy you."

"Indeed!" replied George. "What is it?"

"I would not touch upon it last night, although I think some immediate action should be taken by you or your friends," continued Chauncey, looking very serious.

"Pray speak out," said George.

"Oh yes. I must do that, for I have no tact, never had, to make an unpleasant matter agreeable. Have you heard from your uncle lately?"

"Yes, two days ago—principally on Mr. Bawk's business," replied George.

"My old boy, your uncle never intended you any good when he shut you up in that log-house of Bawk's. He put you there for his own selfish purpose, and nothing else."

"Why do you say that?" asked George.

"He has led you to suppose that you were to be his heir some day, has he not?"

"He has never said *that* in direct terms; but he certainly has hinted at such a possibility."

"Then he's an old scamp, if he don't deserve a harder name," said Chauncey, thumping the table. "Two days ago he did his best to disinherit you. You may stare, but I saw with my own eyes, heard with my own ears, that old ragamuffin marry a bouncing woman of thirty."

"Marry! Uncle Silas marry!"

"Fast as St. Mary Axe could do it, to a snuffseller's daughter;" and then Chauncey, to the astonishment of his friend, narrated what we already know of the wedding at which Mr. Chauncey had so officiously assisted.

"This is indeed a terrible blow," said George, "an unexpected blow."

"Yes; I am afraid, knowing the hands he has fallen into, that he won't have a will of his own when a few months have passed," said Chauncey. "I found out how the matter came about. Old Silas was very ill, and wouldn't have a doctor; but a beadle, I call him, got at him, and then introduced his daughter as nurse. They first physicked him nearly to death, and then brought him round with bottled porter. They told the old fool they had saved his life, and he believed it; and out of gratitude, and the want of a nurse, he proposed to Miss High-dried, and married her."

"This hits me harder than you know, Chauncey—much harder. Poor Letty and I can never hope now ——"

"Oh, nonsense!" replied Chauncey. "Keep your uncle's secret, as he will if he can, marry Letty, and let Mother Green storm afterwards."

George shook his head, and then said,—

"Chauncey, you advise that which is dishonourable."

"All fair in love, old boy," replied Chauncey, with a laugh; "and if I were you, to gain the woman who loves me, and whom I love, I'd KILL MY UNCLE."

"Great Heaven! what do you say? But I see—you were joking. No; my course is perfectly clear so far as Mrs. Green and Letty are concerned. I go to them at once, and tell what has taken place. If I am forbidden to continue my visits by Mrs. Green, she shall be obeyed. Letty, I know, will be always true to me; and when I can make a home for her, I can claim her with honour."

"Devilish pretty speech," said Chauncey, "and all right, I have no doubt. I still say, kill old Silas Cheeseman, and get married: or, stay—perhaps—yes—you shall write to him, now that he's honeymoon-struck—tell him you want to follow his example, and require ten thousand pounds to do it."

"I understand this nonsense, Chauncey," replied George, with a sad smile. "Your friendly chaff is well meant; but my case is very serious. And so good-bye for an hour or two. You will find me here after that time."

The road to Mrs. Green's cottage never seemed so long before to George Poynter as it did now that he felt his fate, the happiness, for a time at least, of his darling Letty, depended upon the interview he was seeking with her mother. He was not without some justification for the misgivings which beset him, as Mrs. Green had more than twice or thrice casually hinted at what a mother's course should be, to prevent a child "marrying into poverty." Indeed, she had once told him, when Letty was not present, how glad she was when his uncle's recognition of him produced such a favourable turn in George's fortunes, as it had spared them all the pain which she should have felt it her duty to have inflicted.

The crisis had only been deferred.

There were tears from Mrs. Green—regrets, and pity; but there were also cold, cruel words, which were not to be gainsaid, unless Letty could disobey the mother who had loved her all her life, and lived only to see her happy.

George spared his Letty and her mother any contest as to the decision to be made. He promised to obey Mrs. Green in all she required of him; but he promised Letty also, when they were left alone, that his love never should change, nor should a doubt ever have place in his thoughts that she could change one tittle in her love for him. And as he held her to his beating heart—not for the last time, no! no!—he told her how he would strive to make a home for both—that their probation would be short if a brave resolution could only find the means wherewith to work. And they would come—they always did, for had they not been promised by the ONE who could not lie?

Poor hearts! they waited very sadly; but a good angel was already busying himself for their reunion. And such an angel!—Chauncey Gibbs!

"He won't write to old Silas? Then I will," said Chauncey, half aloud, when George had left him. "He won't KILL HIS UNCLE—an old fool; then I will." He opened the long blade of his penknife, and—trimmed a quill which he found on George's desk.

There were paper and ink, as may be supposed, and there was also the ready writer, Chauncey, who began,—

"St. Gnats, Dec. 20, 18—.

"DEAR SIR,

"As my friend, Mr. George Poynter, is unfortunately suffering at this time from a severe blow in his chest—('That's perfectly true')—I have placed myself at his service; and although I shall not express myself as he would have done on the subject—('That's true again, I fancy')—I hope you will take the will for the deed. News has reached us here, dear Sir—('He'll like that dear Sir')—that after many years of deliberate calculation—('No, not calculation')—consideration, you have discovered that man was not made to live alone, and therefore, with a wise regard for your own happiness, you have sought connubial felicity at the altar of St. Mary Axe—('Very good,' muttered Chauncey; 'the name of the church will show that his secret is known to us.')—I know not whether it is your wish that your blissful union should be made generally known ; but I cannot hesitate (on the part of my friend, I mean) to offer you my sincerest congratulations, and to wish you all the happiness you deserve. —('That's true ; and I should like to add, all you are likely to find.')—I am aware that what you have done must necessarily interfere largely, if not entirely, with those expectations which you once or twice—(shall I say promised ? No !)—encouraged me to entertain ('What would old George say to that ?') And though I descend from the clouds of hope—('Good figure, that !')—to the sub-stratum of daily toil and permanent anxiety, I shall know that you are sitting happy at your domestic hearth, smoking the pipe of peace—('It wants something else to round off the sentence.')—and—and—('Oh, blow it !')—rocking the cradle.

"May I request, if not asking too much at this blissful period of your life, a line to tell me that I may add to my affectionate remembrances an Aunt Cheeseman?

"I remain, dear Sir,
"Your affectionate nephew,
"For GEORGE POYNTER."

Chauncey paused. "It wont do to sign my name, or Mrs. C. will remember it. Yes—I have it—they never heard the name of

"C. GIBBS."

Having sealed and directed his letter, Chauncey proceeded to post it.

In travelling down from London, Chauncey had learned that a projected branch railway from St. Gnats was in high favour with all the moneyed interest of the place ; and when he suggested the propriety of killing old Silas, he had this railway in his mind, as on the following day the allotment of shares was to take place. Chauncey knew, as he knew everybody, Mr. Golding, the banker, and chairman *pro. tem.* of the projected company. Without the least misgiving or hesitation, he called upon that highly respectable gentleman, and, after a few minutes' interview, gave the conversation an extraordinary twist, or jerk, as thus,—

"You've heard of the great windfall to our townsman, George Poynter, I suppose," said Chauncey. "No? Well, perhaps it was hardly to be expected, seeing what a retiring fellow he is."

"What is it?" asked Mr. Golding. "He is a young man for whom I have the greatest respect. I shall be glad to hear of any good fortune to him."

"And it is a good fortune! His uncle, you know, was immensely rich," said Chauncey. "The *old bachelor* is no more—went off three days ago—and my friend George was long ago his appointed heir."

"Silas Cheeseman gone!" remarked Mr. Golding, with a shrug: "a very money-getting man; and must have died very rich—very rich."

"E-nor-mously rich! Single man many years; no expenses, you know," said Chauncey. "I witnessed the last moments of the old bachelor at St. Mary Axe. Went off quite composedly after his will was accomplished. By-the-bye, it strikes me you might secure the interest of young George."

"How, my dear Sir?" asked Mr. Golding; "we are always glad to secure a good client ——"

"And with such wealth!" said Chauncey. "You allot shares in the St. Gnat's Junction to-morrow, do you not?"

"Yes," replied the banker; "and the applications exceed anything I ever knew: the shares will be five or six premium before to-morrow is over."

"That's your plan, then! Secure him a thousand."

"A thousand!" exclaimed Mr. Golding.

"Well, half-a-thousand—say five hundred—for George Poynter; I'll let him know whose influence he has to thank for them. You'll be the banker of his immense wealth—his friend—adviser."

"But he has not applied," said Mr. Golding.

"But you have. What's a paltry five hundred to you, in comparison to after gain—or to him? He won't care for the money, but the friendliness of the thing," said Chauncey, with a flourish of the hand, as though he were proposing the merest trifle of a sacrifice.

"And you, my dear Sir?" asked Mr. Golding.

"Oh, nothing; I want nothing; and you may rely upon my secrecy."

Mr. Golding pressed Chauncey's hand, and thanked him for the friendly suggestion.

Mr. Golding had but one *confidant*, Mr. Baxter, who at that moment entered the bank, and was announced as being there.

"Do you object to my naming the matter to my friend Baxter!—great influence at the Board," said Golding.

"Not in the least: perhaps he may help you to make the allotment a thousand?" replied Chauncey.

"Oh, impossible, my good friend," said the banker. "Show in Mr. Baxter."

Chauncey's communication having been repeated to Mr. Baxter, the diplomatist thought he had better retire; but he had not gone many yards from the bank, when Mr. Baxter overtook him.

"Delighted to hear what you have told us concerning your friend Poynter—an excellent young man, and deserves all he gets."

"I am sure of that," said Chauncey, "whatever good it may be."

"He'll reside in St. Gnats, I suppose?"

"Yes," answered Chauncey.

"And will want a house suitable to his new position?"

"Yes."

"Now I am wanting to sell Prospect House yonder—fine garden, abundance of water, and all that—would it suit him, do you think?"

Chauncey was rather posed by this inquiry, and said, therefore, "Perhaps."

"I think it would: £3,500 is what I ask—and could get it, but I dislike the man. You know Captain Ranger?—of course you must," said Baxter, with emphasis.

Chauncey did not, and would not know Captain Ranger.

"He is a troublesome fellow, and I should be glad if he would leave the place," said Mr. Baxter. If Mr. Poynter will buy, he shall have the preference."

Chauncey saw no objection to that, and promised to speak

to his friend if Mr. Baxter would make the offer in writing; but £3,000, he thought, would be the utmost that Mr. Poynter would give for a house.

Mr. Baxter paused for a moment, and, as they were opposite his counting-house, he invited Chauncey in, and subsequently gave him a letter to Mr. George Poynter, containing an unconditional offer of Prospect House for £3,000. Chauncey carefully put away the letter, and bade Mr. Baxter good day.

Poor George had returned to his lodging when Chauncey had transacted all the important business we have recorded, and not all his friend's good spirits could rouse him from almost despondency.

"My old boy," said Chauncey, "you'll sink down, down, if you show the white feather in this way. You're young enough to work, and like it—I never did."

"It is not hard work—hard fighting with the world that I am fearing; it is the effect of this day's cruel trial upon poor Letty."

And then George told Chauncey all that had passed.

"Well, you would be so hastily honourable," replied Chauncey; "you had better have been advised by me— waited a day or two until you had killed your uncle."

George looked at his friend and saw a cunning twinkle in his eye; but Chauncey had his own reasons for saying no more on the subject.

George was very ill the next morning—too ill to go to the timber-yard; so Chauncey offered to see Mr. Bawk, and, if business pressed, to supply George's place for a day or two. Mr. Bawk declined Mr. Chauncey's services, and was so excessively polite and anxious in his inquiries about Mr. George, that Chauncey thought the story of yesterday had reached Mr. Bawk.

It was not so; but Captain Ranger had been to the timber-yard to see Mr. Poynter, and had surprised Mr. Bawk by assuring him that his clerk must have come into money, as he had bought Prospect House, at a sum which he (Captain Ranger) had refused to give. He had, however, left a commission with Mr. Bawk; and Chauncey wormed out of the timber merchant the following particulars.

Captain Ranger, it appeared, had married a lady with money—not always a desirable exchange for a man's life and liberty—and the lady never allowed him to forget the

pecuniary part of their engagement. She had taken a
fancy — the word is not strong enough — a longing for
Prospect House, and the captain had undertaken to obtain
it; but, being fond of a bargain, he had disgusted Mr.
Baxter with a tiresome negotiation, and the house had slipped
from him. To confess this to Mrs. Captain Ranger would
be to invoke a conjugal tempest ; and in this extremity he
had come to Mr. Bawk to intercede with his clerk to transfer
his purchase.

"Well," said Chauncey, " George is a good-natured fellow
—too good-natured—and I will undertake to say that the
Captain shall have Prospect House for £4,000."

" Four thousand pounds !" exclaimed Mr. Bawk.

"And not one shilling less," said Chauncey firmly. "The
house is worth it as it stands ; but compute its value to
Captain Ranger and it is cheap at any money."

Mr. Bawk pleaded to a stone agent when he tried to
soften Mr. Chauncey ; and Captain Ranger coming into the
counting-house at the moment, heard the terms proposed,
raved like a maniac for ten minutes, and then consented
to be swindled — robbed, for the sake of peace and
quietness.

Chauncey could be a man of business when he pleased ;
and he was now in a business mood. He therefore trotted
off the angry captain to an attorney's, made the transfer, and
secured a prospective 1000*l*. for his friend George by KILLING
HIS UNCLE.

As the day wore on, Chauncey waited upon Mr. Golding,
and found that gentleman writing to Mr. Poynter, and expressing the great pleasure it gave him to hand him a letter
of allotment for five hundred shares in the St. Gnat's
Junction, etc., etc., etc., Railway ; adding a hope that
the firm of Golding, Silverton, and Co. might have Mr.
Poynter's name on their books as an honoured client.

Chauncey undertook to deliver the letter, and to use his
influence with his friend to make the only acknowledgment
he could for such disinterested generosity.

Poor George was very ill at ease when his friend Chauncey
returned, and at first was disposed to be angry at what he
felt to be his inconsiderate raillery.

" I am serious, old boy, quite serious," said Chauncey,
throwing Golding's letter and the transfer on the table ; " I
have killed old Silas Cheeseman, and there are some of the

proceeds of the transaction. Open — read and satisfy yourself."

George opened the envelope containing the transfer, and then Mr. Golding's letter. He was in a mist. He thought he was delirious and had lost his reason ; and Chauncey was a long time making him comprehend how he had come to be possessed of—

Profit on transfer	£1,000
Profit on 500 Shares ; premium £4 per share	2,500
Total	£3,500

and all by killing old Silas Cheeseman !

Poor George was hard to satisfy that these large gains were honourably come by ; and when he went to sleep he dreamt that he had robbed the bank and had set Prospect House on fire. The following morning brought a letter from Uncle Silas.

The poor old dotard expressed himself so pleased at his nephew's forgiveness of an act which he had thought would have provoked only revilings and wicked wishes, that he enclosed a cheque for £1,000, and his avuncular blessing.

Was ever another fortune made by such means? George had all the money ; Mr. Golding begging his retention of the shares, as his commercial acuteness might be damaged by a disclosure of the trick which had been practised upon his cupidity ; and Captain Ranger was submissively satisfied, having told his *cara sposa* that he had bought Prospect House a decided bargain.

Mrs. Green would have had to endure many mortifying reflections had it not been Christmas time, when Letty and George, and all other estranged friends, are willing to forget their old grievances, and, in thankfulness that such a season was vouchsafed to erring man, humbly imitate the Great Forgiver.

THE GHOST DETECTIVE.

"YOU take an interest in Christmas legends, I believe?" said my friend Carraway, passing the claret.

"Yes, I think they are as good as any other," I replied.

"And have faith in ghosts?"

"Well, I must answer that question with an equivocation. Yes—no."

"Then if you care to listen, I can, I fancy, remove your scepticism," said Carraway.

I professed my willingness to be converted, provided I might smoke whilst my friend talked, and the conditions being agreed to, Carraway commenced:

"When I first came into the City—now some thirty years ago—I formed an intimacy with a young man in the wine trade, and we passed most of our leisure time together. He was much liked by his employers, whose principal business was with publicans and tavern-keepers, and after a time my friend became their town-traveller—a position of trust and fair emolument. This advancement enabled my friend, James Loxley, to carry out a long-cherished desire, and that was to marry a fair cousin to whom he had been attached from his boyhood. The girl was one of those pretty *blondes* that are so attractive to young fellows with a turn for the sentimental, and a tendency to sing about violet eyes and golden hair, and all that. I was never given that way myself, and I confess Loxley's cousin would not have been the woman I should have chosen for a wife, had I ever thought of taking to myself an incumbrance. I had had a step-mother, and she cured me of any matrimonial inclinations which I might have had at one time. Well, Loxley thought differently to me, and his marriage with his cousin Martha Lovett was settled, and I was appointed best man upon the occasion.

"The bride certainly looked very pretty in her plain white dress—very pretty, though somewhat paler than usual, and perhaps made me think more than ever that Martha was not the wife my friend James should have selected, knowing as I did that they would only have his salary to live upon, and that much would depend upon her to make his means sufficient for decent comfort. However, they were sincerely attached to each other, and that, I was told, was worth one or two hundred a-year, which I did not believe. Martha was greatly agitated at the altar, and at one time I thought she would have fainted before the ceremony, as they call it, had finished. As it was, she had a slight attack of hysteria in the vestry, but the pew-opener told me that was nothing unusual with brides, especially with those who had been widows.

The wedding-breakfast was a quiet affair—nothing like the sacrificial feasts of the present day—and we were all merry enough until the happy pair were to leave for their own home, and then poor little Martha hung about her mother's neck and sobbed—much more than I thought was complimentary to her new husband—but then I was not a fair judge of the sex, having been worried all my life by a stepmother.

"When Loxley and his wife were fairly settled in their new home, I used frequently to pop in for a game at cribbage or a chat with my old friend, and a more loving couple I never saw in my life. Not being by any means rich, they had babies, of course, and in less than three years there were two most charming creatures—when they didn't cry or poke out their eyes with the tea-spoons, or perform any other of those antics which are the delight of parents, but can only be designated as inflictions to unattached spectators.

"I have thought it only fair to mention these little matters; you will see wherefore by-and-by.

"Loxley had invited me to take my Christmas dinner with him, and a pleasant day we had! He was partial to keeping Christmas with all the honours, and his little dining-room—it was his drawing-room also—was sprigged about with holly, even to the picture-frames. He had only two oil paintings — portraits of his father and mother, both long deceased, but the likenesses, he said, were so good, that he could always fancy his parents were present.

"Well, as I have mentioned, we passed a happy day and night; Loxley had arranged to go with me for a couple of days into the country, on a visit to a good old uncle of mine, as an atonement for keeping me away from the family dinner.

"The visit was paid; but I was rather annoyed at the effort which Loxley evidently made to appear entertained, and I thought he was home-sick, or vexed that I had not invited his wife to join us, as there were lady visitors at my uncle's. Whatever was the cause of his frequent abstractions, I could only regret it, as I had given him such a good character for cheerfulness and pleasant companionship, that one of my cousins twitted me, with rural delicacy, for having brought a thorough wet blanket from London.

"During our journey back to town, Loxley was silent and thoughtful, and I longed to ask if anything troubled him. But we had passed such a jovial Christmas-day together, that I could not suppose he had any other anxiety than what the restoration to the arms of his Martha would remove. We parted, however, without any explanation being asked or volunteered.

"On the second day after our return, I was astounded at receiving a message from Loxley to come to him at the Mansion House. The officer who brought the note told me that Loxley was in custody, charged, he believed, by his employer, with no less an offence than embezzlement.

"Such an accusation seemed at first, to me who had known Loxley so long, so intimately, preposterous — impossible. As I walked to the Mansion House a cold sweat seized me, and for a moment I thought I should have fallen, as the strange conduct of my friend during the past two days came to my recollection. Had he found his means too small for his home requirements? Had he been tempted, and yielded as good men had done before him? No, no!— a thousand times, no!—if I knew James Loxley rightly.

"He was standing at the prisoners' bar when I reached the Mansion House, and I was not permitted to speak to him. He saw me, however, and knew his friend was with him.

The junior principal, who had recently joined the firm of X. and Co.—by-the-bye, he had, for some reason, never taken kindly to Loxley—was giving his evidence. He said: 'That John Rogers, a customer of the house, had caused a great deal of trouble with his over-due account, and that it was thought he would prove a defaulter. Mr. X. (the prosecutor) had heard accidentally that Rogers had received a large sum of money, and as Mr. Loxley was away from business, Mr. X. had called upon the debtor to demand payment of his debt. Mr. X. was received with much insolence by Rogers; and his conduct was accounted for subsequently by the production of Loxley's receipt for the money, dated the 24th of December. The man had paid £40, by a cheque to Loxley, and no such amount was credited in the book of X. and Co. Rogers produced his banker's book, and the cheque, with Loxley's signature on the back. It was found, also, that a person, answering by description to Loxley, had received two notes of £20 each, one of which had been paid at the Bank of England in gold early on the morning after Christmas-day.

"This evidence was confirmed by John Rogers, who had given the cheque; by the bankers' cashier who had paid it; and by the Bank of England clerk, who had given gold for the note.

"Loxley was asked—having received the usual caution—if he wished to say anything.

"He answered:—

"'Yes; and he thought he had been hardly used by his employers, that an explanation of the matter had not been required from him by them before he had been taken into custody as a thief. He had also heard of Rogers's accession to money; and having the interests of his employers in view, went at once to the man, and with great difficulty succeeded in obtaining payment of the debt. He received the cheque, but fearing that Rogers might stop the payment of it at his banker's, he, Loxley cashed it immediately, placing the notes he received, as he believed, in his pocket-book. As it was Christmas-eve, he did not return to X. and Co.'s, the house being closed, but walked home with a friend he had met in the banking-house when he received the money for Rogers's cheque. On the morning of the 26th he had intended calling at X. and Co.'s on his way to his appointment with me; but finding he was late, he attached no consequence to the omission, having a holiday. When he was at his journey's end, and in his bed-room, he was looking in his pocket-book for some matter or the other, and for the first time missed the bank-notes he had received for the cheque. He was completely perplexed, being certain that he had placed the notes in the case, and that he had never lost possession of them. He had employed the morn of his return to town in searching—vainly, he knew—all conceivable places at home for the missing notes, and of course without success. Before he could go to X. and Co.'s offices he was taken into custody.

"'One of the notes was cashed at the Bank of England early on the morning of the 26th, was it not?' asked the Lord Mayor.

"The Bank clerk who cashed the note said 'Yes, it appeared so, but he could not remember exactly whether it was presented by a man or a woman. He thought it was not paid to the prisoner.'

"'But it was paid, and in gold,' said the Lord Mayor. 'The embezzlement of employers' money is one of the gravest offences against the law, and must be severely punished and put a stop to. The statement of the prisoner is very plausible —very feasible, perhaps I should say—but I cannot feel it my duty to decide upon its truth or falsehood. He must be comitted for trial.'

"Loxley bowed his head and remained immovable, until a shriek in the passage of the court reached him, and he started as from a dream. He instantly looked to where I had been standing, and I understood his meaning. He was right. He had recognised the voice of his wife, who having heard where they had taken her husband, had followed after. I found her as I had seen her on her wedding-day — hysterical, but the attack was very violent; it was with great difficulty I conveyed her to her mother's, and thence to her own home.

"I said all I could to comfort her. I told her my own conviction of Loxley's innocence, my full belief in the explanation which he had given, and the certainty of his speedy liberation. But I spoke to a stricken woman, to a distracted wife, a half mad mother. She sat for some time with her children in her lap, rocking to and fro, and sobbing as though her heart would burst. She cried to me to succour her husband, to bring him home ; if not for her sake, for that of her innocent children. She would not let her mother speak, but continued to appeal to me, until—yes, I own it—until I fairly broke down and could not answer her. And all this while the green holly garnishing the room, and the faces of the father and mother looking on placidly from the walls."

The recollection of the painful scene he had been describing made Carraway silent for a time, and I remarked that he had the satisfaction of knowing he had done his duty to his friend, whether he proved guilty or innocent.

" Yes," continued Carraway, " I had that satisfaction, though I did not desire to blow my own trumpet in what I have said. Well, when the elder X., who had been away from town, heard of the matter, he was inclined to believe Loxley's statement, and blamed his son for his precipitancy. The matter, however, was beyond his control now, and the law had to vindicate its supremacy.

" The trial came on, and the gentleman whose professional business it was to prove Loxley guilty necessarily did all that was possible to show the weakness of the defence. He asked why Loxley had not instantly returned to town when he had discovered the loss of the notes ? Why had he not written to his employers ? Why had he not mentioned his loss to me,—the friend whom he had called to speak to his character ? No satisfactory answer could be given for such omissions. What had become of the other note ? If a dishonest person had found the notes—supposing them to have been lost—would they not have changed both of them for gold ? The most favourable construction which could be placed upon the case was the supposition that the prisoner had need of twenty pounds, and had taken his employers' money, intending, very likely, to replace it. That was no uncommon case. The pressure of what seemed to be only a temporary difficulty, had often led well meaning men into such unpardonable breaches of trust. And now, having placed the case as fairly as he could before the jury, his duty was done, and it rested with the twelve intelligent men in the box to pronounce their verdict.

" ' Embezzlement,' the judge said, very properly, ' was a

serious crime, and must be repressed by the punishment of offenders. The jury had heard the prosecutor's statement—proved by highly-respectable witnesses ; and the prisoner's defence—unsupported by any corroborative evidence. The jury had to judge between them.'

"Without leaving their box the jury, after a brief consultation, pronounced a verdict of 'Guilty,' and my friend—my dear friend, James Loxley—was sentenced to transportation.

"This terrible sentence was almost fatal to Mrs. Loxley, Her delicate constitution would have give way under her excess of grief had not—well, had not I set before her the duty she owed to her children, who had a right to a share in her affection. Poor thing ! she struggled bravely to overcome her great sorrow, but I doubt much if she would have succeeded but for what I am now about to relate to you. Stay—I must mention one or two matters before I tell you that portion of my story.

"The Loxleys occupied only part of the house in which they lived. They had their own furniture, but the landlady of the house provided servants, excepting a little girl who acted as nurse.

"The general servant who waited upon the Loxleys was one of those patient drudges often found in lodging-houses. Her name was Susan, but Loxley had given her the sobriquet of ' Dormouse,' as she was a drowsy, stupid—perhaps sullen is the better word—girl, who moved about more like a piece of machinery than a living being. She never showed any feeling, either of displeasure or gratification, excepting in her strong attachment to Loxley's children. That arose, perhaps, from her womanly instinct. But when Mrs. Loxley's great trouble came, when the girl had come to understand what had befallen Mr. Loxley, and that misery and ruin had overtaken them and their children, Susan's whole nature appeared to undergo a change. She seemed to watch every want, every movement of Mrs. Loxley. More than once she was found sitting on the stairs near Mrs. Loxley's door, when that poor lady was in her paroxysms of grief, as though desirous to lend what aid she could in subduing them. I was so struck by the devotion and sympathy of this poor, stupid creature, that I could not help noticing her, and on one occasion offered her money. She refused to take it.

"' No, thank'ee, Sir,' she said ; 'that's not what I want ;

but I should like to be of use to poor missus, if I could, Sir.'

"I told her she had been of great use, great comfort to Mrs. Loxley, who had seen, as I had, how much she felt for her misfortunes.

"'Yes, Sir, that's true enough. And what will they do to Mr. Loxley, Sir?' she asked.

"'He will have to suffer a great deal, Susan—great misery; but neither you nor I can help him.'

"The girl burst into tears, and cried so bitterly, that Mrs. Loxley overheard her, and I have no doubt questioned her when I was gone.

"Mrs. Loxley's mother was staying with her, the elder Mr. X. having insisted upon making a temporary provision for the unhappy wife of the man he still believed to be innocent —I say, Mrs. Loxley's mother was staying with her daughter. She had gone to bed in an adjoining room, as Mrs. Loxley frequently begged to be allowed to sit alone, as she found it difficult to sleep. I have reason to believe that after her mother had gone to rest, Mrs. Loxley had an interview with Susan; but, for reasons which will appear, I never questioned her on that point. It was past midnight, according to Mrs. Loxley's statement, when, sitting with her head resting on her hands, she saw the door of her room open, and her husband enter; saw him as plainly and like himself as she had ever seen him. She rose up; but the figure motioned her to remain where she was. She complied; now conscious that it was not her husband in the flesh upon which she looked. The figure sat down in his accustomed place, and then appeared to gaze stedfastly on the portrait of his father, still ornamented with the faded holly twigs which had been placed there at Christmas-time. This continued for some minutes. The figure then rose up, and looking towards Mrs. Loxley with a most loving expression on its face, walked from the room, opening and closing the door after it.

"Mrs. Loxley tried to follow, but could not. She was not asleep; she had not been even dozing; she was sure of that; but had seen with her waking senses the apparition of her husband then lying in Newgate prison.

"What followed seemed equally inexplicable, to me who had more than once witnessed her tendency to hysteria and fainting. She said she had felt no alarm at what she had seen. She was stupefied for a few moments, but not alarmed.

She went to her mother; but finding her quietly sleeping, Mrs. Loxley lay down beside her without disturbing her. In the morning she narrated to her mother what she had witnessed during the past night, and subsequently repeated her story—word for word, her mother said—to me, in the presence of her landlady and the maid Susan.

"The effect upon the poor, dull-witted servant was very remarkable. She fixed her eyes on the portrait which had attracted the notice of the apparititon, as though she were fascinated by it. She then asked Mrs. Loxley, with a voice and look of terror, 'Did you speak to the ghost, missus?' and when Mrs. Loxley replied 'No,' Susan inquired, 'And didn't the ghost speak to you?'

"Mrs. Loxley answered that she had told all that had occurred, adding nothing, keeping back nothing; and this assurance seemed to have a consolatory effect upon the girl, who then busied herself with her work. I had made inquiries at the prison, as Mrs. Loxley foreboded illness or death to her husband, and learned that my unfortunate friend was in health, and had become more resigned to the cruel future which awaited him. Mrs. Loxley appeared to be satisfied with this account of her husband.

"The night which succeeded, Mrs. Loxley proposed to pass in the same manner; but her mother insisted upon remaining with her, and that night no apparition came.

"Mrs. Loxley was disappointed, and attributed the absence of the spirit to the presence of her mother, and it was now her turn to insist. Mrs. Lovett went to her room, having promised to go to bed, and not seek to watch or return to her daughter. It was impossible, however, for the old lady to sleep, and she listened to every noise in the street, and to those unaccountable sounds which we have all heard in our lonely rooms.

"It was again past midnight, and Mrs. Loxley had, she admitted, worked herself into a high state of expectancy, when, without the opening of the door, the figure of her husband stood in the room. Again it regarded her most tenderly for a few seconds, and then fixed its gaze on the portrait of Loxley's father. It had not seated itself, as on the former visitation, but stood, with its hands folded, as though in supplication. It then turned it face to Mrs. Loxley, and opened its arms, as if inviting her to its embrace. Without a moment's hesitation she rose, and almost rushed to the bosom of the shadow. But the impalpable figure offering no resistance, she dashed herself against the pannelling of the room, and the withered holly sprigs in the frame of the picture above her fell rustling to the ground. The shade was gone !

Mrs. Lovett, hearing the noise against the panel and the scratching of the falling holly, immediately went to her daughter. Mrs. Loxley had not borne the second visitation so bravely as she had done the former one, and it was necessary to call for assistance, as a violent attack of hysteria succeeded the vision.

"The 'Dormouse,' usually most difficult to arouse, was the first to hear the calling of Mrs. Lovett, and to go to her assistance.

"'Has she seen it again?' asked Susan, almost directly she had entered.

"'Yes.'

"'And did he speak to her this time, missus?' asked Susan. Mrs. Lovett could not satisfy the girl's curiosity, but when Mrs. Loxley revived sufficiently to tell what she had seen, Susan repeated her inquiries. and appeared to be relieved when she heard that the ghost had been silent.

"I was sent for early in the morning, and having despatched what pressing business matters I had, I went to Mrs. Loxley. She was, as before, perfectly circumstantial in her account of what she had seen, not varying in the least from her first statement; and she and her mother believed that she had seen with her corporeal eyes the spirit of her living husband. I could not bring myself quite to this conclusion. I therefore suggested that it was possibly the association of the portrait with her husband, acting upon her over-taxed brain that had conjured up these shadows. Mrs. Loxley admitted the possibility of such a solution, and readily acceded to my proposal to take down the portrait which had attracted, as it seemed, the attention of the figure, and then to abide the result of another night, if Mrs. Loxley felt equal to courting the return of the vision.

"I rang the bell for the maid, and requested her to bring the steps.

"'What for?' she asked quickly.

"'To take down one of the pictures,' I replied.

"'There ain't no steps,' she said, firmly.

"I could have sworn I had seen a pair in the passage as I

entered, but I might have been mistaken, and I did not press the request. The picture was easily removed by my standing on a chair.

"As I turned to place the picture on the floor, I was perfectly thunderstruck to see the change which had come over Susan. She stood transfixed as it were, her mouth and eyes distended to the full, her hands stretched out, as though she were looking upon the ghost which had disturbed us all.

"'What is the matter with the girl?' I exclaimed, and all eyes were directed to her.

"'Susan fell upon her knees and hid her face almost on the ground, and screamed out, 'I'm guilty, missus! I'm found out! I knowed why the ghost come! I'm guilty!'

"We were all astounded! After a few moments, as I stood on the chair with the face of the portrait towards me, Mrs. Loxley uttered a shrill cry, and rushed to the picture. From the inside of the frame to which the canvas was attached she took out a note for 20*l*.—the note which had formed part of the forty which Loxley had received and had lost so mysteriously!

"There was no doubt who had been the thief. Susan had already confessed herself guilty, and I did not hesitate to obtain what other confession I could from her. It seemed that Loxley had been mistaken in supposing he had placed the notes in his pocket-book. Owing to his surprise at meeting the friend he had spoken to at the bankers' he had placed the notes in his trousers-pocket, and the force of habit had induced him to think he had otherwise disposed of them. These notes, so carelessly placed, he had drawn forth with his hand whilst ascending his own stairs, and Susan had found them. The half-witted creature showed her prize to an old man employed to clean shoes and knives, and he counselled the changing of one of the notes, with what success we know. Susan received none of the money, as the old scoundrel declared himself a partner in the waif, and told Susan she might keep the other note. But what Susan saw and heard subsequently had so terrified her and filled her with remorse, that she dared not dispose of her ill-gotten money, but, strangely enough, concealed it behind the portrait of Loxley's father.

"My friend, by the exertion of X. sen., was soon liberated, and by the honourable conduct of the same gentleman, who did all he could to repair the wrong unwittingly done to

Loxley, an excellent appointment was found in Australia. There James and Martha and their progeny are now, and thriving, I am glad to say.

"I'll trouble you for the claret," added Carraway. "And now, do you believe in ghosts?"

"I must make the answer I did before," I replied. "Yes— no. I think the apparition was provoked by the cause you at first suggested—namely, the association of Loxley's with his father's portrait and Mrs. Loxley's overtaxed brain. You have heard, no doubt, of the well-known case of M. Nicolai, the Berlin banker, who, according to his own account, having experienced several unpleasant circumstances, saw phantasms of the living and the dead by dozens, and was yet convinced they were not ghosts. Mr. Loxley might have also been dreaming, without being aware of it, as others have done; and it is rather against the ghost, if he appeared only to discover the lost note, that he came not when Mrs. Lovett was present."

"But the note was found behind the portrait at which the ghost looked so earnestly. How can you account for that?" asked Carraway.

"Well, I am so much a doubter of spiritual manifestation that I can satisfy myself, though not you, perhaps, on that particular. Suppose this stupid Dormouse had taken it into her silly head that Mr. Loxley's ghost had come for Mr. Loxley's money, and under that impression had placed the note behind the picture after she had heard Mrs. Loxley's account of the first visitation, in order to get rid of the money which the ghost wanted?"

"I don't believe that!" said Carraway. "I believe it was a real, actual ghost!"

"I don't," I replied, "and so we end as we began. I'll thank you for the cigars."

A CHRISTMAS DAY IN A JEW'S HOUSE.

E always "keep Christmas" in our village, although it is the fashion somewhat, now-a-days, to sneer at the custom and profess to discover no reason for rejoicing at that particular season. Our neighbours are no better than other folk, but there are many acts of kindness performed by rich and poor, and some small feuds forgiven because of the usages of the time and the remembrance of the great event which they celebrate. No dwelling, however humble, but has its sprig of green holly in its windows, and when the inmates comprise both young and old, a bough of mistletoe is seldom absent. All this, perhaps, would be out of place in London, but we should miss those indications of Christmas-time sadly.

Our rector is a stickler for all pertaining to Christmas observances, in and out of church; and he makes it a rule to invite certain of his friends and neighbours to make merry with him on Christmas Eve, not seeing anything sinful or uncanonical in "a liberal hospitality" which embraces egghot and elder wine, and a round game of speculation. Sometimes, of later years, speculation has been voted too noisy, and one or other has ventured to tell a story, dull enough often, but we are good-natured critics generally, and especially on Christmas Eve, when under the genial influence of the rector's brewage.

Our doctor (he bought the practice some six years ago) has a reputation amongst us as a story-teller, and we now propose to narrate all that we can remember of an account he gave us last Christmas, after supper, of the way in which he came to have a Christmas dinner in a Jew's house.

It was to this effect :—

"After passing my examination at St. Bartholomew's, I was assistant for some years to a gentleman, part of whose practice lay about the neighbourhood of Covent Garden and Drury Lane, and as the patients in those localities were not very aristocratic, they usually (except in cases of danger or difficulty) devolved upon me. It was in my professional capacity that I became acquainted with the story I am about to tell.

"There are many faded streets in the neighbourhood of Covent Garden—streets which, in time past, had inhabitants whose names will be ever associated with the arts and literature of our country ; but their places are now occupied by less distinguished persons, although many of them are engaged in pursuits similar to those which developed the genius of their great predecessors. On the second floor, in one of those houses, lived Mr. Maul, an artist, who managed to earn a limited income by portrait painting. His powers of execution were by no means commensurate with his ambition, but they satisfied the class of sitters whose homely faces he transferred to his canvases. He was, in fact, the artist to a portrait club, established at one of the adjoining taverns, and his patrons were content to accept distinctness of expression and gorgeousness of attire for finish of manipulation ; and Mr. Maul was always prodigal in those particulars, never allowing a portrait to leave his easel until he had adorned the subject of it with a waiscoat of chrome yellow and a coat of Prussian blue, profusely ornamented with buttons almost equal in appearance to original brass. Watch chains and bunches of ponderous seals were prodigally bestowed ; and when finger-rings came in fashion with the vulgar, he never painted a hand without a carbuncle worth ten times the money paid for the introduced digits, and hands were always charged extra. Mr. Maul's remuneration was not excessive ; but his engagements were regular, and he contrived to maintain a respectable appearance and to pay his way like an honest man that he was. Mr. Maul might, it must be confessed, have been a little more provident ; but singing a good song, and having other social qualifications, he was induced, rather too frequently, to stay late at his tavern and to spend more money than he ought to have done, considering the precariousness of his employment, more especially as his pretty daughter Grace had no one in the wide world to care for her but himself, as her mother had died many years ago, when Grace was only a very little child, so young and plump, that her mother called her 'Dumpling,' and this name for the sake of her, perhaps, who had bestowed it upon the child, had been retained, although modified somewhat into 'Dumps' and 'Dumple.'

"It was not in the least applicable to Grace Maul when she was 'sweet sixteen,' as she had grown to be a most graceful maiden, her form quite perfect, and her face pretty enough for her beautiful blue eyes and rich auburn hair. Her disposition was worthy to be lodged in such a casket, as she was always kind and gentle, and loved her father so dearly, that she thought the good people who appeared in blue and yellow on his easel were quite equal to any of the much bepraised portraits which she saw on the walls of the Royal Academy when she paid her annual visit to that painters' paradise (or *inferno*); and nothing could be stronger proof of a blind love than such an opinion, for Mr. Maul was rather hard in his outline and usually flat in his colour. He was great, however, at expression, as the portrait of the landlord hanging up in the bar-parlour of the ' Early Potato' in Covent Garden Market testified to all comers.

"Dumple was very clever with her needle, and Mr. Maul's shirt-fronts were the envy of his acquaintances. She was a capital housekeeper, and made the weekly earnings sufficient for all their wants and a few luxuries besides, as their sitting-room—it was Mr. Maul's studio also—was ornamented with such flowers as would grow in a London second-floor when carefully nursed; and Grace was such a watchful attendant that her plants lived out their natural lives, and made, at proper seasons, the otherwise dull room look like a country bower. Nothing could be neater or more becoming than Dumple's dresses, or prettier than her bonnets, and yet she was her own dressmaker and milliner, and had acquired the 'art and mystery' of those important callings without the aid of an instructor. She made herself useful also to the great artist, 'setting his palette,' for him in the morning and cleaning it in the evening when he had done work, being very careful of the colours. At times, when other sitters than those connected with 'the club' presented themselves, and artist-work increased, Dumple would 'scumble in' the blues and the yellows, leaving the master hand to insert the lights and shadows, the buttons and jewellery, with effect no other hand could produce—so Dumple thought, dear child. As soon as daylight failed in winter, and long before in the summer-time, Mr. Maul found his dinner ready for him; and though it rarely consisted of more than two courses, it was prepared so cleverly, and served so neatly, that it might have 'put an appetite beneath the ribs of death,' even as it did beneath those of the great artist who had won a right to it by his genius and his labour. Now and then, owing to the theatrical tendency of the locality, Mr. Maul was presented with 'an order for two' to the play, where Dumple enjoyed herself to the utmost, and for days after, as it served her as the subject for conversation with her father, who knew many of the lesser histronic luminaries off the stage, and also for her morning's reading, as she selected the play she had witnessed, and it was her custom to read aloud to her father while he sat at work; and by so doing she had gained more knowledge than usually falls to the share of a poor girl who could not be spared to go to school at an age when she would have profited most by her studies. Dumple and her father were very happy together; and though Mr. Maul had his professional jealousies and sense of genius unappreciated, he pursued the even tenour of his way pretty quietly.

"But there came a need for the doctor. The painter's hand would not work so obediently as it had been wont to do, and a numbness seized it every now and then which alarmed both father and daughter. It was incipient paralysis, no doubt, and the remedy was rest.

"Rest! Leave work!

"Why that meant more than the bodily discomfort. To rest from work implied an empty cupboard, or the beginning of debt, which might go on increasing and increasing until it became too heavy to bear, and could only be laid down within the walls of a prison. Rest! Impossible!

"The unsteady hand worked on, more slowly every day, until at last the brush dropped from the powerless fingers, and the toiler's work was ended. Poor Dumple had watched daily the insidious approach of the terrible enemy, and, like a brave girl, had cast about to meet the consequences. Her skill in embroidery was now so employed as to help the wearied bread-winner, as she worked early in the morning and late into the night; but her gains were very small compared with the lessening earnings of her father. When those ceased altogether, her position seemed almost desperate; but Dumple had a brave heart beneath her graceful bosom, and she would not despair. Not she, though only eighteen.

"It wanted three weeks to Christmas, and Dumple had noticed lately, when on her way to the City, where she sold her embroidery, a number of young girls passing in and out of the stage-door of Drury Lane Theatre. She wondered what their business could be, and whether they were earning money. One day, after she had thought thus, she stood on the opposite side of the street earnestly gazing at a group of young girls who had just left the theatre, and who remained chatting together until they separated with laughter and smiling faces, going their different ways. As she continued looking after them, a Jew of some fifty years of age stopped suddenly near her and seemed to have found an interest in her pretty wondering face. He was not a very presentable person, being unshaven, and his face, hands, and wardrobe would have been improved by a thorough ablution. He, too, had come out of the theatre; but Dumple had scarcely noticed him, her thoughts having been with the happy laughing girls.

"'What are you looking at the stage-door for, my dear?' said the Jew to Dumple; "is you waiting for anybody to come out? everybody's gone almost.'

"'No, Sir,' replied Dumple, not feeling in the least afraid; 'I don't know any one connected with the theatre;' adding, after a pause, 'I wish I did, Sir.'

"'Why, my dear?' asked the Jew; 'is you in the profession?'

"'The profession?' inquired Dumple, with a great stare.

"'Yes—they calls it "the profession" do the actors,' replied the Jew. 'Is you wanting an engagement in any line?'

"'I should be very glad to ——' Dumple paused, for her brave heart beat quickly at its own boldness. 'Yes, I should be very glad to get an engagement if I knew how'

"'What as, my dear? Chorus? Bally? or only to go on?' asked the Jew.

"'I presume only to go on,' answered Dumple; 'I have not been educated as a musician, nor can I dance, I'm afraid.'

"'Oh, dear! oh, dear! that's not a very good look-out for you: only fifteen bob a week, and find your own shoes and stockings,' said the Jew.

"'Fifteen shillings a week?' asked Dumple, with great interest; 'as much as that?'

"'Yes, at Christmas-time,' said the Jew.

"'And could you—could you tell me how to apply for such an engagement?' asked Dumple, boldly at last.

"'Well, I don't think the number is made up, as I haven't measured half they says there's to be,' replied the Jew; 'and Mrs. Bellair, the bally-missus, won't let 'em wear no shoes but mine. There she is, a coming out of the the-ā-tre, and if you'll wait here, I'll ask her the question.'

"The dirty little Jew ran across the road in a strange shambling manner, and having had a few words with the lady to whom he had referred, suddenly presented himself in the muddy gutter, and beckoned Dumple to come over to him. As she obeyed his summons, picking her way carefully from stone to stone, the shoemaker's professional eye glistened as he noticed her pretty feet—

> "Which like two little mice peeped out,
> From underneath her petticoat."

The ballet-mistress stared into Dumple's face, and then rapidly surveyed her figure.

"'Yes, Myers, she has a good face and figure, and as we want most of our small ladies for Cupids, and the tall ones for pages, I think I can engage her to go on. What's your name, my dear?' asked Mrs. Bellair.

"'Maul, Ma'am,' replied Dumple.

"'Maul, no; your Christian name, my dear?'

"'Dum ——' she had nearly said Dumple, but replied 'Grace, Ma'am.'

"'Grace!" cried Mrs. Bellair; 'oh, that will never do. What names have we got to spare, I wonder?' pulling out a very soiled roll of paper. 'O-ah! yes—here's "Mathilde" vacant. You call yourself Mathilde, dear, and come to rehearsal to-morrow at ten. Of course, she knows she won't be paid for rehearsals, and that I expect a fee of one shilling a week for teaching her her business to the end of her engagement.'

"Poor Dumple understood little of what she now heard, as she was quite overcome with her good fortune, although she knew she had to wait three long, long weeks before she inherited.

"Mr. Myers undertook to explain matters to his *protégée*, and proceeded to do so in the manner following:—

"'There, my dear, you's engaged for the run of the pantomine at half-a-crown a night, but you'll find your own shoes, and fleshings, and hornaments for your 'air if you wants any, except wreaths, and them you'll get in the wardrobe. You'll come to rehearsal to-morrow at ten, and mustn't mind being put at the back 'mongst the ugly ladies and awkward ones. You'll soon make your way to the front if I isn't mistaken. Your shoes will be three-and-six pence a pair, unless you chooses to have satin, which'll be five-and-sixpence with sandals. I shall be at the the-ā-tre to-morrow at twelve, and will measure you for ready money, dear, as I works cheap, and am too poor to give credit.'

"Dumple thanked her new-found friend, and then hastened home, fearing, however, to tell her father the new life which was before her. The poor painter was seated as she had left him, in his chair by the window, gazing every now and then at his empty easel, until he closed his eyes as though to shut away the present and the future. He would then look out vacantly into the street, regarding neither sight nor sound, as though all human sympathy had left him. Not so when Dumple spoke, as she entered the room. Her cheery voice went at once to the father's heart, and a smile played about the sad distorted features of the poor painter like a sunbeam upon a grave.

"She kissed him tenderly, and having taken off her bonnet and little cloak, showed him triumphantly the money she had received for her last three days' work at embroidery, clapping her hands as though the jangling of those two half-crowns was music to last for ever. The bright look had left her face when she had opened a drawer and added her hard earnings to the small sum which had been saved before the painter's hand was paralysed, and which every week had made less. Now that she knew her parent's restoration was hopeless, she had determined to quit their present lodgings and seek some that were cheaper; but she delayed communicating the necessity for this step to her father, fearing that it would convey to the old man a conviction of his own helplessness and a dread of the uncertain future, and so she remained silent. The poor artist had nothing more to learn—nothing more to fear, as he had long known his fate—the tired old bread-winner—sitting there through the long day with his palette within his reach, and without the power to stretch forth his hand and labour.

"The next day Dumple was punctual to the hour of rehearsal, and found herself much more at home among her stranger comrades than she had expected, although she had been rather dismayed when she first entered the dark, dismal theatre, so unlike the bright place she had seen it on those happy evenings when she had sat in the front with her father, and which had haunted her for days after. There was little time for such remembrances, as the practice preliminary to the rehearsal began. Her grace and quickness soon attracted the attention of Mrs. Bellair; and before the week was ended Dumple had been promoted to dance—yes, to dance in the second row with the prospective salary of eighteen shillings a week. When she told the dirty little Jew of her advancement, he seemed as delighted as though some great advantage had accrued to himself.

"'Well, Miss Matildy,' he said, 'I'm as pleased as Punch to hear on your good fortin. Second row and eighteen shillin' a week. You'll have satin shoes next pair, Miss, and I shall take off the hodd sixpence.'

"'Thank you, Mr. Myers,' replied Dumple, 'but I am compelled to be very saving indeed. You have been so kind to me, that I don't mind saying so to you. I have a poor, dear, helpless father to support, and ——' she paused, smiling sadly.

"'Don't say another word, Miss; I shall make 'em you for four shillin' and lose money,' whispered Mr. Myers.

"'Oh, I was not thinking of the shoes but of something else, and in which you can, perhaps, help me. My father was an artist, but illness has now incapacitated him for his work, and as we have no friends, I must take care of him, Mr. Myers.'

"Dumple smiled again, but very pleasantly.

"'Yes, Miss,' said Myers, clutching his fingers as though he longed to embrace her; 'I knowed you was a good girl, I was sure on it.'

"'I am only doing my duty, Mr. Myers,' continued Dumple. 'We have hitherto lived in lodgings in —— Street, but our means are gone, and I want to find some cheaper rooms near the theatre.'

"Mr. Myers took a small piece of chalk from his pocket and began figuring on the back of the scenes. He was not satisfied at first with a calculation he had made, and it required some further time to make it right. When he had effected it he exclaimed, 'Yes, that'll do.' Dumple saw that the various items and the figures attached which he had chalked upon the scene, amounted exactly to eighteen shillings.

"'I can't see, Miss,' said Mr. Myers, 'that arter you have paid other expenses you can anyhow afford more nor three shillings a week for your lodgings, and rents is high about Doory Lane and Common Garden, leave alone taxes.'

"'I suppose they must be,' said Dumple, with a sigh.

"Now I've this to say, Miss Matildy," continued Mr. Myers, 'we've—that's me and my sister Naomi—we've a second floor back and front, which we lets out to single men, but if them rooms 'll suit you we'll say three shillin' a week for the two and nothing for the water-rate.'

"Dumple hesitated to accept this liberal proposal with the readiness with which it had been made, for should Mr. Myers's house, she thought, want washing, painting, and repairing as much as himself, it could not be a very desirable tenement. She therefore promised to think over the matter and call upon him the next day.

"Having kept her word, Dumple was agreeably surprised to find that Mr. Myers resided in a broad court (I forget its name), and that his house, though dingy enough without from age and weather, was cleanly within, as Naomi, the dirty little Jew's sister, was the most tidy contrast to her hardworking brother.

"The rooms were light and airy considering the locality, and Dumple gladly closed with the Jew's proposal that she and her father should occupy them henceforth at the weekly charge of three shillings. As she went back to her old lodgings she turned over in her mind how she should break the matter of removal to her father, and inform him also of the important step she had taken ; and so difficult did the task appear that she had to pause at the door before she could come to a decision.

"There was the old odd smile to welcome her when she entered the room, as though her presence had brought 'sunshine to a shady place,' and she acknowledged her welcome by a tender embrace.

"'You have thought me a sad truant to-day, haven't you,' she said.

"Mr. Maul nodded in reply.

"'Wait until I have put away my things, and then I will tell you what I have been doing,' she continued, evidently delaying the communication she had to make as long as possible. Having put off her walking attire, she placed a stool at her feet and sat down. Taking his cold powerless hand in her own, she pressed it to her lips, and then looked up into his distorted face, her own beaming with all the love she had in her heart for the poor sufferer.

"'I am going to tell you a secret, father,' she said, 'one which I have kept from you for some days, and only because I thought, if I failed in the experiment I was making, I would not distress you with the knowledge of my failure. I have succeeded, nowever, and so much better than I had hoped for, that I have come at once to make confession.'

"Mr. Maul again nodded his head, but his smile had gone, and his eyes expressed only wonder.

"'You have known—I am sure you have—that my earnings have been less than enough to supply our wants. Don't look so sad! I am going to tell you how I intend to make them enough, quite enough, dear father."

"Again she kissed the cold, powerless hand as though to thank it for all the work it had done in years past, now, that she, 'Little Dump,' or 'Old Dumple,' was about to become the worker.

"'Your savings, father, have dwindled and dwindled under my care until I blush to say there is hardly more than enough to pay our rent here and help us to remove to a new lodging.'

"Wonder again and sorrow in the old man's face.

"'But did I not tell you I can provide for our future? Do not, therefore, look so very sad at leaving this old room, which now has more painful than pleasant memories connected with it. Our new lodging is quite as cheerful, and shall be quite as happy as this has been' (she did not believe herself or she would not have sighed so silently and deeply). 'The rent will be quite within our means. Ah! you may look surprised, but I shall have employment next week —constant employment—which will bring in—oh! I hardly know what at present when added to my embroidery.'

"Mr. Maul muttered feebly—

"'What employment, Dumple, dear?'

"'Duchesses, ladies, good women, have worked at it, dear father; kings and queens, and all sorts of good people have praised and rewarded it, and therefore Old Dumple need not hesitate to take part in it. Do you guess what it is?'

"Mr. Maul replied in his usual manner, and shook his head.

"'I thought you would not. I am engaged as a young lady to go on the stage at Drury Lane.'

"This announcement was startling indeed to Mr. Maul, and his whole frame was affected, whilst a flush overspread his usually pallid features.

"'You do not, must not disapprove what I have done, dear father!' said Dumple, observing these changes. 'It is the only employment I can find at present, and it is honourable to those who choose to make it so. You can trust "Old Dumple," can you not? I have therefore, taken lodgings not two minutes' walk—not one minute's run—from the theatre, so that I shall be there and home again in no time scarcely. I have arranged to leave here on Saturday next, so we shall have plenty to do to pack up and get settled in our new home.'

"The tears ran down the cheeks of father and daughter, but not from sorrow, as they were smiling also. Dumple set to work at once to prepare for their exodus, and when I called to visit my patient the next day, I found her struggling so nobly with a four-post bedstead that I could not refrain taking off my coat and helping her to overcome the troublesome monster. Did you ever try to dissect a four-poster? Don't if you are wise. Castors, wrenches, and screws; legs travelling all over the room, and will not be disjointed; head-boards and laths tumbling about and finding rest nowhere and everywhere. Don't dissect a four-poster unless you have the patience and good temper of Dumple Maul. (The doctor's wife, whose name by-the-bye, is Grace, called him a 'silly fellow' for this commendation of her namesake.)

"The last chair but one, and all the rest of the worldly possessions of the Mauls were safely stowed on the hired van, and the little dirty Jew and Dumple waited to assist the now nearly helpless artist to descend, for the last time, the stairs he had trodden so often. They gently raised him up, and when the van-man had carried away his chair, Mr. Maul looked around the room for a few moments and burst into a passion of tears. Dumple could not restrain hers either, and from a clean streak observed on both cheeks of the dirty little Jew, when the party reached the street, it was conjectured that he also had yielded to lachrymal sympathy.

"No one who had seen the rooms in the Jew's house during their former occupancy could have believed in the 'transformation scene' they presented when Dumple and her father had been settled there a few days. There were green plants, though it was Christmas time, and neat curtains, well-ordered furniture, and a small bright fire in the grate. An old easel stool near one window, and at the other, in his easy-chair, sat the old artist, who had worked before it many and many a pleasant hour, looking out upon the world of the broad court and feeling that he had no longer a part in its struggles. Not directly, certainly, as Dumple had taken up all his burthens except his sufferings, which he bore meekly and patiently himself, and never obtruded them upon his brave, loving daughter, after one brief conversation with her, and with me when I had described—compelled thereto by an earnest appeal from him—the probable termination of his case. He had spoken to her with great difficulty, and his manner had made his words more painful to her.

"'Grace, dear,' he said, 'the doctor has told me that my life is near its close. Since I have sat so much alone—powerless for work—thinking of the past and of the future, I blame myself greatly for many improvident acts. Well, if to say so gives you pain, I will not dwell upon the irretrievable past, dear child, but believe that I have done my duty in part since you love me so dearly.'

"Grace knew that he could not doubt that she did love him, and therefore she was silent, only kissing him.

"He then spoke many solemn words of hope and thankfulness, which Grace always remembered when she felt doubtful or sorrowful and a lonely woman.

"'There is one weakness I cannot overcome, Grace,' he continued, 'knowing how little it matters what becomes of this poor body when the spirit has left it, but—but where I laid your mother fifteen years ago I would ——'

"Grace understood his wish, and promised that it should be accomplished, trusting in her heart that aid would be given her when it was needed, and saving week by week, and little by little, for an object which was henceforth regarded as a sacred duty.

"It was near Easter time, and tribulation came to the house of Naomi and Abraham Myers in the shape of a bad debt. The treasury of the Theatre Royal, Squashborough, had collapsed, and the manager was indebted to Mr. Myers no less a sum than nine pounds and some shillings. Mr. Myers had calculated upon this money to buy stock for his Easter orders, and having scant credit himself, he saw only ruin in the loss of his money and the impossibility of carrying on his business. The few valuables he possessed when sold or pawned did not meet the difficulty, and he was on the point of abandoning the construction of several pairs of 'pink fairies' and 'blue pages' when a real FAIRY came into his dark dirty workshop (the only dirty place about the house) in the graceful form of Dumple Maul.

"Two pounds! Only two pounds would enable him to go to work and maintain his proud position of fancy bootmaker to the Theatre Royal, Drury Lane.

"He could hardly believe his eyes when he saw Miss Matildy bring forth from a small purse two glittering pieces of gold and place them on his lapstone, saying—

"'Mr. Myers, you have been so kind to me in many ways, helping me so often, that you must let me help you a little in return. That money I have saved by sixpences and shillings for a very solemn, sacred purpose, and I am sure you will repay me when you can.'

"'I can! I will, Miss Matildy,' said the dirty little Jew, his tears almost washing his face quite clean. 'I think I know what the money is for, and I would die—starve myself to pay it back to you.'

"So the fairy held out her pretty white hand, and the gnome took it between his own dirty paws and pressed it to the leather apron which covered his heaving bosom.

"Oh, how exacting was old Myers that Easter time! No credit to page or fairy on any account (except to one young girl whose mother was sick), and he had been heard to threaten an advance of sixpence a pair if he were only asked to take a moiety on account. Poor little fellow! he scarcely rested until he had repaid those two pounds into the sacred treasury, and with interest — a gratitude never to be exhausted.

"The money was not needed until the last month of the year. And the poor artist took a farewell gaze at his old easel and his young daughter's face and closed his eyes in death. Before he was borne away to rest by the side of his wife the sacred treasury was emptied—quite emptied—of its contents, as the undertaker was a 'man who had had losses,' and cared not to have more.

" Drop the curtain and shut in the graveyard, and raise it again to the merry Pantomine!

"Why had Mrs. Bellair called 'Mathilde' into her own room and been so long in conference with her? Well, if ever! not twelve months in the profession and going to be Columbine!

" Such was the fact. The grace and intelligence displayed by pretty Dumple had obtained for her this distinction and profitable engagement, as it was usual at that time to pay the principal pantomimists a guinea a night in consequence of the great exertion required from them. Six guineas a week during the run of the Pantomine!

"'May it run for ever and ever, Miss Matildy,' cried Mr. Myers. 'May you get as rich as you deserve to be, and then you needn't envy the Bank of England, my dear! Only to think! Columbine your first season, as one may say! Who would have thought it the day ——' The dirty little Jew paused suddenly, and so Dumple finished his speech.

"'When you saw a young girl with a sad face looking for help from some one, and your kind heart understood her want, and came to offer her the aid she needed; who would have thought that she would have come to this good fortune, and have had her first kind friend still beside her to be made as happy as she is herself by the news?'

" The fairy hand was again in the paws of the gnome, who, having wiped his lips on his leathern apron, kissed the pretty white fingers more than once.

" Naomi Myers had become quite a friend to Dumple Maul, and knew all her little anxieties and pleasant thoughts, and the condition of the empty purse also.

"'What's that matter,' said Mr. Myers, who, wonderful to relate, had arrived at a state of semi-cleanliness, having been asked to tea twice in one week in Miss Matildy's room, where Naomi had been at work (gratis) for Dumple—'what's that matter! Miss Matildy sha'n't stand for nothing! She shall look the beautifullest Columbine that's ever been seen, and I knows where there's some loveliest wreaths that's to be had cheap for ready money.'

"'Ah, ready money? ready money!'

"'That's to be had too, Miss Matildy. Ain't it, Naomi? Think how you trusted me once on a time. You'll want two pair o' fleshings, and such shoes you shall have! Fifteen shillings a pair I charge to the Hopera! Satin thick as a board, and fitting your pretty foot, Miss, like a kid glove. Don't you fidget about nothing.'

"Could Dumple decline all this kindness, needing it so much? No.

"The approaching Christmas day would fall on a Saturday; and on the Wednesday preceding it, Dumple, having nothing to do at the theatre, was to try on her columbine's dress at her own lodgings, Naomi having obtained permission from the theatre to make it, she being very skilful in such matters.

"How had I known this? Why, Naomi had told me so when I had called upon—Naomi—in the morning; and more, she had invited me, with Dumple's kind permission, to be present in the evening to judge of the general effect.

"Never was Columbine half so lovely! The delicate pink skirt, looped up, displayed a gauze petticoat covered with silver spangles, and short enough to disclose two of the prettiest feet in the world, and which set off to the greatest advantage Mr. Myers's very best handiwork. Her beautiful face, glowing with excitement, was surmounted by one of those 'loveliest wreaths' of which we have heard, and any one who had gazed upon the graceful being, must have envied the happy Harlequin."

(The doctor's wife was fairly angry at this glowing description of Dumple, the Columbine, and some of us thought her very ill-natured, despite her own buxom looks. The doctor only laughed and went on).

"Some cheerful-minded philosopher has said that, 'wherever pleasure is, pain is certain not to be far off,' and so it was to be with poor Dumple. During the next day's rehearsal she trod upon a loose trap on the stage, and sprained one of her ankles, to the consternation of the manager and the distress of all in the broad court. I had the responsibility of attending that ankle, and, knowing how many bright hopes would fail to be realised ; guessing, also, how much after-care would come if Dumple should be incapacitated from exertion, I would have given all I then possessed to have been spared the case.

"Dumple bore her misfortune, as she had borne her other troubles, most bravely, her greatest uneasiness being caused by the inconvenience she feared she was causing Mr. Myers, who had provided 'the ready money.'

"'Don't mention it, my dear Miss Matildy, don't think of me, but—it won't matter a great deal—I don't think anybody will press me for the little I owe, and I shall only work the harder—but I won't believe you won't appear. Mr. Doctor won't let you not get well, will you, Sir?'

"I could not promise confidently that Dumple would be able to assume her new character ; but, secretly, I had hope that she would do so ; and I neglected shamefully two chronic patients, who were annuities to my employer, to attend to that pretty injured ankle. To make matters rather worse, the undertaker had heard of the accident, and, fearing for the small balance due to him for Mr. Maul's funeral, wrote to poor Dumple, and demanded an order on the treasury for the small sum coming to her for salary. Mr. Myers most unselfishly and indignantly insisted upon Dumple's compliance with this request, and when Christmas day broke it found the poor dancer lame and penniless.

I did not suspect all this at the time, for I was young and thoughtless, and Mr. Myers and Naomi had invited me to take my Christmas dinner in Dumple's room, as they had concluded that the great holiday which Christians make of Christmas day ought not to be passed in loneliness and sorrow by the good lodger whom they both loved so much.

"Just before the hour appointed for dinner, Mr. Myers, as clean as he could make himself, entered the room, followed by Naomi, each bearing a small basket.

"'Here we are, Miss Matildy,' exclaimed Mr. Myers, opening his basket ; 'here's two pound of roast beef from the best cookshop anyways near Common Garden, and here's a lump of plum-pudden, all over reasons, and would do Mr. Rothschild good to look at it ; and here's browny potatoes and greens, and mustard—rale Durham mustard, 'cos I tasted it —and here's Mr. Doctor as I invited. You not have a Christmas dinner on Christmas day! I never heard of such a thing, and we'll eat it together, and so God bless us all with charity!"

"Yes, Abraham Myers, dirty as you generally were, there was a bright soul burning within you, and there were good angels about your house on the day I ate my Christmas dinner within it.

"Rest and great professional skill (hem!) overcame the trifling sprain (for trifling it proved to be) which had caused so much anxiety and brief sorrow, and on Boxing Night our Columbine's success was nothing short of 'triumphant' *(see the public papers)*.

"Since that day, however, she has never partaken of a Christmas dinner but at my table, as some of you may have heard before, and which I now declare with thankfulness, for such a good wife as Dumple Maul has been."

Of course! The name of the doctor's wife was Grace, and he had bought the practice when his predecessor retired and came to live among us, bringing with him a pretty pleasant wife and four blooming children. How stupid not to have guessed this at once!

A CHRISTMAS HOLIDAY LESSON.

CHAPTER I.

CHRISTMAS EVE.

THIS is to be a Christmas story, and those had better pass it by who do not care to acknowledge the jocund season, as it tells of one who affected to care nothing for Christmas and its doings, and whom we would call a would-be young "Scrooge," did we not fear to provoke comparison. His name was Richard Hobart, a good fellow enough, as he was neither mean, uncharitable, nor unfeeling; but he had a weakness—he could not stand being laughed at; no, not even when he knew he was in the right. He belonged to a small social club called "The Coming Men," and most of the members had their own private opinions of themselves, opinions in general more favourable than the rest of the world entertained of them. They were anxious, all of them, to be considered original, and to set down the experience of their elders—especially the "governors"—at nought. They laughed, very properly, at many old-world notions; and, amongst other, were irresistibly ironical against Christmas customs, and those who took pleasure in observing them. Dick Hobart had an old uncle, and an older grandmother, who always made a Christmas gathering of friends and relatives—old and young, poor and well-to-do—and appeared to enjoy the year which succeeded all the better for their Christmas holidays. Dick was chaffed by "The Coming Men" on this family peculiarity, as they called it, and the foolish fellow actually became ashamed of keeping Christmas, and would have foregone it the preceding year had he not had expectations from granny and his uncle, and from no one else.

It wanted but two days to the Christmas Day of 186—. No invitation had come from Dick's uncle, Mr. Evered Gore, and the weak young fellow, having the certainty of receiving his quarter's salary on the morning of the 24th, had made up his mind, in deference to the opinion of "The Coming Men," to give the family party the slip. With this intention he was busy packing his portmanteau, when a friend, young Goodenough, called upon him.

"Off to Holly Lodge for your Christmas dinner, I suppose?" said Goodenough.

"No, my boy; I've got a reprieve this year," replied Dick.

"A reprieve? what do you mean?" asked Goodenough.

"Why, I've not had any annual ukase to the family gathering, I'm glad to say."

"And you rejoice at that? Well, I always envied you at Christmas time," said Goodenough. "A poor devil like me, without kith or kin, might well do so, seeing that I have no prospect of a Christmas dinner except at a chop-house."

"Then come with me to Paris," said Dick.

"To Paris, at this time of the year?" asked Goodenough. "If I could afford it I wouldn't go there."

"Why not?"

"Why, they don't keep Christmas in the least," said Goodenough; "and, though I don't share very much in the festivities of the season, I do get a little of them, besides the pleasure of looking on."

"What a queer chap you are!" exclaimed Dick; "the festivities of the season bore me to death, and I'm going to Paris because they keep Noël like rational beings."

"You are *the* queer chap, I fancy," replied Goodenough, "to run away from kind friends and a prospective legator."

"Well, it is their fault, and not mine," said Dick; "granny has been rather unwell some time, and so I suppose Uncle Evered intends to be quiet this Christmas."

But as he spoke the servant brought a telegram for Mr. Richard Hobart, and it read as follows:—

"Mind you come to-morrow. Letter omitted to be posted."

Dick let the telegram fall from his hand; but whether from real or affected disappointment, we are not prepared to say. Whether his annoyance was real or assumed, he was compelled to obey the invitation, as the morning brought the delayed letter, and granny's message contained in it news not to be neglected.

Holly Lodge was about forty miles from London, and Dick, therefore, started from one of the London Bridge stations in the afternoon, his fellow-passengers being a very pretty girl and her brother, both of whom were in high spirits at the Christmas holidays before them.

Dick had passed through the streets on his way to the station with a sneer upon his lips at the indications of Christmas festivity which everywhere met his eyes—butchers' shops bursting almost with fat beeves and mutton—grocers' windows piled with luscious raisins, citron, and currants—cheesemongers crowding almost into the streets with their prime Stiltons, and double Glo'sters, and fat Cheshires. Even ready-made clothesmen, who had paid starvation prices for the garments in their windows, had stuck sprigs of holly in button-holes as a sort of Christian garnish to their un-Christian-paid wares. But Dick would not recognise these evidences of rejoicing, but took his place in the train like a sulky cub, and tried to feel disgusted with the world and all in it—even with the pretty smiling girl and her bright-looking brother who were his fellow-passengers, because they were jollier than usual under the influence of Christmas time.

Dick fairly growled at the newspaper lad who brought the Christmas numbers of popular serials and newspapers to the carriage window, but, feeling a little ashamed of his rudeness, called the lad back and invested sixpence in a *Bradshaw*, which he afterwards affected to study until he fell asleep. He woke up at the first station at which the train stopped, and looked out. There were signs of Christmas lying about —hampers with turkey-heads peeping out; baskets filled with game, and apples, and other common niceties, worth little money, perhaps, but becoming of much value when delivered to sons and daughters, friends and relations, old fathers and mothers, long separated from the donors in town and country.

Dick tried again to feel disgusted, and endeavoured to produce lowness of spirits by reading his *Bradshaw*, and nearly succeeded.

A great hulking boy, who got into the carriage at one of the stations, nearly came to sorrow by bringing with him a bunch of mistletoe; but, luckily for him, the pretty girl blushed and giggled so at the sight of the kissing-bough, that Dick thought it would be the pleasantest thing in the world to salute her rosy cheek; or, better still, her laughing mouth, since, as Barry Cornwall sings—

"Mouths were made for kissing."

Dick was again driven to *Bradshaw* for doldrums; but, having opened the page at the advertisements, and dropped on one headed "Picnics and Wedding Parties," he could not help wondering if the pretty girl ever went to the one or would some day play the principal part at the other.

At every station there were friends expecting friends, and Dick could not brutalise himself sufficiently to feel no sympathy with the honest pleasure which filled almost every face when hands were shaken or cheeks were bussed.

Dick was rather pleased—he knew not wherefore—to find that the pretty girl and her brother got out at the same station as he did, and almost expected to see "Passenger to Holly Lodge" affixed to their luggage. Such an incident would have been quite natural at Christmas time, we know; but it was not to be so on this occasion. The brother and sister's destination was quite in an opposite direction to Dick's; and what made that circumstance of some consequence was the fact that Mr. Gore's prevision had secured the only fly disengaged at the station to bring on his nephew to Holly Lodge.

"Well, it's Christmas time, you see, Sir!" said the fly-driver, about to put Dick's portmanteau on the box-seat of his vehicle, "and we could let double what we has. It's Christmas time, Sir!"

"That's awkward, Clary?" said the brother; "no fly to be had!"

"Oh, it's only four miles to the rectory," replied Clara, "and I can walk that, Rory!"

"And it's only three to Holly Lodge," thought Dick, "and I could walk that."

"But your luggage, dear!" said the brother. "You can't dine and spend the evening that fright!"

"Oh, yes, I can! Aunty won't mind, and I'm sure I don't," said the pretty girl, laughing and showing—oh, such pearly teeth!

"But you sha'n't," thought Dick. So, without giving a moment's consideration whether it was Christmas time or not, he made his very best bow, and said—addressing the brother, of course—"I have only a mile or two to go, and if you will take the fly I shall be much obliged."

"You are very kind," replied the brother; and the pretty sister said the same thing by the smile she called to her lips. "But you have luggage, even if ——"

"Only a portmanteau," said Dick, as though he thought no more of carrying the great roomy, patent expanding convenience, that was fitted up like a complete dressing-room, than he would have minded shouldering a knapsack.

"And there's lame Jemmy, with his donkey cart, as 'ud take that," said the flyman, as though he gave the preference to the pretty girl as a fare. Perhaps he was a man of taste, though of humble occupation.

So it was settled forthwith, and Dick opened the door himself, just scratching his cheek with a sprig of holly which the flyman had stuck in the pocket in honour of the season.

Clary thanked him both with smiles and words—she had a sweet, musical voice—"How very good of you. Thank you very much!" And Dick had a peep—only a peep—at what he had not seen before. It was something in a smart kid boot, and looked as though it could dance like a fairy.

"Well," thought Dick, as he waved his hand gracefully to the brother when the fly was driven away, "I've not begun the day badly, and a walk will do me good, and give me an appetite for my dinner."

Lame Jemmy, by the aid of the railway porter, had stowed away Dick's portmanteau in his little donkey-cart, and had taken his perch on the front, ready to start when he knew where to go.

Dick loitered a minute or two just—oh yes—just to ask when the next down-train came in, and who those young people were who had gone off in the fly.

"The next down would be at 6.30," the porter said; "and the young lady and gentleman wasn't knowed to him, but they ordered to be druv to Sithewell Rectory—that's all he could say."

It was not much for the shilling which Dick gave the man, but he was satisfied with it, and so was the recipient, as he not only thanked the donor, but wished him a merry Christmas. Dick was so abstracted that he replied, "the same to you, my man—a Merry Christmas and a Happy New Year."

Lame Jemmy touched his weather-beaten any-coloured hat to his new employer, and said, in rather a diffident voice, "You wouldn't like to ride, would you, Sir? Jacky could draw us both, Sir."

But Dick declined adding to Jacky's labours, and, having mentioned Holly Lodge as his place of destination, walked quietly by the side of the donkey-cart.

"I knows Holly Lodge well, Sir," said the man, again touching his hat to intimate that he did not intend to be familiar. "And well I ought to, Sir ; Mrs. Gore it was as guv me this donkey last Christmas was two year, when I could get about after I had my accident and broke my kneepan. Good lady she is, Sir, and so's her son."

"Yes," replied Dick, preparing to light his pipe.

"I know'd Mr. Gore and Mrs. Gore's brother, Sir—him as died in Ingy, when they was boys, I did," said Jemmy. "Nice lads they was. Lor, what fun they used to make at Christmas up at the Lodge, they did !"

"Oh !" observed Dick, not quite liking the remark.

"Beautiful Christmas weather this, Sir," said the old man ; "I likes frost and snow at Christmas time."

"Do you ?" replied Dick ; "I should have thought that was the sort of weather you would not have liked."

"Well, just for a day or two, Sir, to put one in mind it *is* Christmas," said Jemmy, giving a short sniff as the smoke from Dick's pipe blew past his nose. "Nice 'bacca that, Sir."

"Yes, very good," replied Dick. "Do you smoke?"

"Why, yes, Sir," answered Jemmy ; "but I don't smoke such bacca as that—'udout it's give me."

"Well, where's your pipe? Oh ! inside your hat," said Dick, as Jemmy, quick at taking a hint or a largess, removed his felt and produced a well-blackened tobacco-pipe.

"It's not a very large 'un, Sir," observed the old man ; "but I've had him more nor a year—ay ! nigh two year, now Christmas has come agin."

Dick gave Jemmy a good pinch out of his pouch, and the old man's eyes sparkled as he received it.

"Lor, Sir! not all this. I'm a robbin' on you! but I thank you kindly, and wishes you a Merry Christmas, and many on 'em, Sir."

"You seem very partial to Christmas, old boy," said Dick. "What difference can it make to you?"

"Well, Sir, not much, as it seems to you, but a deal to me. I get a trifle here and a trifle there from the gentlefolks, and a bit and sup acos it's Christmas time. And all the folks, high and low, seems to be more good-natured and affable like; and the church is done up, and there's sprigs of holly in the windows and places; and altogether, Sir, I'm always sorry when Christmas is gone."

"Ah!" said Dick, not knowing what to say, exactly; "ah! you've no Christmas bills to pay."

"Oh, yes, I has, Sir! I owes a little at the shop, sometimes—almost always, like—and then what I 'arns and gets extra at Christmas wipes off the score. I don't know what I should do without Christmas."

"I'm glad it does good to somebody," said Dick, though he wouldn't have said as much as that in favour of the season if Jemmy had been one of "The Coming Men," and not an old threadbare donkey-driver, thankful for small mercies.

"This here's a short cut over the heath to Holly Lodge, if you don't mind the rough walking, Sir," said Jemmy; "and I wants to go this road, as it passes by my cottage."

"Oh, very well!" said Dick; "though, as you say, it is rough walking, thanks to the frost."

"You should see it in summer and autumn time, Sir," observed Jemmy, anxious to cover any objection to the road. "When the heath and gorse is in bloom it smells like a nosegay, then, Sir; and don't the bees come to it; I believe you, Sir; for miles they comes."

"Ah! but not at Christmas time," said Dick, exultingly. "Had him there," he thought.

"No, Sir, not then; but the poor folks comes a-grubbin' it for firin'. Lord of the manor gives 'em leave to do that, and many on us is warmer for what we grubs on Mosly Moor," said Jemmy, adding, "We allus drinks his health, and wishes him a Merry Christmas."

Dick was getting rather tired of Jemmy's reference to the

festive season, and was almost inclined to think that the old man had been "put up to it" by Goodenough some way, and was doing it on purpose to reprove him. They had come to a hollow in the heath, from which smoke had been seen ascending.

"That's my home, down there," said Jemmy, pointing to a rude cottage, made of mud and heather. It belonged to no order of architecture; it was too large for the pig-pen, and too small for the cottage proper, and had been built, Dick learned, by an old squatter years ago, and had come into Jemmy's tenancy by the kindness of the lord of the manor last Christmas three years. It was called Frog's-hole. There was a shed for Jacky and a small residence for half-a-dozen cocks and hens, then pecking their way to roost. The various buildings appeared to be in partnership, and, if one had failed, the whole firm would have "gone to smash." There was a patch of garden ground, much of it bare at present; but one part looked lively with winter cabbage, interspersed with headless stumps.

Jemmy pulled up Jacky, or rather Jacky pulled up Jemmy, being under the mistaken idea that his day's work was over; and he was permitted to remain under this pleasant illusion, whilst his master communicated with his household.

"Bessy! Bessy!" bawled the old man as loudly as he could; and in a moment or two a rosy-faced girl, with moderately tidy hair, opened the door and answered:—

"Yes, gran'dad."

"I'm agoin' with this here gentleman's portmantel to Holly Lodge, so don't wait your tea any longer," said Jemmy.

"Am I to eat the herrin'?" asked the girl.

"Yes, my dear, eat it all if you can. I am sure to get a bit and a sup at the Lodge. Just bring Jacky a drop o' water, as he mayn't like to go on if he's adry."

The girl soon complied with the gran'dad's request, and Jacky, who didn't care at first to be bribed into further progression, took two or three "go downs" of water, and, having cast a wistful look at his peaceful shed, put his shoulder to the collar and walked on as leisurely as before. Dick had not waited for these arrangements, but had stepped on until the appearance of two roads made him pause for the old man's coming, as he was uncertain which led to Holly Lodge.

"To the left, if you please," said Jemmy. "The right

leads to Farmer Jackson's. I allus goes to him on Boxin' Day, and he gives me sixpence and a mug o' beer. That's because it's Christmas time, Sir."

Dick began to understand why the old threadbare, battered-hatted donkey-driver thought lightly of the present frost and the possible snow, which would come, whether regarded or not, at other times when sixpences and mugs of beer were not their accompaniments.

"That was your granddaughter, I suppose?" said Dick, striving to change the tune of the old man's voice.

"Well, no, Sir; she isn't no relation to me, through she calls me gran'dad. I ought to have had a grandchild, but she died along with her mother, Sir, last June six year," replied Jemmy, refilling his pipe, as though to excuse a short silence.

"And this girl is no relation, you say?" asked Dick, rather interested to know why the girl consented to live in such a lonely place.

"You see, Sir," said Jemmy, blowing out a cloud of smoke with the sigh he gave, "my poor old wife, Sir, was bedrid a year afore she died—she's been dead two year come next grass, Sir." Jemmy puffed out two or three clouds in succession. "Well, Sir, about a year after our daughter died—cold, caught arter her confinement, Sir—my missus and me was crossing the heath—we didn't live here then—when we hears a woman moan and a child a-crying. We soon found where it came from, and there was a tramp, as sold tapes and things, lying on side of the path, too ill to walk. She'd tried her strength too far, Sir. She'd been ill of some'at as had brought her down. My missus said she looked like death, and I run for the doctor. But he warn't no use; he said when he got there as she was dyin'; and so she did."

Dick almost wished that he had not been quite so curious, and had spared himself the unpleasant recital.

"Bessie, as you seed, Sir, was that woman's child. As it was Christmas time, Sir, my missus says, 'Jem,' says she, 'I'm very lone when you're away, sometimes'—I was a carrier then, Sir—'and if you don't mind, I'd like to keep that girl, because'—I'd seed it, too—'she's so like what our Johannah was;' and so we took to her."

"Very kind of you both," said Dick; "but you'd have done that all the same if it had not been Christmas time."

"I don't know that, Sir," said Jemmy; "but the snow was

on the ground, and there'd been that hard frost, you may mind of it, Sir; and — — No; I think Christmas time had a deal to do with it."

"Well, anyway, it was kind of you," said Dick. "Have you smoked all the tobacco I gave you? Oh, yes, you have! Here, take this."

"Thanks, Mister, I'm sure," replied Jemmy, emptying the pouch into his old hat, which seemed to be as general a receptacle as was Dick's patent expanding portmanteau. "It was lucky for me as we did take that gal, Sir," continued Jemmy, "seeing how carriering failed altogether when the rail come, and my old missus fell sick with fretting, I think; then Bessy helped her in the house; and, ever since my missus died, and I got lame, and matters went all wrong with me, Bessie has done for me almost as well as anybody could ha' done. If I've luck this Christmas time, I means to send her to school a bit, Sir."

When Holly Lodge was reached, old Jemmy had a good hansel of what was in store for him, in the tip he received from Dick; it looked like half-a-sovereign; but, mind you, "Coming Men," Christmas time had nothing to do with it. Old Jemmy thought it had; and so, when he had given Jacky a surprise (by the desire of Mr. Gore), in the form of a feed of oats, and had refreshed himself with a few slices of cold beef, and a mug of honest malt-and-hop-made beer, he returned to Frog's-hole, chirruping a Christmas carol, and laden with a supper for Bessy, and their Christmas dinner for the morrow.

There was the old Christmas gathering at Holly Lodge, and the party was sufficiently mixed not to be monotonous. The two maiden cousins of Uncle Evered, who lived in the next market town, on small annuities, which held out very well, owing to the circulation of certain baskets between the market town and Holly Lodge—they were there, as spotless in appearance as they were in reputation. There was cross old Dr. Bowler, who had been angry with himself for twenty years because he had sold his practice and lived idly since. He was a cousin by some family ramification, of no consequence to our story. There were two cousins—very good fellows—and their two sisters, sons and daughters of a deceased aunt of Dick, and who were to have fortunes when they came of age. There was Julia Gore—"Giddy Gore," as she delighted to style herself, being forty-nine, with her hair *à la crop*, and very thin, owing, as she said, to a fever which no one remembered her to have had. She was always giggling and making faces at Dick, who really and pardonably detested her.

Poor Giddy was a finely-preserved specimen of a schoolgirl, and would have dressed in a frock and trousers had that custom still prevailed with young ladies of sixteen, as it did when "George the Fourth was King." As it was, she indulged in many prettinesses of her youth, and always wore a sash of rose-coloured ribbon, and sandals to her shoes. She affected a lisp, and showed her pretty teeth when she smiled. She always tripped out of a room and entered with a sort of gush. She made dreadful play with her eyes, and discovered compliments which were never intended. She annoyed Dick awfully by little taps on the arm, and her exclamations of "Oh, what nonthense, Wichard!" Giddy was always in great force at Christmas time. She could cry forfeits capitally, and her condign sentences were largely composed of kissing in corners, and through backs of chairs, or between tongs; and as she herself was generally a great defaulter, she was thought to consult her own inclinations in these selections of redemption. The mistletoe was "her horwor," so she said; but, by some accident or other, she was always under it. Alas! poor Giddy! She had outstood her market, and is now open to an offer.

There was a round game after dinner, at which Dick made more noise than any one. There was one game at forfeits, and a snap-dragon, which, as usual, terrified the old ladies, who thought they should be "set on fire, and were not insured." There was a great jorum of egg-flip, which the old ladies did not shirk in the least—which set Giddy Gore into ridiculous hysterics, and which she worked off in the hall, "unpitied and alone," until the housemaid put the door-key down her back and gave her the shivers. The men got properly hilarious, and would kiss the ladies, as it was Christmas time; and Giddy Gore, having recovered herself at this crisis, rushed, by mistake, into the arms of Dick, who provokingly kissed the back of her head, being obliged by the occasion to kiss somewhere. Then Uncle Evered would sing his old comic song, which was not quite a Christmas carol; and all the servants, being called in to listen to it, made such a chorus, led by Dick, that it must have been heard in Frog's-hole, far away on Mosly Moor.

All to bed at last; and Dick was fain to acknowledge, as he snuggled beneath the heavy bed-clothes, after taking his last look of the bonny fire blazing in his grate, that he had been very jolly, whatever "The Coming Men" might say. He had only one disturbing thought. He knew that the hearty dinner he had eaten, the few glasses of wine which he had taken, in combination with the nappy, glutinous egg-flip, were conducive to dyspepsia and terrible dreams, and he feared that he might have a night-mare in the shape of Giddy Gore. With this oppressive thought uppermost in his mind, he dozed for a little time, and then, tumbling down the steps of his uncle's cellar, woke with a start, and found himself, as he thought ——. But Christmas Eve has a bad reputation for dreams, and Dick might have been dreaming.

CHAPTER II.

CHRISTMAS TIME.

THE moon was shining brightly—Dick told Goodenough when he returned to town—as he followed the boy who had been sent to him, on his way to Frog's-hole. The heather on Mosly Moor looked like a sheet of snow from the hoar frost which had gathered upon it, and glistened in the moonlight. As he drew nearer to Frog's-hole, he saw old Jemmy standing at the entrance to the hollow, evidently expecting him.

"She is gone, Sir!" exclaimed the old man, as soon as Dick was near enough to hear him. "She is gone, Sir! The old woman, her grandmother, has taken her away. You can see them yonder."

Dick looked in the direction indicated, and could plainly discern two figures walking forward.

"Bring her back, Sir! She didn't want to go. If you take the road to Jackson's farm, you will soon come up to them."

Without further instructions, Dick started in pursuit; but as the road was rough and slippery with the frost, he walked with difficulty, whilst the two figures in advance appeared to be umimpeded by the state of the ground over which they travelled.

Before Dick could overtake them, they had reached a quaint-looking old house, that stood out black against the moonlight and showed a strong light in one of the lower rooms. The door of the house was immediately opened, and the two figures passed in, and all was black as before. Dick wondered what he ought to do, whether he should knock and demand the restoration of the girl, or wait until she and her grandmother again came forth. A sound of voices issued from the lighted window, and when Dick approached it he was surprised to find it open, in spite of the coldness of the night, and the lateness of the hour. He could, by this unexpected discovery, see into the room, and hear all that was said.

At one side of a table sat a man somewhat advanced in years, whose heavy eye-brows, and sharp, piercing eyes, made an unfavourable impression upon Dick. On the opposite side was the girl; but Dick would hardly have known her again, had he met her, without his previous conviction that it was old Jemmy's Bessy, as she was older in appearance, and much handsomer than he should have supposed, from the brief glimpse he had had of her in the afternoon. The grandmother had folded her cloak about her head and shoulders, and seated herself on a low stool by the side of her grandchild.

"You are a very obstinate, self-willed girl," said the man, "to refuse such an offer as mine."

"I don't care," replied Bessie; "I can never love you, not if you were a hundred times as rich; and I don't want to be married."

"But why can't you care for me?" asked the man. "I will be kind to you, and give you whatever you desire—good clothes, plenty of food, and this house. I will be kind to old Jemmy, and set him going again some way or the other."

"Ah! think of old Jemmy!" said the grandmother. "You'll be kind to him and to me, won't you, Sir?"

"Yes," said the man.

"I don't believe it," replied Bessy. "You never were kind to any one yet."

"How dare you say that?" exclaimed the man. "But for me old Jemmy would be turned out of his kennel yonder, and sent to the workhouse—your old grandmother would be sent to gaol as a vagrant."

"Think of that, Bessy!" said the old crone. "Think of me in gaol, living on bread and water!"

"I don't believe he can do harm to either you or gran'dad," replied Bessy, rising up; "and I can't believe he will ever do anybody any good."

"Sit down, girl!" said the man, fiercely.

"I shall not stay here," replied Bessy, firmly. "When did you ever help a poor man or woman, except to gaol and the workhouse? When did you ever give a shilling of your wicked money to any poor soul who wanted food or shelter. Never! never!"

The man rose up and clenched his hand, as though he would strike the girl, who did not appear in the least dismayed. "Do you think I am afraid of you?" she said. "You let me go. I came because my gran'mother made me come, and I was resolved to tell you what I have told you, and now let me go."

The man made a movement as though to approach the girl, but at that moment the light was struck down—possibly by Bessy.

Dick strove to call out, but the scene he had witnessed had so surprised him that he lost the power of utterance. Before he could quite recover himself he heard the door open, and Bessy came out alone. She instantly closed the door after her, but did not run, as Dick expected she would have done, but walked leisurely away in the direction of Frog's-hole. Dick soon overtook her, and she did not appear disturbed or surprised when she saw him. "You're the gentleman from London, from Holly Lodge?" she asked.

"I am," replied Dick, "and sent by your grandfather to bring you home."

"He told me he had sent for you," said the girl, "and I knew you would come."

"Yes, I followed you, but could not overtake you before you entered yonder house. I was at the window."

"I guessed that," said the girl, "and that made me as bold as I was. That wicked man wants to marry me, but I would die sooner."

"Is he so very wicked?" asked Dick.

"You shall see with your own eyes, if you like. Come with me," replied Bessy.

The girl made her way to a small copse, which Dick had not noticed before, and, taking a path which seemed to lead into it, walked on. Dick followed until they came to a miserable hovel, partly unroofed. There was a dim light burning within, and through one of the many broken panes in the window Dick saw a wretched-looking woman sitting on the ground, and, lying upon her knees and in her lap, three haggard children.

"All those have been moaning through the day and night, wanting food," said Bessy. "The woman is still awake and suffering, but the children have cried themselves to sleep. That man yonder is the cause of their misery."

"How so?" asked Dick.

"The husband and father was fever stricken not long ago, and the brutal fellow you saw turned them out of their cottage into this place of death. He said the man was a poacher—it was a lie—and set everybody against the poor wretch, who died, and all the other sorrows followed."

Dick had some confused notion that the parish ought to have looked after this miserable household; but Bessy was again walking, and he followed her. They were approaching a neat-looking cottage that appeared to be the abode of comfort and peace. Before they were at the garden gate, Dick heard the noise of loud contention, and an old white-headed man rushed out, followed by an infuriated woman. She was young, it seemed, from the clear sound of her voice and the violence of her gesticulations. What she said was incoherent and terrible in blasphemy and threatenings.

"The woman is mad!" said Dick.

"No doubt of it, and may some day lay violent hands upon herself or her poor father. That man we have left did it; he sowed strife by his wicked calumnies, which drove away from her the youth who one loved her and whom she loved, and, knowing that many believed in her shame, she became what you see her."

Dick was about to enter the garden, but the woman had become silent; and, as Bessy had walked on again, he hastened after her, and was surprised to find, by a sudden turn of the road, that they were at the entrance to Frog's-hole, and that old Jemmy was waiting their return.

The girl did not stay to bid good-night to Dick, but went straight to the mud cottage. Jemmy said a very few words that Dick could not comprehend, although he understood the old man to offer him the services of Jacky to convey him back to Holly Lodge. Dick declined the offer, and Jemmy—a little huffed, Dick thought—went to his cottage also, leaving his late liberal employer to cool himself in the frosty air, or to walk home. Before Dick could determine what to do, Bessy again appeared at the door, and she, who had recently looked so like the pretty girl in the railway carriage, now resembled both in giggle and feature, Dick's *bête noire*, Giddy Gore,

Of course Dick had been dreaming all this, and might have gone on dreaming, had not his feet escaped from under the bedclothes, and then Jack Frost took him by the toes.

"What could ever have put such a rigmarole into my head," thought Dick. "I know before I went to sleep I half repented of my abuse of Christmas time, which seems to soften men's hearts, I confess, and I had thought of that old donkey driver's story, and that day and night mare, Giddy Gore."

Dick rose, early as it was, dressed himself, and went out to see how far his dream of Mosly Moor was realised by the actuality. He had got to the outskirts of the village when he met the doctor, whom he knew, coming from a cottage, in whose window was a sprig of red-berried holly. The place looked neatly kept, and Dick little suspected the sorrow there was within.

"Early astir, doctor," said Dick, after they had exchanged greetings and wished each other a Merry Christmas.

"Yes," replied the doctor. "I want to get over my round before church time, as it's Christmas Day. I am going to the Lodge to beg a Christmas dinner for these poor patients of mine."

"Why, the place looks tidy ——"

"Oh, yes," interrupted the doctor, "and so it is; but there's an empty cupboard for all that. The man, who is ill, wants other medicine than I can supply—good living and peace of mind, poor fellow! Such cases as his are among the most painful we doctors have to cure. We are not rich enough."

"Is he in want of food? Why don't he apply to the parish?" asked Dick.

"No! he would die rather than sacrifice his independence, as he fancies. Very foolish; but you can't beat it out of such men. He can earn good wages, when in health; and a fortnight's good living would set him to work again. I know I can ensure him that to-day, as it is Christmas time. Good-morning, Mr. Richard."

Dick became very thoughtful, remembering what he had seen and heard in his dream. He then tapped at the cottage door, which was opened by a woman neatly but very poorly clad; and Dick saw wrapped up in an old, well-patched blanket, a man seated by a few smouldering sticks, and evidently very weak, if not ill otherwise. Two small children were lying near the mockery of a fire, watching a pot, which, as yet, scarcely sent forth a show of steam.

"I am Mr. Gore's nephew," said Dick, by way of apology. The woman dropped a curtsey.

"The doctor tells me that your husband is very weak—more weak than ill; and he looks it, poor fellow!" said Dick, kindly.

The man had fixed his eyes on Dick, but he now closed them, and sighed heavily.

"What's his trade?" asked Dick.

"He's a clogmaker—makes wooden soles for clogs—I should rather say, Sir!" replied the poor woman, in a feeble, sorrowful voice, adding, "when he's well enough to work."

"Just the thing!" said Dick; "just the thing! I want a lot of wooden soles; so make me a dozen or two, and there's a sovereign on account."

"Oh, Sir," cried the man, "I'm too weak to work!"

"Well, you won't be when you have transformed that money into mutton-broth and bread and butter, and I'll send you a little wine to wash them down," said Dick. "Good-morning!"

Dick heard the woman's words of blessing and the sick man's sobs of thankfulness, as he hurried out of the cottage, and thought what a weak, unworthy member he was of "The Coming Men" Club.

It was time to turn back to Holly Lodge, as breakfast would be ready, and Dick was more than usually hungry, he fancied. Nothing was said, either by Mr. Gore or Dick about the doctor and his patients, as both, we fancy, cared not to boast of their small charities.

When the morning service at the church was over, Dick left his friends, being still anxious to have another look at Frog's-hole, and it wanted an hour to luncheon. He had not reached the moor when he saw an elderly woman embracing a stout, well-dressed young man, and had little doubt but a mother and son had met to pass their Christmas Day together.

"I'm so glad you've come, dear," said the mother; "but, as you didn't write, I was afraid you wouldn't."

"Well, I didn't quite make up my mind until last night, mother," replied the son; "but then I thought of old times, and that it wouldn't be Christmas time again for twelve months, and that you'd be sorry not to see me."

"That I should," said the mother; "for though I get your letters, it ain't like seeing you, Tommy," and she kissed her son again.

Dick had stood, very impertinently, listening to this conversation, and, as the speakers did not take exception to his conduct, he continued to listen.

"There's one thing I want to ask," said the son, becoming rather red in the face, "Is Bill and his wife going to be here to-day?"

"I hope so, my dear," replied the mother, turning very pale.

"Well, then, I sha'n't stop," said Tom. "I won't meet them!"

"Oh, my dear boy, don't say that!" replied the mother. "You are quite wrong in bearing ill-will to Willie and his wife."

"Am I?" asked Tom, rather sharply. "After the way they treated me. Bill's a deceitful, unbrotherly fellow, and I won't meet him!"

"I'm sure you are mistook, Tommy," said the mother; "and I'll put it to this gentleman" (referring to Dick, who was rather startled at being appointed arbitrator in a family quarrel; but, remembering his dream he made no objection).

"Well, put it to this gentleman," said Tom, boldly. "This is it, Sir:—I was very much attached to a young person down here. I loved her—that's the fact; and my brother—Bill's his name—takes advantage of my absence for a few days, cuts me out, and then goes and marries her, Sir."

"He didn't know that you cared for Bella," said the mother.

"Oh, yes, he did! He knowed it well enough," replied Tom.

"How do you prove that?" asked Dick, folding his arms, and looking as sharp as a Q.C.

"Well, because everybody else knowed it," replied Tom.

"Had you ever told him so?" asked counsel.

"No; I hadn't told anybody; but everybody knowed it," replied witness.

"Had you proposed to the young lady?"

"No; but she must have knowed it. She must have seen I was fond of her," said Tom.

"I don't agree with you," replied Dick. "If you had never told your brother that you were in love, and had never told the young lady you loved her, I can't see that either of them was to blame."

"They ought to have guessed it," said Tom, "and not made me miserable."

"You don't look so," observed Dick, with a smile. "You seem well-to-do, well fed, and in good bodily health."

"Well, I'm all that," said Tom. "I'm much better off than I should have been staying at home here; but then they oughtn't to have done it."

"Come," said Dick, "you are a sensible fellow, I know, in a general way, and you'll see, after a little proper reflection, that you are wrong in this matter. You had left the young damsel ignorant of your regard for her, or who knows but she might have given you the preference. *You* only were to blame there. You never told your brother that you loved the girl, or, I am sure, he would have looked out for another wife. Are not those deductions resonable"?

"Well, I can't say they are not," said Tom.

"Then you can't say you've been ill-used; and as it is Christmas time, you'll shake hands with your brother and kiss your sister-in-law under the mistletoe, and be friends all round."

"Well," said Tom, grinning rather than smiling. "I suppose I was the fool, after all; and so, mother, let 'em come, and, as it is Christmas time, I'll do as the gentleman says. But I'll kiss Bella—mind, that's in the bargain!"

Dick shook hands with the young man, and turned back to Holly Lodge to luncheon; and, as he did so, who should drive past him but the pretty girl and her pleasant brother, both recognising him with "nods, and becks, and wreathed smiles." So lighthearted was Dick throughout the remainder of the day, that he actually took Miss Giddy Gore in to dinner, pressed her to take wine, when she declared it would make her "titsey;" and compounded for a kiss, under the mistletoe, by sipping out of Giddy's glass, and compelling her to return the compliment.

Dick had his full share of the Christmas banquet; but "his bosom's lord sat lightly on its throne" that night, and he dreamed he was swimming in a sea of peacock's feathers. His first business the next day was to send in his resignation of membership to the Club of "The Coming Men :" and then, as though to assure himself of his conversion, he stuck a sprig of holly in his button-hole, and walked about, "gaily whistling, and singing, and fancying for him that he heard the bells ringing" for returning to the ways of his good old English fathers.

Three more Christmas Days have been passed at Holly Lodge since the one we have recorded, and, strange to say, the pretty girl has been Dick's fellow-passenger on the two last occasions. When they parted at the station, Dick called the young lady Clara, and she said, "Good-bye, Richard." What will such familiarity lead to when another Christmas time has come and gone? We fancy we have propounded no riddle if the world keeps rolling round as it has done since the sun shone upon Paradise.

AUNT SALLY'S CHRISTMAS-BOXES.

CHAPTER I.

JOHN CRASS.

THE meanest-looking street in London is Lottery Place. It is mean in the style of its architecture, mean in the proportion of its houses, mean in its very knockers, and bears unmistakable evidence of having been built by contract and at the lowest tender. And so it was; for the proprietor of the property, being an ignorant man, who had the luck to draw a prize in the last lottery in England, A.D. 18—, invested his gains in this unsightly pile of bricks and mortar. The houses are called "private," and some of their interiors look smart enough when viewed from the outside. Many of the inhabitants transact their greengrocery business on their doorsteps, and a certain vendor of shrimps and periwinkles boasts of a regular connexion in Lottery Place. Its pinched and parsimonious appearance found favour in the eyes of Mr. John Crass some ten years before the commencement of this story, he being a thrifty man, and by no means particular as to outward appearances. The whole aim of his life was to make money and keep it. He was called a "Commission Agent," and dealt in every conceivable commodity by which he could turn a penny. He was great at "job lots" and bargains, and it was thought impossible for any man to rise early enough to get the best of him. He owned several small tenements, the rents of which he collected weekly ; and woe to the unfortunate who fell into arrear. Nevertheless, Mr. John Crass was looked upon as an honourable man, and always paid his way with scrupulous exactness, thereby setting a good example to many of his more careless neighbours. Mrs. Crass was worthy to be the wife of her husband. She was the best of marketers, and would get more for her shilling than less-experienced housewives would for thirteenpence. She came out strong during warm weather—more ways than one—in the article of butcher's meat ; and her little back-yard was quite a sight sometimes (her neighbours would say) in the matter of fish, especially when flounders were plentiful. She would then festoon her little domain with strings of those piscatorial delicacies, and thus diffuse a marine odour to the circumambient air during the process of drying them. She was learned in exchanges, and knew to a fraction the value of an old waistcoat in barter for the Jew-boy's crockery. I am thus particular in describing the fitness of Mr. and Mrs. Crass to Lottery Place, as I want you to dislike them at once and for ever.

They had only one domestic, a pale, blue-eyed girl of eighteen, and who must long ago have sunk under the labour of her daily life but for the aid of a charwoman and a strong sense of duty to be done and sorrow to be borne for the sake of a widowed mother. Mr. Crass had taken Lucy, when she was only thirteen years old, " to live with him," as he told every one who had known her dead father in his prosperous days ; and soft-hearted men and women, who had been acquainted with the departed, were often loud in their praise of John Crass for his humanity. I wonder what they would have said had they looked into John Crass's kitchen of a cold winter's night, as late as nine or ten o'clock, and found poor Lucy, unkempt, cold, and lonely, still pursuing some drudgery by the feeble light of a miserable candle ; or seen her in the morning raise her still weary body in obedience to the noisy jangle of the cracked bell which hung at her bed-head, and whose wire communicated with the sleeping-chamber of Mrs. Crass ! Poor Lucy !

There was an old friend of Lucy, who told an odd tale about her father, Philip Norton, and John Crass ; and what was more, John Crass admitted it to be true. This old friend said thus :—That Philip Norton had by hard toil and provident care saved as much as three hundred pounds, and, knowing John Crass to be a safe man, who was willing to pay a better interest than could be got in the funds, he had lent him those hard savings on John's note of hand. When Philip Norton was on his death-bed he sent for his debtor, and what passed between them no one knows. John Crass says " nothing particular ;" but the note of hand could not be found among poor Philip's papers. John always professed his readiness to pay when the note of hand could be produced, but no man could expect him to run the risk of doing so without, as an "acceptor is always liable." Nay, John Crass had done more than that ; he had offered to pay the money without the note of hand, provided always that some substantial person would indemnify him against loss. But, as poor Lucy and her mother had not a friend who was sufficiently substantial and confiding, why, John Crass kept his money. And possibly this odd state of matters was the reason why John had taken Lucy "to live with him," so that busy people should nor hear this story too often, and the more so that Philip Norton's widow was thirty miles from London, keeping house for an only brother not much richer than herself.

There were times, however, when Lucy might have been seen with a smile on her face, and her dress neatly arranged and cared for. On those occasions Mr. and Mrs. Crass were making holiday either at the theatre, when orders were obtainable, or when the steamboats were taking people to Gravesend and back for a shilling, or some other very cheap amusement was to be had ; or, perhaps, the Crasses had gone to take tea or a rubber with their particular friends, the Wrangles ; but that could only have occurred when the Wrangles were on terms of amity with each other, which was not always the case. For twenty years they had lived together man and wife, and twenty times they had been on the eve of a dissolution of their connubial partnership. And so they would have continued to do until the end of the chapter had they not made confidants of their friends Mr. and Mrs. Crass ; but from the hour they were admitted as seconds into the domestic ring the word on either side was " No surrender !" And why ?

Mr. Wrangles was the absolute possessor of £300 a year, and was the last male of his line. Indeed, he never had any but poor relations, and these he had discarded long years ago. Mrs. Wrangles had at her own disposal nearly an equal sum, and, having quarrelled with an only sister over the division of the family plate—a silver teapot having been, as she said "the bone of contention"—she appeared to be equally destitute of a residuary legatee as her husband.

It therefore, occurred to our ingenious friends of Lottery Place that if the Wrangles could be effectually separated, and made to consider John Crass and Johanna his wife as their best and truest friends, they (J. and J. C.) might figure advantageously in the last wills and testaments of the W.s.

Very mean all this; but it is needful to be told, although the reason for Lucy's smiling face and smart appearance remains a mystery.

CHAPTER II

AUNT SALLY.

"WHERE'S your missus?" said Mr. Crass as he arrived home very unexpectedly one afternoon early in November; and without waiting for a reply, he passed by Lucy, bawling aloud, "Johanna! Johanna, my dear! where are you?"

A distant "Here I am!" guided Mr. Crass to the little back-yard or garden which Mrs. Crass was then festooning with flounders, a profusion of that delicacy having visited Lottery Place on a barrow that morning.

"Why, what has happened to bring you home so early?" said the lady, evidently surprised, if not alarmed, at the unexpected appearance.

"Very important news, and good news, my love," replied Mr. Crass. "'Our' correspondent at Melbourne" (he always spoke of himself as "our" and "us") "has written 'us'—now take it easy—that your uncle, Jerry Slagg, is dead; and, what's more, he has died e-nor-mous-ly rich."

"Left us anything?" inquired Mrs. Crass, taking it very easy, certainly, and still continuing her tasteful employment.

"No," answered Crass.

"Then he might as well have lived, for what I care," remarked the gentle Johanna.

"Perhaps not, dear," observed Mr. Crass. "Perhaps not, as he has left all he possessed to his only sister and partner, your Aunt Sally, who has sold up everything they possessed—farm, stock, shares, and I don't know what—and is now on her way to England to see us, if she is not here already."

Mrs. Crass actually dropped a flounder, as she exclaimed, "No!" so great was her astonishment and delight.

"I say yes, darling. You are her only known relative, my dear, and who else can she be coming to see, my love?" said Mr. Crass, his wife never having appeared to him so desirable as at that moment.

Before Aunt Sally arrives it may be as well to communicate her antecedents.

Her father was for some time a prosperous farmer and maltster in Essex, but falling into difficulties, and owing £4,000 came, as a matter of course, to be considered a rogue, and unworthy of the notice of his more prosperous friends and relations.

No, not by all, for one old friend stood by Peter Slagg, and lent him £400 to take him to Australia, and help him to make a home for his wife and two children in the New World. Peter Slagg had to struggle very hard for it at first, but before the end of the fourth year he had nearly repaid the friend who had trust in him, and by the sixth he had remitted the balance—"All he owed him," Peter said, "except his gratitude." So the rogue was not a hardened one, at any rate. Both Peter and his wife died soon after this time, and left all their possessions, their sheep-runs and their sheep, their cattle and their stockyards, their log-houses and their clearings, to Jeremiah and Sarah Slagg, their children. Thriftly yet hospitably, hardly yet cheerfully, lived both brother and sister, neither seeking to woo nor be wooed, but apparently resolved to increase their store and lay up riches; and they succeeded, despite droughts, and bush-fires, and bushrangers; and at the time of Jerry Slagg's demise, it was well known that they could reckon their flocks by thousands, and their money invested in many ways by a similar combination of numerals. It was not to be wondered at, therefore, that Miss Sarah Slagg should tire of accumulating and living a lonely life in the backwoods, and should feel a desire to visit the old country, the birthplace of her parents, who had never ceased to talk of the old house at home, the village church and its green graveyard, wherein the names of many a remembered friend must now be recorded. So Miss Sarah Slagg converted all her worldly possessions into money or its representative, and set sail for England, where she arrived after a prosperous voyage, and found her relatives' kind invitation awaiting her.

Miss Slagg, or Aunt Sally, if you please, was an oddity. She was very tall and thin, and those personal characteristics she did not seek to disguise by wearing that uncomfortable folly, crinoline. Her complexion was a deep brown, her features pretty and cheerful, partly concealed by a bonnet invented about 1821, and carried to the colony by her beloved mother. Her hands were somewhat large and bronzed by labour, but their hearty pressure had made many a wanderer feel at home in the distant bush, and the "God speed" to many a parting guest sound more than words of formal ceremony.

Such as she was, she presented herself at the door of her relatives, Mr. and Mrs. Crass, and completely astonished the cabman by her accurate knowledge of her fare thither from the City, which he had, by some error of calculation, made double the amount.

"My good man," said Aunt Sally, "your summing has been neglected shamefully if you make three miles, at sixpence a mile, come to three shillings. I am a woman of business, and you may take my word for it your claim is only eighteenpence for the hire, and twopence extra for the box. So there's one shilling, one sixpence, and two pennies; and good day, driver!" The astonished cabman gazed for nearly a minute at the various coins as they lay on the palm of his hand, and then, placing them carefully in the very depths of his pocket, looked up at the house with all his eyes, and drove off silently.

Aunt Sally's reception by John Crass and Johanna, his wife, was of the warmest. The best bed-room was swept and garnished; the little sitting-room adjoining had a bright fire blazing in its long coal-less grate; and a banquet, in which vegetables and flounders might have been thought to preponderate, welcomed her in the parlour.

Wines of many vintages, home and foreign, sparkled on the board, and none who knew John Crass in his ordinary life, would have believed the recklessness with which he "pushed the bottle round," as he said, though the only drinker was himself. Warmed up by this unusual indulgence, he could not refrain telling his esteemed guest how, many and many a time, he and his Johanna had spoken of the absent ones, and longed to grasp their honest hands, and see their happy faces; how he had looked into his wife's face, and wondered if it resembled dear Aunt Sally's, as it always did in his dreams; and now, sitting there—the most welcomed guest that could sit there—he traced the resemblance a child might bear to its mother, making allowance for a difference of complexion, and a disparity in weight. Aunt Sally was welcome to the roof that covered her, and to the prayer he offered up, and the libation he poured down.

Aunt Sally replied, "Much obliged," and nothing more. Was she thinking of the miscalculating cabman, and fancying that he was not the only man who was disposed to overcharge her? Aunt Sally was, as we shall see, a capital woman of business.

CHAPTER III.

COURTING.

MONTH had passed away since Aunt Sally had become an inmate of Lottery Place, paying (after a short parley with her relatives) a fair sum for her board and lodging. She made daily visits to Mr. Gregory, a broker in the City, and usually passed some hours every day in her own little room, no one could tell how employed, as she invariably locked the door, and requested not to be disturbed by any one. Mr. and Mrs. Crass, therefore, pursued their old course of life very much the same as before the advent of the Australian lady, and one day made an excursion to Rosherville Gardens. Aunt Sally declined their invitation to be one of the party, and set off on her usual visit to the City, intimating to Lucy that it was more than probable she should dine at some place of entertainment, and not return until late in the evening. Why did Lucy's face brighten up at this information? Could the prospect of a respite from her daily drudgery be so very acceptable that her eyes should sparkle and her bosom heave visibly? Aunt Sally had been very kind to her, and given her little presents, and, what was kinder still, had spoken gently, and held many a woman's talk with her, as though she were not the dull, sulking girl that Mrs. Crass always said she was, and had been always.

I cannot part with my mystery yet, and so shall take you to the City with Aunt Sally, and introduce you to her broker. Mr. Gregory was a widower, and had realised a small competency by his business—only a small one, having been led unwisely into ventures on his own account, and lost large sums thereby. How true it is that the experiences of others are useless to ourselves, and even a stock and share-broker, who has known so many consume themselves at the taper of speculation, will sometimes burn his own fingers: Mr. Gregory had been terribly singed. So, when Aunt Sally empowered him to convert Australian shares and bills, and other securities, into hard cash, amounting to nearly £20,000, he had strange thoughts pass into his mind, and all more or less connected with Aunt Sally. He evidently expected her visit, for a substantial luncheon was on a small table, and a more than ordinary blazing fire was in the grate, by whose side a cosy arm-chair was placed to receive the new client. In due time Aunt Sally arrived, her capacious cloak and bonnet covered with flakes of snow, which were then falling without.

"Dear me, Mr. Gregory!" she said, shaking the fleecy particles from her dress, "one would fancy this was June and not December, were one in the colony. Last Christmas day I had my dinner in the verandah, and sat out until nine o'clock hearkenin' to the laughing jackasses and singing magpies."

"But," said Mr. Gregory with a smile, "we in England must do as England does. So take a chair by the fire, and warm yourself, before we have lunch, and proceed to business."

To all these propositions Aunt Sally consented; and, when they were ended, rose to depart.

"Stay one moment, my dear Madam," said Mr. Gregory, laying his white hand on Aunt Sally's ungloved brown one, "I wish to say a few words on my private business. It is now twelve years ago since I lost a most excellent partner." He paused and sighed.

"In your business!" asked Aunt Sally.

"No, not exactly," said Mr. Gregory, "I allude to my wife, and I have hitherto thought that her place was not to be supplied."

"And is it?" inquired Sally.

"Possibly. I am tired, Madam, of this daily drudgery, this endless toil; and could willingly realise the small property I have and retire."

"Then why don't you?" asked Sally.

"Because I should be a miserable man, living alone, consulting only my own comforts, fancies, interests. You know what it is to live alone in the great forest ; but no wilderness so dreary as a home without a wife ; none so lonely as a wifeless man."

" Then why don't you marry again ?" asked Sally. " Gals ain't scarce in England, I am sure."

" What should I do with a girl for a wife ?" said Gregory. " No, my dear Miss Slagg, what I seek is a matured mind, a contented helpmate, to whom home would be the world. From the first moment I saw you, I felt I had found the woman."

" Me !" exclaimed Aunt Sally. " Come, don't talk nonsense to a woman of forty-nine."

" It is not nonsense ; it is earnest, truthful sense ;" and Mr. Gregory was about to kneel when Aunt Sally held him up by the collar.

" Don't make a goose of yourself! I came here on business, I'm a woman of business, and ——"

Gregory would not be denied. On his knees he went, and poured out vows and protestations enough to have won a convent.

"Very well," said Sally, "if you prefer that position keep it, and hear what I've got to say. If you'll keep steady to work, and don't speak to me again upon this subject until I ask you to dinner at Christmas time, I won't say 'No' at present. Is it a bargain ?"

It was a bargain ; so they shook hands, and Aunt Sally left the office, satisfied that she, as a woman of business, had made a discovery.

It was not to be her only one ; for on arriving at Lottery Place, and after letting herself into the house with her latch-key, she heard a strange voice in the parlour. The door of the room whence the sound proceeded being open, she saw Lucy, in her best, seated by the side of a handsome young fellow, to whom she was repeating the multiplication-table. The young man's arm was round Lucy's waist, and seemed so much in place, that the fair pupil was not the least disturbed by it.

"That will do for this morning," said the instructor; "you get on famously, considering the few opportunities you have for practice, and I shall reward you with a kiss."

Lucy received her prize upon her forehead with all proper modesty. And the young pair, looking up, saw, to their dismay, Aunt Sally sitting quietly in a chair by the door, regarding them attentively.

After a moment's careful examination of George Waters, the young gentleman before her, a smile passed over her gentle face as she said :—

"Very pretty, indeed, young folk; very pretty, indeed!" and that was true enough, for a handsomer couple, now Lucy was herself, could hardly be found in London.

"I feel," said George, "that some explanation is necessary."

"Well, if you like," interrupted Aunt Sally, "tho' part explains itself. You like that young gal, and that young gal likes you—isn't it?"

George acknowledged that it was so, and then went on to say "that he had known Lucy all her life, when she had a happy home, and received the nurture due to her gentle nature, before death came and robbed her of her father, and ever since (he half hinted) some one had robbed the mother of the little that remained to them of worldly goods. That, always loving her as a play-mate, he had grown to love her as a man, and, being too poor to find her another home, he had paid her many, many stolen visits, and endeavoured to impart to her such knowledge as he had himself acquired, in the hope that, at some day, he should reap the harvest of his happy labour, when he should call her his wife. And there was hope that that day would come, the sooner if he should succeed in getting the secretaryship of a certain City company of which his father had been a freeman. One person's influence, he knew, could secure it to him, and he had that day written to Miss Slagg to obtain it, knowing that Mr. Gregory was her broker."

"Mr. Gregory can do it, can he?" asked Sally.

"Most certainly." And, as the salary would be a fortune to George, he had made bold to say this.

"Very well," said Aunt Sally, "we will see Mr. Gregory. Eh! hum! When you have done your courting, come up into my room, Lucy, and let me have a chat with you. Goodday to you, young man," and the strange, kind old maid, left the young lovers together.

Time passed more swiftly with them than with Aunt Sally, who, for some reason or other, could not bring herself to her book of figures, and so she shut them up, and then opened one of her huge trunks. From its inmost recess she brought out a small japanned box, and, having unlocked it with a little key attached to a black ribbon which she wore round her neck, she produced the miniature of one whom she had loved in secret years ago, and had seen go down in the cruel sea when his ship was in sight of land. She had loved no other, and, if she knew her heart, never could; and the happiness and sorrow that her love had brought her were remembered now. Long intervening years were as though they had never been, and Aunt Sally felt a young maid's sympathy with Lucy and her lover.

And Lucy, when she had bidden George good-bye a dozen times at least, came to Aunt Sally's room, and told her all her sad story of death, and wrong, and suffering, cheered now and then by such scenes as Aunt Sally had witnessed.

"Your mother approves of this, of course?" said Aunt Sally.

"Oh, yes! and George goes down and sees her every now and then, as I am not allowed any holidays. George goes again next Sunday."

"Then he shall take me with him," said Aunt Sally, kissing Lucy very sisterly, for the memory of the past had made her old heart young again.

More discoveries, you see, and more still; for when Aunt Sally went with George to see Lucy's mother, she found, to her delight and surprise, that they had been playmates together when they were little girls, and before Sally had been taken away to the New World, thousands of miles away. This was a pleasant discovery indeed, for it gave Sally a right to help the oldest friend she had, to meddle in her tangled matters and see if they could not be put straight.

Sally never liked, as she said, to "let the grass grow under her feet," so the next day at breakfast she "tackled" John Crass and Johanna his wife.

"Niece," said Aunt Sally, "you and John have no secrets, I believe?"

"Oh, none!"

"So much the better—what's one's the other's. Very well. So, consequently, as I'm your aunt, whatever affects you must necessarily affect me."

"How kind of you to think so," said John Crass, partly rising, as if with the intention of embracing his generous relative by marriage.

"No thanks at present; leave them to the future,"

"Long distant be the day!" exclaimed John Crass; whilst Mrs. Crass could only trust herself to breathe "Amen."

"Very well, then," said Sally. "Now, I've been obliged to hear that some doubt exists in the minds of some people as to the propriety of your keeping £300, which *morally* belongs to Widow Norton."

"Oh, the malicious slanderers?" cried Mrs. Crass.

"Calm yourself, my dear," said John Crass, wiping his lips on the tablecloth. "If we have done anything which is legally wrong ——"

"I said morally," interrupted Aunt Sally.

"Well, the same thing, only differently expressed," continued Crass. "I was about to add, I should be sorry. But this is the case;" and, laying a finger in the palm of his hand, he prepared himself for the mystifying speech he had delivered frequently before.

"I know all about the case," said Sally; "the bill can't be found, and you won't pay without an indemnity."

"And you don't blame us, dear aunt?" said Mr. Crass.

"Not in the least; if you thought you run any risk?"

"I assure you I do run a risk, or I should be delighted to get rid of the matter," remarked John.

"Consider it done," said Aunt Sally. "I suppose I am good security for three hundred pounds?"

"You security to us? You ask a thing we could refuse?" exclaimed John Crass, plainly seeing that he could not do so in this instance. "No, aunt; give us your word that I am held harmless, and the £300 shall be placed in your hands on Monday next."

"Agreed," replied Sally. "I promise, and I am rejoiced in your decision. So, good-morning. I have a little writing to do before I go into the City."

"Oh, by-the-bye, aunt," said Mrs. Crass, "I hope my old desk answers your purpose?"

"Quite the thing," replied Sally, "if you don't want it."

"Not any use to me; do what you like with it."

And Aunt Sally did that very morning, and made another discovery, of which you shall hear in due course. She made it in an old tortoiseshell snuff-box which had belonged to her grandmother, and which she found in Mrs. Crass's desk, it having been taken out of John Crass's tin dressing-case by Johanna and placed where it was found, as a family reminder to Aunt Sally.

CHAPTER IV.

ONE OF AUNT SALLY'S DISCOVERIES.

IT was now the middle of December, and all sorts of people were talking of Christmas holidays and Christmas gifts to be given or received. Aunt Sally seldom went to the City, and then rarely to call on Mr. Gregory, but employed herself continually in figuring and writing about what no one could tell, until John Crass and Johanna his wife were let some way into the secret by receiving a special invitation to dine with Aunt Sally on Boxing-Day at no less a place than the Bedford Hotel, Covent Garden, celebrated from the days of Sheridan for its good cheer and urbane management. "Boxing-day" the letter was headed. What did that mean? John smiled at Johanna, and said :—

"Odd creature! Isn't she?"

Mr. Gregory had also received a similar invitation. His probation was drawing to a close. Upon the receipt of the invitation, even before he could write to accept it, Aunt Sally herself was announced by the office clerk, and Mr. Gregory's heart actually thumped against his ancient ribs as it did when, at the age of sixteen, at the Mansion House, he danced with the lovely daughter of the Lord Mayor of London. Like a true gentleman, he had kept his promise to Aunt Sally, and had never "told his love" again to her or any one else; and to-day—all women are riddles, more or less—Aunt Sally was the suitor. How she throve we shall learn by-and-by, although Mr. Gregory's parting words were very indicative of a favourable result.

"My dear Miss Slagg, you have made me the happiest of

men. Be assured your wish shall be accomplished; and I believe I am the only man who could at this moment boldly say as much. Adieu! adieu!"

"Gregory, I trust all to you," were Aunt Sally's parting words as she went out once more into the snow.

When Aunt Sally returned to Lottery Place she found the unhappy Mrs. Wrangles waiting the return of her dearest friend, Johanna Crass, who had left home early, catalogue in hand, to attend a sale of furniture at the west-end of London. Mrs. Wrangles was in tears, as usual; but, as those pearly drops (as they are called by the poets) failed to empty her overladen heart, she soon began to pour into Aunt Sally's ears her connubial woes.

"Why, my dear woman," said Aunt Sally; "why should you and your husband be separated? All matter of temper. You won't and he would — he would and you wouldn't. Nonsense. Kiss and be friends."

"Never, Miss Slagg. You don't know—of course you can't—what it is to be the wife of such a man; but my dear friend Mrs. Crass can fully appreciate my position, and urges me to pursue the course I have adopted. Oh, if woman ever had a true friend, Johanna Crass is one! A sister! More than a sister; for my sister gave me up for an old teapot. All I have in the world I have left to Johanna. Would it were ten times as much!"

"Oho!" said Aunt Sally. "You've something to give away, have you?"

"Not much; only £300 a-year," sobbed Mrs. Wrangles.

All the sympathising woman had disappeared from Aunt Sally's face, and "business" was written there in a bold text hand.

At this moment Lucy came into the room with a note, which, she said, "Mr. Crass had left for Mrs. Crass, shou'd Mrs. Wrangles call."

"Oh! business, perhaps," said Aunt Sally; and, without a moment's pause, she opened the note.

Now, this was perfectly indefensible on the part of Aunt Sally—perfectly; but she had passed all her life in the backwoods of Australia, and had acquired some very rude manners.

Sally very nearly whistled as she read the lines there written. Yet she said they were nothing very particular at present, and resumed the conversation by saying—

"Now, Mrs. Wrangles, it's quite clear to me that you're a wretched woman (a sob from Mrs. Wrangles); that you're making yourself so unnecessarily (a shake of dissent from Mrs. Wrangles); and that you must go with me to Mr. Wrangles."

Mrs. Wrangles preferred going to her family vault at Highgate Cemetery.

"Very well. Then Mr. Wrangles shall come to you. Meet you shall; and if you part any more for such a trumpery cause as now separates you, why, say Sarah Slagg knows nothing of business. Where's Wrangles located?"

Mrs. Wrangles gave the address of her recusant husband, and off started Aunt Sally once again through the snow.

A very similar scene was enacted with Mr. Wrangles as had just occurred with his wife, only substituting the name of John for Johanna Crass, and with a very similar result.

"Very well," said Aunt Sally, "I should have been glad to have brought you to reason without betraying the secrets of even John Crass. I must save the dupes at the expense of my relatives. Read that," and she handed Wrangles the note left by John to Johanna.

Mr. Wrangles read as follows :—

"If Mrs. Wrangles calls, you must work her up to indignation-point, as I am half afraid that Wrangles is melting, and wants to go home again. That won't do at no price. So go it strong, as £300 a-year is worth playing for.
"J. C."

Now, this conduct was wrong again; but need I say that Wrangles went at once with Aunt Sally to his long deserted home, and that he and his wife ate their Christmas dinners together from that time to this? That was the last of Aunt Sally's discoveries until after her banquet given on Boxing-Day, when she astonished other people, and was not surprised herself.

CHAPTER V.

THE CHRISTMAS-BOXES.

CHRISTMAS DAY was close at hand, and Aunt Sally had shut herself up in her room every morning after breakfast longer than usual. What could she be doing? Mr. Crass was not a man to be deterred by any nice considerations of propriety from satisfying his curiosity, especially where he considered his pecuniary interests were concerned; and so, being the mean fellow I have described him, he ventured to bore a small hole through the door, and then stooped to peep through it. He might have walked into the room for all that Aunt Sally cared, only she liked to take her own course in all she did; and now she was merely drawing a few cheques and placing them in envelopes arranged upon the table and numbered from 1 to 5.

Mr. John Crass was delighted with what he saw, and told Johanna so, adding "Generous old creature! My dear, it must be our duty to direct her benevolence into proper channels, my love—eh, love?"

The nod which Mrs. Crass gave in reply would have indicated a simple affirmative had it not been for the smile and the wink, and the snifile which accompanied it. Depend upon it, Aunt Sally's relatives meant mischief.

The Crasses never made much of Christmas Day. They were of those who thought it no better than any other day in the year, and never cared to set it apart for any of the pleasant uses which from time out of mind have been said to belong to it. No old grudge was forgiven, no old love renewed ; no unselfish thought admitted within their home on Christmas Day ; but Mr. Crass usually employed it in looking over his list of debtors, and arranging little schemes of annoyance for the defaulting ones.

Aunt Sally, to their great satisfaction, had refused an invitation to dine with them, and had arranged to pay a charwoman to attend in Lottery Place, so that Lucy might spend the day with her in the country. " Could they refuse any request that would give pleasure to dear Aunt Sally? especially as the day after Christmas Day was Boxing Day, and they had to dine with her at the Bedford ! "

Of course they could not ; therefore Lucy, and Aunt Sally, and George found themselves in the back parlour of a grocer's shop, in the village of Crackleton, whilst the shop itself was so choked up with customers—the stock being all new and tempting—that Widow Norton and her brother had enough to do to serve them. But it was Christmas Eve, and neighbours did not mind waiting, as there was no lack of subjects for conversation about former Christmases, and those who had helped to make them pleasant halting-places on the road of life. The shop was cleared at last, and George assisted his uncle (Well ! he would be his uncle in course of time) to put up the shutters ; and then, despite the long day's work, the merriest party in Crackleton was in the grocer's little back parlour.

Aunt Sally had never passed such a Christmas Eve. Can you doubt that she had contributed largely to its happiness?

The Christmas Day which succeeded was bright and frosty ; the old church, from the porch to the altar, was a bower of greenery ; and the day might have been passing in Australian heat, to see how the church-goers would stop in groups on their way ; although some of the children tried to bury their ears in their worsted comforters, and were too cold to use their pocket-handkerchiefs, still bearing up bravely, and wondering why their parents could loiter so, knowing that the roast beef or the roast goose and the plumpudding were nearly ready at home.

Aunt Sally and her party were as happy as any of them over their Christmas dinner, and only one uncharitable speech was made throughout the day, and that was by the old lady herself.

" I wouldn't," she said, very emphatically, " I wouldn't have eaten my Christmas dinner in Lottery Place for half the

Bank of Australia. I couldn't have done it for the life of me, and that's a fact."

A chorus of "Bravo! bravo!" was sung by the whole party in admirable time.

But we must back to town by the first train in the morning, for Aunt Sally had to pack her two large trunks and lock them securely, and write her name in a bold round hand on the labels attached to them, having to receive her guests at the Bedford at the mechanical hour of two o'clock on Boxing-Day. The whole party were very punctual, and more numerous than Mr. John Crass and Johanna his wife expected. They had arrived the first, and were somewhat puzzled when Mr. Buckminster was announced. He was a portly gentleman, and evidently a new acquaintance of Aunt Sally. Mr. Gregory came next, smiling like the sun, which tried in vain to put him out of countenance as he marched boldly up to Sally, and placing a packet in her hand, said, "There it is, my dear Madam, and most happy am I to be the humble means of obliging you."

Aunt Sally went to the window, opened the large envelope, satisfied herself of its contents, like a good woman of business, and then held out her hand to Mr. Gregory, saying, "Mr. Gregory, I am very much obliged to you—very!"

John Crass and Johanna his wife did not half like that.

Mr. Grayfoot and Mr. Martingale, both men of substance evidently, and well known on the Corn Exchange, were duly announced. "Mr. and Mrs. Wrangles" made John stare at Johanna with surprise, and actually bleached them both to an old parchment complexion when those snapping turtles entered the room arm-in-arm together. They warmly shook hands with Aunt Sally, and then passed on to John Crass and Johanna his wife, saying—

"Weak! weak!—we know we are, weak, but we are only human."

George Waters, considering himself nobody, had come in unannounced, and been placed on her right hand by Aunt Sally, who did the honours of the table in a way that showed she had always a liberal hand and had been accustomed to carve for people with good appetites.

At the proper and appointed time Aunt Sally "rose on her legs," as the phrase goes. I know what horrible inflictions after-dinner speeches usually are, how many a man owes chronic dyspepsia to listening to such disturbing influences immediately after a good meal; nevertheless, as the whole gist of this Christmas story is contained in Aunt Sally's, I must beg "silence for the chair."

"My good friends and relatives," she began, "I have no doubt that some of you were rayther surprised to be asked here to take your dinner, and came like good-natured people because you thought me an oddity, and wondered what I should do. You'll perhaps be surprised more when I tell you that I am about to realise the most ardent wishes of four people's lives, three of them are now at rest in a far-off Australian forest, and I, a woman, have come from there also to perform an act of duty—of love to the memories of them that are dead. More than forty years ago my father, in his desire to do his best for his wife and children, made an error of judgment and became a ruined man—ruined in more ways than in pocket, for many who had shared his prosperity not only turned their backs on him in his poverty, but called his misfortunes roguery, and him a rogue. He could never have held up his head again in the Old World, so, like a brave-hearted man as he was, he looked over the thousands of miles of water which were between him and the New World, and he resolved to get there if he could, and in the depths of the forest he had heard of, hew himself a home for his wife and children, and, if God prospered his labours and his thrift, buy back the honest name filched from him. One friend was found to help him, and I would he sat here to-day that I might tell him how often his name was heard in the prayers of the backwoodsman's family, even to the day I turned me away from the place which I loved, and which will know me no more. God prospered my father in his labour, now and then checking our greediness by droughts and bush-fires, but always heaping up the measure of His mercies until it ran over. At last my father died, and she who had followed him to the wilderness could not stay behind when he had gone on to heaven, and my brother and myself were left together. My father's creditors were three rich men, who were not harder than they should have been; and I have the sons here to-day to tell them how often their debts have been paid through years of toil, and by the substantial purchase-money of four willing bonds-people in the lonely clearing, and which I am here to pay.'"

So saying, Aunt Sally handed to Mr. Graysfoot and Mr.

Martingale and Mr. Buckminster each one of the envelopes John Crass had seen through the hole in the door.

"You will find there, gentlemen," continued Aunt Sally, "a cheque for the sum my father owed your fathers, with compound interest, added up correctly, I believe; for I have given much time and care to the calculation. Don't thank me; they are Christmas-boxes which are your due. The sum total is set down under this envelope (and Sally presented one to Mr. Gregory), and amounts, my good friend, to ——"

"Fifteen thousand four hundred pounds!" exclaimed Gregory, starting up, "Why, you've not enough left to buy ——"

"A small annuity," said Aunt Sally. "Oh, yes I have, and something more. Do you wish to renew a conversation we had once in your office?"

"No, Madam," replied Gregory; "most emphatically no, Ma'am. I thought you a sensible, careful woman ——"

"But not a woman of business," added Sally. "I am not wrong, then, in supposing you consider that note an answer to your interesting communication?"

"Pray spare me any further mortification, and consider the service I have rendered Mr. Waters an equivalent for any annoyance I may have occasioned you. I accept my Christmas-box with thankfulness." And Mr. Gregory rose, shook hands with Aunt Sally, and left the room muttering, "What an escape I have had!"

The service he had rendered George was contained in the packet presented to Aunt Sally before dinner. 'Twas George's selection to the situation he had named in his first interview with Aunt Sally, and which enabled him, before three years had passed, to marry his loving pupil Lucy.

"John Crass and Johanna Crass," said Aunt Sally, her whole manner and tone changed, "I came to England and hoped to find kinsfolk I could love and honour. You are all that I have known to be of my own blood, and I find you mean, cruel, and dishonest."

"Hallo! hallo!" said John Crass; "I don't understand all this. If I guess right, you have been fool enough to pay away all you are worth, and only left yourself with an annuity."

"Quite true," answered Sally. "What then?"

"Why, this," said John, "that I ain't satisfied with that

undertaking I hold of yours, and I shall consult my attorney."

"You had better open this envelope first and see what you have for a Christmas-box."

John tore open the envelope presented to him by Sally and read what follows—to himself, you may be sure :—

"John Crass,—Your wife gave me a writing-desk to use as I thought fit. In it I found an old tortoiseshell snuff-box ['That was in my tin dressing-case,' thought John] belonging to my grandmother. I opened it and found ['The bill, of course; Johanna, you're a fool,' thought John] which you can have on returning my memorandum, as I am a woman of business."

"Are you satisfied with your Christmas-box?" asked Sally.

"Quite; and I'll thank you to take away your trunks."

"They are already in this hotel," said Sally, calmly.

"Are they? Very well; then I shall take myself off," said John, preparing to be as good as his word, utterly forgetful of Johanna.

Mr. Wrangles rose with great dignity and said,—

"Stay, Crass, and hear your victim."

"First hear me, Mrs. Crass, you deceitful crocodile!" exclaimed Mrs. Wrangles.

But, as the parties addressed were no strangers to the pertinacity of their ill-used friends, John Crass and Johanna his wife left the room, to the great relief of the rest of the party.

Aunt Sally still lives with Widow Norton in the little village of Crackleton, and her annuity—not a large one, I believe—is known to benefit many besides herself; and George and Lucy come at Christmas-time (and at other times also) to make merry in the little parlour, and once during their visit always ask this question "Oh! Aunt Sally, don't you remember your Christmas-boxes?"

CHRISTMAS-EVE IN A NIGHT TRAIN.

SOME few years ago we met casually a clever friend who was manager of a certain railway, and found, after the usual greetings, that we were both suffering from a very common annoyance, usually known as "depression of spirits," although neither of us was able to assign any substantial reason for our condition at the moment.

"Come with me," said our friend. "Whenever I am in 'the blues' I adopt a simple but efficacious remedy, and you shall try it."

"And canst thou minister to a mind deceased?" was, of course, the natural and time-honoured rejoinder.

"Yes, I can; and I'll tell you what I do. I wait until the line is clear, and then jump on a pilot-engine, run fifty or sixty miles down, and return again under a couple of hours. The excitement of the journey always puts the demons to flight."

The absurdity of this proposition had the effect of dispelling our own megrims, as we laughed heartily at the notion of consigning our invaluable body to a pilot-engine, steaming along at the rate of sixty miles an hour.

We did not accept our friend's invitation, but subsequently, acting upon his discovery, have more than once sought the excitement of Thames Street when business was at its height, and have found that a walk down that river-side thoroughfare has dispelled every other feeling but one of thankfulness for a safe deliverance from danger and death. Let any *malade imaginaire* try it. The bags, barrels, and bales swinging over-head from every gradation of height, the jamming of carts and cabs, the unparliamentary "checking' (we believe that is the word) of cabmen, carters, and truck-haulers—the bawling of grimy coal and corn-porters (who certainly ask, "By y' leave," but require such an immediate compliance that if you hesitate a moment you are pirouetting in the gutter), the roaring which comes from the open windows of gloomy tap-rooms, filled with half-tipsy fellows, emitting clouds of most villanous tobacco, are a combination of exciting causes sufficient to stimulate the most desponding.

On the river-side of the street are numerous alleys which lead down to the Thames, and in one of them a country friend of ours (let us call him Jack Tracey), when in London, with the intention of visiting an aunt, found himself during a thick November fog, and continued to follow its course until he tumbled off the end of a landing-stage, and fell plump into the river. It was fortunately low water, and the mud-bath which received him would certainly have been his death had not two or three coal-heavers carousing in the tap-room of the "Pickled Herring" heard his cries and come to his rescue. When Jack was dragged ashore and examined by the light in the tap-room, he appeared to be clothed from head to heel in a suit of coagulated fog: so that after he had been taken into the back yard and scraped, he looked not unlike the grey monster in "Frankenstein," and "smelt so," as Hamlet says, that *patchouli* might really have been considered an agreeable perfume by comparison.

It was lucky that Jack had found such quarters, as it was questionable whether any less dirty hostelry would have received him in the filthy condition he was then: but there were other odours than those from "Araby the Blest" pervading the "Pickled Herring," and Jack's muddiness, was, perhaps, an addition to the *bouquet*.

The landlady having stipulated that Jack should be valetted in the kitchen before he was taken up-stairs, prepared for him a warm bed, with two hot bricks for his feet, and then administered copious doses of bad rum-and-water softened with salt butter. The effects of her treatment, combined as they were with the shock, fog, and rough hauling of his rescuers, were apparent in the morning, and eventuated in a state of fever which kept poor Jack an inmate of the "Pickled Herring" for nearly three weeks, his condition being unknown to his friends for more than a fortnight of that time, owing to the untrustworthiness of the pot-boy — a drunken old fellow of fifty—who had spent the shilling with which he had been entrusted to pay the postage of a letter, and having afterwards lost it, had sufficient shame to keep his own counsel.

When Jack was convalescent enough to amuse himself by reading, he was kindly allowed the run of the library at the "Pickled Herring," which, however, was very limited in extent, and not particularly interesting in choice of subjects, as it consisted of several ancient "Moore's Almanacs," two odd volumes of the "Newgate Calendar," illustrated, a mutilated copy of "Tales of Terror," and an old "ready reckoner," much thumbed and soiled at the pages referring to dry and beer measure.

As Jack had rewarded his deliverers on the night of his rescue, their interest in him had ceased, and having no other acquaintance in the neighbourhood, the poor solitary invalid had plenty of time at his disposal for his literary pursuits. By the time a second letter had brought his Aunt Hester to his bedside, he knew every tale of blood by rote, and was quite familiar with the exploits of Mr. Richard Turpin and Jack the Pirate.

Aunt Hester lived at Hoxton, wherever that may be, and Jack was removed to her house as soon as he was strong enough to bear the journey, and a cabman could be found who knew the locality.

Good nursing soon restored Jack, not quite to his pristine vigour, as the phrase runs. His early rum-and-water treatment, or the fog and the mud, had left him with an impaired digestion, which was a great affliction, as Christmas time was close at hand, and it being the custom at Jack's home, near Portsmouth, to keep the festive season with plain but prodigal hospitality.

Aunt Hester, a married branch of the Portsmouth tree, had been grafted with a similar reverence for Christmas cheer, and it was generally supposed that she had won the heart of her husband, an eminent exciseman, by her incomparable mince-pies, which she compounded with as much secrecy as is known to attend the manufacture of Day and Martin's blacking.

If Jack Tracey had a predilection—no! more than that—a positive passion for anything in the world, it was for mince-pies; and defying dyspepsia and its attendant agonies, he abandoned himself recklessly to the gratification of his appetite on Christmas-Eve, preparatory to his departure by the night mail train for Portsmouth, where he was expected to eat his Christmas dinner.

Aunt Hester had dressed her little parlour in holly and mistletoe, so that the portrait of the exciseman, hanging in the place of honour on the wall, looked like a Jack-in-the-green peeping out of his "bower of greenery" on the merry party—three neighbours and Jack—assembled at an early supper, whereat Aunt Hester's mince-pies made a liberal display, and commanded the earnest attention of her nephew. Aunt Hester knew that Jack, by his free indulgence, was taking misery to his—well!—his bosom, but her hospitable heart would not permit her to raise a warning voice, and the devourer after a time was filled and happy. Yes, quite happy, for the eminent exciseman was as much an adept at composing gin-punch as his wife was at compounding mince-meat; and so insinuating in its character was the mixture, that, like other tricksy spirits, it beguiled frail mortals occasionally, leading them into strange adventures.

Jack Tracey had taken, at his uncle's earnest solicitation, that treacherous "one glass more," as a specific against the dangers of night air and the tedium of night travelling, not that Jack was any way "fou," nor had he "just a drappie in his e'e," which so poetically expresses incipient intoxication; he was only comfortable and happy—nothing more.

As Jack drove to the station through the busy streets—busy despite the snow which had fallen—he regarded with admiration the grocers' windows, bright with gas-lights, and bursting almost with currants, raisins, and citron-peel, piled therein, garnished all about with holly-sprigs, until he wished in his heart of hearts, that Christmas time came oftener than once-a-year, and that mince-pies were never out of season.

Jack had been franked in a cab to the station by the eminent exciseman, but found it impossible to avoid giving the driver an extra sixpence in honour of the season, although his illness at the "Pickled Herring" had drained his exchequer almost, and made it advisable for him to travel by a third-class carriage, as he was too independent to borrow money of his relatives.

There was considerable bustle at the station, which amused Jack after he had taken his ticket, much kissing and shaking of hands between friends and relations, and one neatly-dressed girl hugged an old woman so affectionately and so long that Jack was almost disposed to ask to be taken into partnership. When the bell rang, however, the young girl took a parting kiss, and entering a third-class carriage, followed by Jack, as though he had a right to escort her, but he found that she was already provided with companions. One was an elderly, rough, seafaring man, who, for some reason of his own, wore the knot of his thick red cotton neckerchief under his right ear, his head being covered by a black fur sea-cap. Next to him sat a smart sailor, and the young girl took her place in a corner on the opposite seat. She appeared to be either tired or thoughtful, as she only replied with a grunt to some remarks about "granny" which the young man made to her, and then she rested her arm upon a pile of bundles and baskets on the seat beside her.

All this Jack saw by the feeble light of the carriage lamp; and then he began to speculate on the probable relation his fellow-travellers bore to each other, deciding that the young people were engaged lovers, and the old man was the father of the pretty maiden.

The train was soon in motion, and Jack Tracey, wrapping himself up in his new railway rug—a present from his aunt—placed his feet upon the vacant seat opposite to him, with the intention of sleeping away some of the tediousness of the journey before him. He found the determination more difficult of accomplishment than he had anticipated, as his " bosom's lord sat " by no mean "lightly on its throne," and some of the tribulations which Aunt Hester had foreboded, in her own mind, as awaiting her nephew, began to possess him. His discomfort was not in any way mitigated when the two seamen lighted short pipes charged with very strong tobacco, and the copious clouds which they proceeded to send forth soon made breathing difficult, nearly obscuring the miserable light blinking above the heads.

Jack did not care to remonstrate with such rough-and-ready-looking offenders, and as the snow was again falling fast, he could not lower the window of the carriage without danger of taking cold. His only hope of deliverance was that the pretty girl in the corner might be inconvenienced by the fumigation, and obtain some cessation on the part of her friends. But she was evidently used to it, or too absorbed by her own reflections to interrupt the enjoyment of her companions.

The old man's pipe was at length exhausted, and Jack, seeing by looking askant from beneath his rug that he had no immediate intention of refilling it, congratulated himself on the extinguishment of one of the volcanoes, little thinking what new misery the old man was fishing out of one of the baskets before him. It came in the shape of a broken egg-cup and a black bottle, which evidently contained rum, as the powerful odour of the spirit soon "o'ercrowed" the tobacco and pervaded the carriage. Jack had a pardonable horror of that popular nautical spirit ever since his adventure at the "Pickled Herring," and by a quick association of ideas, be instantly recalled his mud bath, his rescue and subsequent scraping and ablution in the kitchen, his frowsy bed, and the horrible rum and water treatment; the exploits of Dick Turpin and Jack the Pirate; the terrific incidents of the "Tales of Terror;" the price of coals; and the number of pots of beer contained in a hogshead.

Those pleasures of memory, however, were of short duration, as the old seaman (having filled the egg-cup and offered it to the girl, who took a modest sip of the contents), reached across his younger companion and proffered the cup to Jack, who politely declined the dram. The old man was not to be so easily denied, and after two or three refusals on the part of Jack, appealed to his gallantry and nationality by hoping "he wouldn't object to the cup after a lady, unless he was too proud to drink with an old salt, who could pay his way, and didn't care for no man as wasn't a man."

There was no resisting such an appeal, as refusal would appear to be a slight to the pretty girl in the corner, and an offence to the rough old fellow who made the request, and who did not seem likely to put up with an indignity very quietly. Jack, therefore, took the egg-cup, bitterly regretting the economy which had placed him in such company.

The rum was new and strong, and Jack had great difficulty in swallowing it; but having done so, and shaken hands with the liberal donor, he was delighted to find, shortly afterwards, that the liquor had had the effect of allaying his previous discomfort, and rendering him less obnoxious to the powerful fumes of the tobacco smoke, which the younger seaman continued to emit in clouds. Jack re-arranged his rug and commenced counting the telegraph posts as they became visible in the light cast upon them from the carriage windows—a very sedative employment, as everyone must have discovered who has tried the experiment.

Time and the train passed very rapidly, and Jack was surprised to find that they had reached Blankton station, but by no means gratified when told that they must alight, as the accumulated snow made further progress impossible until the line was cleared.

The authorities at the station had done their best to alleviate the discomfort consequent upon the disaster, and the passengers were shown into a large room, garnished in the most approved Christmas fashion, and in which an abundance of Christmas cheer was laid out for their entertainment. Jack and his party occupied one end of the table, but there was a confusion among the other passengers for which Jack could not account—neither could he discover much flavour in the mince-pies, which, resembling in size and conformation those delicacies made by Aunt Hester, wanted all their other gratifying properties. The attendants were the railway porters, who, considering the novelty of their duty, appeared to discharge their ministerings with much tact and readiness.

By degrees the room was deserted by all the passengers except Jack, the two seamen, and the pretty girl who accompanied them; and he was not surprised, therefore, when he saw the porter putting out the lights and heard the station master announce that the waiting-room must be cleared for the night. Jack's companions took the matter so easily that he was ashamed to make any remonstrance, and therefore he went out with them, feeling strangely indifferent as to where they were to pass the remainder of the night.

The seamen and the young girl were evidently acquainted with the locality, as they strode away briskly over the snow, now hardened by a sharp frost, which had succeeded the fall, and Jack thought he could not do a wiser thing than keep in their company.

At last they came to a house lighted partially from within,

and resembling strangely enough the "Pickled Herring" externally. Without waiting to knock, the whole party entered, and found themselves in a large room also decorated for Christmas time, and wherein burned a bright fire, as though to give them welcome. The house appeared to be in charge of one of the railway porters, as the only person to receive them was a man dressed in the uniform of the company, and who shook them all by the hand, telling them, at the same time, that he had been expecting them since the train had stopped at Blankton station.

When they were seated, the old seaman produced the remainder of his rum and tobacco, and Jack was too glad to renew his acquaintance with the potent spirit, and even to venture on a pipe of tobacco, as his walk over the snow had chilled the marrow in his bones. The soothing influence of the spirit and the narcotic soon displayed themselves on the assembled party, and Jack was glad when the railway porter invited him to go to bed, leading the way up a broad oak staircase, afterwards ushering him into a larger panelled room, in which was a bed of considerable dimensions, hung with ample curtains of faded chintz, and covered with a railway rug in lieu of a counterpane.

The porter bade him good-night, after placing upon the table the bull's-eye lamp which he had carried instead of a candle, and Jack proceeded to make a survey of his apartment. The floor was of rough dark boarding, which had sunk here and there under the weight of years, and was not altogether firm beneath his feet. The dark panelling on the walls, cracked and even wanting in places, being entirely without ornament except over the great fire-place, and there hung a rude painting of Dick Turpin in the act of placing an old lady on the fire to make her confess where her money was concealed.

In the large grate which occupied the ample chimney, a few embers of a wood log smouldered, but there were no materials for continuing or renewing the fire. Jack was less disturbed than might have been supposed by these uncomfortable appearances, until he discovered that the door would not close, and that its large wooden lock was broken, apparently having been forced from without at some time or the other. He was no coward, however, and he had seen nothing which ought reasonably to have give rise to any suspicion of sinister intentions on the part of his new acquaintance. He determined not to undress himself, but to wrap himself in the rug, and lie down outside the bed placing the bull's-eye lamp on the great arm-chair beside him.

Jack could not sleep, at least not for some time, but he must have dozed, as the room had become perfectly dark, and he had no recollection of the lamp having gone out. As he lay with his eyes wide open, perfectly conscious of his situation and of all about him, a light from without defined the outline of the door, and streamed through the large keyhole in the great lock. Before he could rise from the bed or make an inquiry, the door was opened very gently, and the young girl entered his room as noiselessly as a ghost. She carried a bull's-eye lamp, and when the light fell upon her face, he saw that she was very pale, and her eyes appeared to be red with weeping.

Jack Tracey instantly rose up, but before he could speak the girl motioned him to be silent, and then retracing her steps very cautiously to the door, closed it nearly.

Again approaching Jack, she said, in a low, sorrowful voice " Mr. Tracey "—(he wondered how she had learned his name) —" Mr. Tracey, no doubt you are surprised to see me here, and at such a time ; but I am in great trouble, and you, I think, will not hesitate to befriend me, if I can show you the way."

" Pray consider me devoted to your service," replied Tracey, not knowing what else to say.

" I have heard something to-night which will almost kill me if it be true, and I must learn the truth at once. May I ask you to come with me—come with me out of this house? All are asleep but ourselves, and you can do what I now require of you, and what else I may call upon you to do, without fear of detection, if we are careful and silent."

Jack Tracey expressed his ready compliance with her request, and the girl having silently opened the door again, cast her light round the landing, disclosing a long passage which Jack had not seen before, and then led the way downstairs to a door which opened into an enclosure at the back of the house, apparently secured from observation by a high wall on either side.

The moon was shining brightly, throwing the deep shadow of one of the walls upon the white snow ; and availing herself of this protection from observation, the girl, closely followed by Tracey, stole stealthily along towards a distant building, which seemed to be a barn. There was a strong wind blowing, though it was not felt in the enclosed space they traversed; but the snow was occasionally scattered from the ridges of the walls and the roof of the building which they were approaching. Tracey fancied he could hear the dashing of waves upon the shore and the moaning of the sea, although he could not account for the proximity of a beach to Blankton.

The girl, stopping before a small door at one end of the great building, lifted the wooden latch, showing by the light of her lamp, which she still carried, a small room, in which were two dusty chairs and a table, whilst upon the wall were some bunches of faded holly, brown and shrivelled. After closing the door and setting down the lamp, the girl motioned Tracey to be seated, and then said, in the same low, sorrowful voice in which she had hitherto spoken, and as nearly as Jack could remember afterwards, what follows:—

"Mr. Tracey, before we proceed further in this night's work, it is necessary that I should tell you my story. The old man with whom you travelled to-night is my father—my stubborn, unfeeling father. Two years ago my dear mother died in the house we have just left, and there, until that sad time, I had lived all my life. When I was seventeen, I was told that I was very handsome, and my vanity made me believe what was so often repeated to me. My too-indulgent mother was proud of her pretty child, and spared nothing to gratify my love of display, and my desire for admiration. I became every day more conscious of my attractions, and delighted to encourage the attentions of the young men of the place, until many, misled by a pretended regard, offered themselves as my lovers, only to be laughed at by me, and to be ridiculed by their rivals. I was that odious, wicked thing called a flirt.

"There was one, however, whom I did love; oh! how dearly I did not know, until it was too late. He believed that I loved him, and bore with my waywardness and unpardonable encouragement of others, sometimes gently reproving me, sometimes avoiding me when his mortification had become extreme, and his earnest love apparently despised. A word or smile from me would always bring him back again, and during one repentant interview, I exchanged with him a token that we were some day to be married to each other. I will not say I ever sincerely regretted making that engagement, but such was my waywardness, that at times I have resented some fancied control of me which he appeared to assume, and have caused pain to his loving heart, which I would now give worlds to know had never been.

"One Christmas Eve we had a merry-making in our humble way, and he was kept away by some unavoidable cause. The young man whom you have seen to-night had been a suitor to me, and never ceased to press his attentions upon me whenever we met. He was a favourite of my father, and so was present on that miserable evening. He took more than one occasion, before our friends, to jeer me on the absence of his rival. I was greatly mortified, my foolish vanity was hurt at the appearance of neglect; I thought I had a right to command my lover's presence; and at last I denied that the absent man had any reason to call himself my lover. The man you saw to-night had become aware, by some means unknown to me, of our exchange of tokens, and challenged me with wearing the gift I have mentioned. In my wicked rage—my shameful weakness—I took the token from my bosom, and threw it upon the floor, stamping upon it, and declaring, in a passion of excitement, that I never would speak to *him* again, or see *him* more.

"When I recalled the words I had uttered, as I lay sleepless upon my bed that wretched night, I did not believe that they were to prove so true—so very true!"

The young girl covered her face with her hands, but the tears stole from beneath them and fell upon her bosom. Tracey tried to speak to her, but the power of utterance seemed to have left him. When the girl could regain command of herself, she continued,—

"Some one told *him* all that had passed, and when he heard it he never uttered one reproachful word. He merely said, 'God forgive her!' and went away. What my own sufferings were, none knew besides myself, for I was too wicked to acknowledge my fault—too proud to ask his forgiveness! I did never see him more! He went away—to sea, I am told—and from that hour no word of his has reached me, until this night.

"I was not to escape the consequences of my sin, for as such I soon regarded what I had done. I was overtaken by a settled melancholy, which I could not conceal nor master. I wasted away until it was thought that my death was certain. And then my dear mother also paid the penalty of her over-indulgent love, and my sufferings became hers; for when it was needful that a nurse should be with me night and day, she would not allow a stranger to undertake the duty, but watched and waited with such constancy, that when I was saved, my mother died."

She took from her bosom a wedding-ring, which was fastened round her neck by a black ribbon, and kissed it, weeping and sobbing violently.

At length she resumed:—

"The young man who travelled with us has again proposed to marry me, although he knows I have no love to give him. My father has listened to his proposal, and insists upon my accepting him as my husband, declaring that he himself intends to go again to sea, and, therefore, I shall need a protector! But, if what I have heard to-night be true, no power on earth shall force me to obey him. If I could have brought myself to have acted such a miserable lie as to have stood at the altar, and become his wife, it would have been only to have escaped from my father's brutal anger and perpetual reproaches—no other course being open to me. If, however, what we are about to see, and know, be as I have heard, I will not do it! I will not do it!"

She looked upwards as she said this, holding her closed hands above her head, her face becoming as white and rigid as marble.

Tracey was greatly perplexed by what he saw and heard, but he could not speak to her, and felt as though a hand grasped his throat to keep him silent.

The young girl now rose up, and, after trimming the lamp, motioned with her head that they must be going. Tracey's bold heart beat quickly, and cold drops of sweat stood upon his forehead. He followed his guide, however, who passed —he could hardly perceive how—through an opening out of the little room into a large chamber—a barn it might have been, but the sides and roof were concealed under holly boughs and other evergreens tied together with black ribbon.

In the centre of the chamber an object was lying covered by a white cloth, and lighted by some concealed means which made even the texture of the cloth distinctly visible. The young girl paused for a few moments by the side of the covered object, and then slowly removing the cloth, disclosed the body of a young sailor neatly clothed in the dress of a man-of-war's-man, but having entangled among his hair and strewed about him clusters of sea-weed, shining as though fresh from the sea.

The young girl appeared to be prepared for this strange revelation, and for a few moments she stood motionless and tearless, looking upon the only one she had ever truly loved. At last she bent over her dead lover, and kissed the cheeks, the forehead, and lips; but her feelings becoming too excited for control, she threw her arms around the senseless form, and cried bitterly.

When this passion of grief had subsided, she raised her head, shaking aside the long curls which had fallen about her face, and said in a tone of exquisite sweetness,—

"Oh, true lover! You have come back to one who drove you forth to shipwreck and to death! You have come back to claim your bride, and will take me with you whether your grave be in the churchyard or beneath the waves of the deep sea."

She then beckoned the astounded Tracey to her, and placed in his hand her mother's wedding-ring, which she had worn about her neck, saying,—

"Take that cold hand, and between its thumb and finger place this, my mother's ring."

Tracey obeyed her, having seemingly lost all free will.

"Now put the ring upon my finger as he might have done had not my wickedness driven him away to shipwreck and to death!—to shipwreck and to death!"

Again Tracey endeavoured to obey her, but the ring fell from his fingers, and before he could regain it, the noise of approaching numbers was heard, and he looked to the quarter whence the noise proceeded. He then became confused or overpowered by what was passing around him, and fancied that the dead man raised himself upon one hand, and opening his closed lids, looked at the young girl with such loving eyes, that all which would otherwise have been terrible in the action, was absent!

What succeeded to this strange scene was equally surprising!

The chamber was suddenly occupied by the two seamen and their friends, who seized upon the young girl and Jack as though they were about to take summary vengeance on both of them.

During the hubbub which succeeded, the bier and its burthen were removed. At one end of the chamber appeared an altar, hitherto unperceived by Tracey, and standing within the rails a venerable clergyman in a snow-white surplice. On one side of Tracey was the old seaman, supported by many of his friends, rough, pirate-looking fellows armed with bludgeons, and on the other side the young girl, downcast and silent.

"What do you require of me?" asked the clergyman, in a gentle voice.

"This, your reverence," replied the old seaman. "This fellow (pointing to Tracey) has inveigled my daughter from my house, and as this young man behind me won't marry her on account on it, I require that the other one does."

"Who? I marry!" said Jack. "The man's mad. I don't want to marry! Besides, the thing is impossible—no banns, no licence!"

"By an old canon of the church," said the clergyman, speaking more gently even than before, "by an old and somewhat obsolete canon of the church, I can dispense with either preliminary; and if you will take your places and say after me, the ceremony can be performed in five minutes."

Jack's head spun round as he felt himself forced towards the altar, but he struggled manfully to free himself from the crowd about him.

The young girl uttered a piercing scream, then another, and another! until Jack began to recognise the steam whistle of the locomotive, and was delighted to discover the old seaman rubbing his eyes with the back of a great worsted muffatee, and the young girl snoring gently, musically, in her corner. The other man—possibly having been left in charge of the rum and egg-cup—had fallen forward quietly enough, and buried his head among the bundles and baskets.

"Oh, Aunt Hester! Aunt Hester!" thought Jack, "those treacherous, though delicious mince-pies of yours! What a pretty dance they have led me through the Land of Dreams! If ever I eat more of them than—I can get, or drink bad rum even on compulsion, may I be haunted as I have been this

Christmas Eve by memories of Dick Turpin, Jack the Pirate, and Tales of Terror!"

Jack Tracey reached his home in safety, and being laid up on Boxing day with a bilious attack, wrote his Aunt Hester a letter containing his adventure on Christmas Eve when he was a passenger by the night train. From that letter this veritable story has found its way into these pages.

POPULAR BOOKS BY GOOD AUTHORS.

THE FAMILY GIFT SERIES.

A cheap issue of Popular Books, suitable for Prizes and Rewards.

Crown 8vo, cloth gilt, price 2s. 6d. each.

1. **The Swiss Family Robinson.** Translated by HENRY FRITH. With Coloured Frontispiece and over 200 Engravings.
2. **Bunyan's Pilgrim's Progress.** With a Memoir of the Author by H. W. DULCKEN, Ph.D., and 100 Engravings.
3. **Robinson Crusoe.** By DANIEL DEFOE. With Biographical Sketch of the Author, and many Engravings.
4. **The History of Sandford and Merton.** By THOMAS DAY. With 100 Engravings by DALZIEL Brothers.
5. **Famous Boys, and How they became Great Men.** By the Author of "Clever Boys." With many Illustrations.
6. **Fifty Celebrated Women**: Their Virtues and Failings, and the Lessons of their Lives. With Portraits and other Illustrations.
7. **The Gentlemen Adventurers**; or, Antony Waymouth. By the late W. H. G. KINGSTON. With full-page Engravings.
8. **Evenings at Home.** By Dr. AIKIN and Mrs. BARBAULD. With many Illustrations.
9. **The Adventures of Captain Hatteras.** By JULES VERNE. Containing "The English at the North Pole," and "The Ice Desert." With Coloured Plates.
10. **Twenty Thousand Leagues Under the Sea.** First and Second Series Complete. By JULES VERNE. With Coloured Plates.
11. **The Wonderful Travels.** Containing "Journey into the Interior of the Earth," and "Five Weeks in a Balloon." By JULES VERNE. With Coloured Plates.
12. **The Moon Voyage.** Containing "From the Earth to the Moon," and "Round the Moon." By JULES VERNE. Coloured Plates.
13. **Getting On in the World**; or, Hints on Success in Life. By W. MATHEWS, LL.D. First and Second Series Complete.
14. **The Boy's Own Book of Manufactures and Industries of the World.** With 365 Engravings.
15. **Great Inventors**: The Sources of their Usefulness, and the Results of their Efforts. With 109 Engravings.
16. **Marvels of Nature**; or, Outlines of Creation. 400 Engravings.
17. **The Boy's Own Sea Stories.** With full-page Engravings.
18. **Household Stories.** By the Brothers GRIMM, W. HAUFF, &c. With many Illustrations.
19. **Fifty Celebrated Men**: Their Lives and Trials, and the Deeds that made them Famous. With Portraits and other Illustrations.
20. **The Wonders of the World**, in Earth, Sea, and Sky. With 123 Engravings.
21. **The Triumphs of Perseverance and Enterprise.** By THOMAS COOPER. With many Engravings.

London: WARD, LOCK & CO., Salisbury Square, E.C.

POPULAR BOOKS BY GOOD AUTHORS.

THE FAMILY GIFT SERIES—*continued*.

22. Keble's Christian Year: Thoughts in Verse for the Sundays and Holy Days throughout the Year. With full-page Engravings.
23. A Face Illumined. By E. P. ROE, Author of "From Jest to Earnest," &c.
24. The Scottish Chiefs. By Miss JANE PORTER.
25. What Can She Do? By E. P. ROE, Author of "A Face Illumined," &c.
26. Barriers Burned Away. By the Same.
27. Opening of a Chestnut Burr. By the Same.
28. Orange Blossoms. By T. S. ARTHUR. Illustrated.
29. Mary Bunyan, the Blind Daughter of John Bunyan. By SALLIE ROCHESTER FORD. With full-page Engravings.
30. The History of Margaret Catchpole. By Rev. RICHARD COBBOLD. With numerous Illustrations.
31. Julamerk; or, The Converted Jewess. By the Author of "Naomi." With numerous Illustrations.
32. Herbert Lovell; or, Handsome He who Handsome Does. With numerous Illustrations.
33. Amy and Hester; or, The Long Holidays. Illustrated.
34. Edwin and Mary; or, The Mother's Cabinet. Illustrated.
35. Wonders and Curiosities of Animal Life. By GEORGE KEARLEY. With many Engravings.
36. Wonders and Beauties of the Year. By H. G. ADAMS. With many Engravings.
37. Modern Society; or, The March of Intellect. By CATHERINE SINCLAIR. With numerous Illustrations.
38. Beatrice; or, The Unknown Relatives. By CATHERINE SINCLAIR. With numerous Illustrations.
39. Looking Heavenward: A Series of Tales and Sketches for the Young. With numerous Illustrations.
40. Life's Contrasts; or, The Four Homes. Illustrated.
41. Nature's Gifts, and How we Use Them. With numerous Illustrations.
42. Pilgrims Heavenward: Essays of Counsel and Encouragement for the Christian Life.
43. The Book of Children's Hymns and Rhymes. Illustrated.
44. Preachers and Preaching, in Ancient and Modern Times. By Rev. HENRY CHRISTMAS. With Portraits.
45. Character and Culture. By the Hon. and Rt. Rev. the BISHOP OF DURHAM, Canon DALE, &c.
46. Popular Preachers: Their Lives and their Works. By Rev. W. WILSON. With Illustrations.
47. The Boy's Handy Book of Games and Sports. With Hundreds of Illustrations.
48. The Boy's Handy Book of Natural History. With about 100 full-page Engravings by W. HARVEY.

London: WARD, LOCK & CO., *Salisbury Square*, E.C.

THE Select Library of Fiction.

PRICE TWO SHILLINGS EACH.

COMPRISING
THE BEST WORKS BY THE BEST AUTHORS,
INCLUDING

CHARLES LEVER,	WHYTE MELVILLE,
ANTHONY TROLLOPE,	AMELIA B. EDWARDS,
HENRY KINGSLEY,	M. BETHAM EDWARDS,
JAMES GRANT,	VICTOR HUGO,
HARRISON AINSWORTH,	MAX ADELER,
HAWLEY SMART,	MARK TWAIN,
MRS. OLIPHANT,	BRET HARTE,
C. C. CLARKE,	&c., &c.

*** *When Ordering the Numbers only need be given.*

- 6 My Uncle the Curate. M. W. SAVAGE.
- 11 The Half-Sisters. G. JEWSBURY.
- 12 Bachelor of the Albany. SAVAGE.
- 17 Jack Hinton. CHARLES LEVER.
- 23 Harry Lorrequer. CHARLES LEVER.
- 27 The O'Donoghue. CHARLES LEVER.
- 32 The Fortunes of Glencore. Ditto.
- 35 One of Them. CHARLES LEVER.
- 40 Belle of the Village. JOHN MILLS.
- 41 Charles Auchester. Author of "My First Season."
- 44 Sorrows of Gentility. G. JEWSBURY.
- 46 Jacob Bendixen, the Jew. C. GOLDSCHMIDT.
- 47 Mr. and Mrs. Asheton. Author of "Woman's Devotion."
- 48 Sir Jasper Carew. CHARLES LEVER.
- 50 Marian Withers. G. JEWSBURY.
- 53 A Day's Ride: A Life's Romance. CHARLES LEVER.
- 54 Maurice Tiernay. CHARLES LEVER.
- 56 The Only Child. Lady SCOTT.
- 58 Master of the Hounds. "SCRUTATOR."
- 59 Constance Herbert. G. JEWSBURY.
- 66 Elsie Venner. O. W. HOLMES.
- 67 Charlie Thornhill. C. C. CLARKE.
- 70 Falcon Family. M. W. SAVAGE.
- 71 Reuben Medlicott. M. W. SAVAGE.
- 72 Country Gentleman. "SCRUTATOR."
- 75 Barrington. CHARLES LEVER.
- 78 Deep Waters. ANNA DRURY.
- 79 Misrepresentation. ANNA DRURY.
- 81 Queen of the Seas. Capt. ARMSTRONG.
- 82 He Would be a Gentleman. LOVER.
- 85 Doctor Thorne. A. TROLLOPE.
- 86 Macdermots of Ballycloran. A. TROLLOPE.
- 87 Lindisfarn Chase. T. A. TROLLOPE.
- 88 Rachel Ray. ANTHONY TROLLOPE.
- 89 Luttrell of Arran. CHAS. LEVER.
- 92 Irish Stories and Legends. LOVER.
- 93 The Kellys and the O'Kellys. ANTHONY TROLLOPE.
- 95 Tales of all Countries. Ditto.
- 96 Castle Richmond. Ditto.
- 99 Jack Brag. THEODORE HOOK.
- 100 The Bertrams. A. TROLLOPE.
- 101 Faces for Fortunes. A. MAYHEW.
- 102 Father Darcy. Mrs. MARSH.
- 103 Time, the Avenger. Mrs. MARSH.
- 110 Emilia Wyndham. Mrs. MARSH.
- 114 Theo Leigh. ANNIE THOMAS.
- 117 Flying Scud. C. C. CLARKE.
- 122 Miss Mackenzie. A. TROLLOPE.
- 125 Belton Estate. ANTHONY TROLLOPE.
- 127 Dumbleton Common. Lady EDEN.
- 128 Crumbs from a Sportsman's Table. CHARLES C. CLARKE.
- 139 Which is the Winner? Ditto.
- 141 Lizzie Lorton. Mrs. LINTON.
- 142 The Mad Willoughbys. Ditto.
- 146 Rose Douglas. S. W. R.
- 154 Riverston. Mrs. G. M. CRAIK.
- 157 Lord Falconberg's Heir. CLARKE.
- 159 Secret Dispatch. JAMES GRANT.
- 163 Sense and Sensibility. J. AUSTEN.
- 164 Emma. JANE AUSTEN.
- 165 Mansfield Park. JANE AUSTEN.
- 166 Northanger Abbey. JANE AUSTEN.
- 167 Pride and Prejudice. JANE AUSTEN.

London **WARD, LOCK & CO.**, Salisbury Square, E.C.

THE SELECT LIBRARY OF FICTION.

168 Beauclercs, Father and Son. C. C. CLARKE.
185 The Brothers. ANNA H. DRURY.
188 Lotta Schmidt. A. TROLLOPE.
192 An Editor's Tales. A. TROLLOPE.
193 Rent in a Cloud. CHARLES LEVER.
195 Geoffry Hamlyn. H. KINGSLEY.
196 Ravenshoe. HENRY KINGSLEY.
197 Hillyars and Burtens. Ditto.
198 Silcote of Silcotes. H. KINGSLEY.
199 Leighton Court. H. KINGSLEY.
200 Austin Elliot. HENRY KINGSLEY.
201 Reginald Hetherege. H. KINGSLEY.
203 Ralph the Heir. A. TROLLOPE.
204 Semi-Attached Couple. Lady EDEN.
205 Semi-Detached House. Lady EDEN.
206 Woman's Devotion. Author of "Margaret and her Bridesmaids."
207 Box for the Season. C. C. CLARKE.
211 Sir Brook Fosbrooke. C. LEVER.
212 Aunt Margaret. E. F. TROLLOPE.
213 The Bramleighs. CHARLES LEVER.
214 Ladies of Bever Hollow. ANNE MANNING.
225 Tony Butler. CHARLES LEVER.
227 That Boy of Norcott's. Ditto.
228 Lord Kilgobbin. CHARLES LEVER.
229 Cornelius O'Dowd. CHARLES LEVER.
230 Bernard Marsh. G. P. R. JAMES.
231 Charley Nugent. Author of "St. Aubyns of St. Aubyn."
234 A Passion in Tatters. A. THOMAS.
235 Old Maid's Secret. E. MARLITT.
239 Hawksview. HOLME LEE.
240 Gilbert Massenger. HOLME LEE.
241 Thorney Hall. HOLME LEE.
242 La Vendee. ANTHONY TROLLOPE.
244 Lady Anna. ANTHONY TROLLOPE.
245 St. Aubyns of St. Aubyn. Author of "Charley Nugent."
263 He Cometh Not, She Said. ANNIE THOMAS.
270 Hagarene. Author of "Guy Livingstone."
271 May. Mrs. OLIPHANT.
272 In the Days of My Youth. AMELIA B. EDWARDS.
274 No Alternative. ANNIE THOMAS.
275 Colonel Dacre. Author of "Caste."
276 For Love and Life. Mrs. OLIPHANT.
277 Last of the Mortimers. Ditto.
278 My Son's Wife. Author of "Caste."
280 Squire Arden. Mrs. OLIPHANT.
281 Lost Bride. Lady CHATTERTON.
284 Wild Georgie. J. MIDDLEMAS.
285 Ombra. Mrs. OLIPHANT.

286 First in the Field.
287 Pearl. Author of "Caste."
289 The White House by the Sea. M. BETHAM EDWARDS.
291 Entanglements. Author of "Caste."
293 Caste. Author of "Pearl."
294 Off the Line. Lady THYNNE.
295 Ladies of Lovel Leigh. Author of "Queen of the County."
296 Madonna Mary. Mrs. OLIPHANT.
297 Queen of the County. Author of "Three Wives."
298 Miss Carew. A. B. EDWARDS.
299 Olympus to Hades. Mrs. FORRESTER.
300 Vicar of Bulhampton. TROLLOPE.
303 Book of Heroines. Author of "Ladies of Lovel Leigh."
304 Debenham's Vow. A. B. EDWARDS.
305 Fair Women. Mrs. FORRESTER.
307 Monsieur Maurice. A. B. EDWARDS.
309 John and I. M. BETHAM EDWARDS.
310 Queen of Herself. ALICE KING.
311 Sun and Shade Author of "Ursula's Love Story."
313 Wild Flower of Ravensworth. M. BETHAM EDWARDS.
315 Lisabee's Love Story. Ditto.
316 Days of My Life. Mrs. OLIPHANT.
317 Harry Muir. Mrs. OLIPHANT.
318 Gold Elsie. E. MARLITT.
321 Broken Bonds. HAWLEY SMART.
323 Heart and Cross. Mrs. OLIPHANT.
324 Two Kisses. HAWLEY SMART.
325 Layton Hall. MARK LEMON.
326 A Charming Fellow. E. F. TROLLOPE.
328 False Cards. HAWLEY SMART.
329 Squire of Beechwood. "SCRUTATOR."
333 Magdalene Hepburn. OLIPHANT.
334 House on the Moor. Ditto.
335 Cardinal Pole. W. H. AINSWORTH.
336 Lilliesleaf. Mrs. OLIPHANT.
338 Blotted Out. ANNIE THOMAS.
342 Constable of the Tower. W. H. AINSWORTH.
343 A Fatal Error. J. MASTERMAN.
347 Mainstone's Housekeeper. E. METEYARD.
349 Mount Sorrel. Mrs. MARSH.
354 Off the Roll. KATHERINE KING.
359 Courtship. HAWLEY SMART.
360 Condoned. ANNA C. STEELE.
361 Bound to Win. HAWLEY SMART.
363 Gardenhurst. ANNA C. STEELE.
364 Cecile. HAWLEY SMART.
365 Sir Harry Hotspur. A. TROLLOPE.
367 Race for a Wife. HAWLEY SMART.

London: WARD, LOCK & CO. Salisbury Square, E.C.

THE SELECT LIBRARY OF FICTION. 3

368 Leaguer of Lathom. AINSWORTH.
369 Spanish Match. W H. AINSWORTH.
370 Constable de Bourbon. Ditto.
371 Old Court. W H. AINSWORTH.
372 Nuts and Nutcrackers. C. LEVER.
373 Myddleton Pomfret. AINSWORTH.
374 Hilary St. Ives. W. H. AINSWORTH.
375 Play or Pay. HAWLEY SMART.
376 A Laggard in Love. A. THOMAS.
377 Lucy Crofton. Mrs. OLIPHANT.
379 All for Greed. BARONESS DE BURY.
380 Dr. Austin's Guests. W. GILBERT.
381 My Heart's in the Highlands. Miss GRANT.
382 Sunshine and Snow. H. SMART.
383 Broken Toys. ANNA C. STEELE.
384 Is He Popenjoy? A. TROLLOPE.
386 Kelverdale. Earl DESART.
387 Tilbury Nogo. WHYTE MELVILLE.
388 Uncle John. WHYTE MELVILLE.
389 The White Rose. W. MELVILLE.
390 Cerise. WHYTE MELVILLE.
391 Brookes of Bridlemere. MELVILLE.
392 "Bones and I." WHYTE MELVILLE.
393 "M. or N." WHYTE MELVILLE.
394 Contraband. WHYTE MELVILLE.
395 Market Harborough. W. MELVILLE.
396 Sarchedon. WHYTE MELVILLE.
397 Satanella. WHYTE MELVILLE.
398 Katerfelto. WHYTE MELVILLE.
399 Sister Louise. WHYTE MELVILLE.
400 Rosine. WHYTE MELVILLE.
401 Roy's Wife. WHYTE MELVILLE.
402 Black, but Comely. W. MELVILLE.
404 An Eye for an Eye. A. TROLLOPE.
408 Cousin Henry. A. TROLLOPE.
409 Dark and Light Stories. M. HOPE.
410 Riding Recollections. MELVILLE.
412 High Stakes. ANNIE THOMAS.
414 Pique. Author of "Agatha Beaufort."
415 Chips from an Old Block. Author of "Charlie Thornhill."
416 Blithedale Romance. HAWTHORNE.
418 Belles and Ringers. H. SMART.
419 Lord Mayor of London. AINSWORTH.
420 John Law. W. H. AINSWORTH.
421 Dr. Wortle's School. A. TROLLOPE.
422 Tragic Comedians. G. MEREDITH.
423 Social Sinners. HAWLEY SMART.
424 Pickwick Papers. C. DICKENS.
425 Jean Valjean (Les Miserables). VICTOR HUGO.
426 Cosette and Marius (Les Miserables). VICTOR HUGO.
427 Fantine (Les Miserables). Ditto.
428 By the King's Command. HUGO.
429 Out of the Hurly Burly. MAX ADELER. 400 Humorous Illusts.
430 Elbow Room. MAX ADELER. Humorously Illustrated.
431 Random Shots. MAX ADELER. Humorously Illustrated.
432 An Old Fogey. MAX ADELER. Humorously Illustrated.
433 The Second Wife. E. MARLITT.
434 The Little Moorland Princess. E. MARLITT.
435 No Sign. Mrs. CASHEL HOEY.
436 Blossoming of an Aloe. Ditto.
437 Evelina. Miss BURNEY.
438 Unrequited Affection. BALZAC.
439 Scottish Chiefs. JANE PORTER.
440 Improvisatore. H. C. ANDERSEN.
441 Arthur Bonnicastle. J.G. HOLLAND.
442 Innocents Abroad. MARK TWAIN.
443 The Squanders of Castle Squander. WM. CARLETON.
445 Never Again. W. S. MAYO.
446 The Berber. W. S. MAYO.
447 The American. H. JAMES, Jun.
448 Opening of a Chestnut Burr. ROE.
449 A Face Illumined. E. P. ROE.
450 Barriers Burned Away. E. P. ROE.
451 What Can She Do? E. P. ROE.
452 A Day of Fate. E. P. ROE.
453 Without a Home. E. P. ROE.
454 Genevieve and The Stonemason. A. LAMARTINE.
455 Debit and Credit. GUSTAV FREYTAG.
456 The Mistress of Langdale Hall. R. M. KETTLE.
457 Smugglers and Foresters. Ditto.
458 Hillsden on the Moors. Ditto.
459 Under the Grand Old Hills. Ditto.
460 Fabian's Tower. R. M. KETTLE.
461 The Wreckers. R. M. KETTLE.
462 My Home in the Shires. KETTLE.
463 The Sea and the Moor. KETTLE.
464 Tom Cringle's Log. M. SCOTT.
465 Artemus Ward, His Book; and Travels among the Mormons.
466 Artemus Ward's Letters to Punch and Mark Twain's Practical Jokes.
467 Leah, the Jewish Maiden.
468 Margaret Catchpole. CORBOLD.
469 The Suffolk Gipsy. CORBOLD.
470 Zana, the Gipsy. Miss STEVENS.
471 The Sailor Hero. Capt. ARMSTRONG.
472 The Cruise of the "Daring." Ditto.
473 The Sunny South. Ditto.
474 Romance of the Seas. "WATERS."

London WARD, LOCK & CO., Salisbury Square, E.C.

THE SELECT LIBRARY OF FICTION.

476 Poe's Tales of Mystery.
477 Wild as a Hawk. KATH. MACQUOID.
478 Margaret. SYLVESTER JUDD.
479 The Gambler's Wife. Mrs. GREY.
480 Forgotten Lives. Mrs. NOTLEY.
481 The Kiddle-a-Wink. Mrs. NOTLEY.
482 Love's Bitterness. Mrs. NOTLEY.
483 In the House of a Friend. Ditto.
484 Mountain Marriage. MAYNE REID.
485 The Conspirators. A. DE VIGNY.
486 Brownrigg Papers. DOUGLAS JERROLD.
487 Marriage Bonds. C. J. HAMILTON.
488 The Flynns of Flynnville. Ditto.
489 Paid in Full. HENRY J. BYRON.
490 Royston Gower. THOMAS MILLER.
491 Briefless Barrister. JOHN MILLS.
492 Chelsea Pensioners. G. R. GLEIG.
493 Eulalie. W. STEPHENS HAYWARD.
494 The Diamond Cross. Ditto.
495 Image of his Father. Brothers MAYHEW.
496 Twelve Months of Matrimony. EMILIE CARLEN.
497 The Brilliant Marriage. Ditto.
498 The Sea Lions. J. F. COOPER.
499 Mark's Reef. J. F. COOPER.
500 Man of the World. S. W. FULLOM.
501 King and Countess. S. W. FULLOM.
502 A Lease for Lives. FONBLANQUE.
503 Waverley. Sir WALTER SCOTT.
504 Kenilworth. Sir WALTER SCOTT.
505 Ivanhoe. Sir WALTER SCOTT.
506 The Antiquary. Sir WALTER SCOTT.
507 Paul Clifford. LYTTON BULWER.
508 Last Days of Pompeii. BULWER.
509 Pelham. LYTTON BULWER.
510 Eugene Aram. LYTTON BULWER.
511 Midshipman Easy. MARRYAT.
512 Japhet in Search of a Father. Captain MARRYAT.
513 Jacob Faithful. Captain MARRYAT.
514 Peter Simple. Captain MARRYAT.
515 Hector O'Halloran. W. H. MAXWELL.
516 Christopher Tadpole. A. SMITH.
517 Pic-nic Papers. Edited by CHARLES DICKENS.
518 Bret Harte's Complete Tales.
519 Shiloh. Mrs. W. M. L. JAY.
520 Holden with the Cords. Mrs. JAY.
521 Nicholas Nickleby. C. DICKENS.
522 Cruise of the Midge. M. SCOTT.
523 A Knight of the 19th Century. E. P. ROE.
524 Near to Nature's Heart. Ditto.
525 Odd or Even? Mrs. WHITNEY.
526 From Jest to Earnest. E. P. ROE.
527 The Backwoodsman. WRAXALL.
528 Almost a Quixote. Miss LEVIEN.
529 Lost and Won. G. M. CRAIK.
530 Winifred's Wooing. G. M. CRAIK.
531 Tales of the Trains. C. LEVER.
532 Paul Goslett's Confessions Ditto.
533 Counterparts. Author of "Charles Auchester."
534 My First Season. Ditto.
535 Clover Cottage. M. W. SAVAGE.
536 Bret Harte's Deadwood Mystery, and Mark Twain's Nightmare.
537 The Heathen Chinee. BRET HARTE.
538 Wan Lee, the Pagan, &c. Ditto.
539 American Drolleries. MARK TWAIN.
540 Funny Stories and Humorous Poems. MARK TWAIN and O. W. HOLMES.
541 Mark Twain's Mississippi Pilot, and Bret Harte's Two Men of Sandy Bar.

Uniform with the above.

BY G. J. WHYTE MELVILLE.

600 Songs and Verses.
601 The True Cross.

HALF-CROWN VOLUMES.

18 Charles O'Malley. CHARLES LEVER.
20 The Daltons. CHARLES LEVER.
23 Knight of Gwynne. CHARLES LEVER.
25 Dodd Family Abroad. C. LEVER.
28 Tom Burke. CHARLES LEVER.
30 Davenport Dunn. CHARLES LEVER.
33 Roland Cashel. CHARLES LEVER.
42 Martins of Cro' Martin. C. LEVER.
116 Orley Farm. ANTHONY TROLLOPE.
120 Can You Forgive Her? Ditto.
186 Phineas Finn. A. TROLLOPE.
187 He Knew He was Right. Ditto.
243 Eustace Diamonds. A. TROLLOPE.
267 Phineas Redux. A. TROLLOPE.
319 Forgotten by the World. KATHERINE MACQUOID.
362 The Prime Minister. A. TROLLOPE.
378 The Wizard of the Mountain. WILLIAM GILBERT.
417 The Duke's Children. TROLLOPE.

London: WARD, LOCK & CO., Salisbury Square, E.C.

STANDARD WORKS BY GREAT WRITERS.

THE WORLD LIBRARY OF STANDARD BOOKS.

A Series of Standard Works, including many of the acknowledged Masterpieces of Historical and Critical Literature, made more accessible than hitherto to the general reader by publication in a cheap form and at a moderate price.

Crown 8vo, cloth gilt.

1. **Hallam's Constitutional History of England.** From the Accession of Henry VII. to the Death of George II. By HENRY HALLAM, LL.D., F.R.S. With Lord Macaulay's Essay on the same. 970 pp., 5s. Library Edition, demy 8vo, 7s. 6d.; half-calf, 12s.
2. **Hallam's Europe during the Middle Ages.** 720 pp., 3s. 6d. Library Edition, demy 8vo, 894 pp., 6s.; half-calf, 10s. 6d.
3. **Hallam's Church and State.** By the Author of "The Constitutional History of England." 400 pp., 2s. 6d.
5. **The Wealth of Nations (An Inquiry into the Nature and Causes of).** By ADAM SMITH. 782 pp., 3s. 6d.; half-calf, 7s. 6d. Library Edition, demy 8vo, 800 pp., 6s.; half-calf, 10s. 6d.
6. **Adam Smith's Essays**: Moral Sentiments, Astronomy, Physics, &c. By the Author of "The Wealth of Nations." 476 pp., 3s. 6d.
7. **Hume's History of England.** From the Invasion of Julius Cæsar to the Revolution in 1688. By DAVID HUME. In 3 Vols. 2,240 pp., 10s. 6d. Library Edition, demy 8vo, 18s.
8. **Hume's Essays:** Literary, Moral, and Political. 558 pp., 3s. 6d.
9. **Montaigne's Essays.** All the Essays of Michael the Seigneur de Montaigne. Translated by CHARLES COTTON. 684 pp., 3s. 6d.; half-calf, 7s. 6d. Library Edition, demy 8vo, 920 pp., 6s.; half-calf, 10s. 6d.
10. **Warton's History of English Poetry.** From the Eleventh to the Seventeenth Century. By THOMAS WARTON, B.D. 1,032 pp., 6s.
11. **The Court and Times of Queen Elizabeth.** By LUCY AIKIN. 530 pp., 3s. 6d.
12. **Edmund Burke's Choice Pieces.** Containing the Speech on the Law of Libel, Reflections on Revolution in France, on the Sublime and Beautiful, Abridgment of English History. 3s. 6d.
13. **Herbert's Autobiography and History of England under Henry VIII.** By EDWARD, Lord HERBERT, of Cherbury. 770 pp., 3s. 6d.
14. **Walpole's Anecdotes of Painting in England.** By HORACE WALPOLE. 538 pp., 3s. 6d.
15. **M'Culloch's Principles of Political Economy.** With Sketch of the Rise and Progress of the Science. By J. R. M'CULLOCH. 360 pp., 3s. 6d.
16. **Locke's Letters on Toleration.** By JOHN LOCKE. 400 pp., 3s. 6d.
20. **Essays on Beauty and Taste:** On Beauty, by FRANCIS, Lord JEFFREY; On Taste, by ARCHIBALD ALISON, LL.D. 724 pp., 3s. 6d.
21. **Milton's Early Britain,** under Trojan, Roman, and Saxon Rule, by JOHN MILTON. With MORE'S England under Richard III., and BACON'S England under Henry VIII. 430 pp., 3s. 6d.
23. **Macaulay: Reviews, Essays, and Poems.** 650 pp., 3s. 6d. half-calf, 7s. 6d.

London : WARD, LOCK & CO., Salisbury Square, E.C.

STANDARD WORKS BY GREAT WRITERS.

THE WORLD LIBRARY—*continued.*

24. **Sydney Smith's Essays**, Social and Political. 550 pp., 3*s.* 6*d.*
25. **Lord Bacon.** Containing the Proficience and Advancement of Learning, the New Atlantis, Historical Sketches and Essays. 530 pp., 3*s.* 6*d.*; half-calf, 7*s.* 6*d.*
26. **Essays by Thomas de Quincey.** Containing Confessions of an Opium Eater, Bentley, Parr, Goethe, Letters to a Young Man, &c. 500 pp., 3*s.* 6*d.*
27. **Josephus (The Complete Works of).** Translated by WILLIAM WHISTON, A.M. With Life of the Author, and Marginal Notes giving the Essence of the Narrative. 810 pp., 3*s.* 6*d.* Library Edition, demy 8vo, 6*s.*
28. **Paley's Works.** Containing "The Evidences of Christianity," "Horæ Paulinæ," and "Natural Theology." By WILLIAM PALEY, D.D. With Life, Introduction, and Notes. 3*s.* 6*d.*
29. **Taylor's Holy Living and Dying.** The Rules and Exercises of Holy Living and Dying. By JEREMY TAYLOR, D.D. With Life, Introduction, and Notes. 2*s.* 6*d.*
30. **Milman's History of the Jews.** By H. H. MILMAN, D.D., Dean of St. Paul's. 500 pp., 3*s.* 6*d.*
31. **Macaulay.** Second Series. Reviews and Essays. 3*s.* 6*d.*
32. **Locke on the Human Understanding.** 3*s.* 6*d.*
33. **Plutarch's Lives.** By LANGHORNE. 5*s.*

Uniform with the LIBRARY EDITION of "Hume's England," "Hallam's England," &c.

Shakespeare's Complete Works. With Life and Glossary. Demy 8vo, cloth, 6*s.*

WARD AND LOCK'S
STANDARD POETS.

The nominal price at which this Series is offered to the public places the works of our greatest Poets well within the reach of all.

Crown 8vo, cloth gilt, price 2*s.* each.

1. Longfellow.
2. Scott.
3. Wordsworth.
4. Milton.
5. Cowper.
6. Keats.
7. Hood. 1st Series.
8. Byron.
9. Burns.
10. Mrs. Hemans.
11. Pope.
12. Campbell.
13. Coleridge.
14. Moore.
15. Shelley.
16. Hood. 2nd Series.
17. Thomson.
18. Tupper's Proverbial Philosophy.
19. Humorous Poems.
20. American Poems.
21. Whittier.
22. Lowell.
23. Shakespeare.
24. Poetic Treasures.
25. Keble's Christian Year.
26. Young.
27. Poe.

London: WARD, LOCK & CO., *Salisbury Square, E.C.*

ETIQUETTE BOOKS.

THE STANDARD ETIQUETTE BOOKS.

THE MANNERS OF POLITE SOCIETY; or, Etiquette for Ladies, Gentlemen, and Families. A Complete Guide to Visiting, Entertaining, and Travelling, Conversation, the Toilette, Courtship, &c. ; with Hints on Marriage, Music, Domestic Affairs, &c. Crown 8vo, elegantly bound, cloth gilt, 3s. 6d.

ALL ABOUT ETIQUETTE; or, The Manners of Polite Society : for Ladies, Gentlemen, and Families ; Courtship, Correspondence, Carving, Dining, Dress, Ball Room, Marriage, Parties, Riding, Travelling, Visiting, &c. &c. Crown 8vo, cloth gilt, 2s. 6d.

THE COMPLETE ETIQUETTE FOR LADIES. A Guide to Visiting, Entertaining, and Travelling: with Hints on Courtship, Marriage, and Dress ; In the Street, Shopping, At Church, Visiting, Conversation, Obligations to Gentlemen, Presents, Dinners, Travelling, Offers and Refusals, Correspondence, Courtship, Marriage, &c. Post 8vo, cloth, 1s.

THE COMPLETE ETIQUETTE FOR GENTLEMEN. A Guide to the Table, the Toilette, and the Ball Room ; with Hints on Courtship, Music, and Manners, In the Street, Attendance on Ladies, Visiting, Dress, Dinners, Carving, Wines, the Ball Room, Buying and Selling, the Smoking and Billiard Rooms, &c. Post 8vo, cloth, 1s.

THE COMPLETE ETIQUETTE FOR FAMILIES. A Guide to Conversation, Parties, Travel, and the Toilette; with Hints on Domestic Affairs. Post 8vo, cloth, 1s.

HOSTESS AND GUEST. A Guide to the Etiquette of Dinners, Suppers, Luncheons, the Precedence of Guests, &c. With numerous Engravings. Fcap. 8vo, ornamental wrapper, 1s. ; cloth gilt, 1s. 6d.

THE "HOW" HANDBOOKS.

Elegantly bound in cloth, gilt edges, with beautifully Coloured Frontispiece, price 6d. each ; or in wrapper, 3d.

1. How to Dance ; or, Etiquette of the Ball Room.
2. How to Woo ; or, The Etiquette of Courtship and Marriage.
3. How to Dress ; or, The Etiquette of the Toilet.
4. How to Dine; or, Etiquette of the Dinner Table.
5. How to Manage ; or, Etiquette of the Household.
6. How to Entertain ; or, Etiquette for Visitors.
7. How to Behave ; or, The Etiquette of Society.
8. How to Travel ; or, Etiquette for Ship, Rail, Coach, or Saddle.

** *These elegant and attractive little Manuals will be found useful Text-Books for the subjects to which they refer ; they are full of suggestive hints, and are undoubtedly superior to any hitherto published.*

London : *WARD, LOCK & CO., Salisbury Square, E.C.*

INDISPENSABLE HANDBOOKS.

SYLVIA'S HOME HELP SERIES
of Useful Handbooks for Ladies.

Price 1s. each.

1. HOW TO DRESS WELL ON A SHILLING A-DAY. A Guide to Home Dressmaking and Millinery. With a large Sheet of Diagrams for Cutting out Dress Bodices in Three Sizes, and Fifty Diagrams of Children's Clothing.
2. ART NEEDLEWORK: A Guide to Embroidery in Crewels, Silks, Appliqué, &c., with Instructions as to Stitches, and explanatory Diagrams. With a large and valuable Sheet of Designs in Crewel Work.
3. HOSTESS AND GUEST. A Guide to the Etiquette of Dinners, Suppers, Luncheons, the Precedence of Guests, &c. Illustrated.
4. BABIES, AND HOW TO TAKE CARE OF THEM. Containing full and practical Information on every subject connected with "Baby." With a large Pattern Sheet of Infants' Clothing.
5. DRESS, HEALTH, AND BEAUTY. Containing Practical Suggestions for the Improvement of Modern Costume, regarded from an Artistic and Sanitary point of view. Illustrated.
6. THE HOUSE AND ITS FURNITURE. A Common-Sense Guide to House Building and House Furnishing. Containing plain Directions as to Choosing a Site, Buying, Building, Heating, Lighting, Ventilating, and Completely Furnishing. With 170 Illustrations.
7. INDIAN HOUSEHOLD MANAGEMENT. Containing Hints on Bungalows, Packing, Domestic Servants, &c. Invaluable for all visiting India.
8. HOW TO MANAGE HOUSE AND SERVANTS, and Make the Most of your Means.
9. THE MANAGEMENT OF CHILDREN, in Health, Sickness and Disease.
10. ARTISTIC HOMES; or, How to Furnish with Taste. A Handbook for all Housewives. Profusely Illustrated.
11. HOW TO MAKE HOME HAPPY. A Book of Household Hints and Information, with 500 Odds and Ends worth Remembering.
12. HINTS AND HELPS FOR EVERY-DAY EMERGENCIES. Including Social, Rural, and Domestic Economy, Household Medicine, Casualties, Pecuniary Embarrassments, Legal Difficulties, &c.
13. THE ECONOMICAL HOUSEWIFE; or, How to Make the Most of Everything. With about 50 Illustrations.
14. SYLVIA'S BOOK OF THE TOILET. A Lady's Guide to Dress and Beauty. With 30 Illustrations.
15. HOME NEEDLEWORK. A Trustworthy Guide to the Art of Plain Sewing. With about 80 Diagrams.
16. CHILDREN, AND WHAT TO DO WITH THEM. A Guide for Mothers respecting the Management of their Boys and Girls.
17. OUR LEISURE HOURS. A Book of Recreation for the Use of Old and Young. Illustrated.
18. THE FANCY NEEDLEWORK INSTRUCTION BOOK. Profusely Illustrated.
19. THE ETIQUETTE OF MODERN SOCIETY. Illust.

London: *WARD, LOCK & CO., Salisbury Square, E.C.*

HEALTH PRIMERS FOR THE PEOPLE.

WARD AND LOCK'S
LONG LIFE SERIES,

Accurately Written and Carefully Edited by Distinguished Members of the Medical Profession.

Fcap. 8vo, cloth, 1s.

The object of WARD & LOCK'S "LONG LIFE SERIES" *is to diffuse as widely as possible, amongst all classes, a knowledge of the elementary parts of preventive medicine. The subjects selected are of vital and practical importance in everyday life, and are treated in as popular a style as is consistent with their nature. Each volume, if the subject calls for it, is fully illustrated, so that the text may be clearly and readily understood by anyone hitherto entirely ignorant of the structure and functions of the body.*

The Authors of WARD & LOCK'S "LONG LIFE SERIES" *have been selected with great care and on account of special fitness each for his subject, by reason of its previous careful study, either privately or as public teaching.*

---

1. **LONG LIFE, AND HOW TO REACH IT.**
2. **THE THROAT AND THE VOICE.**
3. **EYESIGHT, AND HOW TO CARE FOR IT.**
4. **THE MOUTH AND THE TEETH.**
5. **THE SKIN IN HEALTH AND DISEASE.**
6. **BRAIN WORK AND OVERWORK.**
7. **SICK NURSING:** A Handbook for all who have to do with Cases of Disease and Convalescence.
8. **THE YOUNG WIFE'S ADVICE BOOK:** A Guide for Mothers on Health and Self-Management.
9. **SLEEP: HOW TO OBTAIN IT.**
10. **HEARING, AND HOW TO KEEP IT.**
11. **SEA AIR AND SEA BATHING.**
12. **HEALTH IN SCHOOLS AND WORKSHOPS.**

THE SATURDAY REVIEW says: "Messrs. Ward and Lock have done good service to the public in procuring, at the hands of highly qualified members of the medical profession, a series of manuals compressing into the smallest possible space the elementary principles and practical rules of healthful living. It is not much to say of them, as a series, that the shilling invested betimes in each of them may be the means of saving many a guinea."

London: WARD, LOCK & CO., Salisbury Square, E.C.

REFERENCE BOOKS FOR THE PEOPLE.

BEETON'S NATIONAL REFERENCE BOOKS,
FOR THE PEOPLE OF GREAT BRITAIN AND IRELAND.

*** In an age of great competition and little leisure the value of Time is tolerably well understood. Men wanting facts like to get at them with as little expenditure as possible of money or minutes. BEETON'S NATIONAL REFERENCE BOOKS *have been conceived and carried out in the belief that a set of Cheap and Handy Volumes in Biography, Geography, History (Sacred and Profane), Science, and Business, would be thoroughly welcome, because they would quickly answer many a question. In every case the type will be found clear and plain.*

STRONGLY BOUND IN CLOTH, PRICE ONE SHILLING EACH.
(Those marked thus * can be had cloth gilt, price 1s. 6d.)

1. *Beeton's British Gazetteer: A Topographical and Historical Guide to the United Kingdom.
2. Beeton's British Biography: From the Earliest Times to the Accession of George III.
3. Beeton's Modern Men and Women: A British Biography, from the Accession of George III. to the Present Time.
4. *Beeton's Bible Dictionary. A Cyclopædia of the Geography, Biography, Narratives, and Truths of Scripture.
5. *Beeton's Classical Dictionary: A Cyclopædia of Greek and Roman Biography, Geography, Mythology, and Antiquities.
6. *Beeton's Medical Dictionary. A Guide for every Family, defining, with perfect plainness, the Symptoms and Treatment of all Ailments, Illnesses, and Diseases.
7. Beeton's Date Book. A British Chronology from the Earliest Records to the Present Day.
8. Beeton's Dictionary of Commerce. Containing Explanations of the principal Terms used in, and modes of transacting Business at Home and Abroad.
9. Beeton's Modern European Celebrities. A Biography of Continental Men and Women of Note who have lived during the last Hundred Years, or are now living.

Beeton's Guide Book to the Stock Exchange and Money Market. With Hints to Investors and the Chances of Speculators. Entirely New Edition, post 8vo, linen boards, 1s.
Beeton's Investing Money with Safety and Profit. New and Revised Edition. Post 8vo, linen covers, 1s.
Beeton's Ready Reckoner. With New Tables, and much Information never before collected. Post 8vo, strong cloth, 1s.
Webster's Sixpenny Ready Reckoner. 256 pp., cloth, 6d.
Beeton's Complete Letter Writer, for Ladies and Gentlemen. Post 8vo, strong cloth, price 1s.
Beeton's Complete Letter Writer for Ladies. In linen covers, 6d.
Beeton's Complete Letter Writer for Gentlemen. Price 6d.
The New Letter Writer for Lovers. In linen covers, price 6d.
Webster's Shilling Book-keeping. A Comprehensive Guide, comprising a Course of Practice in Single and Double Entry. Post 8vo, cloth, 1s.

London: *WARD, LOCK & CO., Salisbury Square, E.C.*

CLASSICS FOR THE PEOPLE.

WARD AND LOCK'S
BOOKS FOR ALL TIME

Literary Masterpieces, such as are included in this Series, take their place among our permanent institutions. They are not only certain to receive the admiration of future generations of readers, but they are rightfully the property of all living admirers of the works of genius, and should be within the reach of all. This is rendered possible by the present issue in a cheap form.

Crown 8vo, wrapper, 1s.; cloth gilt, 2s.

1. Macaulay. Reviews and Essays.
2. Sydney Smith. Essays, Social and Political.
3. De Quincey. Confessions of an Opium Eater, &c.
4. Lord Bacon. Essays, Civil and Moral, &c.
5. Macaulay (Second Series). Reviews and Essays.
6. Lord Bacon (Second Series). New Atlantis, &c.
7. Sydney Smith (Second Series). Essays, Social and Political.
9. De Quincey (Second Series).
10. Josephus. Antiquities of the Jews. 1s. 6d. and 2s.
11. Josephus. Wars of the Jews. 1s. and 1s. 6d.
12. Macaulay (Third Series).

THE BOYS' ILLUSTRATED LIBRARY OF
HEROES, PATRIOTS, AND PIONEERS.
The Story of their Daring Adventures and Heroic Deeds.

In this series Biographies are narrated exhibiting the force of character of the men and the remarkable adventures they encountered, and these records can scarcely be perused without exciting a feeling of admiration for the Heroes and of wonder at the magnitude of their achievements.

In picture boards, 2s.; cloth gilt, 2s. 6d.; gilt edges, 3s. 6d.

1. Columbus, the Discoverer of the New World.
2. Franklin, Printer Boy, Statesman, and Philosopher.
3. Washington, Hero and Patriot.
4. The Puritan Captain; or, The Story of Miles Standish.
5. Boone, the Backwoodsman, the Pioneer of Kentucky.
6. The Terror of the Indians; or, Life in the Backwoods.
7. The Hero of the Prairies; or, The Story of Kit Carson.
8. The Spanish Cavalier; or, De Soto, the Discoverer.
9. Through Prairie and Forest; or, De Salle, the Pathfinder.
10. The Shawnee Prophet; or, The Story of Tecumseh.
11. The Buccaneer Chiefs; or, Captain Kidd and the Pirates.
12. Red Eagle; or, The War in Alabama.
13. The Rival Warriors; Chiefs of the Five Nations.
14. The Indian Princess; or, The Story of Pocahontas.
15. The Mexican Prince; or, The Story of Montezuma.

London: WARD, LOCK & CO., Salisbury Square, E.C.

BOOKS FOR YOUNG MEN.

THE FRIENDLY COUNSEL SERIES.

In the Volumes of the FRIENDLY COUNSEL SERIES, *the object has been kept in view to spread abroad for the reading public the good words of the present, and preserve for them the wisdom of the past. From first to last the effort has been, and will be, to make the* FRIENDLY COUNSEL SERIES *a practical illustration of the homely truth that* "*A Friend in Need is a Friend Indeed.*"

Crown 8vo, fancy wrapper, price 1s. each; cloth gilt, 1s. 6d.; cloth gilt, gilt edges, price 2s.
(Those marked thus (*) can also be had in cloth, extra gilt, side, back, and edges, price 2s. 6d. each.)

1. *Timothy Titcomb's Letters addressed to Young People.
2. *Beecher's Lectures to Young Men on various Important Subjects. By HENRY WARD BEECHER, Author of "Life Thoughts."
3. *Getting On in the World; or, Hints on Success in Life. By WILLIAM MATHEWS, LL.D. First Series.
4. *Cobbett's Advice to Young Men, and incidentally to Young Women. With Notes and Memoir of the Author.
5. Christians in Council; or, The Pastor and his Friends. By the Author of "Stepping Heavenward."
6. How to Make a Living: Suggestions upon the Art of Making, Saving, and Using Money. By GEORGE CARY EGGLESTON.
7. The Art of Prolonging Life. Translated, completely Revised, and Adapted for all Readers, from the celebrated work by Dr. HUFELAND.
8. *Foster's Decision of Character, and other Essays. With Life of the Author and Notes.
9. *Getting On in the World; or, Hints on Success in Life. Second Series. By W. MATHEWS, LL.D.
10. *How to Excel in Business; or, The Clerk's Instructor. A Complete Guide to Success in the World of Commerce. By JAMES MASON.
11. *Todd's Student's Manual. By Rev. JOHN TODD, D.D. New and Revised Edition, with Notes by the Author.
12. How to Excel in Study; or, The Student's Instructor. By JAMES MASON, Author of "How to Excel in Business," &c.
13. Money: How to Get, How to Use, and How to Keep It. New and Revised Edition.
14. Oratory and Orators. By WILLIAM MATHEWS, LL.D., Author of "Getting On in the World." Edited by J. W. KIRTON, LL.D., Author of "Buy Your Own Cherries."

Crown 8vo, bevelled boards, cloth gilt, gilt edges, 5s.
The Friendly Counsellor. Containing "Timothy Titcomb's Letters to Young People," "Cobbett's Advice to Young Men," and "Beecher's Lectures to Young Men."

London: WARD, LOCK & CO., *Salisbury Square, E.C.*

ERCKMANN-CHATRIAN'S STORIES.

WARD, LOCK AND CO.'S
ERCKMANN - CHATRIAN LIBRARY.

Either to the young who are learning history, to the old who desire to gain lessons from experience, or to the more feminine minds who delight in stories of entrancing interest, the exquisite volumes of MM. ERCKMANN-CHATRIAN *appeal in tones of wholesome and invigorating effect.*

Post 8vo, picture wrapper, price 1s. each; cloth gilt, 1s. 6d.; cloth gilt, those marked thus (*), with page Engravings, 2s. 6d. each.

The addition to these volumes of the charming Illustrations of SCHULER, BAYARD, *and others, render them in every way perfect.*

*1. Madame Thérèse.
2. The Conscript.
*3. The Great Invasion.
4. The Blockade.
*5. The States-General.
*6. The Country in Danger.
7. Waterloo.
*8. Illustrious Dr. Matheus.
*9. Stories of the Rhine.
*10. Friend Fritz.
*11. Alsatian Schoolmaster.
*12. The Polish Jew.
13. Master Daniel Rock.
*15. Year One of the Republic.
*16. Citizen Bonaparte.
*17. Confessions of a Clarionet Player.
*18. The Campaign in Kabylia
*19. The Man Wolf.
*20. The Wild Huntsman.

DOUBLE VOLUMES. Crown 8vo, picture boards, 2s. each.

1. Under Fire. ("Madame Thérèse," and "The Blockade.")
2. Two Years a Soldier. ("The Conscript," and "Waterloo.")
3. The Story of a Peasant, 1789-1792. ("The States-General," and "The Country in Danger.")
4. The Story of a Peasant, 1793-1815. ("Year One of the Republic," and "Citizen Bonaparte.")
5. The Mysterious Doctor. ("Dr. Matheus," and "Friend Fritz.")
6. The Buried Treasure. ("Stories of the Rhine," and "Clarionet Player.")
7. The Old Schoolmaster. ("The Alsatian Schoolmaster," and "Campaign in Kabylia.")
8. Weird Tales of the Woods. ("The Man Wolf," and "The Wild Huntsman.")

In new and handsome binding, cloth gilt, gilt top, price 5s. each.

The Story of a Peasant, 1789-1792. Containing "The States-General," and "The Country in Danger." With 57 full-page Engravings.

The Story of a Peasant, 1793-1815. Containing "Year One of the Republic," and "Citizen Bonaparte." With 60 full-page Engravings.

London: WARD, LOCK & CO., *Salisbury Square, E.C.*

BOOKS FOR YOUTH.

THE YOUTH'S LIBRARY OF WONDER AND ADVENTURE.

Crown 8vo, picture wrapper, 1s. each; cloth gilt, 1s. 6d.; ditto, gilt edges, 2s.

Healthy literature for Boys is here provided in a cheap and popular form.

1. A Journey into the Interior of the Earth. By JULES VERNE.
2. The English at the North Pole. By JULES VERNE.
3. The Ice Desert. By JULES VERNE.
4. Five Weeks in a Balloon. By JULES VERNE.
5. The Mysterious Document. By JULES VERNE.
6. On the Track. By JULES VERNE.
7. Among the Cannibals. By JULES VERNE.
8. Twenty Thousand Leagues Under the Sea. Part I.
9. ——————————————————————— Part II.
10. Two Years Before the Mast. By R. H. DANA.
11. From the Earth to the Moon. By JULES VERNE.
12. Round the Moon. By JULES VERNE.
13. Sandford and Merton. Illustrated.
14. Baron Munchausen: His Life, Travels, and Adventures. Illust.
15. Robinson Crusoe. By DANIEL DEFOE. With many Engravings.
16. Around the World in Eighty Days. By JULES VERNE. Illust.
17. A Boy's Life Aboard Ship, as it is. Illustrated.
18. Life in a Whaler; or, Adventures in the Tropical Seas. Illust.
19. Household Stories. By the Brothers GRIMM, &c. Illustrated.
20. The Marvels of Nature. With 400 Engravings.
21. Wonders of the World. With 123 Engravings.
22. The Boy's Own Book of Manufactures and Industries of the World. With 365 Engravings.
23. Fifty Famous Men. With Portraits and other Illustrations.
24. Great Inventors. With 109 Engravings.
25. The Boy's Handy Book of Games. Hundreds of Illustrations.
26. The Boy's Handy Book of Natural History. Illustrated.

DOUBLE VOLUMES.

Crown 8vo, picture boards, 2s. each; cloth gilt, 2s. 6d.; cloth extra, gilt, 3s. 6d.

1. The Adventures of Captain Hatteras. ("The English at the North Pole," and "The Ice Desert.") With Coloured Pictures.
2. Twenty Thousand Leagues Under the Sea. First and Second Series, Complete. With Coloured Pictures.
3. The Wonderful Travels. Containing "A Journey into the Interior of the Earth," and "Five Weeks in a Balloon." Ditto.
4. The Moon Voyage. Containing "From the Earth to the Moon," and "Round the Moon." With Coloured Pictures.

London: WARD, LOCK & CO., Salisbury Square, E.C.

GARDENING BOOKS.

THE STANDARD GARDENING BOOKS.

Gardening, properly managed, is a source of income to thousands, and of healthful recreation to other thousands. Besides the gratification it affords, the inexhaustible field it opens up for observation and experiment commends its i teresting practice to everyone possessed of a real English home.

BEETON'S BOOK OF GARDEN MANAGEMENT. Embracing all kinds of information connected with Fruit, Flower, and Kitchen Garden Cultivation, Orchid Houses, Bees, &c., &c. Illustrated with Coloured Plates of surpassing beauty, and numerous Engravings. Post 8vo, cloth gilt, price 7s. 6d.; or in half-calf, 10s. 6d.

The directions in BEETON'S GARDEN MANAGEMENT *are conceived in a practical manner, and are, throughout the work, so simply given that none can fail to understand them. The Coloured Plates show more than a hundred different kinds of Plants and Flowers, and assist in the identification of any doubtful specimen.*

BEETON'S DICTIONARY OF EVERY-DAY GARDENING. Constituting a Popular Cyclopædia of the Theory and Practice of Horticulture. Illustrated with Coloured Plates, made after Original Water Colour Drawings copied from Nature, and Woodcuts in the Text. Crown 8vo, cloth gilt, price 3s. 6d.

ALL ABOUT GARDENING. Being a Popular Dictionary of Gardening, containing full and practical Instructions in the different Branches of Horticultural Science. Specially adapted to the capabilities and requirements of the Kitchen and Flower Garden at the Present Day. With Illustrations. Crown 8vo, cloth gilt, price 2s. 6d.

BEETON'S GARDENING BOOK. Containing full and practical Instructions concerning General Gardening Operations, the Flower Garden, the Fruit Garden, the Kitchen Garden, Pests of the Garden, with a Monthly Calendar of Work to be done in the Garden throughout the Year. With Illustrations. Post 8vo, cloth, price 1s.; or with Coloured Plates, price 1s. 6d.

KITCHEN AND FLOWER GARDENING FOR PLEASURE AND PROFIT. An Entirely New and Practical Guide to the Cultivation of Vegetables, Fruits, and Flowers. With upwards of 100 Engravings. Crown 8vo, boards, 1s.

BEETON'S PENNY GARDENING BOOK. Being a Calendar of Work to be done in the Flower, Fruit, and Kitchen Garden, together with Plain Directions for Growing all Useful Vegetables and most Flowers suited to adorn the Gardens and Homes of Cottagers. Price 1d.; post free, 1½d.

GLENNY'S ILLUSTRATED GARDEN ALMANAC AND FLORIST'S DIRECTORY. Being an Every-day Handbook for Gardeners, both Amateur and Professional. Containing Notices of the Floral Novelties of the Current Year, Articles by Eminent Horticultural Authorities, Directions for Amateurs, Lists of London, Provincial, and Continental Nurserymen, Seedsmen, and Florists, &c. With numerous Illustrations. Published Yearly, in coloured wrapper, price 1s.

London: WARD, LOCK & CO., *Salisbury Square, E.C.*

NEEDLEWORK BOOKS.

THE STANDARD NEEDLEWORK BOOKS.

The Art of Needlework has from time immemorial been the support, comfort, or employment of women of every rank and age, so that any addition and assistance in teaching or learning Needlework will be welcomed by the Daughters of England. In this belief, the Publishers offer to the public the " STANDARD NEEDLEWORK BOOKS.*"*

New and Revised Edition.

BEETON'S BOOK OF NEEDLEWORK. Consisting of 670 Needlework Patterns, with full Descriptions and Instructions as to working them. Every Stitch Described and Engraved with the utmost accuracy, and the Quantity of Material requisite for each Pattern stated.

Contents:—

TATTING PATTERNS.	EMBROIDERY INSTRUCTIONS.
EMBROIDERY PATTERNS.	CROCHET INSTRUCTIONS.
CROCHET PATTERNS.	KNITTING AND NETTING INSTRUCTIONS
KNITTING AND NETTING PATTERNS.	LACE STITCHES.
MONOGRAM AND INITIAL PATTERNS.	POINT LACE PATTERNS.
BERLIN WOOL INSTRUCTIONS.	GUIPURE PATTERNS.
	CREWEL WORK.

New and Revised Edition. Crown 8vo, cloth gilt, gilt edges, price 7s. 6d.

*** *Just as* THE BOOK OF HOUSEHOLD MANAGEMENT *takes due precedence of every other Cookery Book, so this extraordinary collection of Needlework Designs has become the book, par excellence, for Ladies to consult, both for Instruction in Stitches and all kinds of Work, and Patterns of elegant style and irreproachable good taste.*

MADAME GOUBAUD'S
SHILLING NEEDLEWORK BOOKS.
Imperial 16mo, ornamental wrapper, price 1s. each.

1. **Tatting Patterns.** With 66 Illustrations.
2. **Embroidery Patterns.** With 85 Illustrations.
3. **Crochet Patterns.** With 48 Illustrations.
4. **Knitting and Netting Patterns.** With 64 Illustrations.
5. **Patterns of Monograms, Initials, &c.** 151 Illustrations.
6. **Guipure Patterns.** With 71 Illustrations.
7. **Point Lace Book.** With 78 Illustrations.

MADAME GOUBAUD'S
NEEDLEWORK INSTRUCTION BOOKS.
Imperial 16mo, ornamental wrapper, price 6d. each.

1. **Berlin Wool Instructions.** With 18 Illustrations.
2. **Embroidery Instructions.** With 65 Illustrations.
3. **Crochet Instructions.** With 24 Illustrations.

Home Needlework. With 80 Diagrams. Price 1s.
Art Needlework. Illustrated. Price 1s.
The Fancy Needlework Instruction Book. Price 1s.
(See also "The Ladies' Bazaar and Fancy-Fair Books.")

London: *WARD, LOCK & CO., Salisbury Square, E.C.*

AN ENTIRELY NEW ETYMOLOGICAL DICTIONARY.

Just ready, demy 8vo, cloth, 5s. WARD & LOCK'S

STANDARD

ETYMOLOGICAL DICTIONARY

OF THE ENGLISH LANGUAGE.

A POPULAR AND COMPREHENSIVE GUIDE TO THE PRONUNCIATION, PARTS OF SPEECH, MEANINGS, AND ETYMOLOGY OF ALL WORDS, ORDINARY, SCIENTIFIC, AND TECHNOLOGICAL NOW IN GENERAL USE.

With 40 pages of Engravings and an Appendix,

COMPRISING

1. ABBREVIATIONS USED IN WRITING AND PRINTING.
2. A BRIEF CLASSICAL DICTIONARY, COMPRISING THE PRINCIPAL DEITIES, HEROES, NOTABLE MEN AND WOMEN, &c., OF GREEK AND ROMAN MYTHOLOGY.
3. LETTERS: HOW TO BEGIN, END, AND ADDRESS THEM.
4. WORDS, PHRASES, AND PROVERBS, FROM THE LATIN, FREQUENTLY USED IN WRITING AND SPEAKING.
5. WORDS, PHRASES, AND PROVERBS, FROM THE FRENCH, WITH ENGLISH TRANSLATIONS.
6. WORDS, PHRASES, AND PROVERBS, FROM THE ITALIAN AND SPANISH WITH ENGLISH TRANSLATIONS.

Messrs. WARD, LOCK AND CO., in announcing this ENTIRELY NEW WORK, which has long been in preparation, desire to call special attention to the several points of excellence to be found in it, and feel sure that this valuable work will command the favour of the public. The following are the principal points to which attention is called:—

1. *Comprehensiveness.*—New words, that the progress of science, art, and philosophy has rendered necessary as additions to the vocabulary, and thousands of compound words have been introduced.

2. *Brevity.*—To ensure this, care has been taken to avoid redundancy of explanation, while every possible meaning of each word has been given.

3. *Pronunciation.*—Those who may use it will not be puzzled and confused with any arbitrary system of phonetic signs, similar to those usually found in Pronouncing Dictionaries. Every word of two syllables and more is properly divided and accented; and all *silent* letters are put in italics.

4. *Etymology.*—The words are arranged in groups, each group being placed under the principal word to which its members are closely allied. Words similarly spelt, but having distinct etymologies, are separated according to their derivation.

5. *Illustrations.*—40 pages of Illustrations of various objects given, to assist students in arriving at a clear perception of that which is indicated by the name.

London: *WARD, LOCK & CO., Salisbury Square, E.C.*

WARD & LOCK'S POPULAR DICTIONARIES.

THE STANDARD DICTIONARIES OF LANGUAGE.

WEBSTER'S UNIVERSAL PRONOUNCING AND DE-
FINING DICTIONARY OF THE ENGLISH LANGUAGE. Condensed from Noah Webster's Large Work, with numerous Synonyms, carefully discriminated by CHAUNCEY A. GOODRICH, D.D. With Walker's Key to the Pronunciation of Classical and Scriptural Proper Names; a Vocabulary of Modern Geographical Names; Phrases and Quotations from the Ancient and Modern Languages; Abbreviations, &c. Royal 8vo, half bound, 5s.; demy 8vo, cloth, 3s. 6d.

"This Dictionary must commend itself to every intelligent reader. . . . Let us add, it is carefully and well printed, and very cheap; and having said so much, we feel assured that further recommendation is unnecessary. It is good, useful, and cheap."—*Liverpool Mail.*

WEBSTER'S IMPROVED PRONOUNCING DICTION-
ARY OF THE ENGLISH LANGUAGE. Condensed and adapted to English Orthography and Usage, with additions by CHARLES ROBSON. To which are added, Accentuated Lists of Scriptural, Classical, and Modern Geographical Proper Names. Cloth, price 2s. 6d.; strongly half-bound, 3s. 6d.

WEBSTER'S POCKET PRONOUNCING DICTIONARY
OF THE ENGLISH LANGUAGE. Condensed from the Original Dictionary by NOAH WEBSTER, LL.D.; with Accentuated Vocabularies of Classical, Scriptural, and Modern Geographical Names. Revised Edition, by WILLIAM G. WEBSTER, Son of Noah Webster. Containing 10,000 more words than "Walker's Dictionary." Royal 16mo, cloth, price 1s.

WARD & LOCK'S POCKET SHILLING DICTIONARY
OF THE ENGLISH LANGUAGE. Condensed by CHARLES ROBSON, from NOAH WEBSTER's Original Work. With Accentuated Lists of Scripture and Modern Geographical Proper Names. Super-royal 32mo, cloth, 768 pp., 1s.

WARD AND LOCK'S SHILLING DICTIONARY OF
THE GERMAN LANGUAGE. Containing German-English and English-German, Geographical Dictionary, Table of Coins, &c. Super-royal 32mo, cloth, 900 pp., 1s.

WEBSTER'S SIXPENNY POCKET PRONOUNCING
DICTIONARY OF THE ENGLISH LANGUAGE. Condensed from the Original Dictionary by NOAH WEBSTER, LL.D.; with Accentuated Vocabularies of Classical, Scriptural, and Modern Geographical Names. Revised Edition, by WILLIAM G. WEBSTER, Son of Noah Webster. Strongly bound in cloth, price 6d.

WEBSTER'S PENNY PRONOUNCING DICTIONARY
OF THE ENGLISH LANGUAGE. Exhibiting the Spelling, Pronunciation, Part of Speech, and Meaning of all Words in General Use among English-speaking Nations. Containing over 10,000 words. Price 1d.; or, linen wrapper, 2d.

London: WARD, LOCK & CO., Salisbury Square, E.C.

PRESENTS FOR YOUTH.

BEETON'S BOY'S OWN LIBRARY.

*** *The best set of Volumes for Prizes, Rewards, or Gifts to English Lads. They have all been prepared with a view to their fitness in manly tone and handsome appearance for Presents for Youth.*

Demy 8vo, cloth gilt, price 5s. each; gilt edges, 6s. each.

1. **Stories of the Wars, 1574-1658.** From the Rise of the Dutch Republic to the Death of Oliver Cromwell. By JOHN TILLOTSON. With Coloured Pictures and many other Illustrations.
2. **A Boy's Adventures in the Barons' Wars**; or, How I Won my Spurs. By J. G. EDGAR. Coloured Front. and many Illustrations.
3. **Cressy and Poictiers**; or, The Story of the Black Prince's Page. By J. G. EDGAR. With Coloured Frontispiece and many Illustrations, principally by R. DUDLEY and GUSTAVE DORÉ.
4. **Runnymede and Lincoln Fair.** A Story of the Great Charter. By J. G. EDGAR. Coloured Frontispiece and many full-page Engravings.
5. **Wild Sports of the World.** By JAMES GREENWOOD, Author of "A Night in a Workhouse." With Eight Coloured Plates and many Woodcut Illustrations.
6. **The Wild Man at Home**; or, Pictures of Life in Savage Lands. By J. GREENWOOD. With Coloured Plates and other Illustrations.
7. **Hubert Ellis**: A Story of King Richard the Second's Days. By F. DAVENANT. With Coloured Frontispiece, full-page and other Illustrations, principally by ROBERT DUDLEY.
8. **Don Quixote.** Translated by CHARLES JARVIS. With nearly 700 Illustrations by TONY JOHANNOT.
9. **Gulliver's Travels.** With Coloured Frontispiece and upwards of 300 Woodcut Illustrations.
10. **Robinson Crusoe.** With Memoir of the Author. With Coloured and other Plates and many Woodcuts.
11. **Silas the Conjuror**: His Travels and Perils. By JAMES GREENWOOD. With many Illustrations.
12. **Scenes and Sports of Savage Lands.** By JAMES GREENWOOD. With Coloured Plates and many other Illustrations.
13. **Reuben Davidger**: His Perils and Adventures. By JAMES GREENWOOD. With numerous Illustrations.
14. **Brave British Soldiers and the Victoria Cross.** Stories of the Brave Deeds which won the prize "For Valour." With full-page Engravings and other Illustrations.
15. **Zoological Recreations.** By W. J. BRODERIP, F.R.S. With Coloured Frontispiece and many full-page Engravings.
16. **Wild Animals in Freedom and Captivity.** With Coloured Frontispiece and 120 Illustrations by HARRISON WEIR and others.
18. **The World's Explorers.** By H. W. DULCKEN, Ph.D. Including the Discoveries of LIVINGSTONE and STANLEY. With Coloured Frontispiece and many Illustrations.
19. **The Man among the Monkeys**; or, Ninety Days in Apeland. With other Strange Stories of Men and Animals. Illustrated by GUSTAVE DORÉ and others.

London: WARD, LOCK & CO., Salisbury Square, E.C.

PRESENTATION VOLUMES FOR BOYS.

BEETON'S BOY'S PRIZE LIBRARY.

No better Library could be chosen for the selection of Prizes for Young Gentlemen, Birthday Gifts, or Anniversary Rewards.

Demy 8vo, cloth gilt, 5s. each; gilt edges, 6s. each.

1. Beeton's Fact, Fiction, History, and Adventure. 1,110 pp., with 33 page Engravings and many Woodcuts.
2. Beeton's Historical Romances, Daring Deeds, and Animal Stories. 1,104 pp., with 34 full-page Plates and 255 Woodcuts.
3. Beeton's Brave Tales, Bold Ballads, and Travels by Land and Sea. 1,088 pp., with 38 full-page Engravings and 320 Cuts.
4. Beeton's Tales of Chivalry, School Stories, Mechanics at Home, and Exploits of the Army and Navy. 888 pages, with 23 full-page Engravings and 255 Woodcuts.
5. Beeton's Hero Soldiers, Sailors, and Explorers. 890 pages, with Coloured Frontispiece, 36 full-page Engravings, and 157 Woodcuts.
6. Beeton's Famous Voyages, Brigand Adventures, Tales of the Battle Field, &c. 1,054 pp., with 38 Plates and 156 Woodcuts.
7. Beeton's Victorious English Sea Stories, Tales of Enterprise and School Life. 1,050 pp., with Coloured Frontispiece, 46 full-page Plates, and 150 Woodcuts.

BOY'S OWN STORY BOOKS of DARING and ADVENTURE.

By GUSTAVE AIMARD. With Illustrations.

Crown 8vo, picture boards, 2s. each; cloth gilt, 2s. 6d.

1. The Foster Brothers. Containing "The Indian Chief," and "Red Track."
2. The Kings of the Desert. Containing "The Insurgent Chief," and "The Flying Horseman."
3. The Forest Chieftain. Containing "The Guide of the Desert," and "The Bee Hunters."
4. The White Buffalo. Containing "The Prairie Flower," and "The Indian Scout."
5. The Chief of the Dark Hearts. Containing "The Adventurers," and "Pearl of the Andes."
6. The Prairie Rovers. Containing "The Last of the Incas," and "The Rebel Chief."
7. The Robbers of the Forest. Containing "The Border Rifles," and "The Freebooters."
8. Red Cedar. Containing "The Pirates of the Prairie," and "The Trapper's Daughter."
9. The Texan Rangers. Containing "The Buccaneer Chief," and "The Trail Hunter."
10. Pale Face and Red Skin. Containing "Stoneheart," and "The Smuggler Chief."
11. Loyal Heart. Containing "The White Scalper," and "The Trappers of Arkansas."
12. The Mexican's Revenge. Containing "Stronghand," and "Queen of the Savannah."
13. Eagle Head. Containing "The Tiger Slayer," and "The Gold-seekers."

London: WARD, LOCK & CO., Salisbury Square, E.C.

"HEPATICUS,"
Registered No. 25,086.
"THE WONDERFUL HEALTH RESTORER."

Purifies the Blood, and effectually cures and prevents Jaundice, Indigestion, Sick Headache, General Weakness, Loss of Appetite, and all complaints arising from a Disordered Liver. Is adapted to all ages of either sex, and those with the weakest constitution may take it with entire confidence. It is a gentle Tonic, and is free from all mineral matter. *No change of diet is required.*

Can be obtained through any Chemist or Patent Medicine Vendor, or direct from the Manufacturers, in Bottles 2s. 9d. each.

SOLE MANUFACTURERS AND EXPORTERS,
TOMLINSON & HAYWARD, Lincoln.

LOWE'S PILLS
FOR THE HEAD, STOMACH, AND LIVER.

Sold in Boxes at 1s. 1½d. and 2s. 9d. each, by all Chemists; or post-free from the Proprietor for 15 or 36 postage stamps. (There is this advantage in having these Pills direct from the Proprietor—*they are fresh made every day.*)

These Pills cure Rheumatism, Gout, Dropsy, Gravel, Fits, Palpitation of the Heart, Indigestion, Toothache, Bile and Liver Complaints, Gastric Fever, Cholera, Pains in the Back, Stomach, and Side. Public Singers and Preachers find great benefit by taking them. Out of a large number of Testimonials we select this for Ladies.

"Prospect House, Beckington, near Bath.
"Miss Thomas presents her compliments to Mr. R. H. Lowe, and will be greatly obliged if he will please forward by return of post a 2s. 9d. box of his pills for the head, stomach, and liver. Miss T. begs to add that before she was induced to try Mr. Lowe's pills, four years ago, she never knew a day's health; but since that time she has enjoyed very good health, and has not once required any other medicine. Miss T. has had much pleasure in recommending the pills to her friends.
"To Mr. R. H. LOWE (the Proprietor), 187, Bilston Road, Wolverhampton,
"September 18, 1870."

London Agents: BARCLAYS, EDWARDS, NEWBERYS, SANGERS, SUTTONS, LYNCH & CO., THOMPSON. Manchester: WOODLEY & SONS. Liverpool: EVANS, SONS & CO. Thirsk: FOGGITT. Coventry: WYLEYS & CO. Leeds: REINHARDT & SONS.

THE UNIVERSAL HOUSEHOLD REMEDIES!!!

HOLLOWAY'S PILLS & OINTMENT

These excellent FAMILY MEDICINES are invaluable in the treatment of all ailments incidental to every Household. The PILLS *Purify, Regulate, and Strengthen the whole system*, while the OINTMENT is *unequalled for the cure of Bad Legs, Bad Breasts, Old Wounds, Sores, and Ulcers.* Possessed of these REMEDIES, every Mother has at once the means of curing most Complaints to which herself or family is liable.

N.B.—Advice gratis at 90, LATE 533, *Oxford Street, London, daily between the hours of* 11 *and* 4, *or by letter.*

BROWN'S SATIN POLISH.

Highest Award Philadelphia, 1876.
Gold Medal, Berlin, 1877.
Highest Award and only Medal, Paris Exhibition, 1878.
Highest Award, Melbourne, 1880.

Put on by Sponge attached to Wire and Cork in each bottle.
No Polishing Brush required. Dries in a few minutes.
Can be used by any Lady without soiling her fingers.

The "Satin Polish" is the most elegant article of the kind ever produced. LADIES' SHOES, which have become Red and Rough by wearing, are restored to their *original colour and lustre, and will not soil the Skirts when wet*. TARNISHED PATENT LEATHER is improved by it.

For TRAVELLING BAGS, TRUNKS, HARNESS, CARRIAGE TOPS, &c., it is unequalled. It will not harden the Leather nor crack. It is not a spirit varnish.

"AMERICAN MAGIC BRONZE"

Is the Best in the Market, and it can be used with good effect on Ornaments, Picture Frames, Iron and Fancy Work generally, as well as for Boots and Shoes.

Kept by all Wholesale Houses, all first-class Boot and Shoe Stores, and Chemists in the United Kingdom.

Factories: 133 and 135, Fulton Street, 154 and 156, Commercial Street, BOSTON; 377, St. Paul Street, MONTREAL; 18 and 20, Norman's Buildings, St. Luke's, LONDON, E.C.

Under Royal and Imperial Patronage.
Pattern Books (Free) with other Fashionable Fabrics.

Pure Wool  *for all Seasons.*

Include the best makes of this indispensable material, and can be relied on to stand Wind and Weather on Land and Sea, in Summer or Winter, for LADIES', GENTLEMEN'S, or CHILDREN'S WEAR. They can be had in any colour or quality, from the finest and lightest, suitable for Tropical Climates, to the warm, heavy makes capable of resisting an intense degree of cold.

Prices for Ladies, 1s. 2½d. to 4s. 6d. per yard.
Prices for Gentlemen, 54 in., from 2s. 11d. per yard.

Carriage paid to the principal towns in England, and to Cork, Belfast, or Scotland.
Goods packed for Exportation. Orders are daily arriving from all parts. Any length cut.

Address: EGERTON BURNETT, No. 6, Wellington, Somerset.
CAUTION.—EGERTON BURNETT has No Agents.
All Orders are executed direct from his Warehouse.

IMPORTANT TO LADIES.
DR. WOOLLEY'S FEMALE PILLS
will speedily correct all Female Irregularities, from whatever cause they may arise. Thousands use them, as they are the best and most effectual Pills sold.

UNSOLICITED TESTIMONIAL.
SOUTH KENSINGTON, *August*, 1881.
SIR,—Enclosed you will find P.O.O. for 5s. 6d., for which please forward per return of post Two Boxes of Dr. WOOLLEY'S "FEMALE PILLS." I may add I find them INVALUABLE for the purpose for which they are required.   Yours, &c., ...

Price 2s. 9d. per Box ; or, post free, securely packed for 33 stamps, of the Proprietor,
G WOOLLEY (Son of the late Dr. Woolley),
116, Oxford Street, or 29, Carlton Street, Leicester.

THE RIGHT NAIL HIT ON THE HEAD AT LAST.
After 18 years of tormenting agony, and no end of money squandered in worse than useless quackeries, RICHARD FOSTER, of Boroughbridge, was entirely Cured of an Ulcerated Leg, with Seventeen distinct wounds, by one month's application of

PROCTOR'S CELEBRATED OINTMENT & PILLS
which have been sold for the last three quarters of a Century, and proved beyond all doubt to be *the only real remedy* known for Scurvy, Scald Head, Itch, Ringworm, Old Sores, Bad Legs, and all diseases of the Skin, no matter of how long standing. Free from Sulphur, without smell, and perfectly safe in use.

Sold by all Medicine Vendors in Pots, 1s. 1½d. and 2s. 9d. Post free from the Proprietor, 56, North Street, Taunton, for 15 or 36 stamps.

GOLD MEDAL PARIS 1878.

FRY'S COCOA
EXTRACT.

"G... ... PURE COCOA ONLY.
entirely a... ... y assimilated."—
V. W. STODDART, F.I.C., F.C.S., City and County Analyst, Bristol.

"Pure Cocoa, a portion of oil extracted."—
CHARLES A. CAMERON, M.D., F.R.C.S.I., Analyst for Dublin.

COCOA POD CUT OPEN SHOWING THE NUT.

FRY'S CARACAS COCOA
Prepared with ... ated Cocoa of Caracas ... combined
... choice descriptions.

"... most ... ... and valuable article."—
Standard.

15 International Prize Medals awarded to J. S. Fry & Sons.

www.ingramcontent.com/pod-product-compliance
Lightning Source LLC
Chambersburg PA
CBHW022120290426
44112CB00008B/748